GÓRECKI IN CONTEXT

ESSAYS ON MUSIC

◎ ◎ ◎

Series

Books on Music

Vol. 2

GÓRECKI IN CONTEXT

ESSAYS ON MUSIC

◎ ◎ ◎

Edited by Maja Trochimczyk

Moonrise Press, 2017

Górecki in Context: Essays on Music, edited by Maja Trochimczyk

© Copyright 2017 by Moonrise Press and, for individual chapters, copyright 2017 by the authors: Kinga Kiwała, Mieczysław Kominek, Anna Maslowiec, Teresa Malecka. Anna Wieczorek, Krzysztof Cyran, Maja Trochimczyk, and Andrzej Wendland.

Cover Design by Maja Trochimczyk from a photograph, the composer's portrait in his studio in Katowice, April 1998 by Maja Trochimczyk All Rights Reserved 2017 by Moonrise Press

No part of this book may be reproduced or utilized in any form or by any means, electronic or mechanical, including photocopying and recording, or by any information storage and retrieval system, without permission in writing from the publisher. This book is simultaneously published in print and e-book editions.

Manufactured in the United States of America

The Library of Congress Publication Data:
Trochimczyk, Maja. 1957– [Music History, Poland]
Górecki in Context: Essays on Music/Maja Trochimczyk, editor, author, and translator. 420 pages (xiv pp. + 406 pp.) 15.2 cm x 22.9 cm. Written in English. Includes 27 music examples, 66 illustrations, bibliography, list of works, and index.

ISBN 978-1-945938-10-8 (paperback)
ISBN 978-1-945938-11-5 (e-book, E-Pub format) I: Ch.1-7
ISBN 978-1-945938-19-1 (e-book, E-Pub format) II: Ch.8-10
ISBN 978-1-945938-20-7 (e-book, E-Pub format) III: Ch.11-13
ISBN 978-1-945938-21-4 (e-book, E-Pub format) IV: Ch.14-end

I. Trochimczyk, Maja, 1957 – Music History. II. Title.

10 9 8 7 6 5 4 3 2 1

◎ CONTENTS ◎

◎ Acknowledgments — Page viii

◎ Maja Trochimczyk - Preface — Page x

◎ Luke B. Howard - Górecki Tribute — Page xi

◎ Maja Trochimczyk - Mountains of Grief (Poem) — Page xiii

◎ ◎ ◎

◎ PART I ◎

GÓRECKI ON LIFE AND MUSIC

◎ Chapter 1 ◎ — Page 3
Conversation with Henryk Górecki: Leon Markiewicz, July 1962 — Translated by Anna Maslowiec

◎ Chapter 2 ◎ — Page 12
"I Am Always Myself" – Says Henryk Mikołaj Górecki in Conversation with Mieczysław Kominek (December 1993) — translated by Maja Trochimczyk

◎ Chapter 3 ◎ — Page 22
About Life and Music: A Conversation with Henryk Mikołaj Górecki (Zakopane, 16 July 1997) — Maja Trochimczyk

◎ Chapter 4 ◎ — Page 45
"Composing is a Terribly Personal Matter:" A Conversation with Henryk Mikołaj Górecki (April 1998) —Maja Trochimczyk

◎ Chapter 5 ◎ — Page 66
"There's More to Life than the Arranging of Sounds" – Henryk Mikołaj Górecki in Conversation with Małgorzata and Marcin Gmys

◎ Chapter 6 ◎ — Page 80
"Music? A Visitor from Another World," (15 October 2008), Henryk Mikołaj Górecki in Conversation with Małgorzata and Marcin Gmys

◎ Chapter 7 ◎ — Page 87
"Music is a Conversation." Henryk Mikołaj Górecki Talks to Anna Wieczorek and Krzysztof Cyran (29 April 2008)

◎ PART II ◎

ON GÓRECKI'S LIFE AND MUSIC

◎ Chapter 8 ◎ — Page 101
Górecki's Life and Music: A Bird's Eye View — Maja Trochimczyk

◎ Chapter 9 ◎ — Page 144
Henryk Mikołaj Górecki's Symphony No. 2 *Copernican:* Word and Sound and the Sublime — Kinga Kiwała — Translated by Maja Trochimczyk

◎ Chapter 10 ◎ — Page 175
Mothers and Motherhood in Górecki's Third Symphony and Other Works — Maja Trochimczyk

◎ Chapter 11 ◎ — Page 234
Górecki and the Polish Musical Tradition. Wacław of Szamotuły, Chopin, Szymanowski, Polish Folk and Church Music — Teresa Malecka

◎ Chapter 12 ◎ — Page 262
Górecki at the Keyboard: The Piano in his Compositional Output — Teresa Malecka

◎ Chapter 13 ◎ — Page 275
Górecki Conducts Górecki in Los Angeles, 1997 — Maja Trochimczyk

◎ Chapter 14 ◎ — Page 310
The Phenomenon and Mystery of Górecki's Fourth Symphony – *Tansman Episodes* —Andrzej Wendland — translated by Maja Trochimczyk

◎ ◎ ◎

◎ Page 355 — *Henryk Mikołaj Górecki - List of Works*

◎ Page 376 — *Bibliography*

◎ Page 393 — *Notes about Contributors*

◎ Page 398 — *Index*

◎ ACKNOWLEDGMENTS ◎

Music examples reprinted by permission, as follows:

Ad Matrem, Op. 29 by Henryk Górecki
© Copyright 1972 by PWM Edition, Kraków, Poland
U.S. Renewal Rights assigned to Boosey & Hawkes, Inc.
Reprinted by permission of Boosey & Hawkes, Inc.

Genesis I, Op. 19 by Henryk Górecki
© Copyright 1963 by PWM Edition, Kraków, Poland
U.S. Renewal Rights assigned to Boosey & Hawkes, Inc.
Reprinted by permission of Boosey & Hawkes, Inc.

Genesis II, Op. 19 by Henryk Górecki
© Copyright 1963 by PWM Edition, Kraków, Poland
U.S. Renewal Rights assigned to Boosey & Hawkes,
Inc. Reprinted by permission of Boosey & Hawkes, Inc.

Genesis III, Op. 19 by Henryk Górecki
© Copyright 1966 by PWM Edition, Kraków, Poland
U.S. Renewal Rights assigned to Boosey & Hawkes,
Inc. Reprinted by permission of Boosey & Hawkes, Inc.

Old Polish Music, Op. 24 by Henryk Górecki
© Copyright 1988 by Boosey & Hawkes Music Publishers Ltd.
for the World except Poland, Albania, Bulgaria, China, Yugoslavia,
Cuba, North Korea, Vietnam, Roumania, Hungary, Czechoslovakia,
and the former territories of the USSR.

Symphony No. 3, Op. 36 by Henryk Górecki
© Copyright 1977 by PWM Edition, Kraków, Poland
U.S. Renewal Rights assigned to Boosey & Hawkes, Inc.
English, French and German translation: © Copyright 1992
by Boosey & Hawkes Music Publishers Ltd.
Reprinted by permission of Boosey & Hawkes, Inc.

Symphony No. 4 by Henryk Górecki
© Copyright 2013 by Boosey & Hawkes Music Publishers Ltd.
Reprinted by permission of Boosey & Hawkes, Inc.

Three Songs, Op. 3 by Henryk Górecki
© Copyright 1977 by PWM Edition, Kraków, Poland
U.S. Renewal Rights assigned to Boosey & Hawkes, Inc. Reprinted by
permission of Boosey & Hawkes, Inc.

Totus Tuus, Op. 60 by Henryk Górecki
© Copyright 1988 by Boosey & Hawkes Music Publishers Ltd.
for the World except Poland, Albania, Bulgaria, China, Yugoslavia,
Cuba, North Korea, Vietnam, Roumania, Hungary, Czechoslovakia,
and the former territories of the USSR.

For the following compositions by Henryk Mikołaj Górecki:

Ad Matrem, Op. 29 for Soprano, Mixed Choir and Orchestra
© Copyright 1972 by PWM Edition, Kraków, Poland

O Domina Nostra, Meditation on the Black Madonna / O Domina Nostra - Medytacje o Jasnogórskiej Pani Naszej, Op. 55, for soprano and organ
© Copyright 1994 by PWM Edition, Kraków, Poland

Old Polish Music / Muzyka Staropolska, Op. 24 by Henryk Górecki
© Copyright 1988 by Boosey & Hawkes Music Publishers Ltd.
for the World except countries listed below and © Copyright 1988 by PWM Edition, Kraków, Poland for Poland, Albania, Bulgaria, China, Yugoslavia, Cuba, North Korea, Vietnam, Roumania, Hungary, Czechoslovakia, and the former territories of the USSR.

Symphony No. 2, "Copernican" Op. 31 for soprano, baritone, mixed choir and large orchestra. © Copyright 1977 by PWM Edition, Kraków, Poland

Symphony No. 3, "Symphony of Sorrowful Songs" Op. 36 for Soprano and large orchestra. © Copyright 1977 by PWM Edition, Kraków, Poland

Three Songs, Op. 3 by Henryk Górecki
© Copyright 1977 by PWM Edition, Kraków, Poland

Totus Tuus, Op. 60
© Copyright 1988 by Boosey & Hawkes Music Publishers Ltd. For the World except countries listed below and © Copyright 1988 by PWM Edition for Poland, Albania, Bulgaria, China, Yugoslavia, Cuba, North Korea, Vietnam, Roumania, Hungary, Czechoslovakia, and the former territories of the USSR.

And
Stabat Mater, Op. 53 by Karol Szymanowski
© 2000 by PWM Edition, Kraków. Poland.

**Extracts are Used by Kind Permission
of the Polskie Wydawnictwo Muzyczne, Kraków, Poland.**

◎ PREFACE ◎

This volume gathers interviews and studies of the music of the Polish composer, Henryk Mikołaj Górecki (1933-2010). Contributors include the composer himself – in a series of interviews spanning his entire career, from 1962 to 2008 – as well as leading Górecki scholars from Poland, the U.K., the U.S., and Australia. The collection includes a list of works, music examples, portraits, photographs, and a bibliography. The value of gathering five interviews in one place cannot be overestimated, as these encounters portray the mind of the composer and capture the changing interests that preoccupied him at various stages in his career.

The project brings together different views at the composer's oeuvre, highlighting three of the four symphonies, each honored by a separate chapter: the Second Symphony *Copernican* (Kinga Kiwała), the Third Symphony *The Symphony of Sorrowful Songs* (Maja Trochimczyk) and the Fourth Symphony *Tansman Episodes* (Andrzej Wendland). Two studies were contributed by an eminent Polish scholar and Górecki's long-time personal friend, Prof. Teresa Malecka of Kraków, including an extensive review of the composer's links to Polish musical traditions, and an overview of his piano music. The studies are rounded up by an introductory overview of Górecki's life and career and a case study of his visit to Los Angeles in 1997, when he conducted his Third Symphony for the first time outside of Poland, and made a huge impact on the musical life of California.

As one of the organizers of the 1997 Górecki Autumn Residency at the University of Southern California in Los Angeles, and the composer's personal translator and guide, I had an unusually close contact with the reclusive composer and was able to present his views in two interviews and several articles, with a focus on the Third Symphony.

I hope that this volume will serve to stimulate further research into the life and music of Henryk Mikołaj Górecki whose oeuvre goes well beyond the world-famous maverick of a piece, his Third Symphony, beloved and misinterpreted in equal measure.

~ *Maja Trochimczyk*

◎ GÓRECKI TRIBUTE ◎

By Luke B. Howard

It was while a graduate student at the University of Michigan from 1994-97 that I started to examine the music of Henryk Górecki in detail—his famous Third Symphony eventually became the topic for my doctoral dissertation. And during those years I had the privilege of meeting and interviewing the composer several times. Over the course of these visits, and other meetings with Górecki, I came to know something about the man himself as well as his music.

Górecki was unfailingly kind, patient, and generous, despite painful physical ailments and an exhausting schedule that would render any normal person decidedly ill-tempered. I recall him literally bounding across the stage from player to player, with that pronounced limp from childhood injuries, cheerfully offering advice and assistance to student performers, while his close friends threw up their hands in frustration because he would not slow down or calm down. He was irrepressibly enthusiastic, almost giddy, when it came to making music. And he was equally reticent when it came to talking about his music. It's true that he could be dismissive of the merely curious journalist who wanted a quick quote or who attempted to pry into the composer's psyche. But the flip side is that Górecki was consistently respectful of the serious musician who sought for musical answers to the profound questions his compositions raise. It was the music, not the ego, that was most important to him. And that kind of integrity in a composer cannot be faked.

When I came to the end of my journey with Górecki's music, it was such a joy to know that my focus on him was not misplaced. His compositions withstood all the scrutiny I could give them, and every impression that I teased out of my analysis confirmed my feeling that he had reached a place of purity—especially with the Third Symphony—that few composers ever glimpse, never mind achieve. That such extraordinary music could come from such a humble, self-effacing soul should not surprise us. Górecki was a master of his craft, certainly. But for music to speak sincerely to the deepest emotions within us, it must spring from a deep well of sincerity and not merely a reliance on sound compositional technique.

Arvo Pärt, the Estonian composer with whom Górecki was most often grouped during the 1990s, once asked, "How can one fill the time with notes worthy of the preceding silence?" If music aspires to break the powerful, divine stillness that Pärt spoke of, then its inescapable duty is to be exceptional. Górecki's music is exceptional; it has earned the right to break the silence. But when Górecki had nothing to say musically, which was often the case in his last years, he respected the silence, too. At precisely the time when he might have sought for commercial gain, notoriety, attention, and honors, or be tempted to write "copy-cat" works in the wake of the Third Symphony's stunning success, he chose instead to remain silent. That eloquent silence, now perpetual, will be one of Górecki's most powerful legacies. For in an age when so many composers exploit their music to honor themselves, Górecki stood out as a composer who, above all, gave of himself in honoring music. And now in return, his music—and his silence—honor him.

~ Luke B. Howard

◎ MOUNTAINS OF GRIEF ◎

By Maja Trochimczyk

~ for Henryk Mikołaj Górecki in memoriam

"Mom, don't cry — Mamo, nie płacz" [1] —
the soprano soars above
lush chords of the orchestra.

Sorrow, my endless sorrow —
Euntes ibant et flebant[2] —

He grew up bitter, alone
at the keyboard, with waves
of sound crashing all around him.

His Mama, smothered with a pillow
on her hospital bed, he was
an orphaned child, sickly,

with a leg damaged by illness,
a limping gait — look,
a great man comes,
truly great

How do I know? He taught me —

to do everything well,
with my whole heart, whole being,
dance despair into frenzy,

---

[1] "Mamo, nie płacz" – the first words of an inscription on the wall of a Gestapo prison in Zakopane by young Helena Błażusiak, used as text of the second movement of the Third Symphony, "Symphony of Sorrowful Songs" op. 36 (1976).
[2] From Psalm 126:6, *The Vulgate,* a title of Górecki's choral work, op. 32, from 1972. The full verse is: "Euntes ibant et flebant portantes semina sua - venientes autem venientes in exultatione..." [He went off, went off weeping, carrying the seed. He comes back, comes back singing.]

relish that last plate of *barszcz*[3]

laugh loudly, play the second fiddle
in *góralska muzyka,*[4] find Chopin's
mazurkas under my fingers,

look beyond the edge of grief,
toward the mountains,
shrouded by the clouds of unknowing

sing lullabies of consolation,
weave music from strands of pain,
sudden glimpses of grace,

seek safety in the cocoon
of timelessness, under gold stars
on the blue cloak of Mother Mary —
sixteen portraits on one wall
in his studio in Katowice

give of myself fully —
a daily offering of bread, crumbs
of mercy, morsels of blessings

Euntes ibant et flebant—

carry the cross, my cross

as I walk towards the glimmer
of light on the horizon,
bearing the fruit of my harvest

In exultatione —

© *2010, rev. 2017 by Maja Trochimczyk*

---

[3] "Barszcz" - traditional Polish beet soup we shared in Katowice in April 1998; cooked and served by the composer's wife, Jadwiga.
[4] "Góralska muzyka" - folk ensemble of four strings playing music from the Tatra Mountains, Górecki's chosen home. His last name means "of the mountains" and he settled in the village of Ząb in the Foothills area (Podhale) after spending most of his life in his native Silesia, in Katowice.

◎ PART I ◎

GÓRECKI ON LIFE AND MUSIC

CHAPTER 1

Conversation with Henryk Górecki: Leon Markiewicz, July 1962

Translated by Anna Maslowiec

Fig 1-1: Górecki (right) and Patkowski (left), c. 1962. Photo by A. Zhorski. Reproduced with the kind permission of Ludwik Erhardt, Chief Editor; *Ruch Muzyczny*.

Translator's Introduction: *Górecki is notorious for his dislike of speaking in public about his life and music; it is very rare to come across an interview with him. His interview with Tadeusz Marek[1] is widely*

---

[1] Tadeusz Marek and David Drew, "Górecki in Interview (1968) — And 20 Years After," *Tempo* 168 (1989): 25-28. According to Marek, this interview

believed to be the first and "only interview with Górecki in any language . . . certainly the only one in English."[2] *However, there is an earlier interview with Leon Markiewicz from 1962, published in* Ruch Muzyczny.[3] *In this interview Górecki speaks at length about his early works, his thoughts on contemporary music, and other composers. My translation follows the format of the original, editing being limited to one correction (see footnotes).*[4]

Leon Markiewicz: I chance upon Górecki as he is correcting the last pages of *Scontri*. While the coffee is brewing I look around the room . . . reproductions of van Gogh, Kantor, Tchórzewski, Vedova, a huge abstract by Andrzej Urbanowicz and even two abstract paintings by the composer himself. Photographs of Chopin and Szymanowski. Festival posters. Black clay pots resembling old Slavonic vases, a relief by Sabała from Dębno. On the grand piano, the *St. John Passion*, a Brahms piano sonata, and *Prince Igor*. On the bookshelf, my eyes light upon works by Tetmajer, Witkiewicz, monographs on van Gogh and Picasso, various books about art, books about Hitler's massacres, and a lot of Highland artefacts.[5] I look through the pile of neatly handwritten scores. Instinctively I look for new ones. There are two. I open the first one: *Elementi*. Under the title there is a motto: "In the beginning was Movement." The staves are full of unfamiliar diagrams, lines and symbols. Next to the scores—something for every theorist!—a few books with detailed composer's notes, which are produced before the final notation on the paper. There are many of them for every piece. I direct my first question to the composer who is just bringing coffee.

LM: Thanks to my indiscretion I have just found out about two new works. Could you describe to what degree they are related

---

originally appeared as "Composer's Workshop: Henryk Mikołaj Górecki," *Polish Music/ Polnische Musik* 2 (1968): 25-28.
[2] Marek and Drew, "Górecki in Interview," 25.
[3] Leon Markiewicz, "Conversation with Henryk Górecki," *Ruch Muzyczny* 4 (1962): 7-9.
[4] Article reprinted from *Context* 14 (summer 1997-98): 35-41. The translator acknowledges the kind assistance of Ludwig Erhardt, chief editor of *Ruch Muzyczny* at the time of writing, in providing the composer's photograph as well as permission to reprint copyright material.
[5] "Highland" refers to the region of southern Poland in the foothills of the Tatra mountains, known in Polish as Podhale.

to the previous compositions, and to what extent they are introducing new problems?

Henryk Mikołaj Górecki: Up to now I would have been seriously puzzled by this question, because I would not have been able to distinguish exactly between old and new. You happen to come at a moment when I have made a sort of reassessment. First of all, I consider my previous compositions, up to *Scontri* [1960] and *Diagram IV* [1961], as the past, in which I emphasized only the individual stages of getting to know the musical material I had come across. However, I knew that this would not last long. Currently, after a long period of reflection, during which I didn't write a single new note, I have given myself the task of trying out the possibilities of sound for myself, possibilities which are still hidden in the performance forces. New works such as *Elementi* for violin, viola and cello, and *Canti strumentali* for fifteen instruments mark the beginning of the period in which I am under strict self-control, not allowing myself any thoughtless moves. These works open a cycle of pieces with the same title, *Genesis*.[6] The works which belong to the cycle are, or will be, individual compositions with separate titles and various instrumental groups. I have already sketched the order: *Monologhi II* for voice and groups of instruments, Second Symphony for strings, a piece for percussion, a piece for choir and instruments, for large orchestra, and finally one for soloists, choir and orchestra.

> **LM:** Let me complete the comment from your notebook and clarify for readers the meaning of individual terms: "The fundamental element linking [the works] into a whole is constantly evolving Energy existing through Movement: a symbol of Manifestation of Life." But this is exactly the most accurate way of describing all your music! Where does the title of the cycle come from?

HMG: In general terms "genesis" describes conditions which contribute to the beginnings of events, from an embryo to fully developed form. I treated this word [*genesis*] as a symbol of individual stages of beginning, realization and development of the three basic

---

[6] The *Genesis* series eventually included three works: *Elementi, Canti strummetali* and *Monodramma*, i.e., the work referred to above as *Monologhi II*. The other projected works were not realized.

elements of music which I consider to be agogics, dynamics and color. This is where the title of the first piece of the cycle comes from, *Elementi*, in which these elements appear in an embryonic form.

LM: It seems that on the basis of works such as the Symphony 1959, *Scontri, Diagrams* or even the earlier work *Songs of Joy and Rhythm* (1959-60), one can assume that emancipation of these elements has been of concern to you for a while. There we find just such movements of sound masses, dynamic explosions and sound complexes. Would I be wrong in saying that what you applied sporadically before, you now want to, let's say, exploit deliberately?

HMG: Yes; however, in the Symphony only the first and the second movements demonstrate this clearly, and in the *Diagrams* only part IV. Besides, back then there were successions of short, single sounds; this I gave up in *Elementi*, using only successions of composite groups, creating fusions which arise from the complexes.

Because *Elementi* opens the whole cycle, what happens there should be treated as an initial movement of some embryonic forms, individual atoms.

LM: How is the musical material organized in *Elementi?*

HMG: The starting point for me is still dodecaphony, or more precisely, serial technique. Despite other people's opinions that serial technique is outdated, I still see possibilities in it. Schoenberg is the creator of a law which governs sound. He can be only compared with Rameau. The harmonic laws discovered, absorbed and described by Rameau served composers for almost two hundred years as standard laws. They became the basis for the realization of thousands of works, and an abundance of styles.

Today nobody thinks of imitating the style of Schoenberg, but despite attempts to reject dodecaphonic technique, more and more composers are using it; it is becoming a common procedure. Dodecaphony interests me not so much as a way of organizing individual sounds, but more in terms of organizing sound groups. It helps in creating the form. In *Elementi*—since we are talking about this piece—the O and R sets of an all-interval series provide the basis for the formal design of the whole piece. These intervals are characterized by the different number of semitones in each. I treat semitones not only as the basic sound complexes but also as the smallest cells.

LM: I'm not quite clear...

HMG: For example, let's consider, the interval C—F-sharp. The six semitones it comprises serve to expose six different sound complexes in six successive time spans. But anyway, why talk about detailed analysis? Personally I'm content that, at least for the time being, I have resolved some constructional problems involving spatial planning and strict control over it. The sound-material—its order, its duration, and dynamics—I regulate exclusively by ear.

LM: As in the major-minor system?

HMG: Yes. Once formal consequences are realized, I'm not following series of notes that are presented at the beginning. I chose what seems best to me at any moment.

LM: Since we are talking about construction it is hard not to mention aleatoricism... The aleatoricism that Cage represents contradicts Art, which should be a consequence of a specific material organization. Here I share Arp's opinion: "Chance means artistic capitulation, chaos is a negation of artistry." The outcomes of Cage's ideas cannot be called Art. They are only attempts to find a new track; they are inventions which one does not know what to do with after a while. I'm against Cage's Piano Concerto [1959-60]. In my opinion aleatoricism only makes sense when the composer's data about musical events rules out any unpredictable realizations. Then it is a sort of directed movement, a particular variant of the old *ad libitum, ossia,* etc. Chance understood in this way is applied in *Elementi.* I'm sure that performers will not find any realizations other than the ones I have predicted. I will come back to the agogics, dynamics and tone color we mentioned previously. But what about melody, rhythm and harmony?

HMG: I take the same position as Boulez: "At last people have understood that it is impossible to create music out of melody, rhythm and harmony." For me these terms are the same thing. What I understand by the term Melody is complex sound events characterized by a certain tension and movement. So it is a product of interaction between all elements. I cannot talk about rhythm alone, since it operates exclusively on relative values; I cannot separate harmony because for me even one note is a fragment of a vertical range. Therefore for me there are only three basic elements: agogics, embracing all events measured in time; dynamics, regulating tension and its release; and color, which I understand as both changes in pitch and its timbral complexity in the usual sense.

LM: How significant is the choice of strings in *Elementi*? Is there a special reason in choosing strings for *Elementi*?

HMG: Naturally. I regard strings as instruments one can still do a lot with. Before working on *Genesis*, I analyzed their articulation techniques. You will not believe it, but there are about 300 of them. And this is without tapping music stands or using the body of the instrument: only bow, strings and fingers. Obviously, this number also includes the common kinds of articulation. This does not mean that I use all of them in one piece. In *Elementi* there are about ten; however, the predominant sound is rough, and achieved through stronger bow-pressure.

LM: I've noticed that the notation of *Scontri*, *Diagrams*, *Elementi* and *Canti strommtali* often resembles the notation of electronic pieces. Some critics have also pointed out the similarity of some sections of *Scontri* to electronic-like sounds. Is there a real influence from electronic music?

HMG: I think that electronic music has attracted the attention of all composers and directed it towards the value of vertical sonorities, as well as horizontal ones. But—even though I still think about trying my abilities in the electronic studio (but for now, I'm pretty scared by montage)—I have never tried to imitate any electronic sounds, soft rustlings, or noises. If, today, percussion instruments are used to produce some rustling sounds, it is a consequence of normal development of music. We simply have a different way of organizing and using the whole sound-scale. But it is true that today's realities—technology, electronic miracles—allow us to notice something different. Have you noticed the fantastic sound event produced by a stadium full of thousands of people? The joyful yell of thousands of throats? ...It's difficult to ignore it. You see, music is not only F-sharp—A—B, but as Debussy said, "the rustle of forests and sounds of sea."

> **LM**: I must say that your last sentence surprises me. You have talked only about musical material and its organization. Extra-musical aspects were foreign to you. The best proof of this is your own comment about *Scontri* in the Warsaw Autumn program in 1960: nothing but the division of a scale, pitch range, complexes, and notes. I can see that the new cycle of pieces does not only bring changes in terms of musical material. Do you believe in non-autonomous music?

HMG: In my firm opinion it is only possible to talk concretely about technical matters; others cannot easily be expressed by words and this is why they are communicated through music. In the twentieth century, the view that what counts is an idea, its expansion and its relationship to the development of musical material, etc. has become particularly popular. But is that all? Let's take Stravinsky, the main proponent of the cult of craftsmanship. I wonder why he couldn't resist music for the stage, texts with huge emotional weight. Why did he choose the *Martyrdom of St. Sebastian*?[7] Why didn't he use syllables instead of words? I agree that up to now I have talked only about technical matters; however, haven't you noticed that most of my pieces have titles which do not merely reflect the formal design of a piece, for instance *Songs of Joy and Rhythm*, *Epitafium*, "Lauda" or "Invocation"?[8] For me art is a manifestation of life to which I try to bring all possible and available means. Some people are fully satisfied by all the things that constitute craftsmanship. But maybe these are people who are devoid of that secret of music that makes music Art?

> **LM**: Does a title characterize the work in a definite way? What about double titles given to one composition, such as *Phase and Obelisk for Auschwitz*? What about the relative metamorphosis of titles, from an abstract one like 8'37" to a deeply realistic one, *Threnody for the Victims of Hiroshima*? I think that what they really amount to is the fact that in the end, the only

---

[7] The *Martyrdom of Saint Sebastian* is, of course, by Debussy. Perhaps, Górecki was thinking of *Persephone* or *Oedipus Rex* (translator's note).
[8] "Lauda" and "Invocation" are the fourth and first movements respectively of Symphony No. 1 "1959."

matters beyond dispute, which exclude all possible interpretations, are the form and all the technical aspects of the piece.

HMG: All these matters are a bit hypothetical, and difficult to talk about. Perfect craftsmanship should always be the first condition for any art work. And as for a creator not having a definite view of his own work, I wouldn't want to get involved in looking for reasons. I can speak only for myself. I decide to write a piece, and I don't expect any surprises concerning either technical matters or "substance."

LM: What is your attitude towards other composers?

HMG: I'm primarily interested in those composers whose craftsmanship has an ideal characteristic: logic interwoven with consequential development and simplicity. Here I can point to Webern and Bartók. I also value the attitude of a composer towards himself and other people: a firmly defined idea and the consequences of its realization, linked with an individual approach to musical material. You can probably guess that I'm talking about Messiaen and Nono. A scarcely lesser impact for me came years ago from meeting a less well known composer, Franco Evangelisti. He pointed out some problems of sonority and technique, which helped me to find something I was looking for. Naturally, we now stand on opposite sides.

I particularly value artistic honesty, which is based on one's ethics, psyche and interests. Unfortunately, with today's developments in music not many composers can stand on their own two feet; often their abilities are overstretched by the ideas they take up. This often goes hand in hand with liking to talk about themselves and criticizing almost every other composer. In this respect, I'm closer to those composers who remain true to themselves and maybe work in the shadows, but work honestly, and what they produce simply has the hallmark of good music.

LM: I would like to ask about your impressions of Paris, but we will have to postpone this for another occasion. . . You are going to be there again for three months. I guess this is your plan for the near future.

HMG: No, I'm not going to France until Spring. I'm spending my holidays as usual, in Podhale. I love the Highlander village: its hospitality, poverty, art and its particular philosophy of life. Every year my wife and I cannot wait for the moment when we can just cast loose. You cannot imagine what interesting people we come across! Such sculptures, such architecture! And music, which I don't spend a night without, in the great company of highland people. Paris can wait. First, Podhale.

LM: Well, enjoy your trip. An on behalf of your readers I should like to thank you for the honesty (so rarely found these days!) of your responses.

~ *July 1962, Leon Markiewicz*

CHAPTER 2

"I Am Always Myself:" Henryk Mikołaj Górecki in Conversation with Mieczysław Kominek[1]

Figure 2-1: Górecki's portrait by Lech Kowalski and Włodzimierz Pniewski from *Studio*, No. 8 (1993): 8. Used by Permission.

---

[1] Translated by Maja Trochimczyk. Originally published in Polish as "Zawsze jestem sobą: mówi Henryk Mikołaj Górecki w rozmowie z Mieczysławem Kominkiem." *Studio: Magazyn Płytowy* 8 (November/December 1993): 8-11.

Mieczysław Kominek: The first polish performance of your Symphony No. 3, *The Symphony of Sorrowful Songs* at the Warsaw Autumn Festival in 1977 elicited strong emotions. The work entered the canon of Polish contemporary music, appeared in concerts, always making an impression, but has never gained such popularity that it has been enjoying right now.[2] Also in Poland, though this popularity came to our country from outside. Is what is happening around the Third Symphony an expression of historical justice?

Henryk Mikołaj Górecki: I'm not the one you should ask.

MK: Did you expect anything of this sort 16 years ago?[3]

HMG: Every soldier has the marshal's baton in his backpack and thinks that he will be a general. I knew right away what I composed in 1977, and I also know it now.

MK: The listeners were disoriented. The Third Symphony evoked the most controversial opinions and judgments; it was greeted with endless enthusiasm by some and with condemnation by others. Some critics and musicologists were delighted with the expressiveness of this work; others were offended for "turning away from the entire European tradition, not only musical but also, culture in general."

HMG: Opinions and judgments expressed about music are terrifying. I read once that orchestral music by Mozart is nothing more than shifting the Alberti bass accompaniment from the piano to the orchestra. Mozart's religious music? Not interesting. He may have

---

[2] The popularity followed the 1992 release of a recording by Nonesuch, with David Zinman conducting and Dawn Upshaw, soprano. Its popularity completely bewildered Polish music critics, who have been deeply divided about the Symphony's merits since its premiere in 1977. See the Appendix to this interview for excerpts from this debate published in *Ruch Muzyczny*. [This and all subsequent notes by the Translator]

[3] The Symphony was composed in October-December 1976, premiered in April 1977 at Royan International Festival (France), and first performed in Poland in September 1977 at the Warsaw Autumn Festival. Both performances resulted in scandals, the first because the critics hated the music, the second because the composer disliked the interpretation and refused to attend the concert.

done something in the opera... I heard once a lecture before the performance of several string quartets by Mozart. The lecturer was talking about one of the later quartets stating that this was the beginning of the "real" Mozart. Apparently, the earlier works were merely primitive beginnings. But Mozart had composed over 400 works by that time! If this lecturer really knew Mozart, he would have never said such nonsense. But he passes judgment, he knows which work is good, and which one is bad. This is terrifying. So if someone has had such an attitude towards Mozart, what can you expect from this person when he is writing about Górecki? Thus, attacks: a revolutionary, a Majakowski. There: frogs are being fried on the frying pan — that was about *Scontri*. Here: the Third Symphony, a Franciscan habit, simplicity bordering on total indolence, two chords multiplied...[4] Once, he composed works in the spirit of the avant-garde of the time, and then he got offended and wrote *Three Pieces in the Old Style* in major-minor. And then: New-Age... A complete confusion.

> **MK**: People want to organize for themselves this extraordinary world of music; they want to understand; they want to tame it. That is completely natural.

HMG: Exactly, people want to. I do not care one bit about what people want to do with Mozart, with Stravinsky, with Górecki, or with Webern. People always hear what they want to hear, and not what they actually hear, in reality. So they heard in the Third Symphony just two chords multiplied. I *do* know, what is there. Something more, even a lot more. Few people notice this, but someone told me that Bach would have been envious about the canon in the Third Symphony; jealous about its construction. Naturally, it is very nice to hear that; though — my God! — Bach. But this person noticed that I had to work really hard to think it all through in order to achieve this result. This does not fall down from heaven.

Did Chopin just sit at the piano and being suddenly inspired, he just composed? He had to perform a certain amount of labor, working out specific structures. In order to do so, he had to be prepared, he had to know, know a lot. People think and imagine that composers just sit

---

[4] Górecki uses a colorful expression as a pun that points to both simplicity and religious content: *dwa akordy na krzyż* means literally two chords on the cross, or crossed out.

down and write. How many problems have to be solved! I always search for solutions; learn something new. I search in Mozart; I learn from Schubert, Ives, Beethoven, Szymanowski, and Chopin. In order to write music, you have to know. There are certain fundamental principles; there is specific knowledge that cannot be just thought about. Music is not only impression, or emotion. I solve specific issues; I construct these structures in one way and not another. This is hard work—not just improvisation, as some people tend to think.

MK: The Third Symphony has been compared to a lump of a field stone that is in the same relationship to the sculptures by Michelangelo as your music is to the works by Palestrina, Bach or Mozart.

Figure 2-2: Górecki's portraits by Lech Kowalski and Włodzimierz Pniewski from *Studio*, No. 8 (1993): 8-9. Used by Permission.

HMG: I have no intention to compete with a lump of field stone, nor with a sculpture by Michelangelo. I really have nothing against stones: I even collect them and have acquired a beautiful collection. Oh, well, perhaps again the simplicity of music is in question. Let me refer to folk music, *górale* music.[5] Someone may say that this is extremely primitive musical material. The harmonic-rhythmic structure is very poor: quarter-notes in simple harmony D major and G major, sometimes in A major. The music from the Kurpie region is much richer, has much more complicated musical material, relationships of words and sounds. But in the music of the Podhale region in addition to this "tangible" element, there is also something else, what you can either discover—hear and feel—or not. You have your sensors aimed at this something; without these sensors, you can notice only this external, primitive structure.

MK: What can be seen behind the structure of your music?

HMG: Always the same Górecki, still interested in the same issues.

MK: The same Górecki even in such different works as *Scontri* and the Third Symphony?

HMG: You, the writers, have several Góreckis because you like boxes and labels: this one from *Scontri*, that one from Sonata, still another one from *Refrain*, and one more from the Third Symphony. It is probably pleasant to arrange reality in such a way, but the true reality is somewhat different. Between *Scontri* and the Third Symphony I wrote many other compositions and I do not see any reason to distinguish any phases, to write about leaps and jumps. If you listen carefully, in all of my works you can hear many similarities. I did not replace the clothes of a revolutionary with a habit of a Franciscan; I have never had the clothes of a revolutionary, nor a habit. I have never needed them.

I have my own world and that is sufficient for me. Mountains take a lot of space in this world. Regardless of where I am, I always see before my eyes and within me, my Chochołów, my Podhale, my fir trees, my streams, my stones. It seems that people with heart illness should not

---

[5] *Górale*, highlanders are the inhabitants of the foothills of the Tatra Mountains, the Podhale region in southern Poland, Górecki's favorite area, as discussed later.

go to the mountains, but I feel really well in the mountains. I have never gone to any resorts, I have never taken a vacation, visited any sanatoria. I always go to the same place. To Chochołów.[6] That is probably why I am who I am. Without Podhale, perhaps, I could be different. But I never wrote anything "górale"-like. Some people say that in the second part of the Harpsichord Concerto there is some mountain music, some *krzesany*.[7] Since Kilar composed a *Krzesany*, Górecki should write one, too. No, I have never written anything in the *górale* style and probably I will never write it. This is not what matters.

MK: Were you pleased with the enormous success of the Third Symphony?

HMG: It would have been hard to get angry, but I look at it as if it were happening somewhere far away, to someone else. I have walked in this world for a while already. This is just chance.

MK: Maybe the time for the Third Symphony has come now? This does happen...

HMG: I do not know who needs what and when. Why do young Englishmen in their discoes need Górecki? Why do they publish Górecki in England, in America, why are they buying it? I do not know, I can only acknowledge this fact. I am wondering, however, how much of it is due to fashion and how much stems from necessity: I nod my head, because others nod their heads. But I know that there are people who experience the Third Symphony in solitude. And I am delighted by this, because a person alone, by themselves, stops pretending, stops to nod his head like others do. This is a success.

Many letters reach me from different parts of the world, even from near the North Pole. Someone wrote to me from Australia, that the

---

[6] Chochołów is a large village in Podhale, about 15 miles to the west from Zakopane, established in 16th century. Górecki later bought a house in the nearby village of Ząb, where he lived until his death.

[7] *Krzesany* is one of the dance genres of the Podhale area; Wojciech Kilar composed a work for orchestra based on this model in 1974. See Timothy J. Cooley, *Making Music in the Polish Tatras: Tourists, Ethnographers, and Mountain Musicians*. (Bloomington: Indiana University Press, 2005).

Third Symphony helped him to survive. And then a doctor from Sweden wrote about his tragedy. His sons died in accidents, he was close to a nervous breakdown, but he listens to my Symphony. The music helps him survive his difficult fate. This really is not about a fashion, this is not about what is appropriate to have at home, a recording just like you have to have an important book that you just put on the shelf and never open, but you can show to your guests and brag about it... If I know that my music helps someone survive dramatic moments in life, this really moves me to tears. I know how such help can be needed.

> **MK**: It seems that would be hard to find a greater satisfaction for a creator than one stemming from an opportunity of such service, wouldn't it?

HMG: Let us not use such grand words. I do not like such grand words and I never use them. But, indeed, I have had some satisfaction recently. I keep hearing that my old works are alive somewhere, that they make an impression, that they are accepted well. Different works, not only the Third Symphony, also the *Refrain*, the First Symphony and *Scontri*. The Second Symphony has become a revelation. Thanks to the Sonata for two violins an ensemble won an international competition somewhere. A work from my youth!

This was not talked about much, but this Górecki was always played around the world. Who wants to would know it? Naturally, at the moment when I joined Boosey & Hawkes in London, everything changed. This is an excellent publisher which publishes music not only just to print it. If they publish it, the music has to be performed somewhere. So it is played. In recent years I have had several dozen or even several hundred performances per year. Some people do not like it, but I say that there is enough room on Earth for everyone. I have my own place.

> **MK**: So what is your place in the new Polish reality?

HMG: A lot is being said about the old times. That now we are free, and then we, composers, were forced to compose some kind of music, forced to draw from folklore... Nobody could ever force me to do anything. I have always been free, I have done what I wanted and I found inspiration where I wanted. You can sit in prison and be a free man.

But it is fashionable now to talk about your suffering. And there is a fashion for different mottos. I have been enraged by one such horrible motto: "Finally in our own home." This is a horrid insult to people who have always lived and worked here. One word was missing: "Finally, we are alone in our own home." I have always lived in my own home, in Poland. I had a tenant that was forced on me, but it is not my fault. The house was mine. This is my place and always will be.

APPENDIX

Excerpts from the Debate about the Third Symphony in *Ruch Muzyczny* in 1977[8]

"A masterpiece, placing its creator among geniuses. Any attempt to argue and prove this statement, would condemn me to make this work more banal."

~ Andrzej Chłopecki, *Ruch Muzyczny*, November 6, 1977.

"I can only be jealous those who, free from any doubts, have called the Third Symphony a work of genius. To identify a genius gives one a great satisfaction, and the risk is low. I find it hard to join this choir — for me beyond discussion is only the "otherness" of Górecki's composition, its ostentatious simplicity of material and construction, the negation of the "artistry" (*kunszt*) which in this work reaches an extreme that has not be experienced before. However, Górecki reached his goal—it is hard to deny a peculiar strength of expression to these three or four chords tuned into a national-elegiac note."

~ Olgierd Pisarenko, *Ruch Muzyczny*, November 6, 1977.

"In this music, turned with its back to modernity, I found something new: an otherness from all Polish music of the postwar period. The only analogy may be found in almost completely unknown here vocal-instrumental compositions by Andrzej Nikodemowicz. This analogy stems from the common source, which are religious folk songs of the village. Thanks to these songs, we enter into this music easily and we feel in it as in a warm house, from which we do not want to leave. Its familiarity [*swojskość*] is its value, perhaps the only value, but certainly more than sufficient."

~ Tadeusz Kaczyński, *Ruch Muzyczny*, November 6, 1977.

"The extraordinary talent of Górecki is being lost, alas, more and more, due to a fundamentally false premise: the composer clearly wishes in his music to reveal the simplest, most elemental, "naked" emotional

---

[8] *Studio: Magazyn Płytowy*, No. 8 (November/December 1993): 12-13.

experience, and to reduce to minimum the whole artistic "remainder" —that unwittingly leads to *reductio ad absurdum.* This is acting contrary to the deepest tradition of European (and probably not only!) art and culture, in which content and form, emotion and the artistry of expression, sincerity and sophisticated taste—have (luckily) never been values that excluded each other."

~ Tadeusz Zieliński, *Ruch Muzyczny*, November 6, 1977.

"Before I heard this work, too many enthusiastic opinions reached me. There were not free from such statements as "the greatest Polish contemporary composer" or, simply, "a genius." So much greater was my disappointment at the concert. So much stronger the irritation, when in place of an experience and emotion, boredom broke in. When the refined simplicity turned out to be mere primitivism... The composer seems to have crossed the border that our culture encircled around the area of human activity that we call 'the arts.'"

~ Ludwik Erhardt, *Ruch Muzyczny,* November 6, 1977.

"All three movements are expressively unified, all are slow and all musical statements are stated to the end. Górecki is like that: he does not leave for us any room for guessing, for the imagination of the listener, whereby a listener could think of things that are not in the score. In his *ostinato* system, the notes that are used are placed next to each other, predominantly in diatonic steps. Whoever will not be exhausted by it, will be delighted—I succumbed to this, I was deeply moved—I jumped into this water, into this world created by Górecki. If not, I would see here only excessive length and an economy bordering with poverty, and unity bordering with monotony."

~ Zygmunt Mycielski, *Ruch Muzyczny,* 4 December 1977.

CHAPTER 3

About Life and Music:
A Conversation with Henryk Mikołaj Górecki

Maja Trochimczyk

Figure 3-1: Henryk Mikołaj Górecki with Maja Trochimczyk in Zakopane, July 18, 1997. Photo by Andrzej Bachleda.

The first part of this conversation took place in Zakopane, on 18 July 1997, in the home of Andrzej and Maria Bachleda. I went there to invite Mr. Górecki to conduct his Third Symphony at the University of Southern California in Los Angeles and participate in the Górecki Autumn Festival the School of Music was organizing. The conversation was concluded in Los Angeles on 8 October 1997 at the end of these festivities.[1]

---

[1] An earlier version of this interview, translated and edited by Anne Botstein, "On Life and Music: A Semi-Serious Conversation. Maria Anna Harley talks with Henryk Mikołaj Górecki" was published in the *Musical Quarterly*, 82/1 (Spring 1998): 60-82. The current translation is closely based on the original Polish text.

Maja Trochimczyk: We don't have much time today, so we cannot delve into technical details and the craft of a composer. Instead, I would like to have a short general conversation. I would like to talk about music and life.

Henryk Mikołaj Górecki: Please, one does not talk about life, one lives life.

MT: So what about music and faith? You composed a lot of religious music which expressed faith. How is faith expressed in music?

HMG: Life and faith... I don't know. I don't understand the question... Let's put it this way. I have the following motto: Life is complicated enough, let's not make it more difficult, let's not complicate it for us even more.

MT: I had in mind the audience, people who write letters to you saying that music gives some sense to their lives, consolation in suffering.

HMG: Please, these are not the things one should talk about.

MT: Let's leave this topic aside, then.

HMG: One shouldn't talk about these things. Except these are the things that are the most important for people—for writers, for creators. Not gloss, not this "fame" in quotation marks—which is here today and gone tomorrow. You may be elevated to the top of the mountain today and fall down tomorrow because some fashion or some ideas have changed. Therefore, we should not attach to these things any significance. An honest creator should not give them any weight. I try to understand and approach it this way: fame may be here today and gone tomorrow. But I have lived for a while and maybe will still live for a while. You know, we don't choose the place and the time of our birth, we receive them. Maybe if we could, we would choose and regulate them. Fortunately, we can't... (*pause*)

So if you received that span of time from someone, you should live it out decently. And this is the whole philosophy: everybody has to do some work here, however modest, whatever it is. There is a place on earth for everybody, and everybody should do something in this world. Only one should do it honestly (*przyzwoicie*).[2] And what does "honestly" mean? Let everyone rack their own brain to figure it out for themselves.

MT: What does it mean "to do honest work" while composing?

HMG: Why do we talk about music? Music is a profession like any other—a carpenter, a cabinetmaker... Bach used to say that he is not an artist, not a creator. Bach always emphasized that he was a servant; that he served. That great Bach! This is service.

MT: So you serve too...

HMG: Of course, I do my part. As I said, God gave me some talent. I don't know whether I multiply my talents. I don't know: I try. I consider music a normal profession and I want to do it the best I can. Nor go beyond myself. Just do my work decently. That's it.

MT: But this "work" is a kind of experience, searching for beauty...

HMG: What is *not* an experience? Or let me put it this way: could anything not be an experience? For me, there is no such thing. No. Not for me. Every second of our life is an experience, an experience of something. And does only music accomplish it? Does it have to be done by a musician?

MT: But in music, to give for example, there is a special experience of time.

HMG: Only in music? Time? There is time in film, too.

MT: In a film, there are images, there is a plot.

HMG: Images, you say. Indeed, these images move and can be stopped. Thus, a film is not an abstraction; we understand these images. But not everybody understands music... I am not an expert about it. Twenty

---

[2] The word "przyzwoicie" actually means "decently" – but "honestly" could also be used in this context.

years ago we would have been talking about it all night, but now I am no longer interested in this topic. Music... I think music is one of the fields that people really need: but much depends on whether people know how to perceive it. Everybody should be prepared to know how to benefit from music. Not only from music, but also from literature, sculpture, or film. You know, film is not only a sequence of moving images, let's say "a gun, one shot, and ten corpses..." A good film is a good film. It can be great art.

MT: For example, Tarkovsky's films.[3]

HMG: Of course—wonderful! Tarkovsky said that art is prayer. This is something I have always stressed. But it is hard to understand; a person has to mature to realize it. Because people imagine that to pray means to say the words of their prayers. But the truth is that one can say tons of *Hail Marys* and that will not amount to any prayer.[4] Olivier Messiaen said during a meeting in Katowice that he was a man of prayer.[5] But... he just writes his notes, listens to the birds. Is that supposed to be prayer?

Or let's look at life in the mountains. Andrzej [Bachleda] talked earlier about these remote times: there was poverty, lack of everything. Indeed, there was poverty, conditions were very hard. The winter was long, nothing grew, and the agricultural technique was just about useless. And still, these people lived in *heaven*. Indeed, from today's perspective, these times were heaven.

MT: Was this heaven the internal peace and silence?

HMG: No, heaven was this normalcy which we forgot completely— heaven was taking life on earth as something normal. Life was not surrounded by some grand philosophy. You just exist, and you do something you feel you were created to do. Whatever you do, you

---

[3] Andrei Tarkovsky (1932-1986) was a Russian filmmaker, author of experimental and philosophical films such as *Solaris, Mirror, Nostalghia,* and *Sacrifice.*
[4] Górecki uses the informal term *zdrowaśka* (from "Zdrowaś Mary," first line of *Hail, Mary,* as an example of high-speed, casual recitation of prayers.
[5] Olivier Messiaen (1908-1992) was a French composer of a mystical and experimental orientation; inspired by Catholic faith, he served as a church organist for most of his life.

should enjoy, whether it is difficult or not, whether it is a burden or not. That is your destiny: you should enjoy your destiny. And now what? We race like dogs after their tails, searching for something. What are we searching for? What do all these people search for? Tell me, really, what?

MT: I think people are searching for success—for something to prove their value.

Figure 3-2: Henryk Mikołaj Górecki in Zakopane, July 18, 1997.
Photo by Maja Trochimczyk.

HMG: No. What is it? It is not "looking for success."

> **MT**: Maybe something else... There is now a lot of greed in people. Everybody wants to have more, always more: more of everything, even more experiences... More and more, to infinity.

HMG: "Me, me, me... If I have a Cadillac, you want a Porsche. If I have a Porsche, you want a Mercedes." And what's the use? "If you have ten suits, I want twenty." And I ask: "What for?" Somebody said it nicely (let me not ruin it): "Live as if you had to die tomorrow, and work as if you could live forever." (*pause*) That is the whole philosophy of life. So what about us? There is a phrase I like a lot that sums this up, and I have been repeating it for so many years, I no longer remember whether I invented it or heard it somewhere: "Your last shirt has no pockets."

> **MT**: So, you can't take all the riches with you.

HMG: Nothing will be left of all of this. A person who has ten or one hundred fifty cars, or many villas or private planes... Such a person is terribly poor, because he has no time to stay in all the villas, drive his cars, or wear his suits. "Wait a minute, stop to think about it. Is that why you are here on earth? For more, and more, and more?" And then a certain moment comes, my God, maybe a disaster. Consider it good luck, if death occurs in a second. But if one is left suffering and has to remain lying down for a long time, then what? Well, you cannot reverse the film and change it. You cannot cut out bad scenes and replace them. There is no editing, no reassembling of life.

> **MT**: But it is possible to live well today and to try make today's "good life" happen daily.

HMG: Give me an example: what is living a "good life" today?

> **MT**: It means always trying to do the best one can, and to, in each moment, choose something that is of real value.

HMG: I think this is devilishly difficult, as there are always hundreds of possibilities, and it is impossible to make the right choice. Maybe one day a computer program will be invented for this purpose. But God forbid... Let me put it another way. Everybody is given some wisdom and some conscience. We forget about it, as we focus on the notion of *Homo sapiens*, the thinking beings. What is missing, is conscience. The worst bandit, the worst murderer, the worst criminal, they all have some hidden feelings, some remorse nagging them. Conscience. This is the best solution: act according to what your conscience dictates. But not for display, not for show. I always wonder how often it happens that somebody does something good, and there is a television crew right there... Isn't it true?

> **MT**: Oh, yes, that happens often.

HMG: "I do something good, I feed poor children in Kenya..." And we watch this benefactor on TV. Why don't you go there without television? Without profiting from human poverty? So, that's what interests me instead: simple, common, peasant philosophy.

> **MT:** We have been talking a lot about life; now it's time for a few words about music.

HMG: I see, you are prepared, with a notebook.

> **MT**: I jotted down a few questions, because I was apprehensive about this conversation.

HMG: Why?

> **MT**: Because I am intimidated by great people.

HMG: But I am not great, I am only 178 centimeters tall.[6] I used to be 180 centimeters: my wife is 164 centimeters, and she also shrank. One shrinks with age. Yehudi Menuhin once phone me: "Are you the great Górecki?" "Oh no," I say, "Because I was 180 centimeters and now I am 178 centimeters." "So maybe I will call later, when you grow great again?" So witty! Why be afraid?

> **MT**: (*laughs*) Maybe I should not be... I only want to ask you some general questions; there is no time for any details.

---

[6] The word "wielki" that Trochimczyk and Górecki used means both "great" and "grand" and may be used to mean "tall."

HMG: You think I would tell you any details?

> **MT**: Not at first. For that I would have had to move in next door, to become your neighbor, see you daily, and keep asking questions.

HMG: Install a listening device? (*laughs*)

> **MT**: I don't think so. I have a question about the ancient Polish tradition in your music. Where does your interest in early music come from?

HMG: It is difficult to answer this question, because I have worked with this tradition all my life. It is hard to summarize. I don't know, I have been thinking about this a great deal, so it is hard to make a quick summary.

> **MT**: But this music is particularly close to you. You quote early music in many works.

HMG: That may be true. But are there others who do not feel as close to it? Maybe some people are ashamed? I do not deny my roots. After all, one grows from a root. I am now an older person and I am aware of some things I did not pay attention to earlier. It seemed to me to be much simpler; I saw the world as a simpler place. But now I see what influences an individual. What can influence a person? We are not even aware that there is something in the subconscious, waiting for the moment when this hidden valve would open. (*pause*)

Let's talk about me: born in Silesia, in a small, fine, wonderful place with a lovely old Polish name.[7] This village is called Czernica; between Rybnik and Raciborz. Old, ancient Polish land. But there were always three cultures in this area: Polish, Czech, and German. Folklore, all the

---

[7] Silesia is a region in southwest Poland, consisting of Upper Silesia (centered on Katowice where Górecki was born), and Lower Silesia (centered on Wrocław, or Breslau). The region belonged to Polish princes in the Middle Ages, but was under German rule for most of its modern history. It was a part of the Austrian partition through the 19th century to World War I, and was later divided between Poland and Czechoslovakia in the interwar period.

arts, knew no boundaries. These boundaries were supposed to exist, but they shifted frequently to the right, to the left. That did not mean that people started thinking differently. No, the land dictated it. The region defined the identity of a person, of its inhabitants. A highlander (*góral*) is always a highlander, first and foremost a highlander. A Silesian is always a Silesian. There is this particular land that transmits certain genes and not others. I did not always realize this. Where does my knowledge of, and my preference for, Czech music come from? My knowledge of German or Austrian music? Why did, for instance, Mozart never speak of his being an Austrian, but only of being a German? What is the reason for my worshipping of Mozart, Schumann, Schubert, Brahms, Beethoven, or Bach? Peculiar, isn't it. So, tell me, why?

> **MT**: It means that place, history, and geography all mold and define us.

HMG: I don't know, but something is there, somewhere in this pot. Why do I love Szymanowski and Chopin? Where did I grow up with them? Because even in the very beginning of my music education, when I had no idea about music—nothing!—these names were floating all around me: Beethoven, Chopin, and Szymanowski. It is not even possible to put them together, it just cannot be done! (*pause*) No, actually you can place together Szymanowski with Chopin. Szymanowski: you know, a Pole from the borderlands (*Kresy*), from the distant Tymoszówka.[8] Beethoven: distant, all the way up at the other end. And from the district of Mazovia,[9] in the middle, we have Chopin, who is also being claimed by the French. I think that you can describe it in the following way.

Should we really consider it and should we think a lot about it? I do not think so. Either you have it, or you do not have it. Either you have the genes, or do not have these genes. Should you admit to this, or not? I cannot imagine cutting myself off from my roots. I do not know if I can. Despite the fact that a child is cut off from the umbilical cord, he is

---

[8] Karol Szymanowski (1881-1937), was born on his family estate in Tymoszówka, in eastern Poland, that is now Ukraine. The borderlands between Poland, Russia, Lithuania, Belarus, and Ukraine were called "Kresy" (Borderlands), and inhabited by a multicultural mixture of ethnicities and religious communities.

[9] Mazovia is the central district of Poland, around the capital of Warsaw.

still a child of his mother and this is still the closest link. There are very rare cases of "renegade" children or "renegade" mothers that would disown each other and not admit to their kinship. Talking about this and explaining this is a normal part of life. Nobody selects a place and time for himself.

    MT: But you chose the mountains...

HMG: Did I choose the mountains?[10] Maybe the mountains were with me all the time? Did I choose them? Sure, some conscious choice was there. When my father built a house after my mother died (they started building it together, she died in 1935), I saw distant mountains in the south, out of my little room upstairs. I saw rain gathering over the mountains far away on the horizon. What are mountains? Seemingly nothing, yet a lot. But what do the mountains mean? Upper Silesia is a very nice region of rolling landscapes, but there are also agricultural plains there. This is not Mazowsze [Mazovia] or the district of Lublin; it is not completely flat. Thus, my mountains originate from there.

And probably, as I said before about the three composers, there is a connection. For instance: Szymanowski – there is Tomaszówka and there is Zakopane[11]... When I played *Highlander Music* (*Muzyka Góralska*) by Szymanowski I had not seen the mountains yet. I did not know anything about them. I did not know musicology. The first booklet I read about Szymanowski was a brochure published by Wiedza Powszechna and written by Gołachowski.[12] You know, because of the terrible poverty in Poland after the war these simple booklets were issued about many topics in science and arts, mathematics, biology, or music... Chopin, Szymanowski, Polish pianists, Polish

---

[10] By "mountains" Poles typically mean the Tatra Mountains, a range in the Carpathians, even though other ranges are found along the southern border of the country: Beskidy and other ranges of the Carpathians.

[11] Zakopane is the popular mountain resort in the Tatra Mountains, discovered by tourists from northern Poland in the late 19th century, with considerable interest of artists and musicians, especially Ignacy Jan Paderewski, and Karol Szymanowski who travelled there, transcribed the music of local inhabitants. Szymanowski owned a villa in Zakopane, called Atma, which is now his museum.

[12] Stanisław Golachowski, *Karol Szymanowski* (Łódź : Spółdzielnia Wydawnicza "Czytelnik", 1948). Series: Wiedza Powszechna., series *Muzyka i muzycy polscy* ;, vol. 16.

violinist, and so on — I still have these booklets. Szymanowski is connected with the mountains, there are elements in common. I don't know anything else, I will not say any more. I don't want to construct a grand philosophy.

Fig 3-3: Maja Trochimczyk, Henryk Mikołaj Górecki and Jane Kedron in the home of Andrzej Bachleda, Zakopane, July 18, 1997.

MT: So maybe we could talk about your songs. I understand there are many songs in your oeuvre.

HMG: I have been writing songs all my life. Many are not published and remain in manuscript. I don't know why I did not publish them. Only some early songs were issued. I also wrote quite a bit of vocal music for choirs, soloists, but songs were what I was composing all my life.

MT: Why did you choose these texts? Słowacki,[13] Norwid[14]... There is a special emphasis on the Polish heritage, on the Romantic tradition....

---

[13] Juliusz Słowacki (1809-1849) was a Polish writer and poet, one of the three so-called national bards: Adam Mickiewicz, Juliusz Słowacki and Zygmunt

HMG: I don't know whether it is just romantic tradition. I always read a lot. In the early 1950s, I bought the first edition of Słowacki, published by Ossolineum. A complete Słowacki! I am terribly in love with him. Not only Słowacki, also Wyspiański.[15] It did not always work; it was very difficult to match their poems with my music. I also wrote some songs to poems by Maria Konopnicka.[16] I always liked her work, even when I was in college. I still value her very much. She was an uncommonly talented poet who is underestimated in Poland by many critics, many historians—completely underestimated. People say that she wrote only for children, that she was boring, didactic. But her verses are pearls. Recently I dug out two of my songs from my student years and we performed them in America with Andrzej [Bachleda] when we were in New York.

MT: That was in 1995, but a third new song was added, right?

HMG: Yes I wrote the third. I thought there were only two, something had to be added—so I wrote it. I am not ashamed of these songs. Why shouldn't there be such songs? Later, I wrote songs to the verses of Norwid, and these were a success. Now I also have the songs to Lorca's texts and a cycle on Słowacki.[17] Quite a collection!

Krasiński, who created the greatest poetry and drama of Polish 19th century. Górecki used his poems in two of *Three Songs / Trzy Pieśni*, Op. 3 for medium voice and piano (1956) and *Two Songs of Słowacki / Śpiewy do słów Juliusza Słowackiego*, Op. 48 for voice and piano (1983).

[14] Cyprian Kamil Norwid (1821-1883) was a late-romantic Polish poet, a Christian mystic and a Polish patriot, who was often considered the fourth "national bard."

[15] Stanisław Wyspiański (1860-1907) was a Polish playwright, painter, and artist, whose original dramas about Polish history and ancient traditions made a major impact on Polish literature. He was associated with the symbolic theater and the *art nouveau* "secesja" period. Górecki used his poems in *Blessed Raspberry Songs / Błogosławione Pieśni Malinowe*, Op. 43 for voice and piano(1980),

[16] Maria Konopnicka (1842-1910) was a poet of the "positivist" period, discussing poverty and solutions to social problems in her work; numerous poems were written for children, and these remained known, whereas her more serious work was forgotten. Górecki used her poems in *Two Songs to Texts by Maria Konopnicka* for voice and piano (1954-55) and *At My Window / U okienka, u mojego*, for voice and piano (1995).

[17] *Dwie Pieśni do słów Lorki / Two Songs of Lorca*, Op. 42 for medium voice and piano (composed in 1956, rev. 1980).

MT: Later there were the songs for Wanda Warska.[18]

HMG: Oh, yes. It was in 1995. Wanda approached some composers to write songs for her, all on the same text. A good idea! So we wrote. I later composed two more songs and now it is a cycle. And so I wrote all my life. I have the complete writings by Wyspiański. I have been reading and reading them; it was too difficult to compose, but sometimes such an impulse may come.

As I said before, the pleasure of music-making travels strange roads. Sometimes a small place, an unimportant concert, brings the greatest joy. I will bypass a big metropolis to go there; to conduct or to play. Of course, a normal person would do the opposite: "Of course, I would go to New York to conduct, and I would skip Sandomierz.[19] What do I need Sandomierz for?" Because, if you say you gave a concert in Sandomierz, what do you gain? But if you say, "New York," it will be obvious. You can brag, you can repeat it in your biography: "New York, New York." However sometimes I have more fun in Sandomierz. I don't know why.

MT: Maybe because it is less egoistic? Sandomierz does not reward you by creating immediate, international fame. On the other hand, it lacks the superficial crowd seeking cheap sensations.

HMG: Maybe there is something to it.

MT: Maybe there is some truth in it, that all the people coming to a concert there really want to hear your music. Just in Sandomierz and not in New York where on these musical occasions thousands of business deals are negotiated.

---

[18] Wanda Warska (b. 1932) is a Polish jazz singer, and composer; wife of composer Andrzej Kurylewicz, she premiered most of his songs. Together, they managed a cultural venue, Piwnica Artystyczna (Artistic Basement) that was well-known for its jazz and sung poetry events.

[19] Sandomierz is a renaissance town on the Vistula river, a popular tourist resort. Górecki cited the name of New York in English, paraphrasing a well-known song.

HMG: I mentioned Sandomierz because it is my favorite city. I did not say it without reason. I do like the city enormously. I have always said that it is the most beautiful city in the world.

> **MT**: I do not know, I have not been in Sandomierz, but I often visited Kazimierz Dolny, which is delightful.[20]

HMG: But I have not visited Kazimierz. So let's return to concert-giving. Sometimes things happen one after another, seemingly without rhyme or reason. From this one concert later emerged an idea to do a whole recital of my songs. Ewa Michalska came up with this plan. Maybe Bohdan Pociej has overestimated in his review what Warska did, writing that this was a new format of a concert... Earlier, there was nothing like that: several composers write songs to the same text and these songs create a whole. There were also recited words that connected these songs in to a unified whole. All of this was by Wyspiański. Later, I wrote two more songs, and it turned out to be twenty or thirty minutes of music—my song cycle to poems by Wyspiański. This was an unusual spectacle, a strange recital, a strange concert. But I have to say that, personally, I was delighted with this and I liked a lot travelling to give such concerts. Maybe we will still go to other places? I accompanied the singer by myself in these songs...

I do not have much pianistic capabilities, because I did not have an opportunity to study piano performance—for many reasons. The vagaries of fate! But I play things for myself and it does not turn out the worst, and gives me a lot of pleasure. I am delighted. I do not know if I were as delighted if we went with these songs to Washington, or to Chicago, or wherever. And isn't it a greater thing? We were in Łańcut, we were in Sandomierz, in Warsaw, in Poznań in a theater, in Kraków in a theater, in Łódź. We were in Katowice; there was also Przemyśl, also somewhere abroad... We also went here to Zakopane... there was also a performance... Well, I do not know. I do not make any philosophy out of this, but as I say sometimes, a place that seemingly does not matter or a time that is not really important gives this impulse that is in the grand scale of things, much more important than a well-known, famous commission, or whatever.

---

[20] Kazimierz Dolny is another scenic renaissance town on the Vistula river.

MT: What counts is the profound quality of the experience. Can we say so?

HMG: It is too strongly worded. What is this profound quality? Life is life. One has to live life to the fullest, one has to live now, live today's life and stop speculating about what is to come. I don't know, there are surprises in life and one has to benefit from one's lot. Let me put it this way: we should not bargain with fate and select one's lot: "Oh, this is unimportant, that is less important, and this, this one is very important, and that is what I will pick!" Nonsense! Sometimes what looks very important, is in reality nor important and what seems to be unimportant at first is actually the most important. Isn't it so?

MT: Yes. Let's return to the mountains. You *do* compose music connected with mountains, for instance in your string quartets there are audible echoes of the "muzyka" of the highlanders, with accented rhythm of basses, sharp timbres, bravado *góral* virtuosity of the violin...

Fig 3-4: Górecki with friends in Zakopane, L to R: Prof. Thaddeus Gromada, then Executive Director of the Polish Institute of Arts and Sciences in America; HMG, Jane Kedroń (Gromada's sister), Theresa Gromada, Henry Kedroń, Andrzej and Maria Bachleda, July 18, 1997. Photo by Maja Trochimczyk.

HMG: But you know, I am not even mentioned in a dictionary of musicians connected with the mountains. Indeed, it seems that I did not write any "góralski"-style works. Kilar wrote them, I did not.[21] Let's look at this highlander music: strings only, it is really a string quartet. So why not compose it as a quartet? Seriously, I would like very much to write a violin concerto for Bartuś Obrochta.[22] I would love to do something for my land, for these mountains. But it would not be stylized music, with quotations. It would be real, great virtuoso violin concerto: a huge orchestra, a huge format – dedicated to "Bartuś Obrochta, an excellent musician, one of the greatest artists from Podhale." But these are only plans. It is too early yet to talk about them.

Figure 3-5: Prof. Thaddeus Gromada with his wife Theresa in a traditional *górale* folk costume of the Tatra Mountains. Thaddeus Gromada Archives.

---

[21] Wojciech Kilar (1932-2013) composed many works based on Podhale and other mountain folklore, to mention only: *Krzesany* for orchestra (1974), *Kościelec 1909* (1976) *Siwa Mgła* (1979) and *Orawa* (1986).
[22] Bartłomiej Obrochta, Bartuś (1850-1926) was the most famous highlander musician and tourist guide, a folk violin virtuoso, and a friend of Dr. Tytus Chałubiński, the discoverer of the Tatra Mountains for tourists. Obrochta is associated with the establishment and codification of the conteporary *górale* folk music style.

MT: Obrochta was from the Tatra Mountains, what about Polish folklore in other areas of the country?

HMG: Polish culture is a wonderful mixture: there are German, Czech, Russian, and even Tatar elements in it. And Jewish of course. Jews were exiled centuries ago from Spain, France and other European countries, and they arrived in Poland. Here they settled and lived. Poland bloomed. Only later came the occupations and then the disastrous time between the wars, the second war, and now we have problem. And yet, when you look at the history of Poland, it is precisely the multi-culturalism and the presence of the so-called minorities that made Poland what it was. The cultural wealth, the diversity, mixed and created a new entity.

MT: Indeed, you are perfectly right, Poland as frontier, as a melting pot of nations—it is a very beautiful picture.

HMG: It is not a picture, it is the truth! And now there are those would claim that Poland is some kind of a monolith, that there is only Polish identity while the others are strangers. That's terrible. It is a lie. After all, there always were Czech and German elements in Polish culture, especially in Silesia, or in the East, where there is a mixture of Russian, Ukrainian, Jewish, and even Romanian elements. Poland is different in every region.

MT: I agree. I don't want to give you a hard time. I have still some questions...

HMG: What else do you have?

MT: On music in general, for instance on rhythm.

HMG: I don't know what rhythm is.

MT: You wrote *Songs of Joy and Rhythm*... There was some rhythm, wasn't there?

HMG: *(laughter)*.

MT: There was rhythm in the repetitions of chords. Sudden changes, proportions between sections of the form. For me the greatest, personal experience of rhythm and time was listening to your First String Quartet. The CD started to play in Montreal, and during a cold Canadian autumn, I found myself back in Poland. When I "fell" into this music, I could not stop listening to it. I listened again and again, maybe thirty times, until I memorized each phrase. It is because there, in exile, with this nostalgia for Poland, I was terribly touched by this: something unusually Polish, something close to the edge of pain... This was a very intimate, very private experience and later I was thinking about it, as a musicologist, taking the experience apart in my thoughts and thinking "why"? Now, I believe that a part of the answer lies in the echoes of highlander folklore and Polish religious songs. First and foremost, though, is the way of shaping time. I took the score later and started counting and comparing: here that many notes, there that many notes... And I still do not know.

HMG: And this is what I wanted to say. It is really good that we cannot capture this phenomenon in words; I myself cannot express it in words and we really should not express it in words. It would be wrong to try. It really would not be right to capture this in words.

MT: There are different philosophies and theories of time.

HMG: We cannot do this... Really, we cannot. This is a conversation for a month. One could talk and talk, invent arguments, digressions, and later you would still not know what and why. I think that many things add to the experience of music and time. Consciously and subconsciously. Sometimes, even despite our controlled consciousness, something comes out from the subconscious. And again, it should not be too controlled, because it is good, if it not too controlled, if it is not too speculative. Because then it becomes business, and the worst enemy of art is business. The worst thing is business in the arts. So many got burnt on that, and they have not even realized that they got "burnt."

Many things contribute to the experience of music, to living of time. Perhaps it would seem possible to be analyzed, to find the primary components, to find the elementary particles—so what? We still know nothing! In spite of analysis, in spite of looking at everything through a microscope... And what? We still stand still! Fortunately, there is this secret. What is it? We still stand and wonder. This also contributes to the fun we have, the joy and happiness of writing!

> **MT**: And there is also a secret of live performance. Whenever you listen in a full concert hall, full of people, with musicians who perform in a unique original way—music sounds quite different. It is a unique experience, one of a kind, not possible to be reproduced. The recording is an ersatz of it.

HMG: Sure we know it—there is something to it. Take an electronic instrument, seemingly you play, but you can't accomplish much because the sound of this instrument is dead. I wondered often whether this sound can be revived. Never mind who takes the electronic instrument—an American, a New Guinean, an African, a Japanese, or a Bolivian—the instrument sounds the same! Press the key and that's it. One sound. But if the same people take a violin, that's different: the instrument sounds differently. The music played by Jabłoński, a Slavic virtuoso, has a different musical coloring than if it is played by a German, Bolivian, or an Argentinian. There is something! The difference is that these performers are six different performers; it is not one instrument but six individuals who are playing it. There you see the character, spirit, mentality—all the items which enable us to say, "Oh, this is a Japanese, or this is a Slavic performer." Each one of these people looks at this world differently.

> **MT**: There are differences in individual personalities.

HMG: But the violin, which is a live instrument, reacts. A string is not a mechanism, even if you have to place your finger in a particular place and not in another. And sometimes if you press your finger a quarter-quarter-quarter millimeter lower, a hairline lower, the sound is different. On a mechanical keyboard nothing will happen. This is a secret *(pause)* but the question was about....

> **MT**: ... about live music and recordings.

HMG: With the "mechanical" recordings, you have only one performance. It can be very good; I do not question the value of recordings, because they are the miracle of technology! The invention of CD is a truly a great discovery! But there are many differences between live music and recorded music. One more thing is important: a professional musician, such as me, listens in a different way than a non-musician. This is my profession, so while listening to a piece of music I pay attention to all the technical things. I listen not to hear how a work is recorded, but to know how it is constructed. I am less interested in performance than in form; sometimes even bad or mediocre performances also interest me because I can see the quality of the work itself. When I know that the performance is mediocre I do not waste any time agonizing over the mistakes of the performer... I only think about the work: "It is a wonderful piece, but it needs to be performed differently!" So, the live contact with musicians is completely different in the concert hall. On a recording you hear one particular performance from the beginning to the end. Moreover, very often you can hear the mistakes in editing.

> **MT**: Yes the position of the sound source, the reverberation, or the apparent size of the hall may suddenly change; there might be abrupt shifts in dynamics...

HMG: And there could also be an echo, or a sudden broadening or narrowing of the frequency band. But in live performance you do not know what will happen next: perhaps the musicians will make a mistake, they may forget something—after all, they are living people, not machines. There are many surprises for live performers, in live performances. However, if the performer is able to reach contact with the audience, we have true communication between the musician and the listener: "Here, we understand each other!" Then, the performer's heart grows and he does his best, and the result is fantastic. It happens very often. On such occasions the greatest musical experiences may occur for both the musician and the listener. The listener will be satisfied and the performer will be happy that someone heard him well, that someone really listened!

> **MT**: True. It means that human beings are the most important in all of this.

HMG: Who would deny it? People are the most important because machines have to be monitored by people. Something breaks on the Mars Pathfinder and the human on earth starts pushing buttons and rescues the machine on Mars. It is a person who does the rescuing, not the machine. I saw it on television. It was beautiful. I liked especially the horizon shown from the camera: a mysterious mountain, with huge rocks. And when the view from above was taken, it turned out that the mountains were only a crater, the edge of a hole. In the hole sits the machine looking around, like a child would look.

Later, the breakdown was very interesting. There was the man who thought, "We have to rescue that thing; otherwise it will be destroyed." It sounds ridiculous, but there was such a man who figured it out. And that is a joy! I think it is one of the greatest achievements of science and the human mind. Penetration of outer space, inventing such a voyage. That's a phenomenal idea. A human machine bounces on Mars like a ball! A wonderful, fascinating event...

And with this optimistic accent, about research on Mars, let us complete this conversation.

MT: Yes, thank you very much for giving me so much time.

Figure 3-6: Górecki at NASA Jet Propulsion Laboratory facility in Pasadena, with L to R: Jane Kedroń, Andrzej Bachleda, Henry Kedroń, and Henryk Mikołaj Górecki. Early October 1997. Photo by Maja Trochimczyk.

Figure 3-7: Górecki at USC in Los Angeles with Jane Kedroń, Andrzej Bachleda and Maja Trochimczyk, 2 October 1997.

Figure 3-8: Henryk Mikołaj Górecki with Maja Trochimczyk on the campus of the University of Southern California, in Los Angeles, 3 October 1997.

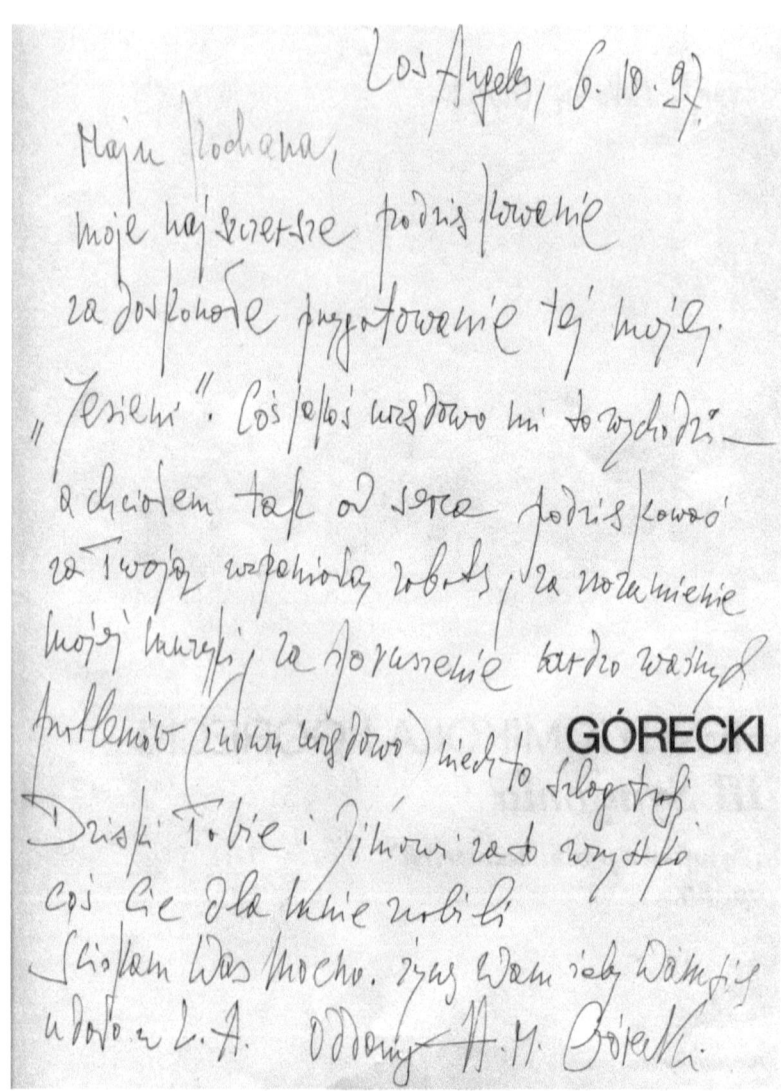

Figure 3-9: Handwritten note on the title page of the Symphony No. 3 by Henryk Mikołaj Górecki, addressed to Maja Trochimczyk, October 6, 1997.

Translation:
Dear Maja! My heartfelt thanks for the perfect preparation of my "Autumn" – it is turning out very official, and I would like to thank you sincerely, from the heart, for your wonderful work, for your understanding my music, for addressing very important issues (again, this is too official)—God damn it! Thank you and Jim for everything that you have done for me.
Lots of hugs!   With wishes that you find success in L.A.
—Devoted —H.M. Górecki

CHAPTER 4

"Composing is a Terribly Personal Matter:" Henryk Mikołaj Górecki in Conversation with Maja Trochimczyk (Katowice, April 1998)[1]

Figure 4-1: Henryk Mikołaj Górecki in his study in Katowice, April 1998. Photo by Maja Trochimczyk.

Maja Trochimczyk: Thank you for agreeing to talk to me today. I have a lot of questions to ask. Where shall we start?

Henryk Mikołaj Górecki: I would like to share with you my excitement about a true musical revolution. Grzegorz Michalski first

---

[1]This interview was published in *Polish Music Journal*, 6/2, Winter 2003. The interview was recorded in Poland, on two 90 minute cassette tapes, transcribed by Adrianna Lis and Blanka Sobuś, and translated into English by Maja Trochimczyk. http://pmc.usc.edu/PMJ/issue/6.2.03/GoreckiKatowice.html.

told me about this discovery which was announced during a small musicology session in Warsaw. During the session, Jan Węcowski—I'm sure you know him—revealed a bit about the mystery that he is working on.[2] In his study he proves that Chopin used Polish religious church songs in his works. I called him up and talked to him on the phone. He confirmed that—and I quote—"Chopin arranges old Polish church songs." But this has never been mentioned before! Never, in no books! Of course, we know about his use of the Christmas carol, *Lulajże Jezuniu* [Hush, Baby Jesus][3] but this is just the beginning. I have never seen anything like it and I have seen a lot of research on Chopin; I have a lot of books. Nobody mentions it.

But if this is true, and it has to be true, because Węcowski is a serious fellow and knows what he's doing—then we have a true Chopin revolution. Węcowski told me: "Do you know what a tragic character Chopin really was?" Of course, we know all the clichés, all the banalities about the Revolutionary Etude: the struggle, the uprising, the bayonets... This is a 90-percent martial matter. We have attached this image of a revolutionary patriot to Chopin. At the same time, we have this image of Chopin as a "ladies' man" who sits at his instrument and reflects about the lost Poland and does nothing really. All these obertas, kujawiaks, are nice, but nothing more than nice. But if you could prove that he actually used church songs, that have texts that mean something, not only the folk mazurkas, but also the expressions of folk spirituality, then we see how Chopin returned to the foundations, to the roots from which all the music grows.

Similarly you have Karol Szymanowski using the material from the Skierkowski's collection.[4] You know, if it weren't for Skierkowski, if it weren't for the Kurpian music, this Szymanowski would be very poor, limited. In the end, he found the material that he had been searching for. And Skierkowski helped him a lot with that. He went beyond

---

[2] Jan Węcowski, "Religious Folklore in Chopin's Works," *Polish Music Journal* 2/1-2 (1999), http://pmc.usc.edu/PMJ/issue/2.1.99/wecowski.html.

[3] The lullaby appears in the Scherzo in B Minor, Op. 20. See Maja Trochimczyk, *Chopin with Cherries blog.* http://chopinwithcherries.blogspot.com/2012/12/on-chopin-and-polish-christmas-carols.html

[4] Władysław Skierkowski, *Puszcza Kurpiowska w pieśni* [Songs from the Kurpie Forest], 2 vols. (Płock: Wyd. Tow. Naukowego Płockiego, 1928-1934).

górale[5] music which is somewhat one-dimensional. It is rich, do not misunderstand me, but it is one-dimensional. One or two melodies suffice to give the whole technical image of this music. In contrast, Kurpian music is built from melodies, melodic structures based on intervals. It is much more complicated; it is certainly not accidental that Szymanowski turned his ear, so to speak, towards this region.

But we have to know that church songs are 90 percent folk songs. These are folk songs that were created over centuries: at first there were old plainchant melodies, already adjusted to the needs of the people. The pastor sang his music and the people while listening to him transformed the music in their own way. They wrote new texts, and so forth. It is also interesting that Węcowski is going to publish a *Dictionary of Polish Church Songs* simultaneously with his study on Chopin. Most probably a lot of these songs were already forgotten. Therefore, for me it is completely different. Or, not completely different. It is the Chopin revolution.

MT: How so? Why is it so important?

HMG: It is a revolution because the whole mystery of Chopin's craftsmanship, of Chopin's music—of this amazing genius—is now explained. You know that geniuses do not fall from the sky. The fact that you have hearing, that you have memory is good, but it is not enough. . . Something else is needed for you, for me to be "myself."

MT: Personality?

HMG: Yes, Chopin—who learned how to move his fingers quickly over the keyboard—had a good memory: he knew almost all music, he was sensitive, attentive, erudite, but that was not all, that was not enough. He knew all the piano literature, but in order to be "Chopin" he had to do something special within himself, inside himself. These sounds were in his mind; one person would say that they were in his heart, someone else that they were in his head. Composers are like that. Somewhere within us the music sounds, we are surrounded by these

---

[5] Górale, highlanders are the inhabitants of the Podhale area of the foothills of the Tatra Mountains, Górecki's preferred region of Poland where he eventually settled. Their folklore inspired Ignacy Jan Paderewski, Karol Szymanowski, Wojciech Kilar and other composers.

sounds. But what would one do with all that music? This is an incredible truth, an incredible discovery. It is clear that it was filtered through his education, his knowledge, but that there was the source for his melodies. There is no other melody like Chopin's.

Figure 4-2. Vintage postcard of Chopin evoking the spirit of Poland with his music. Kraków, 1890s. Maja Trochimczyk Collection.

MT: It is often said that Chopin's melody is derived from the opera, especially from Bellini.

HMG: But it has nothing to do with Bellini! Look: Chopin's harmony naturally develops from his melodies. Just look how different he is from his contemporaries: Hummel, Spohr, Field. There are lots of them, yet, he is different. He did not fall down from heaven here; he did not come out of nowhere. He knew the music literature. He had to know it. He collected all these new things and distilled them into his own harmonic language. Actually, Bach also collected and distilled the religious music of his time.

Chopin alone collected Polish songs. After Chopin it was all over. After Chopin one could not go further along the same path, because he did it with such genius. There were many other composers in his time:

Kalkbrenner, Field... Hummel will remain Hummel, Bellini will remain Bellini... But Chopin's music was not about Bellini! This is a half-truth that someone heard somewhere and which keeps recurring. But they do not repeat that Chopin played and remembered Bach's fugues and preludes until the end of his life. Nobody talks about the fact that once, after a concert, he gave his favorite student the score of Beethoven's *Fidelio*, not of any Bellini. He bought this score for his student; so, he knew what *Fidelio* was. He also knew what Bach's fugues were.

Now, consider this: Bach's head was also filled with his Protestant chorales and with his own church songs. You can see it everywhere, every note of Bach's music stems from this source, not from the music of other composers that surrounded him. And now let us look at Chopin: It is truly amazing to discover that he did the same thing as Bach, that he turned to his own religious folk songs for sources of material, for inspiration. I am very grateful to Jan Węcowski for his work on Chopin's use of Polish church songs. I regard musicological studies of this kind highly, studies that I can take and use, studies that teach me something.

Interestingly, I was often annoyed with Węcowski in the past. He publishes a lot of material on religious music and I know his work quite well. I often teased him because when he edited songbooks, he selected the first, third or fifth strophes and omitted the second, fourth or sixth strophes. It upset him: but if you publish a song like that, why can't you print all the strophes of the text? I remember the times when one was not allowed to use "anatomical" terms in church songs. For instance, the Mother of God could not have breasts in such a song, the word "breast" had to be removed. But as a Mother was she really without breasts? How did she feed the baby Jesus, may I ask?

Other deletions in the songbooks were of simple folk expressions that were deemed unsuitable for publication by the editor. There are many enemies of simple folk poetry, people who hate simple, regular rhythms and call them "rymy częstochowskie."[6] The term is derogatory and means poetry of no literary merit and very simplistic

---

[6] "Rymy częstochowskie" [Rhymes of Częstochowa] is the Polish term for "doggerel" poetry of very low artistic quality and extreme simplicity of form. The term is associated with religious folksongs sung at the shrine of Our Lady of the Bright Mount in Częstochowa.

form. It refers to Częstochowa, where the Marian cult is expressed in a variety of popular religious songs with texts of this kind. But why should one apply such literary criteria to folk expressions of piety? Do these critics want old beggars who panhandle in Częstochowa to recite the poetry of Miłosz, or Mickiewicz, or Norwid? I thought about it for a long time. It has to be that way: the old beggar is no more than an old beggar, the singing church hag is nothing else but a singing church hag... If you read Mickiewicz's *The Forefathers' Eve*[7] and notice what the old people sing in the Lithuanian cemetery, you realize that this folk song is nothing but doggerel.

But it all depends on how this poetry is used. Mozart also had texts that were true doggerel and he was able to compose phenomenal operas to such horrid libretti. If you also write bad music, everything is wrong. But if you, as a composer, are able to distill from the folk songs, from this doggerel, what is the most important in them, then you may create something of lasting value. Therefore, it is very important how the folk material is used, not cited, but used as raw material for the creation of the work. Chopin did not like quotations, but was able to use musical material from religious folklore as a source for his works. Węcowski claims that traces of these songs may be found in such diverse pieces as preludes, etudes, and mazurkas. Even in the nocturnes in G Major or in E-flat Major there are so-called chorale sections that should be called plainly and simply church songs.

> **MT**: I can see that you are very enthusiastic about this issue. Perhaps you find it so important because that is what you do yourself: you use old Polish church songs as source material for your music. Let me ask the next question about *Bogurodzica*. Did you know it from church liturgy? Is there a moment when you learned about this song? I heard it first in my music history classes, but it was also sung in St. Martin's Church in Warsaw by the Franciscan Sisters. Did you sing it in the church? Did you learn it in live practice, or from books?

HMG: In my neighborhood, where I was growing up in Silesia, this song was not known. I never heard it in the church in those early years. I learned it during my music studies, I read about it in books and articles, the study by Hieronim Feicht, the volume edited by

---

[7]*Dziady*, the most famous Polish romantic drama, published in separate sections between 1822 and after the author's death, by Adam Mickiewicz (1798-1855).

Woronczak that you see over there on my shelf. These were my sources.[8]

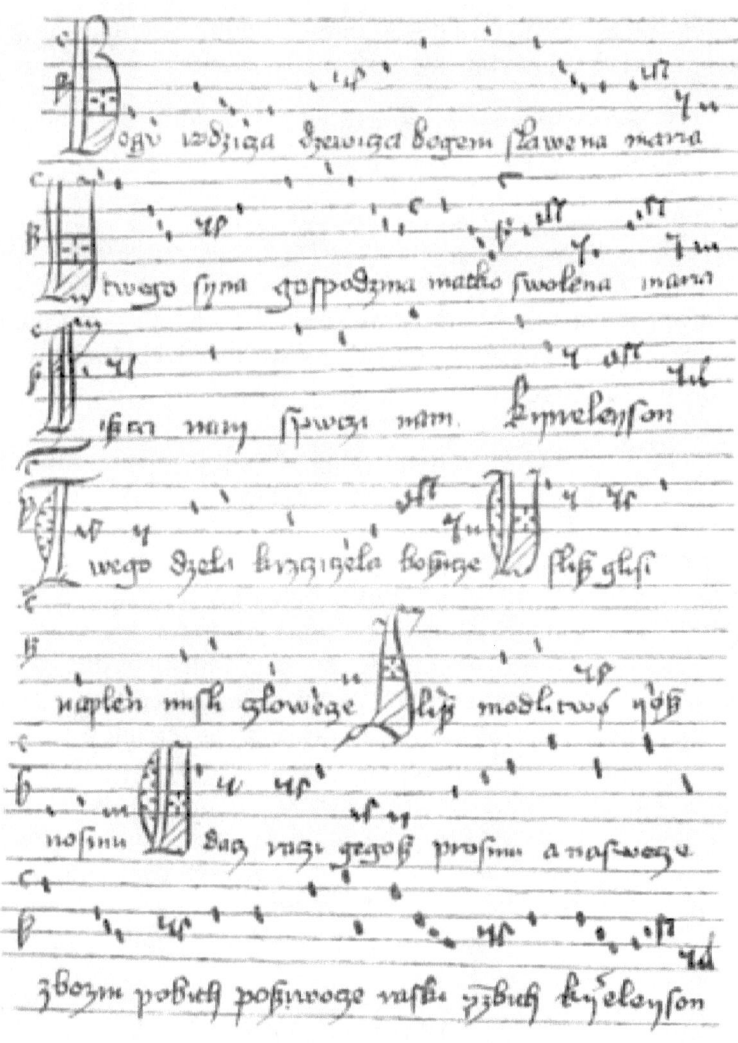

Figure 4-3: *Bogurodzica*[Mother of God] manuscript from 1407, cited by Hieronim Feicht, *op. cit.*

---

[8] Jerzy Woronczak, *Bogurodzica* (Wrocław: Zakład Narodowy im. Ossolinskich, 1962); Hieronim Feicht, "Bogurodzica," in Hieronim Feicht, *Studia nad muzyką polskiego średniowiecza* [Studies in the Music of the Polish Middle Ages] (Kraków: Polskie Wydawn. Muzyczne, 1975).

MT: But even Siedlecki's *Church Songbook*,[9] so popular before the war and repeatedly reprinted, includes a version of *Bogurodzica*...

HMG: Yes, but Siedlecki was not so popular in my neighborhood, in my youth. I do not recall having ever heard it in church.

MT: So why did you grow so attached to it and why did you use it in so many works?

HMG: Somehow. Even in St. Adalbert [i.e., *Salve Sidus Polonorum*][10] there is a lot of *Bogurodzica*, but it is transformed there, used my way. Let me put it this way: I do not like to create elaborate theories about this. I have come across this melody and liked it a lot. I liked the text, I liked the melody, I liked this song as a historical document, a proof of how ancient Polish culture really was.

MT: What was more important for you in this hymn: the text or the music?

HMG: It depends, sometimes the sounds, at other times, the words. It depends on what I want to use. But I remember only one thing, that I was annoyed with the existence of so many different versions of this song, both the text and the music: so many manuscripts, so many versions. I know that there are many different editions, different copies, that it is so ancient that we really do not even know who wrote it. Some people even claim that St. Adalbert wrote it and that he composed *Chwała Tobie Gospodzinie* [Praise to You, o Lord]—a Czech song. If he could write that one, he could also write *Bogurodzica*. But, because of the different versions, you cannot even be certain whether what you have is the real hymn, or a distortion. What is important in this song for me is its melodic contour, its pitches, not its rhythms or

---

[9] Jan Siedlecki, ed., *Śpiewnik kościelny z melodjami na dwa głosy* [Church Songbook with Melodies, for two Voices] (Lwów-Kraków-Paris: Missionary Fathers, 1928).
[10] *Salve Sidus Polonorum*, Op. 72 for chorus and ensemble was composed in 1997-2000 and was not premiered in 1999. The work lasts for 25 minutes, not an hour and the texts come from Catholic liturgy as well as the composer. The work was premiered on 21 June 2000 at Garden Church, Hannover, by a chorus and instrumental ensemble from The National Philharmonic, Warsaw conducted by Henryk Wojnarowski

durations. The sounds could be sustained for longer or shorter intervals, there was no stable rhythm in the notation. I have all the different versions gathered in my book on *Bogurodzica*. Knowing this material, I wanted to allude to it, but not cite extended fragments from it. It is so characteristic and so well known that it would be hard to place it in a new musical context. There is the major second and the fourth at the beginning; these intervals are so obvious.

    MT: Many composers have quoted it, though: Andrzej Panufnik in *Sinfonia Sacra* (1963), Wojciech Kilar in *Bogurodzica* (1975), Marta Ptaszyńska in *Conductus, A Ceremonial for Winds* (1982), and others.[11]

HMG: For me it is too serious a matter to make it into a sort of easily recognizable musical sign, almost a joke. It is a great thing and we should leave this song alone the way it is. It is an incredible, fantastic historical document. Only let us consider the following question: Whose document is it? Is it ours? Is it from Poland? We know that it was used and sung during the battle of Grunwald. But what if it turns out that the song itself is of German-Bohemian origin? What if we borrowed it? Would it be good or bad to find out? So I think that these political uses of the song are dubious; they are more political games than valuable artistic artefacts.

    MT: This issue is highly politicized in the Grunwald battle scenes in *The Teutonic Knights* where the Polish and Lithuanian forces sing *Bogurodzica*, while the Teutonic Knights respond with *Christ ist erstanden* and both songs clash.

HMG: In the novel by Sienkiewicz or in the film by Ford?[12]

---

[11] See Maja Trochimczyk, "Bogurodzica Reborn: A Medieval Anthem in Contemporary Polish Music," in *Mittelalter-Sehnsucht?*, Dorothea Redepenning and Annette Kreutziger-Herr, eds. (Kiel, Germany: Wissenschaftsverlag Vauk Kiel KG, 2000), 131-152; "Sacred/Secular Constructs of National Identity: A Convoluted History of Polish Anthems," in Maja Trochimczyk, ed., *After Chopin: Studies in Polish Music* (Los Angeles: Polish Music Center, 2000), 246-268.
[12] Henryk Sienkiewicz's novel, *Krzyżacy* [The Teutonic Knights], written in 1900, was filmed by Aleksander Ford in 1960, with the music by Kazimierz Serocki. The film is distributed in English as *Knights of the Teutonic Order*.

MT: Sienkiewicz cites *Bogurodzica*, but the clash of two religious songs, addressed to Christ and his Mother respectively, appears only in the film. However, according to historians, Grunwald was not the only battlefield where *Bogurodzica* was sung. It was heard during the battle at Varna, where Polish prince Władysław IV (Vladislaus IV) was defeated and killed by the Ottoman army. It was also used on more ceremonial occasions. Jan Łaski placed it at the beginning of the *Statutes of the Polish Kingdom* and it was sung during the crowning ceremonies of the Jagiellonian dynasty. It appeared in many contexts, but it was transformed into a military hymn in Sienkiewicz's novel. This patriotic and militarized image was later referred to by such composers as Panufnik and Kilar.

HMG: Right. But I do not like it. For me it is a song about the Mother of God. It is not a martial song. I guess one can use it for just about anything. Why can't it be a funereal song? It could be used the way the *Stabat Mater* is used. It is a wonderful church song, a religious song. Why can't we find another patriotic song in its place? Here, let me return to the main subject of our conversation: what religious songs did Chopin absorb from the church? You have to admit that he was a tragic man, not some atheist bozo, even though he did not often participate in liturgical practices. He was born here, had parents here, lived here in Warsaw. Here, he was formed before he left. I cannot believe that he then dreamed and remembered only folk dances and folk ensembles [*kapele*]. He had to remember also church songs. How could he leave without taking these songs with him, at least in his memory? I have these songbooks at home.

But, I am sorry to say, as a society, we really neglect this repertoire. We forget about it. Why are these songs not published? So, if Chopin took this folk poetry and music from Kujawy, Mazowsze, he also took with him the religious songs of his youth. He was not deaf! He played the organ in the church. He attended services as a student. And these songs have remained in the church repertoire until today.

I remember my conversations with Bolesław Szabelski.[13] In the 1950s and 1960s, at a festival we heard a piece in which *Bogurodzica* was

---

[13] Boleslaw Szabelski (1896-1979), Polish composer from the Silesia region, Górecki's composition professor at the State Higher School of Music in Katowice,

played with the banging of drums, with the screaming of trumpets. For me it was a cheap effect. This melody is so characteristic that its appearance in the music is too obvious. I believe that we should leave it for special occasions. Instead, let us use individual sounds and intervals from this melody. If you play the note "D," then you really want to play "C"—and with these two sounds you already have the beginning of *Bogurodzica*. It is obvious for us, Poles. Then, if you add the third and fourth note "F" and "E" - now it becomes so clear that it is no longer the *Bogurodzica*, but an apparition.

Figure 4-4: Our Lady of the Bright Mount from the shrine in Częstochowa, Poland.

---

whose music took a sharp turn from neoclassicism to pointillistic serialism inspired by Webern in late 1950s.

> **MT**: Are the initial intervals the most important, then? Adrian Thomas finds the initial motive of *Bogurodzica* in numerous fragments of your music.

HMG: I have not read his book yet, it was not translated into Polish. I discovered the motive that Adrian calls the "Skierkowski turn"—it is one of the most beautiful melodies that exist. It appears in Szymanowski's music, too, but I took it from somewhere else. There is a little book called *Melodie Puszczy Kurpiowskiej* by Antonina Woraczyńska. It is a very beautiful book, but it is too short, it only reveals the tip of the iceberg... We should do more than that; we should publish the whole Skierkowski collection, which is filled with amazing melodies. I love, for instance a song called *Boże obiady* [God's dinners]; it is astoundingly beautiful and funereal at the same time.

While composing the Third Symphony, I was looking for a theme, for a very long theme. I had this idea: to use not a short, little theme, but a really long one, even longer than the longest subject in a fugue. This theme was to serve as the basis for the canon at the beginning. Therefore, I decided to use a religious song; I thought that perhaps a whole song could provide the theme for my canon. So I looked, and looked, and looked... Naturally, I needed a particular structure for the theme so I browsed through all these collections for a long time. Finally, I found the songbook by Woraczyńska and noticed these fascinating melodic "turns," with a minor third and a fourth.

> **MT**: A similar motive appears in *Bogurodzica*, only there it is inverted...

HMG: Yes, but I did not cite *Bogurodzica* here. I did a lot of research while preparing the theme for the Symphony and this is where I found it. I call it the "Kurpian motive." This does not mean that I simply quoted the whole, unchanged melody from the Kurpian folklore. Not at all. I composed it myself in this way. Why not? Szymanowski did this, so can I! I should make it clear here that this is not a folksong, but a melody that I composed on the basis of all the references that I reviewed, all the church songs that I studied. I wanted to construct a true folk "church song" and it seems to me that I succeeded in this task.

Figure 4-5: Górecki in his study in Katowice, with crosses, religious artwork, wood carvings from Podhale, and a photograph of his mother above him. April 1998. Photo by Maja Trochimczyk.

Figure 4-6: Górecki's study in Katowice, a close-up of the wall behind his desk. The metal box on the books on the left was made in a concentration camp. The wood shelves and sculptures are from Podhale, the „ryngraf" metal plates are of Mother Mary. April 1998. Photo by Maja Trochimczyk.

MT: There are similar motives at the beginning of the Second Symphony.

HMG: You know, I really, really like these thirds and seconds. I think these intervallic relationships have a great potential, you can invert them and still recognize the motives. I based a whole massive section in *St. Adalbert* on *Bogurodzica*, but it is presented only by instruments. There is one additional reason for citing this hymn in the oratorio: St. Adalbert was considered the author of this hymn. In my work the melody emerges in a pretty natural way. It starts from a sixth and gradually appears in the texture of the music. I was always opposed to straightforward, obvious quotations. *Bogurodzica* is *Bogurodzica* and will remain this way. Using it in its entirety as a quotation seems to be almost blasphemous. It is cheap; it is banal. The same effect could be created with another song: why waste *Bogurodzica*?

MT: Is the piece completed already?

HMG: It is still in manuscript. It is going to be premiered in June 1999 during the visit of the Holy Father to Bydgoszcz. During this trip he will stop in Toruń, Łowicz, Gdańsk, Częstochowa, Kraków... I still have to write a letter to His Holiness, because this oratorio is the second part of the whole cycle. The first part was *Beatus Vir* which I wrote when he became the Pope. The second part is *St. Adalbert*, the third will be about St. Jadwiga [Hedwig]. I would like to have a whole cycle of Polish saints. At first I wanted to start with martyrs, but then I changed my mind. The fourth part will be about St. Maksymilian Maria Kolbe. The fifth part will be about all saints, from Vespers, with the title *Święci Twoje Pana zakwitną* [Your Saints, O Lord, Will Blossom]. This is a wonderful title, again with doggerel rhymes. St. Jadwiga's oratorio will last for half an hour, St. Adalbert for an hour. It will be very long, I do not know if you would be able to play the whole cycle in one night. Who would survive that?

MT: Perhaps, you could divide the cycle into several concerts.

HMG: Perhaps. We'll see how it turns out as a whole. However, the cycle has to have an overall form, I envision it in the outline of a massive symphony.

MT: Does it mean, then, that *Beatus Vir,* the first movement, is the equivalent of a symphonic Allegro?

HMG: Yes, and St. Adalbert is the Adagio. I do not yet know what St. Jadwiga will be.

MT: Perhaps she should be a dancer, it is time for a scherzo...

HMG: Perhaps I could have five movements in the way Shostakovich arranged them in his String Quartet No. 15. That is: Adagio, Adagio, Adagio, Adagio... I could do it that way, too.

MT: I would like to ask you now about *O Domina Nostra.*[14] What type of "victory" do you refer to when you call the Mother of God "Victoriosa" in this work? Is this "victory" in the extra-temporal, spiritual dimension?

Figure 4-7: Our Lady of a Bright Mount (with a blue background) and paintings of Polish churches in Górecki's study in Katowice. Photo by Maja Trochimczyk, April 1998. With the Nonesuch CD of the Third Symphony.

---

[14]*O Domina Nostra. Meditations on Our Lady of Jasna Góra / Medytacje o Jasnogórskiej Pani Naszej* for soprano and organ (1985); ca 35'.

HMG: She is "Victoriosa" because she is from the Bright Mount, Jasnogórska. But stop these questions. It is an illness, or something: you would want to know so much. But I will not tell you everything, other than it was a very definite piece composed for a definite occasion. I consider this work as being extremely difficult. I am afraid as to whether I will be able to find singers, if I will be able to find two musicians who would want to do what is there to be done.

MT: Is it because the music is so slow?

HMG: Yes, it is slow, but you could perform anything if you wanted to. The whole trick is in the organ part. I did not provide registration for it; perhaps later I will add these markings. But everything in this work is so simple, it seemed to me that a good organist would be able to intuitively recognize the intention of the composer and chose the proper registers for the various sections of this piece. I started composing it in the year celebrating the 600th anniversary of the shrine. Our Lady of the Bright Mount was a national symbol for us for so many centuries. Whether one likes it or not, the whole history of the Black Madonna is a great thing. It is fantastic and dramatic in every respect.

MT: I would like to change the subject now and talk about your idea of human motherhood. In my study of the Third Symphony I referred to the concept of the lullaby, the slow, soothing, rocking motion implied in its rhythm, the comforting character of the song that brings tranquility and rest.

HMG: If I wanted to say something wise about it, I would not want to explore technical aspects of the lullaby's rhythm. It is a lullaby whether it is in 3/4 or 4/4 or 6/8 or even 9/8. A lullaby is not the rhythm by itself; a lullaby is the emotional quality that the rhythm and melody create with the words . . . I wrote three Lullabies as a set. For one I used a text from Kolberg, the texts for the other two I found in a little book. The lullaby *Uśnij, że mi uśnij* [Sleep, for me, sleep] has a lot of versions.[15] I wanted to use two strophes of the text. I have all the details in my notes.

---

[15] *Three Lullabies*, Op. 49 (1984, rev. 1991) for mixed choir. For a discussion of the lullaby in Górecki's music see Maja Trochimczyk's article in this volume.

MT: But I do not want you to talk about these details now; let's focus on the "idea" of the lullaby as it appears in other works, not just in the specific "Lullaby" settings.

HMG: This is a form that interests me more as an inspiration. I do not know how not to name it. It is not what is outside, but what is inside. What is a lullaby? It starts from a relationship between the mother and the child, could be the father and a child... There is always a child and a parent, male or female. And what else? These are, if one were to define them, the most wonderful, tranquil moments of human life. When singing the lullaby, there is no teaching, no discipline... It is the most happy, blissful moment between the parent and the child. This is it and this is what I am interested in, not in particular rhythms, motives and so forth.

MT: There is very little happiness and tranquility of this kind in *Ad Matrem*.[16] While studying this work I introduced the images of the process of childbirth and an awakening from a nightmare. Do you think I was right? Could one find such imagery in your music?

HMG: Neither childbirth, nor nightmares. You are going too far. I do not want to create legends associated with my music. It is obvious that everyone will have certain images, that there is no such thing as pure, absolute abstraction. So there are various associations that emerge while listening to music. For me it was my life. My case was very tragic, very dramatic. This is where it comes from. It seems to be a different thing when you hear someone saying: "His mother died" and when they say: "A young girl died." But my mother was a young girl when she died: what is 26 years? Then, there were all these tragedies I lived through: the broken family, no home, illnesses, the war... Everything was superimposed in my memory. This is my experience...

I composed this piece in 1971. Mikołaj was born on 1 February that year and was three months old when I went for my kidney operation, one in a series, to the same hospital where my mother died. I am sure staying in that hospital that May brought all these thoughts back to life. Her death was a tragedy, an unexplained, mysterious tragedy. I

---

[16]*Ad Matrem / Do Matki,* Op. 29 (1971) for soprano, choir, orchestra, to a text by the composer based on *Stabat Mater*.

searched for information about it for years, I found some partial documents, memoirs of family members, vague recollections...

MT: So that is why *Ad Matrem* sounds so tragic.

HMG: Yes, but as I said, I do not want to create a legend for this work. I started composing from the central section, based on Bach's Prelude in E-flat Minor. Later I wrote the introduction with all these "biological" elements, with the heartbeat of the mother, the first cry of the newborn, and so forth. I wanted to write this kind of a piece and I did it. That is all. I have to say that I wrote this piece without a conscious effort to express my feelings about parenthood. But whether conscious or subconscious, these ideas are still there. It is a reference to *Stabat Mater*, but the roles are reversed here: not the mother, but the son is standing under the cross... You know, I have this ideal image of my mother. You should also know that she really wanted to become a nun. But enough of that.

MT: You mention the "biological" sphere here. Let me change the subject to other ideas borrowed by composers from nature. Bartók was fascinated with the golden section and its manifestations in shells, cones, sunflowers, etc. Did you do anything of this kind?

HMG: I was always fascinated by it and liked reading about Bartók, but during my youth when I was interested in this subject there were no books in Polish about him. I remember reading an article in *Ruch Muzyczny* about his work, but it was rather superficial. By the time Zieliński wrote his huge study of Bartók,[17] I had stopped being interested in him in that sense. I was fascinated with the golden section, with the series of proportions summarized by the Fibonacci series – you know – the relation of three to five, then eight to thirteen, and so forth. When using these proportions in my works, I sometimes counted the measures and sometimes the rhythmic values. I do not have the notes here, but for every work I made descriptions of its structure that included such numbers.

MT: These notebooks would be a gold mine for researchers.

---

[17]Tadeusz Zieliński, *Bartók* (Kraków: PWM, 1969).

HMG: Yes, but I am not sharing my secrets. At the end of my life the first thing I will do while I am still able to walk is to burn all of this material. I understand the musicologists; I know that it is important for them. But for me it is such a personal matter: the ordering of material, deciding upon a method of structuring a new piece. Serialism is just one of the many possibilities. I invent my own order and this is how I work.

Figure 4-8: Górecki with Maja Trochimczyk in Katowice, April 1998.

MT: You did go through a serial period yourself, though, so your method was not always that different.

HMG: In the past I invented and worked out detailed frameworks for my pieces. I had everything prepared and described before the work was composed. This started with the First Symphony; also in *Monologhi* and *Elementi* I introduced different ways of structuring the pieces. Later I just knew—I had a technique and then other ideas came in. Composing is a terribly personal matter: the overcoming of difficulties, gaining knowledge, deciding upon a certain order, a certain method of constructing a new piece. This is important. You have to choose your way; you have to pick a proper path from an infinite number of possibilities.

    MT: Are you saying that all of these works are based on the golden section?

HMG: No, the technique differs from one work to another. I come up with many different ways of structuring my compositions. Let me put it this way: you scholars would want to know too much. Of course it is important to know how a piece is constructed and how it was made. But later this mechanism, this architecture ceases to be all important; the composer thinks about the forms that the music should be "poured into." Thus, you could reverse the order between the structure and the music. On the one hand, you invent the form and the construction for the whole work; on the other hand, you begin with the music that could be written down and structured in different ways.

What I am trying to say is that all music begins with sound. It is always based on some musical association, a musical theme or a structure. Now it is fashionable to say that there are no themes, but they continue to exist. At times I even treated a 12-tone series as a theme. When composing, I always begin with introducing some order. I have many things prepared much, much earlier when I actually begin to compose a piece. In this way I have researched and analyzed the possibilities provided by my materials. However, many pieces that I have worked on have never been finished. I only ordered the materials without composing them out into pieces. It is very important for composers to think these ideas through. If Chopin did not think through and consider all his options, he would not have been able to compose any music. Schubert, Beethoven. . . There would be nothing. You have to create an order in your work; you have to start from order. But we have to end now; your three hours are up.

    MT: Thank you very much for sharing with me some of your secrets.

CHAPTER 5

„There is More to Life than the Arranging of Sounds" Henryk Mikołaj Górecki in Conversation with Małgorzata and Marcin Gmys (31 August and 1 September 2002 in Ząb, near Zakopane)

Małgorzata and Marcin Gmys: In 1990, for the famous Kronos Quartet, you composed your Second String Quartet, subtitled *Quasi una fantasia*. Twelve years later, at the request of the Adam Mickiewicz Institute in Warsaw, you agreed to present a new composition for large string orchestra, bearing—on the one hand—a new opus number in the list of your works, yet—on the other—the same title as years before: *Quasi una fantasia*. Does this mean that the audience of the concert in Madrid will be the first in the world to hear a transcription of a work written earlier?

Henryk Mikołaj Górecki: In order to answer that question, we must first establish what a transcription is. It is the strict transferal of a given composition from instrument X for which it was originally intended to instrument (or group of instruments) Y; strict, that is, respecting in the minutest detail the pattern of the movements (in the case of a cyclical form) and the architectonic construction of each of those movements taken separately. Or are certain deviations from the original permitted? If we deem the former definition to be correct, then the orchestral *Quasi una fanasia* is not a transcription; if the latter—then, on the contrary, we will be able to speak of a sort of transcription.

M&MG: From what you say, we may conclude that there are similarities between the first and the second Fantasy, but there are also differences. In that case, could you describe them to us?

HMG: What links these compositions is the pattern of the movements, which has not changed, and their form. And surely we are also not dealing there with a transcription in the sense of the practice that was formerly cultivated by such conductors as Herbert von Karajan, Leopold Stokowski, or Jan Krenz. The essence of the orchestral *Quasi una fantasia* does not involve simply reinforcing the sound of the string quartet or increasing the number of first and second violins, violas and cellos, to which the part of the double basses is mechanically added, as in classicism. That was not the point. The fundamental change in this work—in the whole of the work— is that it is intended to be the sound of a grand string orchestra, and not the multiplication of a string quartet. The prototype was the string quartet, in which certain sections (which I did not want to relinquish, as I already had the string orchestra „in my head") are virtually impossible to perform.

  M&MG: Which sections of the composition do you have in mind?

HMG: Above all, the third movement, mainly the part of the second violin, during the performance of which the musician has been obliged, up to now (and still will be when performing the version for string quartet) to simplify this section.

  M&MG: The title *Quasi una fantasia* suggests to the listener a clear link between your composition and Beethoven, who wrote two sonatas to which he gave exactly the same name (the reference here, of course, is to Op. 27—the Sonata in E-flat Major and the famous „Moonlight" Sonata in C-sharp Minor). Indeed, this is not your first allusion to the last of the Viennese Classics; suffice it to mention *Lerchenmusik*, in which you quote passages from your great predecessor's Fourth Piano Concerto in G major. Could you outline for us the connection between your *Quasi una fantasia* and its Beethovenian forerunners?

HMG: Well, there is not actually much to describe. Quite simply, I like very much the title devised by Beethoven, which reads in full „Sonata quasi una fantasia," or „Sonata almost a fantasy." At this point we must therefore consider what is a *sonata* and what is a *fantasy*. After all, the construction of a sonata, in principle a cyclical work, is completely different from that of a suite, for example, to say nothing of the fact that we associate the term *sonata* with a specific form, usually composed of an exposition, development, reprise, and so on. And a fantasy? What has that been during the different periods in music history? For we are familiar with Bach's magnificent organ fantasias, with which our Beethoven works have nothing in common. Beethoven was already creating what was essentially a kind of a Romantic fantasy. From Opus 27, I am particularly fond of the E-flat Major Sonata which, incidentally, I have played; a wonderful sonata, but I cannot not point to any specific dependencies between it and my work. Again, I was charmed above all by the title. Naturally, one may ask whether *Quasi una fatasia* is already a „string quatet" or still „music for string qurtet," which is analogous to the question that, were it possible, we would willingly ask Beethoven, namely whether his work is still a „sonata" or already a „fantasy." In a word, the title taken from Beethoven sugests to us a very capacious and, from a formal point of view, hybrid phenomenon, standing on some invisible, yet intuitively perceptible, borderline. And it has two more virtues, by no means inconsiderable. Firstly, it is quite simply a very lovely, poetical title and secondly, its semantic capacity means that it apears commensurate with the substance or content of the work

> **M&MG**: In that case, would you say that one may distinguish in the musical work the formal from the substantial layer?

HMG: If you'll allow, instead of deliberating such questions I shall quote an utterance that is much closer to me, by the great Polish poet Zbigniew Herbert. When asked to give his own definition of art, Herbert replied that art is the conveying of important spiritual experiences.

> **M&MG**: Let's return to *Quasi una fantasia.* The British musicologist Adrian Thomas, the first monographer of your oeuvre, discerned in the Second Quartet „Beethovenian chords," the presence of which would appear to testify that this work's links with the great Viennese, contrary to what you said earlier, go beyond just the title. Where did these chords come from?

HMG: I have no idea! I don't even know if they are „original" Beethoven chords, or if they were simply created by me as my own vision of Beethoven's music. They were certainly not taken in a conscious way from any of his compositions in particular, although I don't deny that they do indeed sound as if Beethoven himself had written them. What is more, I'm not at all ashamed of this fact, and consider that during the composing of this work my ideas were running in a very good direction.

M&MG: And did Beethoven's quartets play some „part" in this?

HMG: No, although I value them extremely highly. But I would not single out any one of them, And I must admit that Im frequently annoyed by those snobbish raptures over the late quartets. Of course, they are brilliant quartets, the greatest works of that kind in history, but let's not forget that for them to arise, Beethoven first had to write the Op. 18 Quartets, or the brilliant „Harp" Quartet in E-flat Major, etc.

M&MG: In *Quasi una fantasia*, before the first movement material appears in the conclusion of the finale, clasping together the dramaturgy of the whole four-movement cycle, there appears unexpectedly a quotation from the carol *Silent Night*. It sounds as if from afar, a little like in Penderecki's Second Symphony „Christmas Eve" where a quotation from the same carol reaching us *quasi da lontano* evokes an „idyllic-angelic" time—the time of childhood. What were your intentions there? Was it an attempt to direct the listener's attention towards the festive mood of Christmas, or perhaps something entirely different, e.g., a sort fo compositional polemic with Penderecki's work?

HMG: That's just how it turned out. I was writing this piece during Advent (I started on St. Nicholas's Day) and at Christmas. The melody of *Silent Night* „came up" by itself; there is not question of any „polemic" with Penderecki's work.

M&MG: You wrote your Second Quartet twelve years ago. Does such a lengthy silence in this domain mean that you have said all you have to say in the genre?

HMG: No. I have already completed the score of another quartet. It will be perfomed by the Kronos Quartet next year, but I would not like to divulge any more details at present.

M&MG: For many years you ran your own composition class, from which there emerged several composers who went on to make their mark on Polish music, including the „1951 generation." Do you consider that the art of composition can be taught?

HMG: Hmm... My answer is that it would be best if all the composition departments of music academies were closed down...

M&MG: So it can't?

HMG: It is a terribly complicated matter. Of course, I can tell a budding young composer what I like about his composition and what he should rework from scratch. But immediately someone else might come along and say something diametrically opposed and—what is worse—each of us will arguably be right. What should we convey to students of this „subject" today? That it is wrong to write thirds and octaves, like a certaing professor of composition at one music academy „teaches"? Today, there are no authoritative criteria whatsoever for assessing a composition. Nowadays, everything is allowed in music, but on one condition: if we speak about.... music.

M&MG: ????

HMG: What I mean is that we can speak about music, about particular works, but not about the teaching of composition. In that domain, we are doomed to failure. For instance, there are no longer any binding rules, like in the Renaissance, which changed gradually, as the great individuals appeared, partly negating the principles elaborated by their predecessors. The only thing that one should demand of a composer today is the ability to play some instrument, as I personally do not trust composers who cannot play anything. It is in some way deranged and false, because how can such a person really foresee the effects of his work, to say nothing of the fact that playing also greatly develops one's imagination. Such a „composer" is essentially capable only of placing lifeless signs on a staff line and that is basically it.

M&MG: Would ou consider that a knowledge of the rules of classical counterpoint and harmony (to limit ourslves to those two aspects of the musical work) might still be of any use to the contemporary composer?

HMG: I could not imagine (since I always relate everything to my own compositional practice) that I would be able to compose anything without knowledge of those Beethovens, Chopins, Scriabins, Szymanowskis, and so forth. How would I supposedly go about it? Would I begin by assuming that music starts with myself? Arrogant nonsense! After all, it surely goes without saying that to invent anything original we have to know what was created before us, if only to ensure that it doesn't turn out one day that we had battered down a door that had been standing wide open for a hundred years; to know, for example, that Richard Strauss achieved a certain effect in such a such a way. With this knowledge, I can consciously seek, for example, to achieve a similar effect by completely different means, or vice versa —by the same means reach a totally different effect. Can we imagine that the elderly Strauss could ever have written such a masterpiece as *Metamorphosen* without a knowledge of Beethoven's *Eroica* and na excellent grouding in the art of counterpoint?

> **M&MG**: A rhetorical question. A propos Strauss's *Metamorphosen*, which seems to be one of your favourite works. Was the mournful, and at the same time, metamorphic character of the first movement of *Quasi una fantasia*, where, as in *Metamorphosen,* Beethoven's music looms somewhere in the background, not, in some general way, at least, inspired by this late, unquestionably brilliant work by the last of the Romantics?

HMG: No. Althought it is indeed an exceptional work, the form of which is a great mystery... for how could an old man create something like this? How proficient must have been his „computer," which sought out for him and proposed the best solutions? It is truly utterly extraordinary and quite astounding: I have envied him and continue to envy him. But that is exactly—paradoxically—a question of training. Thus we return to the riddle that runs: "What is composition and how to learn it"? Let's look at Olivier Messiaen, who taught music analysis. When you went to him, when for example, Wagner's *Parsifal* was „on the carpet," you had to bring with you that score, which was subjected to almost X-ray exposure during lessons that lasted for hours. And now let me ask how many composers today, especially those of the younger generation, have a thorough knowledge of that work? How many of them have read that score? (I would emphasize the score and not the piano reduction). At once, I have the impression of hearing them answer in chorus, in one voice: "We don't need it today, we can live without Wagner!" Well, I agree! One can live without Wanger, but that is not what I'm getting at! The crucial thing is whether you have an idea what Wagner did? I might not like something, find something unappealling—for example, I can live without Wagner or Debussy—but it is my duty to know what they did and what they achieved.

> **M&MG**: So far in our conversation the names of numerous composers from the past have cropped up. Do you still have your own personal masters?

HMG: I remember, during my studies, being fascinated, not so much by the works of the most fashionable Western composers of those times, but by the works of Bartók, especially the second movement of his Piano Sonata. My first encounter with this work was something of a shock, the like of which I have never experienced before, or since. I literally had the impression that the whole world was caving in on me. I had not the slightest idea that music could be constructed from such sounds, from such structures—and such wonderful music!

Szymanowski's Third Piano Sonata also proved to be very important for me. And the work of Ives and Messiaen made a huge impression on me. Not to mention the early Romantics, or the other Viennese Classics. Although perhaps it is worth mentioning that a few years ago I once again—and to a large extent thanks to my son, Mikołaj, who is also a composer—discovered for myself the music of Mozart. That doesn't mean that I didn't know it well before. No. His operas, piano concertos and chamber works had always been the most profound experiences, but then I opened myself up to this oeuvre completely, as it were. Nevertheless, the composer who has been my most faithful, most reliable, „helper," so to speak, to whom I have always turned when I have been unable to resolve something, and a „helper" who has ALWAYS given me invaluable advice in such moments of „oppression" is Johann Sebastian Bach. Contact with his art always brings a breath of the most invigorating inspiration, even if one is composing in a style that is very far removed from Baroque counterpoint.

> **M&MG**: Our converation is taking place in a room which, besides „offering" a breath-taking panorama of the Tatra Mountains, possesses the additional attribute of being a library, in which countless scores by various composers sit shoulder to shoulder with books devoted to the Tatras, art albums, works on history and—doubtless—hundreds of volumes of Polish poetry. Would you say that, besides an

extensive musical context, a composer also needs his horizons expanded by knowledge from other fields?

HMG: I can only answer for myself. Yes, I need it very much. Indeed, I often repeat that we are all—myself included—dreadfully undereducated. For this reason, since I said to myself while still a youngster that I would do everything to avoid dying in ignorance, in order to keep that pledge I decided to collect all the scores that were important for me (even those, as I said, that I am not particularly fond of). No computer program, for example, will take care of this for me, until I personally come into contact with what has been truly important in the history of music. But that's just one side of the coin, the musical side. The books that I've gathered have created a living library, which I am constantly mining and without which it would be impossible for me to imagine life. After all, reading books opens a person towards other people like nothing else. It is thanks to the pearls of wisdom which they contain that there spreads out before one a space for fascinating conversations (on anything but music!), which can be had with everyone—bakers, professors, doctors, carpenters, and so on. And these conversations are always—at least for me personally—hugely enjoyable. And one more thing: they keep me from forgetting that there is more to life than the arranging of sounds, and music is by no means the hub of the universe. The great Norwid once said that what remains when we're gone will be goodness and poetry...

M&MG: Virtually from the beginning of your compositional work, you have been one of the most esteemed of Polish composers. But it was the unprecedented success of your Third Symphony, *The Symphony of Sorrowful Songs* that brought you mass popularity around the world. We would ask you to speak a little about this work, to reveal, as far as possible, the intentions which accompanied you while composing it and the inspirations which were then—in the second half of the seventies—stimulating your imagination.

HMG: Hmm... I've spoken on that subject so many times already that I wouldn't like to repeat myself yet again. But I'll tell you something else, instead, which is strictly related to the second movement of that work. Some thirty years ago, give or take, I bought a book by Alfons Filar and Michał Lejko entitled *Pałace. Katownia Podhala* [*The Palace. The Torture Chamber of Podhale*], published in 1970, which contains photographs from the cells of the Gestapo prison in Zakopane (the so-called Palace, a beautiful pre-war guest house), the walls of which were covered with numerous inscriptions scratched out by the Poles who were imprisoned and often tortured there during the Second World War. Most of these inscriptions contained pleas for remembrance, not infrequently for the avenging of the wrongs that were experienced there. But my attention was caught by one inscription, made in 1944 by the then eighteen-year-old Helena Błażusiakówna, which stood out for its content, more specifically for the fact that it was completely lacking in any desire for revenge (incidentally, I managed to see this cell myself, before some idiot came up with the barbaric idea of painting over these inscriptions). Many years ago, when I decided to use this text in the second movement of the Third Symphony, I tried to find out something about this girl's fate—but without any success. It seemed that all trace of her had disappeared irretrievably; it was not even known whether she had managed to survive.

Still in the seventies, following the first Polish performances of the Third Symphony, I received letters from Poles who once lived in Lwów.[1] They informed me that the text which I had attributed to Błażusiakówna was a fragment of a much earlier song of the Eaglets of Lwów [a division of Boy Scouts], that was very well known before the war and told the story of Jurek Biczan, a young hero who perished during the battle of Lwów in 1918. Hence, my enduring presentiment that Helena Błażusiakówna, since she knew that song, may have been a girl guide. In the eighties, I happened upon a small volume entitled *Droga wiodła przez Spisz* [The road led through Spisz] by Józef Bieniek, from which I learned that Błażusiakówna was imprisoned in the Palace in Zakopane in September 1944, together with a group of partisans. After a month-long interrogation she was freed. Further attempts at picking up this woman's trail, following the Third Symphony's international success were made by British journalists, but, alas, with the same effect as before.

And then, approximately two years ago, I received various materials from Doctor Wincenty Galica, an expert on Podhale. From these materials I learned that Helena Błażusiakówna survived the war and

---

[1] Lwów, Lemberg, now Lviv, was the largest Polish city in the province of the Ukraine.

had subsequently married and settled in Wadowice, the home town of Karol Wojtyła. Unfortunately, I also learned that she had recently died. Incidentally, her life had not been easy after the war, either, since, ddue to her active role in the partisan Home Army, she was subjected to many vexations in the Polish People's Republic. By some irony of fate, while living in Chochołów for many years we would travel through Wadowice sometimes as many as four times a week. Somehow, that meeting was never meant to be...

> **M&MG**: But did Helena Błażusiakówna at least know that the inscription she made had been immortalised in your symphony?

HMG: That I don't know, and I doubt that it will ever be established...

> **M&MG**: The Third Symphony, apart from forming the backdrop to many feature films, some by world famous directors (such as Peter Weir's *Fearless*), has also been the „protagonist" of two films. In one of these films—*The Symphony of Sorrowful Songs* by Tony Palmer—a series of extremely graphic images from various tragic events of the twentieth century, including the Holocaust, is superimposed onto the cotinuously flowing music of this work. Do you agree wich such an interpretation, as we must call it, of your work?

HMG: Absolutely not. I regard Palmer's film as scandalous, as it has absolutely nothing in comon with the substance of my work.

> **M&MG**: What do the Tatras mean to you—one fo the most myth-producing places in Polish culture, where throughout the twentieth century many writers, artists, and composers (including among the last group, your predecessors Mieczysław Karlowicz and Karol Szymanowski) have worked?

HMG: Let's leave that subject for another conversation.

> **M&MG**: If we were to glance through the list of your compositions, it would turn out that a substantial part of it would comprise vocal-instrumental works. As for the texts fo these works, the most common are folk texts, or poetry from Polish romanticism and modernism. Hence the degree of surprise that the list also includes two songs to words by

Federico Garcia Lorca. Could you unveil the secret of how the verse of this Spanish poet came to inspire you?

HMG: I believe it was in 1955, when I came across several poems by Lorca in the *Tygodnik Powszechny*, in a translation by Mikołaj Bieszczadowski. One of these—*Nocturne*—I set to music in December 1956, but I was paticularly electrified by another poem entitled *Malaguena*, in which I read the exceptionally poignant, piercing words: „Death goes in/ and death goes out /of the tavern./ Black horses/ and sinister people / roam the hidden trails / of the guitar/ and there is a scent of salt / and woman's blood / in the febrile flowers / on the beach. / Death goes in /and death goes out / and death goes out /and death goes in/ to the tavern."[2] I don't know how this poem reads in the original, but in the translation it is a masterpiece. In Polish, this poetry is so suggestive that it is actually hard to imagine that its author was not Bieszczadowski himself.

M&MG: In spite of this, you did not compose music to these words straight away, off the cuff, so to speak...

HMG: In the fifties, I felt that I had not yet fully matured into setting such a keen, intense poem, and so it lay in one of my drawers for almost a quarter of a century. Not until 1980 did I muster the courage to set this poetry to music.[3] And so I have at present two songs to words by Lorca to my name.

M&MG: These songs have yet to be published. Is there any chance of them seeing the light od day and entering artists' vocal repertoire?

HMG: They'll most likely be printed by Boosey & Hawkes, a publishing firm to which I've been attached for many years.

M&MG: After the world premiere of your Third Symphony, which took place in Poland in 1976,[4] the critics essentially split into two camps, one of which praised the work highly, while

---

[2] Transl. Sandra Forman and Allen Josephs, *Only Mystery Federico Garica Lorca's Poetry in Word and Image* (University Press of Florida, 1992).
[3] *Two Songs of Lorca*, Op. 42, published by Boosey & Hawkes.
[4] This is an error; the world premiere took place at the Royan Festival France, in April 1977, followed by the Polish premiere at the Warsaw Autumn Festival in September 1977. See the List of Works for more details. [editor's note]

the other belittled it. Then, for many years, little was heard of this compostion in Poland, although it cannot be said to have fallen into oblivion. But it was the work's recording in 1992, by Dawn Upshaw and the London Sinfonietta under David Zinman, which met with a success that was absolutely unprecedented in the history of twentieth-century music, measured even in typically show-business terms (the CD sold over one million copies). As a result, your name began to be seen alongside the most outstanding composers of that century. Would you agree with the statement that it is difficult to be a prophet in one's own country?

HMG: I have never thought about it, and honestly speaking those things are of no interest to me whatsoever. To tell you the truth, when I'm composing I never give a thought to whether that new work will be to anyone's liking or not. For me, the most important thing is the personal satisfaction, even immense delight that I feel when I become convicted that I have composed something in the way that I had previously heard it in my imagination and planned to write. But the question of popularity, and especially of whether I'll be played at prestigious festivals of contemporary music, has left me absolutely indifferent.

M&MG: How, from a present day perspective, would you assess the output of the avant-garde of the sixties, to which you belonged?

HMG: But what is an avant-garde!? Because for me it's an empty label, artifically created by critics who are scared that, Heaven forbid, they should become lost in the jungle of disparate phenomena. Personally, I have never „ascribed" myself to any avant-garde; and neither, even more so—as critics ill-disposed towards my work have asserted over the last thirty years—have I ever „betrayed" it (after all, how can you betray something to which—at least intentionally—you have never consciously belonged, or which does not even exist?) As I said, I have always written that which, at a given moment in time, I have wanted to write; so-called musical fashions have never interested me.

M&MG: Thank you for talking with us.

Figure 5-1: Morskie Oko in the Tatra Mountains; by Op. Wikimedia Commons.
https://upload.wikimedia.org/wikipedia/commons/2/2c/Tatry_-_MOko.jpg

Figure 5-2: Zakopane at night, Photo by Mgiganteus. Wikimedia Commons.
https://en.wikipedia.org/wiki/Zakopane#/media/File:Zakopane_at_night.jpg

Figure 5-3: Pages from the Program of the 8th Festival of Polish Composers in Bielsko-Biała, celebrating the 70th Birthday of Henryk Mikołaj Górecki.

CHAPTER 6

„Music? A Visitor from Another World"

Henryk Mikołaj Górecki in Conversation with Małgorzata and Marcin Gmys

(15 October 2008 in Ząb, near Zakopane)

M&MG: More than six years have already passed since our conversation ended. Just for a moment, we would like to return to one of its earlier threads. You previously evaded the question of the significance that the Podhale region holds for you—as a man and an artist. Perhaps now, since we find ourselves once again in the same room with a view over the Tatras, you might be persuaded to pick up that thread again?

HMG: Not for all the world! Not only do I not intend to pick up that train of thought, but please delete the whole question from our conversation!

M&MG: ???

HMG: [*sigh*] It's enough to take a look around to notice—immediately, on every level—this whole deluge of sloppiness and factiousness. I'll say just so much: I'm getting off that „train," I don't understnd that „speech" at all. That's my whole reply...

M&MG: Over the last six years, the greatest event in your musical biography has been the premiere of your Third String Quartet '*...songs are sung*' – a work, the existence of which you confirmed during our previous conversation. This quartet—like your previous works for these forces—was premiered by the phenomenal Kronos Quartet. We already have three recordings of this work made by the same American musicians. Which of these recordings do you prefer: the first, a recording of the premiere performance in Bielsko-Biała, or perhaps the recording from the Festival of Polish Music in

Kraków, released on DVD by Polskie Wydawnictwo Audiowizualne, or—finally—the studio recording?

HMG: I cannot answer that question. And that's not at all because I am undecided. I simply do not know those recordings: both the discs—compact and DVD—are lying in my workshop not even unwrapped and that's probably how it will stay.

M&MG: You are a very busy composer...

HMG: In this case, it's not even a question of a lack of time. I'm simply not, and never have been, in the habit of listening to my music at home. If I have a free moment for myself, which happens very rarely, I enjoy listening, but always to other composers. Without any special reason, I don't like reaching for my own music. After it is written, performed and recorded, it already constitutes for me a chapter that's definitively closed.

M&MG: And you never feel the temptation to listen to your works a little—if only to change, improve or clarify something in them?

HMG: The temptation for improvement certainly lies in every artist, but I concluded long ago that' it's a waste of time. There's no sense in looking back—one has to march onward, forward. That's the only „journey" that makes sense.

M&MG: Your last quartet has a rather enigmatic title, but on the occasion of the premiere you already mentioned that this ttile comes from a quatrain by Vladimir Khlebnikov, which in Adam Pomorski's translation reads as follows: „Gdy umierają rumaki—dyszą / Gdy umierają zioła—schną/ Gdy umierają słońca—nagle gasną / Gdy umierają ludzie—śpiewają pieśni" [„When horses die—they breathe, and pant / when grasses die —they wither / when suns die—they go out / when people die —they sing songs].

HMG: I know this poem from a different, much earlier, translation, which *Życie Literackie* published in the fifties.

M&MG: Given the contemplative, and at times even mournful character of all your music, could one risk the statement that the Third Quartet, is in its own way, a work inspired by that poetry?

HMG: Actually no, one could not. I wish to emphasize this most strongly: my composition has, apart from the title, NO connection with this beatufiul poetic fragment. I have to say that a sort of plague has spread for comparing the Third Quartet to this poem. But first I wrote the whole quartet, then it lay on a shelf for several years and only after I'd taken the decision to release it into the world did I start to search for some title for it. And then, unexpectedly and a little by chance, I remembered that quatrain, already perfectly familiar to me earlier. What is more, at the same time I was also considering a number of other possible titles, but I was anxious to include the word „song" in the quartet's title, hence my choice.

M&MG: But you won't deny that there exists some afffinity between the general mood of the two works.

HMG: That's just a matter of individual reception. Essentially, each person sees in my work what he himself would like to see in it. Regardless of my corrections or explanations, musciologists will write what they want to, anyway.

M&MG: So, let's drop the question of the possible influence of the Russian poet's words on the Third Quartet. Yet proceeding somewhat in spite of your expectations, we would like to ask whether you would agree with a reading of your work as a composition of a sombre character which may constitue a sort of homage to Podhale?

HMG: But on what grounds might I think so?

M&MG: On the one hand, on the grounds of the pessimistic diagnosis of the Tatras today which you hinted at yourself a moment ago; and, on the other hand, on the basis of the overall expression of this work (comprising, as it does, four adagios divided by a central scherzo) and a number of universal signs which it contains...

HMG: What signs?

M&MG: For example, the entire first movement is grounded on a rhythm that is deceptively similar to the „mournful" chaconne from Beethoven's Seventh Symphony, the rhythm of which could, incidentally be identified with the motif of the „journey to nowhere" (or to death) from Schubert's *Winterreise*. The finale contains the cello's exceptionally moving recitative, which seems only to enhance the funereal atmosphere....

HMG: For me these are not unversal signs. In writing the Third Quartet I was not thinking about such symbols and I certainly did not have Beethoven's Seventh Symphony in mind.

M&MG: But you would surely not deny the presence of a quotation from the Second Quartet of Karol Szymanowski, who to a certain degree was inspired by highland music?

HMG: Of course not. But what has that to to do with your whole „theory?" There is nothing of the highlands in the Szymanowski chords I quote!

M&MG: Quite so, and yet it is difficult to believe that this „sequence of musical meanigns" (the chaconne, distant echoes of the playing of highland bands, the Szymanowski chords, the recitative, and the domination of a „largo rhythm") was solely the work of coincidence...

HMG: Well, there you go—I was right! Regardless of what I might have to say, musicologists will always „know better" and will always expound their theories.

M&MG: All right—we give in! But let us remain with this work for a while, or rather with the string quartet as a genre. What does thie composing of a string quartet really meant for you?

HMG: In the twentieth century, a whole mass of string quartets were written. Yet to my mind the clear majority were works for four string instruments, and not, as in Shostakovich, for example, compositions for string quartet, that is for an ensemble which has its own, unique sound. I intuitively sense the great difference between writing for the first and second violin, viola and cello, and writing for the string quartet.

M&MG: Is it something like the difference between writing for orchestra and writing a symphony?

HMG: More or less.

> **M&MG:** „More ore less" means that in your differentiation there is only a grain of truth...

HMG: Only and as much as a grain. Because art must contain an element of mystery. I'm immediately reminded of a wonderful conversation with Gustaw Holoubek, which I read quite recently in a single breath.[5] Holoubek—allow me to quote his words straight from the book—recalled, among other things, this event from his biography:

> I was playing once the Beggar in Giraudoux' *Electra*, directed by Kazimierz Dejmek.[6] An impressive role, grand monologue. In the premiere, I played it quite successfully. After a dozen or so performances, Dejmek comes up to me backstage and says: 'Mr Holoubek, the way you are playing that beggar now, you can play it at home. All those gestures, the miming, the drawn-out vowels, are artificial. Please go back to how it was in the premiere!?' But how was it in the premiere?' 'I don't know,' replies Dejmek, 'But there was a sparkle in your eye, something that carried me into a completely different world. I didn't know where it came from, but I felt that you were a prophet, and now nothing of that remains in your playing.'

For me that extract could be a motto for every artist! Because that is exactly what often happens in art, at least in Art with a capital A. In order to achieve that „sparkle in your eye" you must have instruments which you received from the Lord God. And not everyone possesses them, and not all the time. If you do have these things, you can occasionally reach inside a word, or a sound. But that cannot be learned from anyone. Indeed, as I often say: the worst things are those that are learned.

> **M&MG:** Some example?

HMG: Let's take Chopin. A question has long been bothering me as to whether, had he not left Warsaw, he would still have been the same great Chopin, or would he have become some provincial Kątski? After

---

[5] Małgorzata Terlecka-Reksnis, *Holoubek—rozmowy* [Holoubek—Conversations] (Warszawa: Prószyński i S-ka, 2008). Gustaw Holoubek (1923-2008) was a Polish actor and director, later member of the Sejm and senator—[Editor].

[6] Kazimierz Dejmek (1924-2002) was a Polish theater director—[Editor].

all, he was taught very little. What could good old Żywny have taught him? An ordinary, average musician. But at the same time an incredibly judicious chap who saw in an instant the diamond he was dealing with and decided „only" so much: to not hinder the lad in his natural development. And what could Elsner have taught Chopin? I ask therefore: How and „from what" could Chopin have dreamed up those mazurkas, ballades, and sonatas of his? We can digress *ad infinitum* as to why Beethoven proceeded in a particular sonata as he did and not in some other way. No Sikorski, Chomiński or Feicht will ever explain that to you. We can always break something down into its component parts, but to answer where „it" came from? Why this or that composer employed a particular modulation and not another? Or—oh, exactly!—are you disturbed by the lack of the first subject in the first movement reprise of the B-flat Minor Sonata? But it was exploited so comprehensively in the development!

> **M&MG**: Perhaps Chopin took this „concept" from the first movement of Beethoven's D Minor Sonata, Op. 31?

HMG: Not impossible. After all, he had an excellent knowledge of the literature of his times from what he read himself (not from school!). But in that case where did it come from in the Beethoven? That we do not know and will never find out. Asked what is music, Leszek Kołakowski replied—and I like this utterance enormously—that it is a visitor from another world. On the other hand—and Michał Heller wrote a book about this—the most wonderful domain of human thinking remains mathematics, capable of proving everything, even phenomena which we don't yet completely understand. But really everything? In music, often compared to mathematics, even mathematics begins to fail us, since no one can mathematically prove why Beethoven composed the opening bars of the *Allegretto* of his Seventh Symphony in just that way or how he arrived at some of the modulations in his Ninth Symphony. Where did it all come from?

> **M&MG**: In our previous conversation you betrayed a secret and revealed the existence of the Third Quartet, which was then awaiting its premiere. Is the score of a Fourth Quartet already lying in wait?

HMG: Yes, but so far only in fragments.

> **M&MG**: Could you tell us something more about that work.

HMG: Six year ago, when the Third Quartet was already complete and waiting to be performed, did I expatiate on it?

M&MG: Unfortunately not.

HMG: Then, let is remain just so.

M&MG: So what—apart, of course, from good health and creative inspiration—may one wish you for the future? What does a seventy-five-year-old, fulfilled artist expect?

HMG: How awful and pathetic that sounds: „fulfilled artist." What to wish me? That, without losing the acuity of my vision, I might not look upon that river of filth that engulfs us.

M&MG: Thank you for talking with us.

Figure 6-1: Portrait of Henryk Mikołaj Górecki from the Program of the 8th Festival of Polish Composers in Bielsko-Biała, celebrating his 70th birthday.

◎ ◎ ◎

CHAPTER 7

„Music is a Conversation"

Henryk Mikołaj Górecki Talks to Anna Wieczorek and Krzysztof Cyran

29 April 2008. The Academy of Music in Katowice. Its new building. The conversation with Prof. Henryk Mikołaj Górecki lasts for five hours. It is a fascinating journey through the hidden corners of the composer's mind. The strands are woven, as if in counterpoint; they surprise each other, and sometimes complement each other. The main conceptual thread for the entire conversation is mathematics. The interview is conducted by two doctoral students of the Academy of Music in Kraków, Anna Wieczorek and Krzysztof Cyran, assisted by their professor, one of Górecki's close personal friends, Dr. Teresa Malecka, as well as by Małgorzata Janicka-Słysz who edited the entire conversation for publication.

Henryk Mikołaj Górecki: I am preoccupied with this question: what is music? I thought that Father Professor Józef Tischner could suggest something. I searched for an answer in his beautiful book, *Thinking In the Element of Beauty* [Myślenie w żywiole piękna].[1] Now, I'm looking at mathematics, reading Father Professor Michał Heller.[2] How fascinating are his writings: the creation—creation, chance and non-chance in the activities of the Creator. Someone would say: the Lord God. Someone else: a mysterious, highly improbable power. I would have loved to talk to Father Heller, I would have been all ears! This man, I think, the first one in Poland, had not opposed science to religion, but instead connected science with faith.

---

[1] Józef Tischner, *Myślenie w żywiole piękna* [Thinking in the Element of Beauty] (Kraków: Wydawnictwo Znak, 2013).
[2] Michał Kazimierz Heller is a Polish professor of philosophy at the Pontifical University of John Paul II in Kraków, Poland, and an adjunct member of the Vatican Observatory staff. A prolific writer on cosmology, cosmogony and theology, he authored, among other titles *Usprawiedliwienie wszechświata* [The Justification of the World] (Kraków: Znak, 1995), or *Wieczność, czas, kosmos* [Eternity, Time, Cosmos] (Kraków: Znak, 1995).

Anna Wieczorek, Krzysztof Cyran: Are numbers beautiful?

HMG: Numbers help me reach the heart of the issue; reach knowledge. I know something about numbers; I know how they have been used. These are not great secrets. When I say „5" everyone knows what it is, but when I say „F-sharp"? And then, when I add from which octave this note comes, and when I specify the instrument... Then, nobody really knows anything...

Teresa Malecka: A mathematician once compared differential equations with the Ninth Symphony of Beethoven.

HMG: Father Heller said that the whole of the Divine Creation is like a perfect symphony. And this floored me. I can teach counterpoint, instrumentation, only I always repeat that you cannot treat these things separately. A „sound" by itself does not exist. A sound has to have a specific instrument and a specific person that will play or sing this sound. These are measurable things.

AW/KC: Did you calculate all the repetitions in the Third String Quartet? These are not repetitions that happened by chance, are they?

HMG: This was by chance... But I'm always tormented by another problem. What is music?

AW/KC: Music can be felt.

HMG: You can feel odors from the kitchen, or stinking, but not music!

Małgorzata Janicka-Słysz: Chopin said that music was a miracle.

HMG: I can agree with that... For me, music is a kind of a conversation. I talk to someone, I communicate something to this person.

AW/KC: But to whom? A universal listener, or a particular recipient? And who should be this recipient?

HMG: That one who needs this. But art is not for boors! And we have an epoch of sanctified rudeness: everything that long ago was in the septic tank has been elevated to the highest shelf. Art is not for crowds. Chopin also did not compose for crowds. He was persuaded:

„Write, Mr. Fryderyk, a national opera!" And to one disciple he gave... guess what? The score of Beethoven's opera, *Fidelio*.

AW/KC: What do you owe to your teacher, Professor Bolesław Szabelski?

HMG: When I was studying, there were only three professors of composition in Katowice. I wanted to study with Szabelski, I really do not know why. Not with Bolesław Woytowicz—a wise mathematician and lawyer. Maybe he could have taught me the craft of composing? Exactly—the craft.

AW/KC: What is the direction of development in contemporary music?

HMG: In the 1920s perhaps, the International Society for Contemporary Music was formed. I am thinking: what for? Because every living composer **is** a contemporary composer: in the 18th and 19th centuries—Mozart, Beethoven, etc. Neither the 18th nor the 19th century needed such a society.

AW/KC: Has the music created „here and now," that is contemporary music, stopped to be a conversation?

HMG: I do not know. I have been circling around this issue, from which we have come. Ah, I'm not Gustaw Holoubek, I'm not Czesław Miłosz. I get lost in all this. I remember the statements of Professor Leszek Kołakowski,[3] statements of Holoubek, conversations with Piotr Mucharski and Katarzyna Janowska in the second volume of *Conversations for the End of the Century*.[4] Phenomenal conversations! I return to the question: what is music? Professor Kołakowski gave his answer: Music is a guest from another world. Genius!

---

[3] Leszek Kołakowski (1927-2009) was a Polish philosopher and writer, a prolific critic of Marxism, who often wrote on religion and ethics, for instance *Moje słuszne poglądy na wszystko* [My Right Views about Everything (Kraków: Znak, 1999); *Mini wykłady o maxi sprawach* [Mini Lectures about Maxi Matters] (Kraków: Znak, 2003); and *O co nas pytają wielcy filozofowie* [What Great Philosophers Ask us about] (Kraków: Znak, 2004)—[Editor].

[4] Paweł Hertz; Katarzyna Janowska; Piotr Mucharski, *Rozmowy na koniec wieku* [Conversations for the End of the Century[(Kraków : Wydawn. Znak, 1997-1999) —[Editor].

AW/KC: But not all music.

HMG: Agreed. Similarly, not every human being is from another world.

AW/KC: The hallmark of the music by Henryk Mikołaj Górecki is a particular experience and impression of time. The flow of time in the symphonies or in *Beatus Vir* is amazing!

HMG: In mathematics there is also a certain time. The strength of the explosion of sound, the duration of this sound, the pitch, the amplitude. Perhaps I could have been a better composer, if I knew math better? I treated it as God's plague. I passed my high school exit exam in 1951. For my math exam I received, I remember, a question: a formula on a formula pushed by a formula. I got all sweaty, I drank two soda waters and nothing. The annoucement of results. I'm called in. The committee: „And what do you want to do?" I say: „Study music." So they let me pass. And this is how music saved my high school diploma.

AW/KC: Do you read texts about your music?

HMG: The best criticism will not spoil me, and the worst will not annoy me. I know what I can do and what I cannot do; what I bungled up, and what I did well. I have stacks of records that I do not listen to, because I do not want to be disappointed. Only after several years, after I play it back, I think: oh, so they understood something after all.

AW/KC: A composer lives in the world of various sounds. Is it true that you listen to jazz?

HMG: Jazz is fantastic music! But true jazz. It has to be an excellent pianist, to the measure of Oscar Peterson, Art Garner... I love Oscar Peterson: a huge man, when he sits at the piano it seems that he will crush the instrument with his legs. And he plays jazz like Mozart. I had a friend, Bernard Biegon, who directed the Fifteen of Poznań. One of the most talented pianists that I knew in my life, only an incredibly lazy bum. I remember we were practicing at the Academy the *33 Variations* by Beethoven. He says: „I'll play and you will tell me what I'm doing wrong." I could not follow while reading the score. He was phenomenal in jazz, but this was a gentle kind of jazz. And that is what I had a passion for.

AW/KC: The jazz pulse, jazz rhythm?

HMG: But also the melody. The ability to develop a melody that is clearly heard.

AW/KC: And what about harmony? Do works have to differ in their harmonic climate?

HMG: They have to and they do not have to. They have to bring with themselves some harmonic image, climate, or aura. For a while I have been thinking about it, I wanted to discuss this with Czesław Miłosz: what are the sounds that we speak with? There are many nations. Let us take the melody of the German language as an example: the seconds, major thirds, everything is clear. But we always cry. A person could save himself/herself in a brilliant way if they could move in the minor material as well as in the major. One could take the essence from mazur, from dance.

M J-S: Szymanowski would say that Chopin took from the mazur what is profound, what is racial.

HMG: He took what is our speech. Mickiewicz is not using the *word* in the minor key; Słowacki, Norwid, Krasiński—do not either. But Sienkiewicz, does so: the sabre, the sabre... Prus—no. I do not intend to insult Sienkiewicz, I only make a statement. When I read as a child [*gówniarz*] his novel *Krzyżacy* [*The Teutonic Knights*], I cried my eyes out... And this is what was supposed to keep up the spirit of Poles?

AW/KC: So how can you express strong and positive emotions in music?

HMG: Strong? Better say: positive. Is Chopin powerful? His mazurkas, nocturnes, waltzes, or ballades are tragic. Not sad, but tragic. It is drama that could have different endings or conclusions.

AW/KC: There is a spot in the second movement of the Third Symphony where the third B-flat—D-flat is resolved into the second B-flat—C. The essence. Simple intervals, but how they sound! How do you understand the keys of major and minor?

HMG: There is no major and minor any more. In my music, I have plenty of sections that are badly made from the point of view of classic harmony. I really like shifting chords in the first inversion. And these are awful chords: I would have been chased out of school for using them. I would have been accused: „Mister, you are moving in parallel, like on skis." But this sounds fantastic: *E—C—G, D—B-flat—F...* My question: can it be like that, or not? Is there a prohibition?

> **AW/KC**: Thanks to the fact that there was the twelve tone system, we do not have to ask about it now.

HMG: In today's music, the major and minor keys create certain motives that have their own melodies and harmonies, their own strength. There is a certain energy in this. When Bach started a theme he already knew how many developments there could be. He knew this, he had this sense of construction. I am interested in this issue: can I make anything out of it?

> **AW/KC**: So what about the canon in the first movement from the Third Symphony?

HMG: Somebody told me once: when you meet Bach, he wil tell you, „a great canon." They say that I use repetitions. There are no repetitions there at all! Not to mention *minimal* or *repetitive music*. I remember when I was working on this canon, I looked through all the responses: tonal, real. The theme was not to be two-or-three notes, it was to be the whole song. Can a song be a theme for a canon? This was the first question. The second question: should the canon be tonal or real? If it were tonal, we would have had the same image from the beginning to the end, and from the first to the last page nothing would have changed. After the second entrance of the theme you would have had enough. It is not important whether there will be 50 or 100 pages, when you know in advance what will be on the fifth page: the same. But in my work it changes: E-minor, G-major, a certain F-sharp. Now, as to the form: here you have to lift the canon up, there you have to interrupt it, and then, again, descend. The canon grows, grows, and then it diminishes, from the inside out. Similarly, the architect draws his form. But what is form? Form is mathematics.

> **AW/KC**: What about the sense of sacred space?

HMG: One thing I do not like: the division into *sacrum* and *profanum*. Was Chopin profane? Was Schubert profane? The simplest song by Schubert is for me an incredible *sacrum*. What was given by God is, in itself, a certain *sacrum*. But do not mess with it, behave like Father

Heller, who does not have a TV, does not listen to the radio, only he sits down and clarifies for us time and space. Our life is like that of a dragonfly in all that. But we have to accept this incredible space—versus our nothingness, fragility.

> **AW/KC**: You attach great importance to the word. Is it lost in contemporary times?

HMG: The tragedy of the arts took place when the word lost its value, when it became trite. But the word has to have value! The tradition is a historical continuity: it is something that we have that is of the highest value. And not „in reference to." There is no need to improve on anything, to think too much about anything.

> **AW/KC**: It is springtime. Nature awakens. Does it favor creative work?

HMG: Utopia. We live in the times of devastation of what we have found. The Tatra Mountains are smaller and smaller, and they cry more and more. I am a person connected to nature. I went up to the mountains despite my handicap; I enjoyed the forest, the stream, the fields, a nice house. I do not know why did I end up there, in Podhale. Maybe because of Szymanowski, maybe because of the music? When I was enrolled in the third year of college, I met people who performed with Szymanowski: Władek Obrochta and Tadek Gąsienica. Władek Obrochta had these humongous fingers, but when he played he was transformed into a Paganini. I hiked in the Tatras, I walked through villages, together with my wife. We drank water without boiling it. Now we are becoming wild. Why? I do not know. Something has to break; something has to explode. There will be events; there will be clashes...

> **AW/KC**: *Scontri...*

HMG: ...But of these clashes there may arise an incredible event. And again, we enter the domain of mathematics. I have always looked at math as a lame evil that impacted my life. I was not taught well. And music has a lot to do with mathematics. And with physics. What kind of music can we write?

> **AW/KC**: Just like the Third Symphony?

HMG: The Third Symphony is a certain digression, but strongly situated in tradition. But can you write five symphonies like that? I wrote the Fourth. It is lying there in a piano reduction. Purely instrumental, with *obbligato pianoforte* and organ. I did write such music before. There are planes—harmonic „stretches" that are connected to space. Do you know that cosmic space is full of sound? There are other suns, much greater than ours. But how does this space sound? I am interested in this infinity, the black holes that break, swallow each other and create anew. And this space continually increases. This is genius! Only in this moment, you can start thinking: who is God? Only then you can see the beginning of the Old Testament.

AW/KC: This is how we feel it, too.

HMG: I wanted to test it on exotic instruments, in Japanese or Arab music. I do not like this music, though; it is foreign to me. Why did this smallest continent, that is Europe, build all this? Asia now replicates what has been made in Europe. Islam is dangerous. Conflict is on the edge of the knife. And what do you want a person to do: write symphonies?

AW/KC: Maybe songs?

HMG: I awfully like songs. I have several not published and not performed yet: song cycles for choir. These are in manuscripts, in notebooks. I wanted to create a chorale from Polish songs with my harmony. I found a very specific harmonic language for choral songs.

AW/KC: What kind of harmony?

HMG: I do not harmonize the melody in accordance with classic principles. Each melody has its own harmonic halo; it carries within itself its own certain harmony. On the one hand, you can do anything today. And I take such common harmonies. Agreed, they are in major-minor, but I use all the keys. I do not care if I write in D Major. I write in the key in which I received the song. Therefore, I take the key in which it was sung or played. To harmonize this very simple song, I have all the keys at my disposal. All! Major, minor, flat, sharp...

AW/KC: So chords may be juxtaposed that come from different keys?

HMG: I brag that I discovered the melody of the Polish language. I do not like translations. I do not like to write in a foreign language.

AW/KC: Szymanowski also selected Polish text for his *Stabat Mater*.

HMG: But this is a translation of a Latin sequence.

AW/KC: Szymanowski composed to Polish texts, though.

HMG: But he was—I think—focused on Palestrina and on the Russian way of leading the choir, of singing...

AW/KC: ...and on *Gorzkie Żale* [Bitter Sorrows]...

HMG: He had this in his blood. I would have had to learn it, but he had it. And in Szymanowski's *Stabat Mater* there is a number of examples from Tchaikovsky. What a sonority! This is his own discovery. I grew up with Szymanowski from the beginning. This beginning was, for me, when I was almost 20 years old. My first scores were the Szymanowski Mazurkas, PWM edition. I memorized them. On the occasion of a certain anniversary in Warsaw, Jarosław Iwaszkiewicz (so strongly criticized by some people, and he is a person distinguished in every way) said that whoever had not seen the steppe, would not understand Szymanowski. I have never been in Russia, I will not go through this border on my own free will, but I would love to go visit Tymoszówka in the Ukraine. And see the steppe.

AW/KC: Does the steppe have its own sound?

HMG: Yes, also the earth, the forest... I have never been to a steppe, but I imagine it, based on films and literature. This heat, the warmth... And this light! Sunny. This has musical sense, too. Szymanowski did not have to discover this; he lived it. If there were no revolution, he could have still lived in Tymoszówka—I am completely convinced. I can see some of this steppe in the *Stabat Mater*. Szymanowski grew out of Skriabin and Stravinsky. He was transplanted to Poland in an artificial, quick and brutal way. And here began... a question mark after a question mark. Bydgoszcz, Warszawa, Paris, Kraków, Podhale, Zakopane...

AW/KC: Italy...

HMG: ... and longing for what he lost. He was forced to search for his own place here, in Poland.

AW/KC: And he was fighting for his mission, for his convictions.

HMG: And how!

AW/KC: He was also fighting with the ignorance of the community.

HMG: In general there is too much ignorance. Yet, we do not need to make a great effort to ensure that things are going well. So this is sad, and as politicians often say it nowadays—deeply shocking. And it is enough that a person be.... well, tell me, what?

AW/KC: Good?

HMG: There is nothing more that is expected of us. The whole Bible can be reduced to this one word. You do not have to be wise, just good. If you are good, you will also be wise. I live thanks to the fact that I had the good luck of meeting the Holy Father, the personification of goodness. The last conversation we had was in Rome in 2003. It was October, Thursday, half past twelve. John Paul II was seriously ill. I held his hand, I pulled on it, I did not let it go, I thought that I would crush it. The Holy Father had a so-so little table. He was sitting there, exhausted. I remember the whiteness and the sunlight that was on him. We were alone... And Father Stanisław. I was explaining why I am not composing the Mass. It was commissioned by the Holy Father. I only have a *Kyrie*—25 minutes of music.

AW/KC: It would be enough...

HMG: But I do not know how a Mass should look like. As a musical composition. Not a liturgical Mass. What is a Mass? Not a text! The Mass is something that grabs you by the throat in the first chord. And whether it is a *Requiem* by Mozart or a Mass by Schubert—it captures you and it holds on to you. This is about a serious matter. *Credo* is the most difficult. A good *Credo* is a catechism.

AW/KC: An explanation of an attitude?

HMG: No, the codex of behavior. „Two times two is four." It is interesting why Olivier Messiaen had never composed a Mass. And he was the closest to this idea.

AW/KC: Perhaps, that's why?

HMG: He knew what it was... And what is the Holy Mass—in one sentence?

AW/KC: Prayer.

HMG: I would call it something else: it is a conversation.

AW/KC: Just like music...

Edited by Małgorzata Janicka-Słysz

Figure 7-1: Cover of a PWM brochure for Henryk Mikołaj Górecki, 1990s.
Krakow: PWM Edition. Reprinted by Permission.

◎ PART II ◎

ON GÓRECKI'S LIFE AND MUSIC

CHAPTER 8

Górecki's Life and Music: A Bird's Eye View

Maja Trochimczyk

I was born in Silesia, in a small, fine, wonderful place with a lovely old Polish name.[1] This village is called Czernica; between Rybnik and Raciborz. Old, ancient Polish land. But there were always three cultures in this area: Polish, Czech, and German. Folklore, all the arts, knew no boundaries. These boundaries were supposed to exist, but they shifted frequently to the right, to the left. That did not mean that people started thinking differently. No, the land dictated it. The region defined the identity of a person, of its inhabitant. A highlander (*góral*) is always a highlander, first and foremost a highlander. A Silesian is always a Silesian. There is this particular land that transmits certain genes and not others.

~ Henryk Mikołaj Górecki, 1997[2]

Born on December 6, 1933, in the village of Czernica in Upper Silesia, (southwest Poland), Henryk Mikołaj Górecki spent his entire life within this and neighboring areas of Silesia, Podhale, and the Tatra Mountains.[3] Górecki's father, Roman (1904–1991) worked at a railway

---

[1] Silesia is a region in southwest Poland, consisting of Upper Silesia (centered on Katowice where Górecki was born), and Lower Silesia (centered on Wrocław, or Breslau). The region belonged to Polish princes in the Middle Ages, but was under German rule for most of its modern history. It was a part of the Austrian partition through the 19th century to World War I, and was divided between Poland and Czechoslovakia in the interwar period.

[2] Górecki in conversation with Maja Trochimczyk, "About Life and Music," see Chapter 3 of this volume.

[3] The best known English language biography of the composer is by Adrian Thomas, *Górecki* (Clarendon Series of Composers, Oxford University Press, 1997). Numerous studies of his life and music have been published by such scholars as Krzysztof Droba, Martina Homma, Luke B. Howard, Leon Markiewicz, Teresa Malecka, Bohdan Pociej, Iwona Lindstedt, and others. A collection of interviews with the composer's friends, students, teachers, scholars, and performers was published in 2013 by Beata Bolesławska-Lewandowska, *Górecki: Portret w Pamięci* [Górecki: A Portrait in Memory] (Kraków: PWM, 2013). Earlier biographies are: Bernard A. Jacobson, *A Polish Renaissance. Twentieth-Century Composers* (London: Phaidon, 1996) and B. M.

station, his mother Otylia (1909–1935) was a homemaker. She played the piano, but died when the future composer was merely two years old. Even though Henryk was discouraged from playing his mother's piano by his father and stepmother, his passion for music persevered. According to his wife, Jadwiga and daughter, Anna, the early death of his mother and the strict, cold atmosphere in the home afterwards, marred Górecki's childhood with feelings of abandonment, rejection and neglect. Being forbidden to touch his mother's instrument or learn how to play was just one of the many incidents that estranged him from his step-family and led him to leaving home early.[4]

During the war, in 1943 he started taking violin lessons from Paweł Hajduga; an amateur musician, instrument maker, artist, and a folk philosopher. Górecki's formal music education continued after WWII at the State School of Music in Rybnik; he enrolled into the music equivalent of a "high school" program at the age of 19. In 1952-55, in Rybnik, he studied clarinet, violin, piano, and music theory—completing a curriculum of four years in three. At the same time, he worked as a teacher in an elementary school in Rydułtowy (1951-53) and studied on his own, collecting books and scores, and later listening to radio broadcasts. This auto-didactic habit persisted throughout his life, as he conducted extensive historical research in preparation for every major composition.

During his college studies at the State Higher School of Music in Katowice (1955-1960), Górecki gained knowledge of neo-classicism and the folklore of the Tatra Mountains, as well as an unwavering commitment to individual creativity, and the highest standards of artistic craft from his composition professor, Bolesław Szabelski (1896-1979), a former student of Karol Szymanowski, who turned to 12-tone composition in the late 1950s.

Górecki's favorite composers at that time were Johann Sebastian Bach, Ludwig van Beethoven (the score of the Ninth Symphony was among his first music purchases), Karol Szymanowski (starting from

---

Maciejewski, *Górecki—His Music And Our Times* (London: Allegro Press, 1994).
[4] See interviews of Jadwiga Górecka and Anna Górecka with Beata Bolesławska-Lewandowska, *Górecki, op. cit.*, 25-26 and 46-7.

Mazurkas) and Fryderyk Chopin.⁵ In college, he added to this list Béla Bartók—an inspiration for his neoclassicist teacher; and twelve-tone composers, Anton von Webern and Alban Berg.

Figure 8-1: Young Henryk Mikołaj Górecki at the Warsaw Autumn Festival, ca. 1959. Probably talking to Krzysztof Meyer.

Górecki's first published compositions were piano miniatures, works for violin and piano, and songs. His life-long interest in Polish romantic poetry manifested itself early, to mention only an unfinished ballad *Świtezianka* of 1952 (a ballad by Adam Mickiewicz) and the third

---

⁵ See interviews with Maja Trochimczyk and as statements by his son, composer Mikołaj, and his daughter, pianist Anna, in Bolesławska-Lewandowska, *Górecki*, *op.cit.*, pp. 27-34 and 35-47.

published opus, *Three Songs/Trzy pieśni* for medium voice and piano Op. 3 (1956); to texts by Juliusz Słowacki (*To Mother/Do Matki; Jakiż to dzwon grobowy/ What a funereal bell*) and Julian Tuwim (*A Bird/Ptak*). The Op. 3 was the first opus dedicated to the memory of the composer's mother, followed by *Ad Matrem* in 1971.

The first two opuses were for piano—Four Preludes for piano solo, Op. 1 (1955) and *Toccata* for two pianos, Op. 2 (1955). These were followed in quick succession by Variations Op. 4 for violin and piano (1956) and Sonata No. 1, Op. 6 (1956/84/90) for piano solo. The three-movement Piano Sonata, initially indebted to Bartók, with its neoclassical formal outline (Fast—Slow—Fast), was revised twice and remains a favorite of many pianists. It is the first in a long string of compositions dedicated to the composer's wife, pianist and teacher Jadwiga Rurańska—Lullaby, Op. 9 (1956-1980); *Monologhi*, Op. 16 (1960); *Two Sacred Songs*, Op. 30 and Op. 30bis (1971); and Symphony No. 3 (1976). Other chamber works with neo-classical titles followed: *Sonatina in One Movement* for violin and piano, Op. 8 (1956); and *Sonata per due violini*, Op. 10 (1957). These early compositions were strongly influenced by the folklore-infused neo-classicism of Béla Bartók and Karol Szymanowski.

Soon, like other Polish composers of this era, Górecki "discovered" 12-tone serialism. Similarly to Bolesław Szabelski, his teacher at the State Higher School of Music in Katowice (currently Karol Szymanowski Academy of Music), he was particularly fascinated with the intricate clockwork mechanisms and sparse pointillistic textures of the music of Anton Webern. Another fascination was the avant-garde constructivism of Europeans, such as Oliver Messiaen and Luigi Nono.[6] Interestingly, neither Górecki himself nor his biographers ever mention Iannis Xenakis whose "sound mass" spatial compositions based on architectural and scientific models expressed a harsh sound world, scarred by echoes of the war that was akin to Górecki's aesthetics of intense dissonance and emotional extremes found in *Scontri* or in the First Symphony *1959*. It would suffice to listen to these works after hearing Xenakis's *Metastaseis* of 1954 or *Pithoprakta* of 1956 to notice their expressive kinship. These and other spatial-architectural works by Xenakis were performed at the Warsaw

---

[6] See the interview with Leon Markiewicz in Chapter 1.

Autumn Festivals where the Greek expatriate composer was among the favorites.

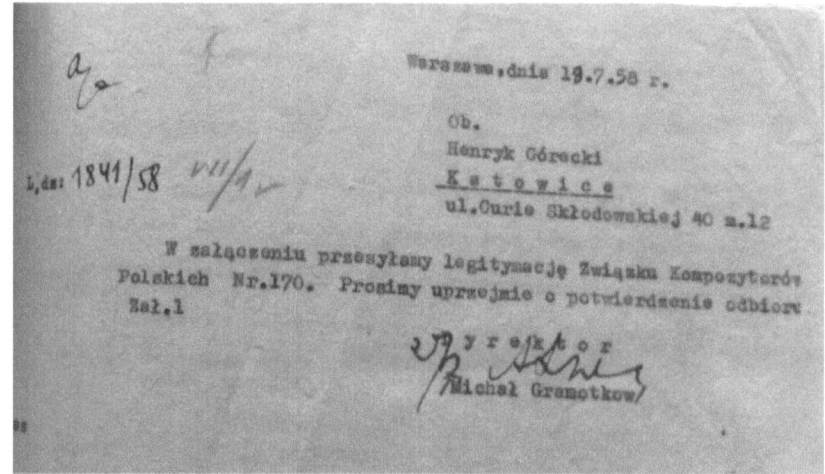

Figure 8-2: Letter about admission to the Polish Composers Union (ZKP), with the ZKP Membership Card as a Student-Candidate; July 1958. The Górecki File, ZKP Library, Warsaw. Used by Permission.

Cultural exchanges and foreign scholarships funded by the Polish government, as well as Polish Radio broadcasts "Horyzonty Muzyki" [Horizons of Music] by Józef Patkowski[7] presenting various trends in the Western avant-garde,[8] allowed Polish composers to gain access to

---

[7] The Polish Music Publishers (PWM) published the scripts from these broadcasts as a series of brochures in a box, The *Horizons of Music* series appeared later, see Józef Patkowski and Anna Skrzyńska, eds., *Horyzonty Muzyki*, Biblioteka Res Facta, vol. 1. Kraków, PWM, 1970. This was a popular resource for composers and historians, including information about *musique concrète* used by Witold Lutosławski in developing his unique compositional technique of "sound planes" – see Maja Trochimczyk, "Witold Lutosławski and *musique concrète:* The Technique of Sound Planes and its Sources," in *Lutosławski: Music and Legacy,* Edited by Stanisław Latek and Maja Trochimczyk. (Montreal: Polish Institute of Arts and Sciences in Canada, 2014).

[8] Józef Patkowski was the director of the Electronic Music Studio of the Polish Radio, travelled widely and gathered information about the most unusual compositional theories and technologies to share with Polish contemporary composers. In 1956, for instance, he published an article "O muzyce elektronowej i konkretnej" [On Electronic and Concrete Music]. *Muzyka* 1/3: 49-68, 1956. However, Górecki was not interested in electronic instruments nor sounds.

recordings and ideas of their Western contemporaries and to develop what soon became known as the "Polish school of sonorism."[9]

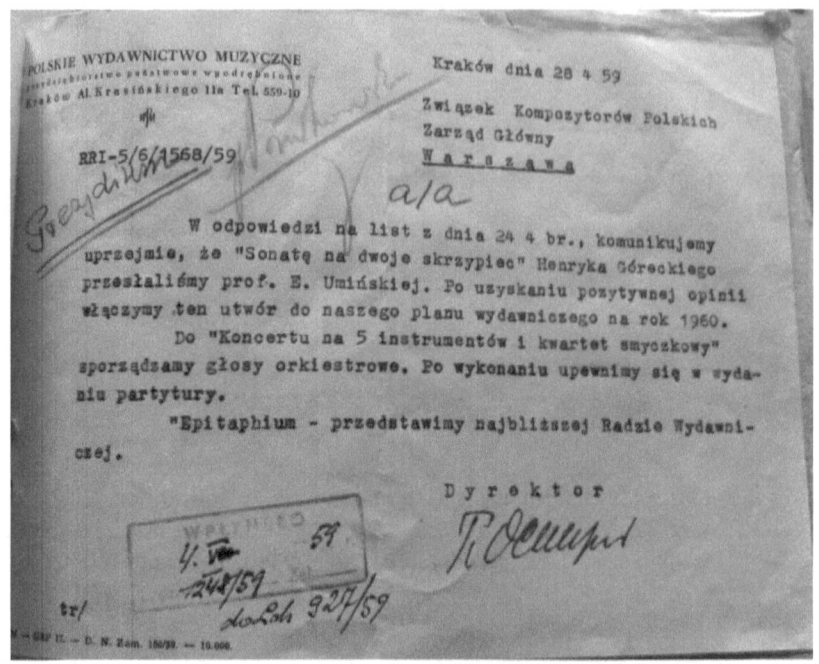

Figure 8-3: Letter about acceptance for publication by Polskie Wydawnictwo Muzyczne PWM of Górecki's Sonata for Two Violins, mentioning also Concerto for Five Instruments, String Quartet, and the *Epitafium*. The Górecki File, ZKP Library, Warsaw. Used by Permission.

Financial and organizational support funneled by the Polish Composers' Union (Związek Kompozytorów Polskich; ZKP) helped Górecki by providing commissions and grants, promoting his music

---

[9] The term "sonorism" was developed by Polish musicologist Józef Chomiński in late 1950s. For the overview of Polish music history of the second half of the 20th century, with a positive emphasis on the aesthetic values and artistic outcomes of the Polish school of sonorism see Adrian Thomas, *Polish Music since Szymanowski (*Cambridge and New York: Cambridge University Press, 2005). For a history of definitions and limitations of "sonorism" as a term see Adrian Thomas, "Boundaries and Definitions: The Compositional Realities of Polish Sonorism," *Muzyka* vol. 53, no. 1 (2008): 7-15. Iwona Lindstedt, *Sonorystyka w twórczości kompozytorów polskich XX wieku* [Sonorism in the Oeuvre of Polish Composers of the 20th Century] (Warsaw: Wydawnictwa Uniwersytetu Warszawskiego, 2010).

through publications and performances, and solving such basic issues of daily life as obtaining an identity card; having a phone installed; gaining access to medical services; or receiving a supply of large music paper, suitable for symphonic scores. The correspondence in the Górecki file in the ZKP Library in Warsaw provides ample proof of these exchanges, along with his applications for membership in the organization, granted in 1958 as a student candidate (Fig. 8-2, 8-3).

A state-promoted and sponsored response to the relentless experimentation by the Western avant-garde, the Polish school of sonorism developed a dissonant, aggressive style of music composed from sound blocks and objects, massive dissonant chords, cloud of percussive sound effects, intersecting glissando lines, etc.[10] Górecki was a key member of this school and, with his "maximalist" compositional aesthetics, he soon became one of its leaders. He created some of the most complex conceptually and most dissonant perceptually compositions of the period, including *Epitafium* for mixed choir and instrumental ensemble, Op. 12 (1958); to a text by Julian Tuwim; *Songs of Joy and Rhythm* [Pieśni o radości i rytmie] for two pianos and chamber orchestra, Op. 7 (1956, rev. 1959), also inspired by Tuwim; Symphony No. 1 '1959' for string orchestra and percussion, Op. 14 (1959); *Scontri* for orchestra, Op. 17 (1960);[11] *Monologhi* for soprano and three instrumental groups, Op. 16 (1960); as well as Op. 19, the *Genesis* cycle: *I. Elementi* for three string instruments (1962); *II. Canti Strumentali* for 15 performers, (1962); and *III. Monodramma* for soprano, percussion and double-basses (1963). Many of these highly structured works were based on mathematical formulas and 12-tone sets, providing musicologists ample subjects for dissertations and research projects, especially the Symphony No. 1, *Scontri* and the

---

[10] See Maria Anna Harley, "The Polish School of Sonorism and its European Context," in *Crosscurrents and Counterpoints: Offerings in Honor of Bengt Hambraeus at 70*, ed. Per Broman, Nora A. Engebretsen, and Bo Alphonce. (Gothenburg: University of Gothenburg, Sweden, 1998), 62-77. Reprinted in Polish as "Polski sonoryzm i jego europejski kontekst" [Polish sonorism and its European context], in *Dysonanse* , no. 0 (Fall 1997). See also Anna Maslowiec, *Sonorism and the Polish Avantgarde*. Sydney Conservatorium of Music, 2008.

[11] Lisa Jakelski, "Górecki's Scontri and Avant-Garde Music in Cold War Poland," *The Journal of Musicology*, 26, no. 2 (Spring 2009): 205-239. See also her history of the early years of the Warsaw Autumn, *Making New Music in Cold War Poland: The Warsaw Autumn Festival, 1956-1968* (University of California Press, 2016).

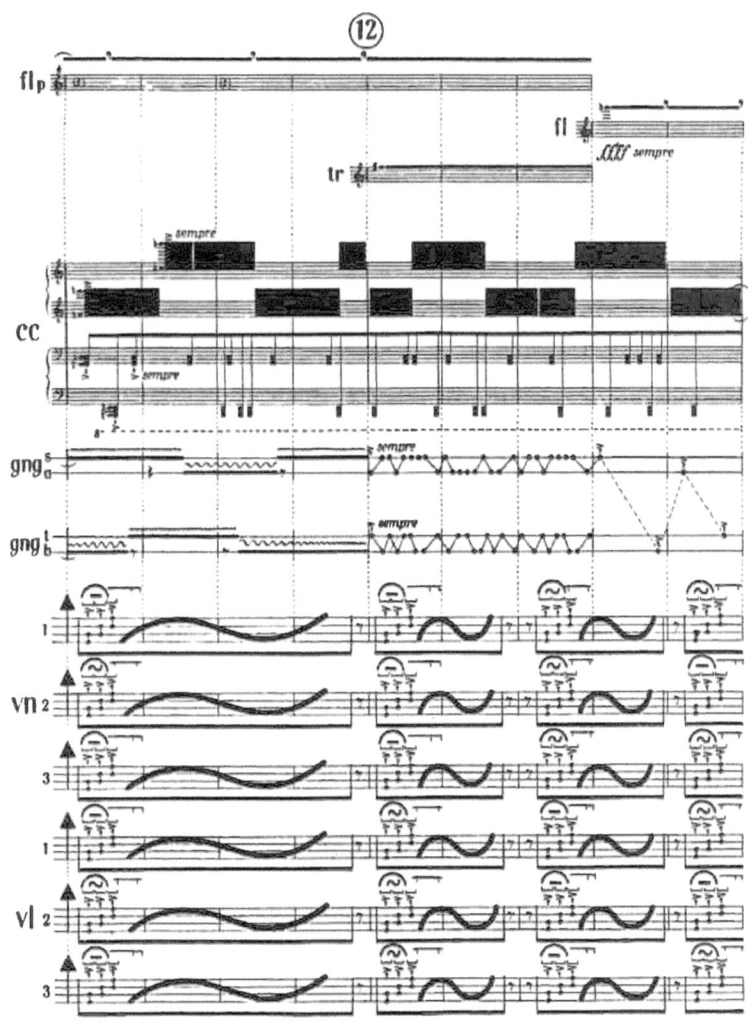

Figure 8-4: Page with graphic notations for cluster and repeated patterns in Genesis II: *Canti Strumentali* (1962). Genesis I, Op. 19 by Henryk Górecki © Copyright 1963 by PWM Edition, Kraków, Poland. U.S. Renewal Rights assigned to Boosey & Hawkes, Inc.

Genesis cycle—where he used performer placement charts (Fig. 8-5) and graphic notation (Fig. 8-4).[12]

---

[12] For a list of dissertations about Górecki's music see the bibliography at the end of this volume. Notable studies of this earlier period include Martina Homma, *Das Minimale und das Absolute. Die Musik Henryk Mikolaj Góreckis von der Mitte der sechziger Jahre bis 1985*; *MusikTexte* 44 (April 1992): 40-58; and Anna Maslowiec, "'The Utmost Economy of Musical Material:' Structural Elements in

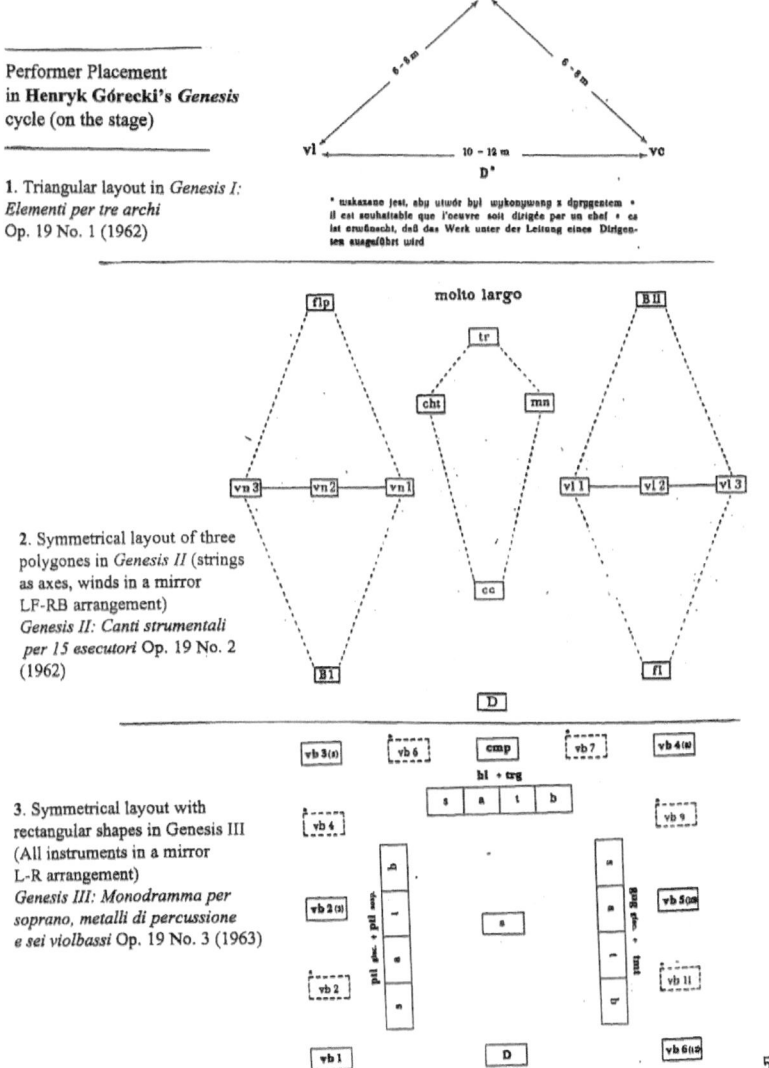

Figure 8-5: Seating charts in the scores of *Genesis I: Elementi* (1962), *Genesis II, Canti Strumentali* (1962) and *Genesis III: Monodramma* (1963). The directional differences and distances (left to right, front to center to back) can be used to enrich the dramatic flow of the music, similarly to antiphonal and responsorial interactions, but the exact

the Works of Górecki from *Refrain* (1965) to *Ad matrem* (1971)," *Contact* 14 (1999). http://pmc.usc.edu/PMJ/issue/6.2.03/Maslowiec.html. Reprinted in *Polish Music Journal* 6, no. 2 (2003).

placement cannot be articulated into a form-shaping element of music. Cited from Harley, Maria Anna [Maja Trochimczyk]. "Spatiality of Sound and Stream Segregation in Twentieth-Century Instrumental Music," *Organized Sound* 3, no. 2 (1998): 147-166.

Figure 8-6: A waveform diagram showing the unconventional dynamic outline of *Genesis II: Canti Strumentali*. A large segment of quiet music is followed by a massive, unpredictably changing central section, leading to silence interspersed with outbursts of musical activity. A traditional work would have a more evenly patterned outline.

In the *Genesis* cycle, for instance, diagrams of elaborate seating plans for the musicians precede every movement (Fig. 8-5). However symmetrical and visually attractive, these patterns cannot be heard: an attempt to transform auditory space into precisely outlined geometric figures is doomed to failure. Simultaneously, the work relies on a block-like, untraditional way of structuring the dynamics of form: this is "sonorism" in its pure state. The waveform diagram of the overall shape of *Genesis II: Canti Strumentali* (Fig. 8-6) reveals its temporal-dynamic outline, made up of strongly contrasted blocks that follow each other in unpredictable fashion. In listening, the most striking feature of this music is its incessant dissonance, coupled with the lack of themes and the absence of regular rhythmic patterns, leading to audible chaos.

The harsh, aggressive and chaotic sound world of these works was in part a reaction to the trauma of the Second World War, which had been denied an expression during the state-sanctioned rule of the optimistic "socialist realism" doctrine, *de rigueur* through the early 1950s. In the following decade, these suppressed dark emotions erupted in avant-garde music, visual arts, and film, permeated with images and sonorities of destruction. Górecki's radical experimentation in this phase, dubbed by Danuta Mirka "musica geometrica,"[13] due to his interest in the use of spatial diagrams for performer placement and spatial designs in pitch space, earned him many performances, recordings, state prizes and honors, to mention only the First Prize at the Young Composers' Competition of the Polish Composers' Union for *Monologi I* (1960); and the First Prize at the Youth Biennale in Paris for Symphony No. 1, *1959* (1961). This second award included a three-month scholarship to Paris and thus had a lasting impact on Górecki's compositional development.

---

[13] Danuta Mirka, "Górecki's Musica Geometrica," *The Musical Quarterly* 87 (Summer 2004): 305-332. The use of this term is not necessary, as these works could be described by the labels of total serialism and spatial music, discussed respectively by Iwona Lindstedt, *Dodekafonia i serialism w twórczości kompozytorów polskich XX wieku* [Dodecaphony and Serialism in the Oeuvres of Polish Composers of the 20th Century] (Lublin: Polihymnia, 2001), and Maria Anna Harley, *Space and Spatialization in Contemporary Music: History and Analysis, Ideas and Implementations*. Ph. D. Dissertation (McGill University School of Music, Montreal, Canada, 1994).

Like many of his contemporaries and successors, Górecki greatly benefited from the support of the state that used contemporary arts as a proof of its benevolence and the proof of "freedom" of its creative citizens that were allowed and encouraged to engage in artistic experimentation. The extraordinary amount of funding allotted to the Polish Composers' Union,[14] and contemporary music performances (extraordinary, when seen from a contemporary American perspective) reached its apex in the first annual International Contemporary Music Festival "Warsaw Autumn" held in September since 1956.[15] The Warsaw Autumn Festivals were initiated upon the initiative of composers **Kazimierz Serocki and Tadeusz Baird with strong Party support** and were designed as a promotional vehicle for the innovative "socialist" culture of the Polish People's Republic.[16] The Festivals offered free tickets, hotel stay, and travel reimbursement to dozens of foreign guests—heads of publishing houses, radio stations, music critics, musicologists, composers, performers and other "tastemakers" who would promote the "socialist" brand of avant-garde music upon returning to their home countries. These annual festivals provided Górecki and other Polish composers an opportunity to hear their own music, while also being exposed to the European trends and fashions, from Luigi Nono to Dmitri Shostakovich.

Górecki's well-received 1958 Warsaw Autumn debut held prior to his graduating from the Katowice's State Higher School of Music placed him in the forefront of the Polish school of sonorism. An American

---

[14] See *50 lat Warszawskiej Jesieni* [50 Years of the Warsaw Autumn] (Warszawa: Związek Kompozytorów Polskich; Międzynarodowy Festiwal Muzyki Współczesnej "Warszawska Jesień", 2007) and essays in the album *50 Lat Zwiazku Kompozytorów Polskich*, especially by Zygmunt Mycielski (Warsaw: ZKP, 1995).

[15] See an impartial analysis of this topic by American scholar, David G. Tompkins, *Composing the Party Line: Music and Politics in Early Cold War Poland and East Germany* (Purdue University Press, 2013). In Poland Krzysztof Baculewski first pointed out the extent of composers' reliance on government commissions and socialist realism ideology, in *Polska Twórczość Kompozytorska 1945-1984* [Polish Compositional Output] (Kraków: PWM, 1987).

[16] Cindy Bylander, *The Warsaw Autumn International Festival of Contemporary Music 1956-1961: Its Goals, Structures, Programs, and People* (Ohio State University, Ph.D. Dissertation, 1989). See also the 2016 history of the first decade of the festival by Lisa Jakelski, *op. cit.*

music critic, James Wierzbicki, wrote later that "Górecki was seen as a Polish heir to the new aesthetic of post-Webernian serialism; with his taut structures, lean orchestrations and painstaking concern for the logical ordering of pitches."[17] According to musicologist Leon Markiewicz, holding a monographic concert at the festival at such an early stage in Górecki's career was a great and unusual distinction. It was possible due to the promotional role of the Warsaw Autumn festivals that Markiewicz and others considered a wonderful cultural phenomenon, stimulating and presenting an explosion of Polish talent and creativity.[18] This political investment quickly brought results: according to Adrian Thomas, the years 1958-59 marked a turning point in Polish music when its avant-garde output began to match in quantity and quality that of the West.[19]

Of the various "-isms," Górecki's involvement with total serialism, a technique in each all aspects of music are organized on the basis of pre-determined 12-element sets, reached its apex in the second movement of the Symphony No. 1 and in *Monologhi* (1960). The explosive, dissonant sound world of Górecki's monumental *Scontri* from the same year, premiered at the 1960 Warsaw Autumn, shocked the audiences and delighted avant-garde-loving critics.

According to Iwona Lindstedt, *Scontri* is the prime example of total serialism, where basic elements of music (pitch, rhythm dynamics, and timbre) are separately organized in 12-item sets and subject to rigid permutations and other serial procedures to create the musical composition.[20] The work consists of six distinct sections, and the form is defined by clashes of two core textures: sonic bands (the equivalent of chords, or vertical structures) and sonic complexes (the equivalent of melodies, or horizontal structures). The musical material is

---

[17] James Wierzbicki, "Henryk Górecki," *St. Louis Post-Dispatch*, 7 July 1991.
[18] See the 1962 interview reprinted in this volume; see also Markiewicz's reminiscences in *Górecki: Portret w Pamięci*, op. cit., 85-108.
[19] Adrian Thomas, *Polish Music Since Szymanowski* (Cambridge and New York: Cambridge University Press, 2005), chapter 7, 107-109.
[20] Iwona Lindstedt, *Dodekafonia i Serializm*, op. cit., 195-200. The first scholar to have access to the composer's sketchbooks where these materials and structures were developed was Adrian Thomas, who wrote about early works in articles published in the 1980s: "The Music of Henryk Mikołaj Górecki: The First Decade," *Contact* 27 (1983): 10-20, and "A Pole Apart: The Music of Górecki since 1965," *Contact* 28 (1984): 20-31.

developed from a basic 12-tone set of pitches, accompanied by similar 12-item sets of rhythmic units (from the sixteenth to a dotted half-note), 12 dynamic units (from *pppp* to *ffff*), and 12 timbres.

ORIGINAL 12-TONE SET IN SCONTRI											
G	B	B-flat	A	G-sharp	C-sharp	D	F	E-flat	E	F-sharp	C
ITS PERMUTATIONS											
1	2	3	4	5	6	7	8	9	10	11	12
9	1	11	8	10	4	3	6	2	12	7	5
10	5	1	11	8	3	2	7	12	6	9	4
8	4	5	1	11	2	12	9	6	7	10	3
11	3	4	5	1	12	6	10	7	9	8	2
6	8	10	9	7	1	5	2	4	3	12	11
12	10	9	7	6	11	1	3	5	4	2	8
4	6	12	2	3	9	10	1	8	11	5	7
2	9	7	6	12	8	11	4	1	5	3	10
3	7	6	12	2	10	8	5	11	1	4	9
5	12	2	3	4	7	9	11	10	8	1	6
7	11	8	10	9	5	4	12	3	2	6	1

Table 1: Permutations of 12-tone set in *Scontri*.

The direct model for this type of formal structure may be found in Olivier Messiaen's *Mode de valeurs et d'intensites* from *Quatre études de rythme* (1949) and Pierre Boulez's *Structures I* (1952), both for piano. The *Scontri* 12-tone set is permutated as shown in Table 1. Similarly rigid was the structuring of the rhythm and dynamics. This abstract conceptual framework was coupled with intense dramatic expression, making *Scontri* one of its composer's favorites, even in the late 1990s, when he became critical of some of his earlier works.

By the early 1960s, the composer reached another turning point in the formation of his compositional aesthetics. During a short postgraduate study in Paris, he did not visit famous composers for whom he had recommendations letters. Instead, he listened to organ improvisations by Olivier Messiaen, connecting the roots of the Catholic musical tradition (the Gregorian chant), with modern, original harmonies, in prayerful serenity and awe at the sublime. The Paris scholarship allowed Górecki to meet with Polish émigré composers,

Roman Palester and Michał Spisak (the latter offered him lodging in his residence, and became a lifelong friend).

After returning to Poland, Górecki continued to develop his radical reductionist style and served on the faculty of his *alma mater* in Katowice (1965-1979), rising through the ranks from an instructor to the president of the entire school. Before becoming a professor of composition in 1975-79, he took another trip abroad. This time, he travelled with his family (since 1959 he was married to pianist Jadwiga; they had two children, Anna, a pianist, and Mikołaj, a composer). The 1973 German DAAD (Deutscher Akademischer Austausch Dienst) fellowship allowed Górecki to live and create in Berlin for a year and a half as a guest artist. The DAAD fellowship recipients in the same year included Klaus Huber of Switzerland and a fellow Pole, Zygmunt Krauze. Established in 1963, the DAAD program supported representatives of music, literature and the fine arts, including, in the sixties and seventies, such luminaries of contemporary music as Iannis Xenakis, Igor Stravinsky, Luciano Berio, Elliott Carter, Louis Andriessen, John Cage, and Alberto Ginastera.[21]

The purpose of such international cultural exchanges that allowed Górecki to visit Paris and Berlin was to strengthen the musical avant-garde and the acceptance of the Polish People's Republic in the artistic circles. Paradoxically, the composer took a different route and did not become an avant-gardist, after all. Inspired by Messiaen's idea of music as prayer and by a vision of building new music on the foundation of tradition (not by destroying this tradition), Górecki turned to early music sources and religious texts. Soon, his fascination with dissonance and abstract mathematical structures gave way to a unique reductionist and minimalistic compositional style informed by his intense religious faith and a fascination with Polish folk and religious music.

Early music inspirations and stylizations flourished in the popular *Three Pieces in Old Style/ Trzy Utwory w Dawnym Stylu* for brass and strings (1963) and in *Muzyka Staropolska /Old Polish Music* (1969) for orchestra. This turn to tradition offered a safe escape from the ideological pressures of the socialist government also to other

---

[21] See the list of guest artists supported by DAAD on the program's website: http://www.berliner-kuenstlerprogramm.de/en/gaeste.php.

composers, like Andrzej Panufnik (*Muzyka Gotycka*, or *Jagellonian Triptych*) or Tadeusz Baird (*Colas Breugnon Suite*). Since, as Maciej Gołąb writes, "for the radical, belligerent avant-garde, break with the past is a radical component of its ideology," by transgressing this rule and returning to ancient themes and melodies, Górecki left the avant-garde behind.[22]

Figure 8-7: Henryk Mikołaj Górecki as a young composer.
Photo by Kazimierz Seka (PAP).

The *Old Polish Music* is based on the 14th century organum, *Benedicamus Domine*, the oldest work of Polish polyphonic religious music (cited in the brass), juxtaposed with *Already It Is Dusk* by Wacław of Szamotuły, a melancholy prayerful exemplar of vocal

---

[22] Maciej Gołąb, *Musical Modernism in the Twentieth Century*, translated by Wojciech Bońkowski (Franfurt am Mein: Peter Lang, 2015), 92.

polyphony from the 16th century (The latter melody later appears in Górecki's First String Quartet, Op. 62, *Already it is Dusk*, 1988).

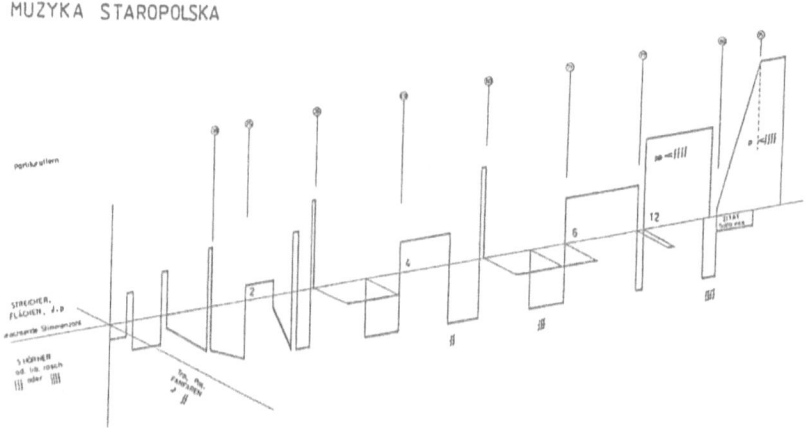

Figure 8-8: An outline of dynamics, timbre and block-like form in *Muzyka Staropolska* (1969) from Martina Homma, "Das Minimale und Das Absolute" *op. cit.* (1992).

Throughout this period, works based on old Polish tradition are interspersed with sonoristic opuses that continue the constructivist and experimental strand of Górecki's style, yet with a notable reduction of musical means. These compositions often feature simplified, block-like, massive textures organized into architectural sound sculptures, evolving in a clearly perceivable direction towards powerful climaxes. *Choros I*, Op. 20 (1964) for string orchestra; *Refrain*, Op. 21 for orchestra (1965); and *Canticum Graduum* for orchestra, Op. 27 (1969) may serve as examples.

The reductionism of textures and the limited vocabulary of musical means are coupled with an intensification of expressive and dynamic contrasts. Ongoing textural, timbral and structural experimentation permeates the *Muzyczka* cycle [*La Musiquqette*, Little Music]. It consists of: *Muzyczka I* (1967) for two trumpets and guitar (later withdrawn); *Muzyczka II*, Op. 23 (1967) for four trumpets, four trombones, two pianos and percussion; *Muzyczka III*, Op. 25 for violas (1967), and *Muzyczka IV* (Koncert Puzonowy), Op. 28 (1970), commissioned by the Warsztat Muzyczny of Zygmunt Krauze and set for four instruments: clarinet, trombone, cello, and piano.

In this period, the composer's technically reductionist and expressively maximalist music continued to be aesthetically related to that by Iannis Xenakis in France and Galina Ustvolskaya in Russia, two composers who captured the trauma, chaos and suffering of the war in abstract musical means. It was a parallel development, though, without any known direct, personal, or artistic interactions.

It is interesting to compare the block-like formal outlines of Górecki's reductionist-constructivist works from this period (based on an analysis by Martina Homma, see Table 2 below).[23]

Title	Year	Formal Outline
Choros I for orchestra	1964	A B C A* Codetta
Refrain for orchestra	1965	A B C B C D C D C A*
Cantata for organ	1968	A A B C B C B A D E D
Old Polish Music/ Muzyka Staropolska, for strings and brass	1969	A B A C ABA C C+A B D+A
Ad Matrem/ Do Matki for soprano, choir, orchestra	1971	A B C B C B A D
Euntes ibant et flebant for choir *a capella*	1972	A A* A B B* A C

Table 2: Outlines of formal blocks in works from mid-60s to mid-70s.
After Martina Homma, "Das Minimale und Das Absolute" *op. cit.*

The sectional-repetitive large-scale structure of Górecki's music resembles the block compositional technique developed by Igor Stravinsky and Oliver Messiaen. Górecki's blocks juxtapose extreme contrasts of timbres, textures and dynamics, creating a large-scale form from the proportions and contours of these monumental sound sculptures. Simultaneously, the uncompromising experimentalist thought little of accommodating performers or performance organizations to his unusual musical visions. The resultant unusual instrumental settings, with massive amounts of percussion, and strange juxtapositions of instruments, definitely posed performance problems for standard instrumental groups. Only well-funded contemporary music festivals could afford to bring such a diverse groups of instrumentalists together to play just one work on a concert program.

---

[23] Martina Homma, "Das Minimale, und Das Absolute," *op. cit.*, 41-50.

For years, the composer avoided using standard ensembles such as a string quartet. Instead, Górecki envisioned assemblages of contrasting and heterogeneous sonorities, saturated with extreme dynamic and expressive contrasts, massive numbers of repetitions, and unusually slow tempi. He could have a musician waiting for most of a work's duration to appear suddenly in a brief, luminous, ecstatic moment (for instance, the surprising appearance of the soprano in the conclusion of *Ad Matrem*). Moreover, his artistic vision was so precise, as to how the music was supposed to sound like, that he was also mostly dissatisfied with performances or recordings.[24] Typically, musicians failed to give justice to his extreme emotionalism and radical sound visions; often they did not understood how much effort is required to sustain one note for an extended period of time—as in *O Domina Nostra*, for instance. Not only to sustain: to saturate with expression and emotion.

According to Górecki's star student and colleague, composer Eugeniusz Knapik,[25]

> With Górecki, nothing is half-way, in his music it is not possible to pretend being expressive, to just play through his piece. This music must be played at the edges of one's capability—not only physical, but also spiritual, emotional—then, sometimes, we may cross the barrier beyond which music reaches a completely new dimension.

Without this intensity of emotion, Knapik added, "the music may become irritating, the endless repetition may annoy, become monotonous or aggressive." Musicologists like Krzysztof Droba or Danuta Mirka like to divide Górecki's oeuvre into distinct stylistic periods, from avant-garde experimentation, to radical reductionism of the years 1961-70, and the expressive constructivism with a focus on monumental vocal-instrumental religious works noticeable since 1971. Droba's entry in the PWM *Music Encyclopedia*[26] distinguishes the following periods:

---

[24] For the composer's view on recordings of his own music, see the interviews with Maja Trochimczyk, Chapter 3 and with Małgorzata and Marcin Gmys, Chapter 6 in this volume.
[25] Eugeniusz Knapik, ed. Beata Bolesławska-Lewandowska, *op. cit.*, 63.
[26] Krzysztof Droba, "Henryk Mikołaj Górecki," entry in *the Encyclopedia Muzyczna PWM*, Vol. EFG (Biographic Part), edited by Elżbieta Dziębowska (Kraków: PWM, 1987): 424-433; Mirka, *op. cit.*

1) the early phase (1955-57) with dynamic, rhythmic and chromatic compositions;
2) the serial phase (1957-1961) with *Epitaph, Scontri, Monologhi,* First Symphony and other exemplars of total serialism;
3) the sonoristic phase (1962-3) with the *Genesis* cycle;
4) the "caesura" transitional phase (1963-4) with *Choros I*;
5) the reductionist phase with *Refrain*; and
6) vocal-instrumental phase of religious music, written since *Ad Matrem* of 1971 to the mid-1980s when the article was written.

Indeed, the years 1962-70 could be described as a transition from the 12-tone serialism and dissonant sonorism of the fifties, to expressive constructivism that begins with *Ad Matrem / Do Matki* for soprano solo, mixed choir and orchestra, Op. 29 to a text by composer (1971). However, Górecki was quite "allergic" to such classifications (according to the interview with Kominek in Chapter 1),[27] and considered each new work as an artifact of its own, developed from unique inspirations, based on extensive research, and presented in highly-structured, well-articulated sonorous shapes. For Górecki, "all music begins with sound. It is always based on some musical association, a musical theme or a structure."[28] As the composer explained:[29]

> I come up with many different ways of structuring my compositions. Let me put it this way: you scholars would want to know too much. Of course it is important to know how a piece is constructed and how it was made. But later this mechanism, this architecture ceases to be all important; the composer thinks about the forms that the music should be "poured into." Thus, you could reverse the order between the structure and the music. On the one hand, you invent the form and the construction for the whole work; on the other hand, you begin with the music that could be written down and structured in different ways.

In mid-1960s, the Messiaen-inspired turn to religious music brought to the surface an undercurrent of Górecki's intense spirituality and

---

[27] Górecki, "I Am Always Myself" *op. cit., (*1993) Chapter 2 of this volume. See also Anna Górecka interviewed by Beata Bolesławska-Lewandowska, *op. cit.*, 35.
[28] Henryk Mikołaj Górecki, "Composing is a Terribly Personal Matter," *op. cit.,* Chapter 4 in this volume.
[29] *Ibidem.*

profound sorrow.³⁰ His mother died when he was only two years old and this early trauma was translated into the painful focus of many works, from *Ad Matrem* to *Kleines Requiem für eine Polka* (1993).³¹ The outpouring of religious choral music permeates the late sixties and early 1970s: *Two Sacred Songs* for baritone solo and orchestra or piano, Op. 30 and Op. 30bis (1971) are settings of poems by Marek Skwarnicki; *Amen* for unaccompanied mixed choir, Op. 34 (1975) takes the basic religious acclamation into a new dimension; and *Euntes ibant et flebant* for unaccompanied mixed choir, Op. 32 (1972) stretches into a vast expanse fragments from Psalms No. 125, 6, and 94. The title of the latter work ("as they walked and cried") captures the primary emotional tone of Górecki's religious music, one of devotion rooted in suffering, joy among tears. Martina Homma describes works from this period and reflecting a similar compositional aesthetics as both "minimal and absolute" in their purity and focus.

Górecki's affirmative artistic-religious statements reached cosmic heights in the monumental Symphony No. 2, *Copernican*, Op. 31 commissioned by the Kościuszko Foundation to celebrate the 500th anniversary of the birth of the famous astronomer, Mikołaj Kopernik (Copernicus, 1473-1543).³² This massive portrait of the Copernican Revolution, the ultimate "fall of Man" from the center of the Universe, to a tiny "thinking reed" below countless stars, based on textual fragments from three Psalms (145, 6, and 135) and an excerpt from Book 1 of Copernicus's own *De revolutionibus orbium caelestium*, is both mystical and contemplative in its repetitiveness, with vast, unadorned surfaces, and massive dimensions.

The Symphony contrasts the sublime power of cosmos, portrayed in the dynamic and sonorous sound masses in the first movement, with the tranquil realization of the harmony and beauty of a well-ordered Cosmos in the second movement. In the words of Krzysztof Droba,

---

[30] Maria Anna Harley, *"To be God with God:* Catholic Composers and the Mystical Experience." *Contemporary Music Review*, 12/2; "Contemporary Music and Religion," ed. Ivan Moody, (1995): 125-145.

[31] See Maja Trochimczyk, "Mothers and Motherhood in Górecki's Third Symphony and Other Works," Chapter 10 in the present volume. See also Maria Cizmic, P*erforming pain : music and trauma in 1970s and 80s Eastern Europe.* Ph. D. Dissertation (University of California, Los Angeles, 2004).

[32] See the study by Kinga Kiwała in the following Chapter 9.

"The first part is the creation of the world still without people, built in an abstract way. The second part is the human being that faces God."[33] Górecki designed the Symphony's overarching narrative as an image of the creation of the universe from nothing, and the creation of human beings to praise its beauty. It spans the trajectory from dissonance and chaos to the serene union of all in the consonant A-flat major chord that swells into its resonant power before fading into silence.

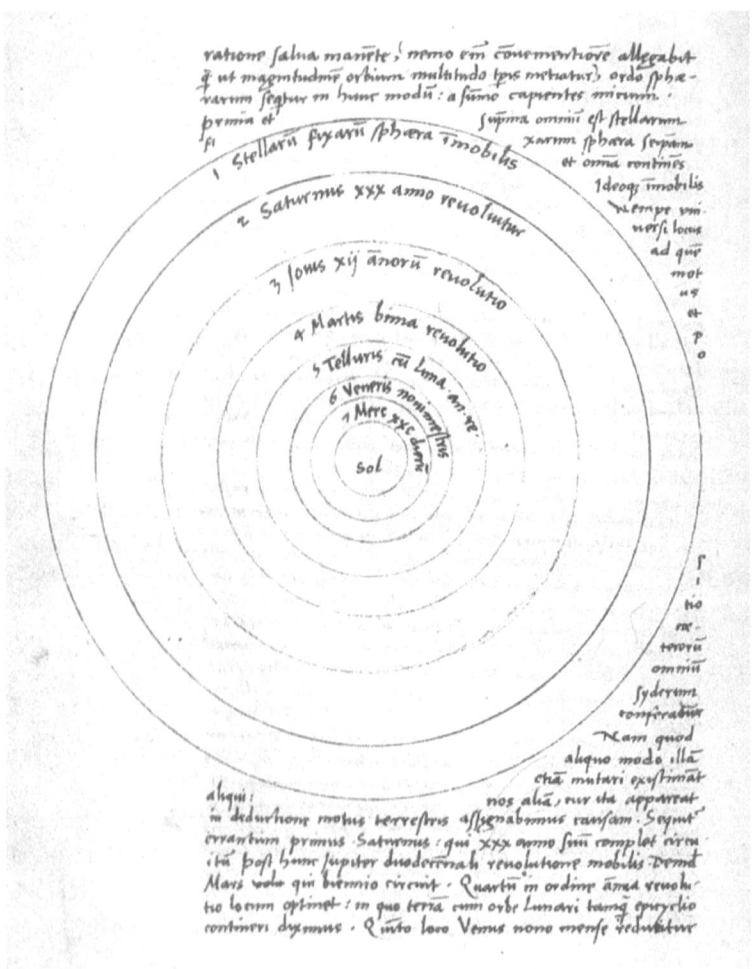

Figure 8-9: Heliocentric system in Copernicus's manuscript of *De revolutionibus orbium caelestium*.

---

[33] Krzysztof Droba interviewed by Beata Bolesławska-Lewandowska, *Górecki*, op. cit., p. 155.

The last four minutes of the Copernican Symphony are remarkable, featuring one of the longest continuously sustained chords in all of classical music. In contrast, the opening is quite dramatic: a series of *fortissimo* chords alternate with sudden percussive crashes of the drums, interrupted by silence. The whole-tone cluster spanning six octaves resolves in step-wise motion into a pentatonic chord. The basic melodic motion is colored by underlying dissonances that make the surface of the music split into a vibrating mass, all the more voluminous that the Symphony calls for huge performance forces: quadruple winds, six percussionists, and 12 strings per section. The irregularity of the drum patterns adds to the chaos of the music and introduces a powerful reset effect after each of the pauses. Here we find ourselves at the beginning of time, at the edge of creation. The music's obvious state of disarray arises from the disordered state of its chords, and sharply articulated, strongly localized dynamics peaks created by the percussion strokes. Against this background of "sonic matter," voices appear to proclaim that God created the heaven and earth, light and everything that exists.

Figure 8-10: Waveform diagram of the extended chord with massive crescendo/diminuendo dynamics at the end of the second movement of the Second Symphony *Copernican*.

In the second part of the symphony, the chorus continues to reflect on the magnitude of the universe and the miraculous creation of the sun, moon and stars. The section ends with a quotation from Copernicus: "What indeed is more beautiful than heaven, which contains all things of beauty?" This final reflection precedes a sustained cadence—a D-flat pentatonic chord building up gradually in a dynamic arch from *pp* to *p – mf – f – ff – ffff – ffff – ff – f – mf – mp* and back to *p*, again. Finally, the chord finds its resolution as it shifts into a stable A-flat major. All dissonances disappear and the sounds fuse into a unified sphere of harmony and balance. In this way, "with a bang, not with a whimper"—to reverse T.S. Eliot's famous phrase,[34] Górecki's music returns to tonal roots.

The respite created by a consonant conclusion after a span of violent outbursts and sorrowful plaints seems to be a hallmark of Górecki's style. Its effect is that of consolation, an arrival—finally!—in the realm of serenity. Similarly uplifting are Górecki's oratorio-like works with chorus, soloists and orchestra. *Beatus Vir*, Op, 39 commissioned by Cardinal Karol Wojtyła to commemorate Poland's patron saint, Stanisław, was transformed into a tribute to Wojtyła, the newly elected Pope John Paul II, and played for him during the Papal visit (1979). The composer selected fragments from Psalms 142, 30, 37, 66, and 33, and used his preferred setting of a solo voice (baritone), with a mixed choir and a large orchestra. He was so late in completing the work, that he ended up conducting the premiere himself, because nobody else could learn it. This concert became one of the most extraordinarily moving moments of his life.

Totus Tuus, Op. 60 for unaccompanied mixed choir (1987), yet again honors Pope John Paul II during his pilgrimage to Poland and proclaims an allegiance to Mother Mary with the Pope's personal motto, *All Yours*—this outward sign of an intense Marian devotion could also be called the motto of the composer himself. *Salve Sidus Polonorum* (1997-2000) the first cantata from a planned, but never completed, series dedicated to Polish saints, honors St. Adalbert (Św. Wojciech), another medieval patron of Poland. Meditative repetitions of prayerful religious texts continue in *O Domina Nostra Meditations on Our Lady of Jasna Góra* for soprano and organ (1985). Nonetheless, the pious composer was not oblivious to politics: *Miserere*, Op. 44 for choir commemorated the suffering of Solidarity activists during a

---

[34] T. S. Eliot's "The Hollow Men" ends with: "*This is the way the world ends / Not with a bang but a whimper.*" See: https://allpoetry.com/The-Hollow-Men.

government-sanctioned assault in Bydgoszcz (1981), and it is dedicated to the suffering city.

The most famous work that assured for Górecki's a permanent and prominent place in world music history was his Symphony No. 3, *the Symphony of Sorrowful Songs*, Op. 36 composed in 1976 for soprano and orchestra. The texts of its three slow movements focus on suffering and grief, the dark side of human existence: a 15th-century lamentation from the Holy Cross Monastery (I movement); a young prisoner's inscription on the wall of her cell in Zakopane's Gestapo prison (II movement); and a mother's lament in a folk song from the Opole region.

Figure 8-11: Mosaic of Our Lady of the Bright Mount, Częstochowa, Poland. https://commons.wikimedia.org/wiki/File:Jasna_Gora_-_Czarna_Madonna_(mozaika).jpg. From Wikimedia Commons.

The Symphony juxtaposes the image of eternal suffering of crucified Jesus and His Mother (first movement) with two embodiments of this transcendental Passion in human history: the torment of a young prisoner during World War II, and the sorrow of a mother grieving the death of her son. The temporal framework of "during—before—after" death, coupled with the symmetrical design of the suffering "mother-child–mother" unites the work beyond the superficial similarity of slow tempi and quietly sorrowful expression of the three movements.

In the first movement of the Third Symphony a remarkable arch structure—with precedents including Bartók's *Music for Strings, Percussion and Celesta* (1936) and Witold Lutosławski's *Funeral Music* (1957), yet reaching far beyond any models—a frame of two monumental canons for strings surrounds the plea of the *Mater Dolorosa* addressed to her dying Son (see Figure 8-12).

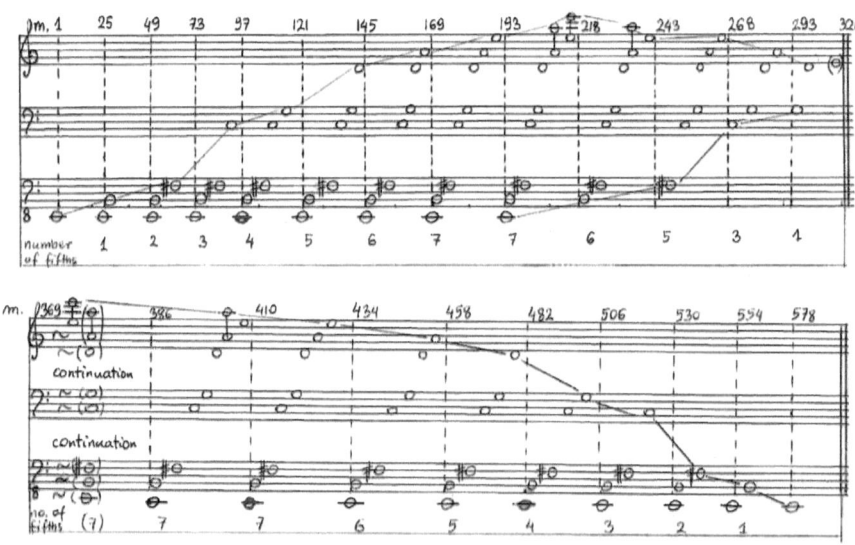

Figure 8-12: The pitch range of the canons in the first movement of the Third Symphony (1976), plotted against the measure numbers, with entries of voices in successive registers, and the outline of the pitch space.

The text of the first movement comes from the Holy Cross lament, a Lenten poem in the tradition of *Stabat Mater*. The monumental scope of the design, the persistent repetitiveness and austere restraint of the music, ascending form an abyss of silence and darkness and receding again after the brief sorrowful apparition, point beyond the realm of temporality. Although the representation of eternity in time is, strictly speaking, impossible, for, to quote St. Augustine in eternity, "all is at once present, whereas no time as all at once present," musical portrayals of timelessness often employ the means described above: vast dimensions, extreme slowness of tempo, repetitions, symmetry, canons, etc. In this way, Górecki invokes the heritage of music symbolism created over centuries. The canons are built on a 24-measure theme that is repeated nine times in the lowest voice. Successive entries of voices follow a series of ascending fifths, using the even pitches of the E-Aeolian mode (Figure 8-12).

The image of *Mater Dolorosa* whose soul is "pierced by a sword" of pain (as foretold in Simeon's prophecy, Luke 2: 35) appears in this Symphony surrounded by a halo of austere instrumental music. This setting petrifies Mary's anguish into a timeless icon of sorrow, cast in the eternal *now*. According to the Church's doctrine, Mother Mary brings relief to suffering people whose ordeals are a part of her pain, and a part of the passion of her Son's.

One such person was Helena Wanda Błażusiak, a young prisoner from Zakopane, held by Gestapo in a cell where she wrote on the wall: "Mama, don't cry. The Purest, Heavenly Queen, protect me forever. Hail Mary, full of grace." This inscription provides the text for the second movement of the Symphony. Helena's initial words ("Mama, don't cry") supply Christ's response to the unanswered plea of Mary at the bottom of the Cross in the first movement. In Górecki's music, the young prisoner's ordeal is strangely peaceful and non-dramatic: "*tranquillissimo—cantabillissimo—dolcissimo—legatissimo.*" The absence of despair, highlighted by the musical setting may result from the girl's intense faith, her humble acceptance of her destiny, and the closeness of human and divine motherhood.

The Symphony's last, even slower, movement follows a trajectory from sorrow to respite in grieving the death of a son. The Opole-area folksong, written during the Silesian Uprisings against the Germans in the 1920s, is a lament of a mother who lost her son: embittered accusations or hatred of his killers are followed by expressions of profound sadness and a resigned acceptance of her fate. The communion of suffering makes human grief a portion of Christ's redemptive Passion.

The music uses a recurring semi-tonal motive C—D-flat—C that is a signature of sorrow and binds the three movements together, appearing in different settings, before giving way to the "yes...yes...yes" sequence of slowly repeated 21 tonal chords that dissolve into silence at the end. The apparent simplicity of the form was a result of painstaking compositional effort; the notebooks for the canon from the first movement include about 200 different versions of the melody and its ascent, interlocking in a chain-like fashion to the climax.

Figure 8-13: Cover of Nonesuch recording of the Symphony No. 3 with Dawn Upshaw and the London Sinfonietta, David Zinman, cond.

Rejected and derided by many critics after its Polish premiere at the Warsaw Autumn Festival in 1977[35] (the composer so disliked the

---

[35] See excerpts from a discussion published in *Ruch Muzyczny* in 1977 in an Appendix to interview with Mieczysław Kominek, Chapter 2 in the present volume. Files in the Polish Composers Union Library indicate that the composer's

operatic-style interpretation by Stefania Woytowicz that he did not attend the concert at all), and taken to pieces by Western music press after the first European performance at the Royan Festival in April the same year, the Third Symphony became an international hit many years later, after the release of its recording with Dawn Upshaw in 1992. Conducted by David Zinman, this interpretation was welcomed by the composer's with approval; he particularly liked the crystalline, luminous voice of the singer, a lyrical soprano without a heavy, operatic vibrato or other traditional mannerism of a prima-donna.[36] What's more significant, her voice and Górecki's slow-slow-and-slower symphony also delighted millions of listeners who purchased the CDs and transformed this obscure work that languished for over a decade, into a celebrated masterpiece. It was used in films; it was broadcast and performed by orchestras world-wide. Today there are dozens of different interpretations available, even though the frenzy of popularity peaked in 1996-97.[37]

The Third Symphony uses the Phrygian mode in the first movement and the triads D-flat Major and A Major in the second movement. *Beatus Vir* juxtaposes harmonic C Minor with the triumphant C Major at the end. The judicious use of modal and tonal harmonic means is one of the main elements of the composer's style since mid-1970s. He also relies on the material borrowed from religious songs, both historic (*Bogurodzica*, late medieval chorales, and Renaissance motets) and folk-style (melodies from the Kurpie and Opole regions in the Symphony No. 3). These often take the form of narrow-range, small motivic cells that are derived from the borrowed materials, and may appear alongside with quotations or allusions to works by Górecki's favorite composers, such as Chopin or Beethoven.

---

protest against the interpretation of the symphony at the 1977 Warsaw Autumn had serious institutional repercussions.
[36] For the history of this recording and its promotion see the recollections of British performers, publishers and scholars in Beata Bolesławska-Lewandowka, *Górecki, op. cit.*
[37] Luke B. Howard, "Motherhood, Billboard, and the Holocaust: Perceptions and Receptions of Górecki's Symphony No. 3". *The Musical Quarterly* 82/1 (1998): 131–159. See also, Howard, "Henryk M. Górecki Symphony No.3 (1976) as a Symbol of Polish Political History" *The Polish Review* 52/2 (2007): 215–222.

The spirituality and simplicity of Górecki's works from late 1970s onward have led to grouping him with other composers of the so-called "Holy Minimalism"—Arvo Pärt from Estonia and the English John Tavener who converted to Easter Orthodoxy. Nonetheless, while the Polish composer's works were intensely spiritual and often used psalm fragments as texts, his musical roots were markedly Central European. He was fascinated with Beethoven, Schubert and Mozart—the Austrians were close to him as he lived, studied and taught in Silesia, not that far from Vienna.

When asked to name some favorite composers in 1998, he recited a long list that included, besides the early favorites of Bach, Beethoven, Szymanowski, Chopin, Bartok and Messiaen, also Schumann, Brahms, Haydn, Wagner, Schubert, Shostakovich, Ives, Dvorak and Puccini.[38] He listened to radio broadcasts all his life and wrote comments about each work he heard: some were harsh, other positive, but all displayed his unique personality and taste. In composing, Górecki created a world of his own. He did not imitate the immense colorful chords and birdsong portrayed by Olivier Messiaen, the Catholic mystic. He reached instead to his own musical roots in *Old Polish Music* (1969) and numerous choral works quoting the medieval Marian anthem *Bogurodzica*,[39] or folk melodies from the Kurpie region and the Tatra Mountains.

The composer found old Polish folk melodies in many songbooks, but was especially partial to a collection he adored and mined for inspiration, the multi-volume cycle of ethnographic works by Oskar Kolberg (1814-1890).[40] During a 1998 interview, Górecki bemoaned the fact that the publication of Kolberg's *Complete Works* was, as yet, incomplete; he thought that this collection, more than any other

---

[38] Górecki, "Composing is a Terribly Personal Matter," *op. cit.* See Chapter 4.

[39] Maja Trochimczyk, "Bogurodzica Reborn: A Medieval Anthem in Contemporary Polish Music," in *Mittelalter-Sehnsucht?*, edited by Dorothea Redepenning and Annette Kreutziger-Herr, (Kiel, Germany: Wissenschafts-verlag Vauk Kiel KG, 2000), 131-152.

[40] Oskar Kolberg, *Dzieła Wszystkie* [Complete Works] were published since 1954 in Poland and over 50 volumes appeared before the establishment of Oskar Kolberg Institute, with one purpose, of completing the edition, now planned for 86 volumes. http://www.oskarkolberg.pl/

[40] Górecki, "Composing is a Terribly Personal Matter," *op. cit.* See Chapter 4.

publication contained the "heart and soul" of Polish music.[41] Simultaneously, he was delighted to hear that a Polish scholar, Jan Węcowski, had apparently discovered quotations of old religious folk songs in Chopin's music: "if you could prove that he actually used church songs, that have texts that mean something, not only the folk mazurkas, but also the expressions of folk spirituality, then we see how Chopin returned to the foundations, to the roots from which all the music grows."[42]

In the Third Symphony and other vocal instrumental compositions, Górecki worked to achieve a direct link between the emotional and spiritual content (both sacred and traditional) and his musical architecture. The focus on vocal music throughout this period led quite naturally to an emphasis on melody, with resulting simplification of the harmonic and textural aspects. This gradual progress away from dissonance towards consonance was not "absolute" as it was followed by an expansion of the composer's personal "bag of tricks" in the 1980s to encompass radical contrasts in tempo, dynamics, textural density, and a return of harmonic dissonance. These elements cooperated to create a unified, highly concentrated musical expression, present in a remarkable series of chamber music works: *Recitatives and Ariosos 'Lerchenmusik'* for clarinet, cello, and piano, Op. 53 (1984); *Already It Is Dusk, Music for String Quartet* (String Quartet No. 1), Op. 62 (1988); *Quasi una Fantasia, String Quartet No. 2*, Op. 64 (1992); *Kleines Requiem für eine Polka*, Op. 66 (1993); *Kleine Phantasie* for violin and piano, Op. 73 (1997), and the *Third String Quartet, ...songs are sung* (1995-2007).

These compositions draw inspiration from colors and rhythms of folk music: the dance patterns and string ostinati of the mountain *kapelas*, the melancholy clarinet tunes of Silesia, the unbridled impetus of the polka... The melodic lyricism and chorale harmonies bring echoes of late Beethoven, whose inspiration is present both in allusions and direct quotations (such as the Fourth Piano Concerto in *Lerchenmusik*). Many of these chamber works seem to be large in scope because of the seriousness of expression. The musical ideas

---

[41] Górecki, *ibidem*.
[42] *Ibidem*. English translation of Jan Węcowski's controversial article, "Religious Folklore in Chopin's Works," was published in *Polish Music Journal* 2, nos. 1-2 (1999).

develop, as it were, on a symphonic scale, for instance the 45 minutes of *Lerchenmusik* require a great intensity of performers and an intense focus by the listeners for its proper interpretation and appreciation. In many ways, it is as intense as the monumental Copernican Symphony, with which it shares some formal gestures. The first movement (A BC BC BC* A), second movement (A A1 A2 A3), and third movement (A A* BA**B* CDE A*** F) bring together distinct expressive and thematic patterns, highlighted at the beginning of the third movement with a quotation from the opening of Beethoven's Fourth Piano Concerto.

> At the beginning of my music education, when I had no idea about music- nothing!—these names were always near me: Beethoven, Chopin, Szymanowski. Does one need to consider it in a special way; does none need to think much about this? I do not think so. Either one has it or one does not. Either these genes are there or not; but do we have a choice to accept them? I do not know if this is possible…. Nobody chooses their time and place of birth.[43]

Fig 8-14: Górecki plays in a *górale* ensemble in the US, with Prof. Thaddeus Gromada (standing), singer Andrzej Bachleda (L), Janina Kedroń (R), wearing folk costumes. October 1997, New Jersey, celebrating the 50th Anniversary of the *Tatra Eagle*, published by Gromada and Kedroń. Used by Permission.

---

[43] Górecki, "Composing is a Terribly Personal Matter," *op. cit*, see Chapter 4.

Górecki spent hours and years crafting pieces with deep connections to the history and spiritual roots of Polish music. The energetic, yet often jarringly harsh performance style of a *góralska muzyka* or *kapela* (a band of four string instruments) echoes in the String Quartets and other works for strings.

While the Catholic Church and its traditional religious music was Górecki's spiritual home, he found his hermitage and refuge in the Tatra Mountains, where he purchased and remodeled a house in the village of Ząb. There, he listened to and performed with *górale* folk string ensembles, enjoyed the natural beauty of the mountains, and the resilience and creativity of their inhabitants. He befriended the grandson of the legendary Podhale fiddler, Bartuś Obrochta, and other górale musicians. Echoes of their music can be heard in many works, though none are named after the mountains, like those of Górecki's contemporary and a fellow Silesian, Wojciech Kilar (1932-2013), such as *Orawa* or *Krzesany*.[44]

Yet, it is impossible to imagine Górecki's quartets without the sound world of the Tatra Mountains. The First String Quartet (1988) for instance, brings to mind an image of dance frenzy, of exhaustion by incessant movement, by the rhythms that become overwhelmingly wild, by the sound colors and chords that are ever more harsh and dissonant. The music is filled with impetuous, strongly voiced emotions, it is aggressive and incredibly moving at the same time, as it dissolves into silence towards the end, following the *Already it is Dusk*" sunset topos of the waning of the day (or life) found in the melancholy Renaissance melody by Wacław of Szamotuły.

A judicious use of quotation amidst extreme emotional and textural contrasts characterizes also the *Little Requiem for a Polka*, Op. 66 (1993). Commissioned by the Holland Festival and the Schonberg Ensemble and premiered in Amsterdam in June 1993, this work initially had a somewhat different title: *Nocna Serenada. Małe Requiem dla Pewnej Polki* [Night Serenade. Little Requiem for a Certain Polka]. The currently used versions do not reflect the ambiguity of the Polish title: the word "Polka" may mean both a "Polish woman" and a folk dance. This fluidity of meaning is intended: the work was written *in memoriam* of someone whose identity the composer did not wish to

---

[44] Górecki, "Composing is a Terribly Personal Matter," Chapter 4, *op. cit.*

disclose, and one of the movements, is, indeed, a polka. The *Little Requiem* is framed by two slow movements, contrasting their resigned tranquility with anguished grotesque of the central section.

As typical in his large-scale works, the music follows the emotional trajectory of *catharsis,* from an intense distress to repose, marred by faint echoes of past darkness to the very end. The first movement invites the listeners into a vast space of silence, drawn out in violin lines and punctuated by sweetly resonating notes of the piano. Soon, the music becomes dramatic: a sudden clamor of bells brings in a premonition of future distress. After the brutal awakening of the second movement, with hits aggressive brass chords, fast tempi, and irregular shifts of melodic and rhythmic patterns, the mood descends again into a trance-like slowness.

The Mahlerian device of contrasting the poignant with the banal underlies the surprising entrance of a boisterous polka in the third movement. The piano part is especially prominent here, with its obsessive ostinati, and garish brightness. The melody in the winds is played in parallel sevenths and seconds (as in Bartók's "mistuning" effects borrowed from the folk music of the Balkans). It evokes the frenzied "out-of-tuneness" heard at so many folk dance parties. The scene is one of dancers intoxicated with their motions and musicians reaching complete exhaustion and stupor. A sudden pause breaks the flow with silence (*à la* Messiaen or Xenakis) and underscores the feeling of a painful unreality of this sonic landscape. The bells toll again, the funereal procession looms at a distance, the lonely horn solo echoes from afar (as in Mahler and Ives, and, maybe, also in Ligeti's *Lontano*) and the Requiem fades away: it is over.

As mentioned above, Górecki served on the faculty of his *alma mater* in Katowice (1965-1979), rising through the ranks from an instructor, to the president. He was a professor of composition in 1975-79; his students included Rafał Augustyn, Eugeniusz Knapik, Andrzej Krzanowski, and his son, Mikołaj. Engaged in teaching and administration, in this period, he composed less often, yet each work was a result of intense, profound reflection. According to his teachers, students, and children, he composed irregularly, in intense spurts, following extensive periods of planning and research.⁴⁵ The perfectionism resulted in long delays of completion of certain works, like the Third String Quartet or the Fourth Symphony. For the composer, the music could not become a business; it had to be done right. (Incidentally, scholar Adrian Thomas goes as far as to blame the success of The Third Symphony for what he sees as a "creative paralysis" of the composer unwilling or unable to compose during over a decade).⁴⁶

Such an uncompromising aesthetical stance did not bide well for the composer's success in an administrative career. Indeed, his term as the President of the Katowice State Higher School of Music was ended prematurely: elected to the post in 1975, he resigned in 1979, while working on the commission for *Beatus Vir*. Adrian Thomas attributes this resignation to a political controversy concerning the refusal of the authorities to allow Pope John Paul II visit Katowice. Another reason cited by Thomas was the meddling of the Party apparatus in the internal matters of the School, such as not allowing Górecki to hire his students, Eugeniusz Knapik and Andrzej Krzanowski. However, according to a testimony of Leon Markiewicz (who served as a Vice President at the School and took over as President after the composer's resignation) and the research by Silesian musicologists, the reasons for Górecki's resignation were most likely artistic.⁴⁷ The composer needed time to complete the oratorio for the Pope, and the administrative duties were too time-consuming. Besides, the two students were already employed.

Thus, the composer left the academic world, while continuing some involvement in cultural, religious and political activism: as a Vice President of the Szymanowski Society in Zakopane (1977-1983), and the President of the Club of Catholic Intelligentsia (1980-1984). Ill health caused a gradual withdrawal from these and all other public

---

⁴⁵ Especially student Eugeniusz Knapik, teacher Leon Markiewicz, and student-son, Mikołaj Górecki, cited by Beata Bolesławska-Lewandowska, *Górecki, op. cit.*

⁴⁶ Adrian Thomas interviewed by Beata Bolesławska-Lewandowska, *Górecki, op. cit.*, 176-180.

⁴⁷ Beata Bolesławska-Lewandowska's 2013 interviews show the ambivalence of Górecki's friends and students about the reasons for his resignation; there are arguments to support both sides, *Górecki, op. cit.*

functions. The composer continued supporting himself and his family with commissions, royalties, and performance fees.

In the late nineties, Górecki was finally able to enjoy the rewards and recognition stemming from the global fame of his music, that resulted in frequent invitations to conduct, perform, approve recordings, or lecture in Europe and America. He was also able to do what he liked, and instead of touring the world or cranking up imitations of the Third Symphony, he composed choral music and songs and toured small Polish town with jazz singer Wanda Warska.[48]

He also helped organize and plan the Festival of Polish Composers in Bielsko-Biala, where his music was featured in 1996, 2003, and 2008, and where he often conducted the orchestra, most notably in his Third Symphony in 1996. The successive festivals were initially dedicated to just one composer: 1997 – Wojciech Kilar, 1998 – Stanisław Moniuszko, 1999 – Fryderyk Chopin, 2000 – Karol Szymanowski, 2001 – Zygmunt Konieczny, Andrzej Kurylewicz, Zbigniew Preisner, 2002 – Mieczysław Karłowicz, 2003 – Henryk Mikołaj Górecki, 2004 – Witold Lutosławski,2005 – Krzysztof Penderecki, 2006 – Grażyna Bacewicz, and Henryk Wieniawski,2007 – Jan Krenz,2008 – Ignacy Jan Paderewski and 75th birthday of Henryk Mikołaj Górecki, 2009 – Krzesimir Dębski and Mieczysław Karłowicz and 2010 – Fryderyk Chopin. Interestingly, Górecki insisted that the 2005 world premiere of his Third String Quartet by the Kronos Quartet took place in Bielsko-Biała, instead of New York, London, or, at least, Warsaw...

The composer also collected many honors, reaching far beyond the First Prize at the UNESCO International Composers Rostrum in Paris for *Ad Matrem* (1973)[49] and many state government awards that he had received earlier. In 1994, he received the Commander Cross of the Order of Polonia Restituta, and in 2003 the Commander Cross with the Star of the same order as well as *Lux ex Silesia* Prize. In 1993 the

---

[48] Wanda Warska commissioned several composers to write music to the same poem by Stanisław Wyspiański; Górecki composed additional two songs and accompanied the singer during tours of small towns in Poland, organized by Ewa Michalska. *Three Fragments /Trzy fragmenty do słów Stanisława Wyspiańskiego*, Op. 69 for voice and piano (1995-96). See Chapter 4.
[49] This was his third award in Paris: preceded by the First Prize at the Second Biennale of Young Composers in 1961 for the First Symphony, and the Third Prize at the UNESCO Rostrum of Composers for *Refrain* in 1967.

Upper Silesia Union (Związek Górnoślaski) presented him with the Karol Miarka Prize and the Wojciech Kofranty Prize. He enjoyed these less-known regional honors as much as those of international stature. In 2000, Górecki was presented with Order Ecce Homo, in 2002—with the Tansman Medal, in 2005— with the Gold Cross Gloria Artis, in 2009—with the Order of St. Gregory the Great by the Vatican and in 2010—with the Order of the White Eagle, the highest distinction granted by the Polish government.

The last decade of Górecki's life was also filled with honorary doctorates awarded by: the Academy of Catholic Theology in Warsaw (1993), University of Warsaw (1994); Jagiellonian University in Kraków (2000), Karol Szymanowski Academy of Music in Katowice (2003), the Catholic University in Lublin (2004), the Academy of Music in Kraków (2008); and from several institutions abroad: Catholic University in Washington, D.C.; Victoria University, in Victoria, British Columbia, Canada; and Concordia University in Montreal, Quebec, Canada. He also received an honorary fellowship from Cardiff University in Cardiff, Wales where Adrian Thomas, his biographer, was a professor. Furthermore, Górecki became the honorary citizen of several Polish cities: Zakopane (1994), Bielsko-Biała (2003), Rybnik (2006), Katowice (2008), and Ostrowiec Świętokrzyski (2009).

When the Kronos Quartet commissioned the Third String Quartet, the work materialized 13 years later. The composer could have written 20 quartets in this time, but he worked on one, the right one: a piece of music in which every note is in its place, every chord belongs, every dynamic sign is exactly what it has to be, as part of a highly-charged emotional and expressive structure. There are no random fillers, materials "just so" — everything has its meaning and its function in the overall design. It may be deceptively simple, but being crafted so well, it will survive centuries. Apparently, the delayed release of the Quartet, subtitled *"...songs are sung"* and inspired by the memory of a young pregnant woman killed in Podhale area during WWII, was due to personal issues; revisions consisted mostly of changed or refined dynamics.

Figure 8-15: Program and Press Clippings from Górecki's Honoris Causa Doctorate Ceremony at the University of Warsaw. The Górecki File. ZKP Library, Warsaw.

The slowing down of the pace of composing was also due to serious health issues. Suffering from a string of illnesses since his childhood, the composer had a particular difficult time in 2004, as discussed in the letter he sent to me, dated 3 March 2004, after I tried to invite him to come back to Los Angeles to give the third annual Paderewski Lecture-Recital at the University of Southern California in the fall of 2004:

> Dear, darling Maja!
>
> Thank you for an extensive letter—the invitation and materials. My dear—I must introduce certain corrections to my life. Quite suddenly, at the beginning of January of this year I landed in the hospital—and I went through a very serious surgery (5 February 2004)—from my stomach a massive cancer mass was cut out, about which I knew nothing, and which was not troubling me at all, while it was attached to my stomach. And what is the most funny, is that the "thing" that I

went to the hospital for was almost completely ignored. Then, on 11 February, I had a huge hemorrhage (I lost several liters of blood, I was "hanging" by the tread—but I was saved). On 19 February, I returned home and somehow, slowly I am gathering myself together. All of this comes with great difficulty, since some "trifles" have also attached to me—so that it were more interesting. Due to the above my life will have to undergo certain changes.

I now have to wait and arm myself in patience and look what the nearest future will bring, only then I would be able to plan something concrete. For now, I'm waiting.

I send you my most heartfelt greetings. Please share my most heartfelt greetings also with the beloved Wilks—Wanda and Stefan. However, I hope that we will still be able to see each other.

Much cordiality and lots of health,

H.M. Górecki

I give you my two addresses:
Ul.   Katowice
or
              near Zakopane.

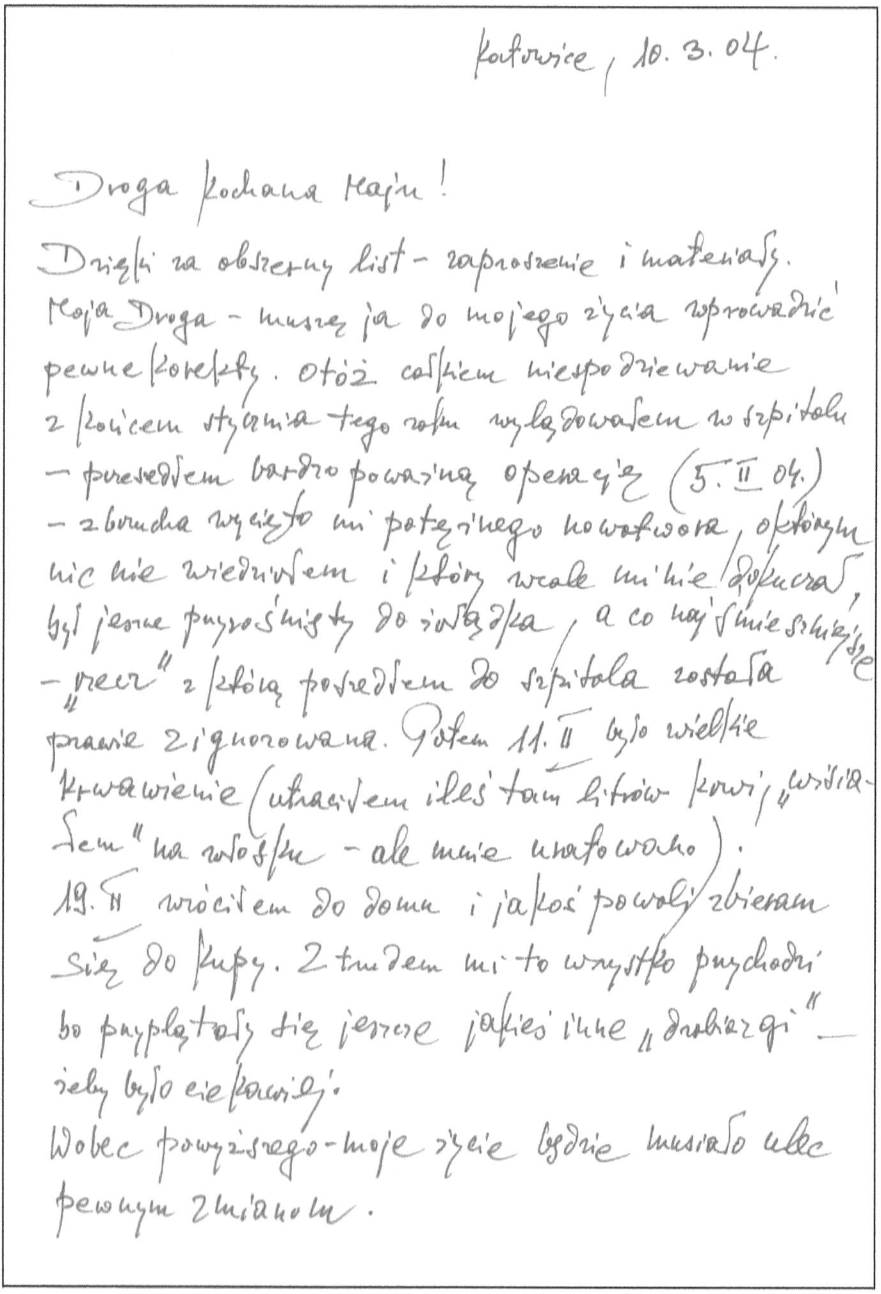

Katowice, 10. 3. 04.

Droga Kochana Maju!

Dzięki za obszerny list - zaproszenie i materiały. Moja Droga - muszę ja do mojego życia wprowadzić pewne korekty. Otóż całkiem niespodziewanie z końcem stycznia tego roku wylądowałem w szpitalu - przeszedłem bardzo poważną operację (5. II 04.) - z brzucha wyjęto mi potężnego nowotwora, o którym nic nie wiedziałem i który wcale mi nie dokuczał, był jeszcze przyrośnięty do żołądka, a co najśmieszniejsze - "rzecz" z którą poszedłem do szpitala została prawie zignorowana. Potem 11. II było wielkie krwawienie (utraciłem ileś tam litrów krwi, "wsiadłem" na wołóżkę - ale mnie uratowano).
19. II wróciłem do domu i jakoś powoli zbieram się do kupy. Z trudem mi to wszystko przychodzi bo przyplątały się jeszcze jakieś inne "drobiazgi" - żeby było ciekawiej.
Wobec powyższego - moje życie będzie musiało ulec pewnym zmianom.

Figure 8-16a: First Page of Górecki's letter to Maja Trochimczyk, 10 March 2004. Maja Trochimczyk Archives.

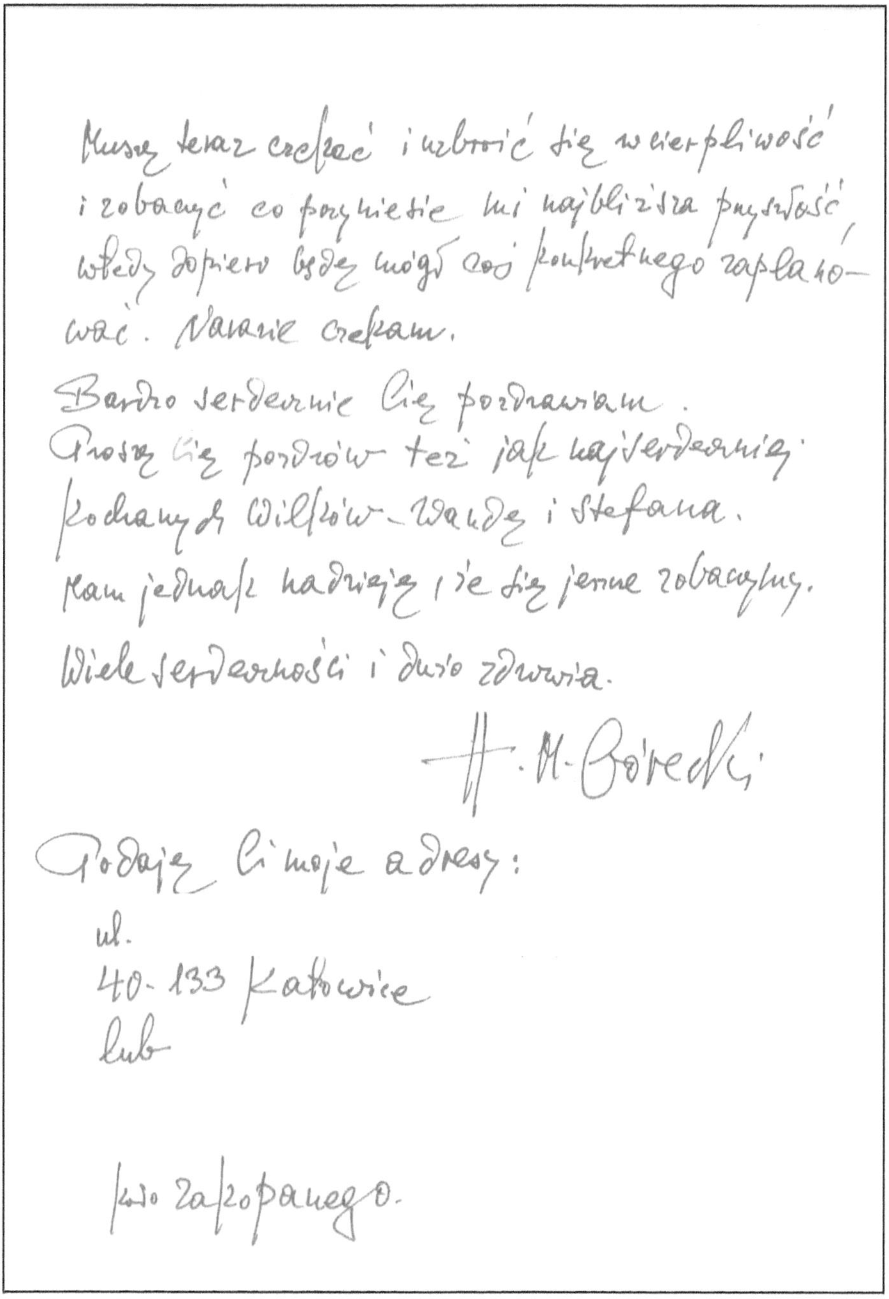

[Handwritten letter in Polish:]

Muszę teraz czekać i uzbroić się w cierpliwość
i zobaczyć co przyniesie mi najbliższa przyszłość,
wtedy dopiero będę mógł coś konkretnego zaplano-
wać. Narazie czekam.
Bardzo serdecznie Cię pozdrawiam.
Proszę Cię pozdrów też jak najserdeczniej
Kochanych Wilków – Wandę i Stefana.
Mam jednak nadzieję, że się jeszcze zobaczymy.
Wiele serdeczności i dużo zdrowia.

H. M. Górecki

Podaję Ci moje adresy:
ul.
40-133 Katowice
lub

k/o Zakopanego.

Figure 8-16b: The second page of Górecki's letter to Maja Trochimczyk, 10 March 2004. Maja Trochimczyk Archives.

The opening of the Fourth Symphony, *Tansman Episodes* (composed in 2006, left in a piano score and completed by Mikołaj Górecki after his father's death in 2010-11), is a great example of the emotional intensity and predilection for harsh, contrasting sonorities that persisted in the Polish composer's oeuvre since *Scontri*. Yet, the massive chords carry a special meaning, as they spell out the name of a Polish-Jewish-French composer, Aleksander/Alexandre Tansman (1897-1986), the dedicatee of the symphony.

Figure 8-17: Aleksander Tansman (1897-1986), 1946 photo, Maja Trochimczyk Archives.

The appearance of this composer in the music is surprising and may be explained by the fact that the work was initially commissioned by the Tansman Foundation.[50] The later "official" co-commission was by the London Symphony Orchestra and the Los Angeles Philharmonic that performed the work in 2014 and 2015. Stylistically, this last

---

[50] Andrzej Wendland, *Górecki: IV Symfonia. Tansman Epizody. Fenomen. żywioł, Tajemnica* [Górecki The Fourth Symphony Tansman Episodes. The Phenomenon, Elements, Mystery] (Łódź: Tansman Cultural Association, 2016). See also Wendland's discussion of the *Tansman Episodes* in Chapter 14.

Symphony continues Górecki's preoccupation with expressive contrasts, emotional arches, and creating complex, large-scale structures from deceptively simple musical means.

◎ ◎ ◎

Sick since childhood, suffering multiple hospitalizations and hip surgeries, and living most of his life in severe physical pain, Górecki died of lung disease in November 2010. His death left a gap in Polish musical world that will be impossible to be filled. The composer created a unique sound world of suffering and revelation. Never moderate or "tame," the composer's intense, extremist personality found a perfect expression in his intense, extremist music that he painstakingly described in some of the most unusual annotations ever found in any score. In Ad *Matrem,* for instance, the expressive quality of *tranquilissimo—cantabilissimo—dolcissimo—affettuoso e ben tenuto e LEGATISSIMO,* provides a diametrical contrast to *ritmico— marcatissimo—energico—furioso—con massima passione e grande tensione* of the work's opening drum motives. Filled with the passion raised to the maximum, his conception of music gradually evolved to become more spiritual and "otherworldly." As defined by Bohdan Pociej, Górecki's favorite musicologist and his staunchest supporter, this was music of another world.[51]

Called "a Pole apart" by Adrian Thomas, the composer created an idiosyncratic musical style and aesthetics that have indeed set him apart from his contemporaries. Similarly, Górecki's disregard for social conventions and expectations of a "successful" composer (especially after the phenomenal global success of the Third Symphony) resulted from his dogged pursuit of a personal spiritual truth, expressed bluntly, yet with profound sensitivity. For Górecki, composing was an expression of a profound internal vision; living—an expression of an uncompromising personal faith.

◎ ◎ ◎

---

[51] Bohdan Pociej, *Bycie w muzyce. Próba opisania twórczości Henryka Mikołaja Góreckiego* [Being in music: An attempt to describe the oeuvre of Henryk Mikołaj Górecki] (Katowice, 2005).

CHAPTER 9

Henryk Mikołaj Górecki's Symphony No. 2 *Copernican*: Word and Sound Facing the Sublime

Kinga Kiwała

> In the arts nearly everywhere the most effective means of representing the numinous is „the sublime."
> Rudolf Otto[1]

1. Genesis and Sources of Inspiration

Górecki's Symphony No. 2, *Copernican* was composed between April and December 1972, on commission from the Kościuszko Foundation in New York, to celebrate the 500th birth anniversary of Mikołaj Kopernik (Copernicus).[2] In his oeuvre of the time, this work was set for the largest performing forces and had the longest duration. According to Adrian Thomas, by tackling a Copernican subject, Górecki could engage in one of his greates passions, the fascination with Cosmos.[3] The composer had the following to say about his grappling with the Copernican theme and about discussions with film director Krzysztof Zanussi that helped him to crystallize the core idea for this work:[4]

> Zanussi said that the story of Copernicus (...) is really one of the greatest tragedies that ever took place in the history of the human spirit: the whole way of thinking was destroyed, the foundation on which the relationship of human beings to their surrounding reality was based. We stopped being the navel of the world; in the face of

---

[1] Rudolf Otto, *Świętość. Elementy irracjonalne w pojęciu bóstwa i ich stosunek do elementów racjonalnych,* Polish translation by B. Kupis (Warsaw, 1968), 102. Originally published in German, *Das Heilige - Über das Irrationale in der Idee des Göttlichen und sein Verhältnis zum Rationalen* (Breslau, 1917). Cited from English translation, *The Idea of the Holy* (Ravenio Books, 1959), online.
[2] Adrian Thomas, *Górecki,* Polish translation by E. Gabryś (Kraków: PWM, 1998), 206.
[3] *Ibidiem,* 102.
[4] H. M. Górecki,„„Powiem Państwu szczerze... ", *Vivo* 1 (1994), 45.

infinity we became nothing. Then, the whole theme became clear to me, obvious for the musical setting. Fromo here comes the two-part design of this Symphony in two movements: first the whole, let's call it, mechanism of the world, then—contemplation.

Thus, Górecki interprets the Copernican discovery not only in „scientific" categories, as one of the greatest revolutions that helped humans discover the true face of Cosmos, but also from an existential perspective. However, a question arises here about the condition of a person facing such a discovery. It seems, that this shift of perspective may fascinate, because space suddenly extended into infinity leads to contemplation; opens new horizons. However, a discovery of this kind must also evoke existential terror, because it means a loss of a fixed, apparently unmovable order of things, in which the human world had a central position in the center of the Universe. The humility, mutiny, fear, or questioning one's own place—all these feelings may arise in a person that is finding himself or herself in such a situation. From the perspective of faith, this person directs his or her anxieties and questions to the Creator. Górecki's own interpretation of the „Copernican Revolution" became the core idea and the point of departure for the construction of the Copernican Symphony.[5]

Stylistically speaking, the Symphony may be placed in the phase called by Krzysztof Droba „the phase of religious music."[6] This phase— considered by Teresa Malecka as the apex of the composer's whole oeuvre to date[7]—was initiated by *Ad Matrem*, created in 1971. The phase encompasses the following works: The Second and Third Symphonies, *Beatus Vir*, and compositions for voice with piano or orchestra (*Dwie pieśni sakralne*) or for chorus *a cappella* (*Euntes ibant et flebant, Amen, Miserere, Totus Tuus*, etc.). In these works, the composer continues and deepens his reductionism of musical materials, a technique that he had initiated in the mid-1960s. He also turns toward modal and tonal harmony and an intensified expression, but—first and foremost—towards the use of a religious text. To quote

---

[5] More about this issue is below in the section on the Symbolic Function of Music.
[6] Krzysztof Droba, *Górecki,* entry in the *Encyklopedia Muzyczna PWM,* vol. 3, E-F-G, ed. Elżbieta Dziębowska (Kraków: PWM, 1987), 429.
[7] See Teresa Malecka, „III Symfonia i Beatus vir – faza szczytowa w drodze twórczej Góreckiego," in *Dzieło muzyczne i jego rezonans,* ed. Anna Nowak (Bydgoszcz: Akademia Muzyczna, 2008).

Krzysztof Droba, this period in Górecki's oeuvre can be considered as a unified expanse of music that „evokes the Word."[8]

2.1. Analytical Remarks — The Text

Górecki started composing the Second Symphony from the verbal layer, by creating his own text instead of drawing from any „standard" ready-made verbiage. This approach is typical for his later oeuvre. The occasion for which this work was commissioned influenced the choice of several psalm verses taken from Psalms 146 (145) and 136 (135), and accompanied by a fragment from *De revolutionibus orbium celestium* by Copernicus. The main idea is the meditation on the beauty of Creation and the contemplation of Cosmos conceived in the classic sense of this term as a harmony of elements that is opposed to the dysharmony of Chaos. The verbal layer of the Symphony is limited in size and the composer often uses repetitions of words. It is beyond any doubt that in the semantic layer of the text the main emphasis is placed on the issue of „light." Here, Górecki follows Copernicus in encouraging the listeners to be delighted by the perfection of the creation: the „luminaria magna"—the Sun, Moon, and stars. Simultaneously, or so it seems, he conceives „light" in a more profound way—in a cosmological, as well as a symbolic, sense. This second meaning of „light" is clarified, to a certain extent, by the final fragment of the text, borrowed from Copernicus's treatise: „What is more beautiful than the heavens, which encompasses eveyrthing that is beautiful?" As Bohdan Pociej writes, „in this sentence we find (...) the old idea about beauty, harmony and the absolute order of the universe."[9]

It is crucial to note that the verses selected from the psalms come from the most solemn hymns in praise of God, the Creator. Here, the composer directly refers to the tradition of the hymn, a poetic-musical genre that is characterized primarily by its laudatory tone. In this context, the genesis of the genre of the hymn is important—it probably stems from religious practice, i.e., prayers recited with musical

---

[8] Krzysztof Droba, „Słowo w muzyce Góreckiego,"[Word in Górecki's music] *Ruch Muzyczny* 22 (1981): 4.
[9] Bohdan Pociej, „Kosmos, tradycja i brzmienie" [Cosmos, Tradition and Sonority] *Ruch Muzyczny* 15 (1973): 3.

accompaniment while making offerings to the deities. These cult-related and liturgical functions are its most primary aspects. Hymns were always performed in the most solemn moments of religious ceremonies.[10] As Father Władysław Borowski reminds his readers, „Hymn (...) in a temple was the highest religious act for a person that lived with and in God."[11]

Already from the start, the appearance of a textual fragment borrowed from the Old Testament songs of praise of the Creator suggests a deeply religious orientation of this composition. Nonetheless, the contemplation of Cosmos does not have a „pantheist" character, but is directed towards a personal God. This aspect is emphasized by the repeated invocations of „Deus" that appear at the outset of the psalm borrowings. The composer added his own invocation to close this segment of the text; this final phrase does not occur in the original psalm verse.

It is necessary to emphasize that the scarcity of words being pronounced coupled with their repetitiveness is typical for meditative practices of many religions, including Christianity; it is also characteristics for prayers deeply rooted in folk religiosity, such as the litanies and the Rosary.

The text of the Copernican Symphony is of an epical-lyrical kind, which also corresponds to the tradition of the hymn.[12] Verses borrowed from psalms „count" all the heavenly bodies created by God and describe their functions. The concluding fragment, however, taken from Copernicus's treatise, consists in a rhetorical quesiton, expressing delight in the beauty of creation. As such, it could probably be considered „lyrical." The words of Górecki's Symphony are also characterized by a certain objectivity: the texts borrowed from psalms are almost completely deprived of adjectives; it is hard to define the subject of the statement in the final fragment; and the Latin invocations „Deus" that permeate the psalm fragments could be understood in two distinct ways: on the one hand, subjectively, as

---

[10] See S. Czajkowski, „Hymn," in *Od psalmu i hymnu do Songu i Liedu. Zagadnienia genologiczne: rodzaj-gatunek-utwór.* Series *Muzyka i Liryka 7*, ed. Mieczysław Tomaszewski (Kraków: Akademia Muzyczna, 1998), 25, 32-33.
[11] W. Borowski, *Psalmy. Komentarz biblijno-ascetyczny* (Kraków: 1983), 18.
[12] See Czajkowski, *op. cit.*, 25.

sighs „Oh, God," and, on the other hand, as objective calling to God. A specific „objectivity, a resignation from emphasizing one's own subjectivity and a focus on the contemplated object, is also characteristic of a religious meditation."[13] All the above-mentioned features of this short text of the Copernican Symphony open a whole palette of interpretitative possiblitities and allow for the text's particular „clarifiation" by the music.

2.2. Analytical Remarks — The Music

Starting from the 1970s, the verbal, meaningful layer in vocal-instrumental works by Górecki is their component that is decidedly at the forefront. The verbal layer is form-bearing and plays a leading role in the shaping of a composition. Nonetheless, in the Second Symphony, this principle operates only to a limited extent, since the core of the drama takes place in the purely musical layer. Music interprets the text; it completes the text and explains it. Interestingly, in large fragments—that is, nearly in the whole first movement—the Copernican Symphony does not have any text at all. As Adrian Thomas writes, „Górecki directs the listener's attention to instrumental images without text, created by a huge orchestra."[14]

The Copernican Symphony consists of two movements performed *attaca*. Singing appears at the end of the dynamic first movement, before flourishing in the diametrically opposed, contemplative second movement, where it plays a primary role. The contrast between the dramatic first movement and the slow and static second movement is the core formative principle for this composition.[15] On the micro-level, the first movement is contrasted internally from the point of view of tempi, expression, and harmony. An intense, and at times even brutal type of expression predominates here, emphasized by all the musical elements—dissonant harmony, decisive articulation, and contrasting dynamics. In the second movement, however, one can observe a shift to creating the form on the basis of a „nuanced contrast" which is typical in later works by Górecki.[16] The second movement is

---

[13] Cited from J. Woroniecki OP, *Pełnia modlitwy* [*The Fullness of Prayer*] (Poznań 1984), 146.
[14] Thomas, *op. cit.*, 104.
[15] Pociej, *op. cit.*, 4.
[16] See Krzysztof Droba, *Górecki*, in *Encyklopedia*, *op. cit.*, 431.

developing in a way that reminds one of the arch form, with a double culmination on the words „luminaria" and „solem." Simultaneously, however, it shows a strong predilection for a teleological orientation, with its inexorable motion towards the finale. Here, Górecki applies a very interesting and quite atypical formal gesture. In the conclusion of the solo parts in the second movement the chorus appears to intone, with words from Copernicus's treatise, a quotation from a four-part chorale from the fifteenth century, *Laude digna prole*. This quotation, borrowed from the Antiphonary of Bożogrobcy from Miechów, creates the „ideological" and expressive climax for the entire Symphony. In the purely auditive dimension, it appears to be the arrival point, the climax and the final statement of the second movement. However, after this final culmination there is yet another sequence, a sustained pentatonic chord lasting for several minutes.

By introducting this „anti-developmental" and static, but simultaneously, internally shimmering and pulsating sonority, the composer achieved an impression of stopping the flow of musical time. The „progress" or „action" of music ends, as it were, with the silencing of the human voices. In this way, there is a certain dissonance created between the large-scale architecture of the work and the perception of the flow of time. The quotation is introduced near the golden section of the second movement (in terms of duration), but it is, in auditory perception, heard as the work's finale, its arrival point.

It is important to emphasize that despite the basic expressive contrast between the first and second movements, there exists, nevertheless, a kinship of materials. In the whole Copernican Symphony the quasi-refrain motive returns repatedly; it consists of chromatically descending dyads and is constructed by shifting two whole-tone complexes by a minor second. This refrain accompanies the invocation „Deus" in the sections of the symphony that use text. This motive also plays a significant, double role in the entire composition. On the one hand, as the „core motive" that constantly evolves, it becomes the source of the melodic layer of the whole work. On the other hand, however, in certain moments it appears in the original dyad-form— and, as such, it may be considered as a kind of a Leitmotif for the whole *Symphony* (see Figure 9–1, a and b).

Fig.9-1a Fig. 9-1b

Figure 9-1, a – b: H. M. Górecki, Symphony No. 2, Op. 31, *Copernican*, beginnings of both mvements. H. M. Górecki, *II Symfonia „Kopernikowska"* na sopran solo, baryton solo, chór mieszany i wielką orkiestrę. © 1974 PWM Edition, Kraków, Poland. Extract Used by Kind Permission of Polskie Wydawnictwo Muzyczne, Kraków, Poland.

While focusing on the function of particular elements in the shaping of the large-scale form, it is important to emphasize that the Symphony's most important, form-generating aspect is the idea of a concrete, characteristic type of sonority that provides the background against which a broad melodic phrase is introduced. This moment marks the appearance of the voice.

This sonority is created primarily from elements of harmony, texture and orchestration. During one of his seminars, Górecki pointed out that harmony is the primary element that determines the uniqueness of a given composition.[17] It is beyond doubt that the sonorities in the Copernican Symphony result from the use of a particular compositional technique, present in the composer's works from the mid 1960s and called „reductionism" by Krzysztof Droba.[18] This technique consists of increasingly greater reduction of the material in subsequent compositions, while simultaneously maximizing the form, and intensifying the expression. The reduction of material in the Second Symphony is not perhaps as radical as in later works (and it also does not pertain to the Symphony as a whole), but it possesses the characteristic features of Górecki's compositional language: repetitiveness of motivic and harmonic structures, limiting the number of distinct sonorities in certain segments of the work, and using carefully selected types of intervals. These techniques are coupled with the frequent treatment of the orchestral apparatus—to use the composer's words—as one voice, a timbral monolith, that appears to be „one instrument," similar to the *tutti* register in the organ.[19]

A manifestation of this reductionist approach is, for instance, the melodic layer in the first section of the first movement—that recurs as a refrain. It is composed merely of four sounds: C-sharp, D-sharp, E, and F-sharp. Another feature of Górecki's „reductionisim" is using one type of sonority or interval in extended sections of a composition, such

---

[17] See *Konwersatorium* with H. M. Górecki dedicated to *Beatus vir*, Baranów Sandomierski, September 1979; in Kinga Kiwała, *Problematyka sacrum w polskiej muzyce współczesnej na podstawie wybranych utworów związanych z osobą Ojca Świętego Jana Pawła II*, M.A. thesis (Kraków: Akademia Muzyczna, 2002).
[18] See Droba, *Górecki*, in *Encyklopedia, op. cit.*, 430-431.
[19] *Konwersatorium... op. cit.*

as the whole-tone sonorities in the first movement; or the pentatonic sonorities and the A major chord in its first inversion that appear in the second movement.

Interpretation

3.1. The Symbolic Function of Music

Górecki's Copernican Symphony is not a work that would have had its essence contained within and limited to its purely compositional aspects. Instead, it carries a profound message that is both ideological and symbolic. At its foundation lies, as the composer revealed himself, an individual intepretation of the Copernican discovery—an event that awakens not only fascination, but also (and primarily) existential terror. This idea was suggested to the composer by film director, Krzysztof Zanussi. Such an interpretation influenced, to use the expression of the composer, a particular „binary" nature („dwoistość") of the Symphony's form—with the first movement portraying the mechanism of the world („mechanizm świata") and the second movement representing its contemplation („kontemplacja").[20]

It seems, therefore, that the essence of the Second Symphony lies in its particular dialectical nature, primarily in its approach to the „Copernican theme" that has a profound impact on the construction of the work. The „cosmic" dynamism of the first movement may evoke, —within the framework of what the composer calls „the mechanism of the world"—the battle of the elements, the clash of some enormous energies, and, at times, also a musical image of chaos. (As an example, see the section *furioso-marcatissimo*, with elements *ad libitum* reproduced in Figure 9-2).

---

[20] H. M. Górecki, *Powiem Państwu szczerze...*, op. cit., 45.

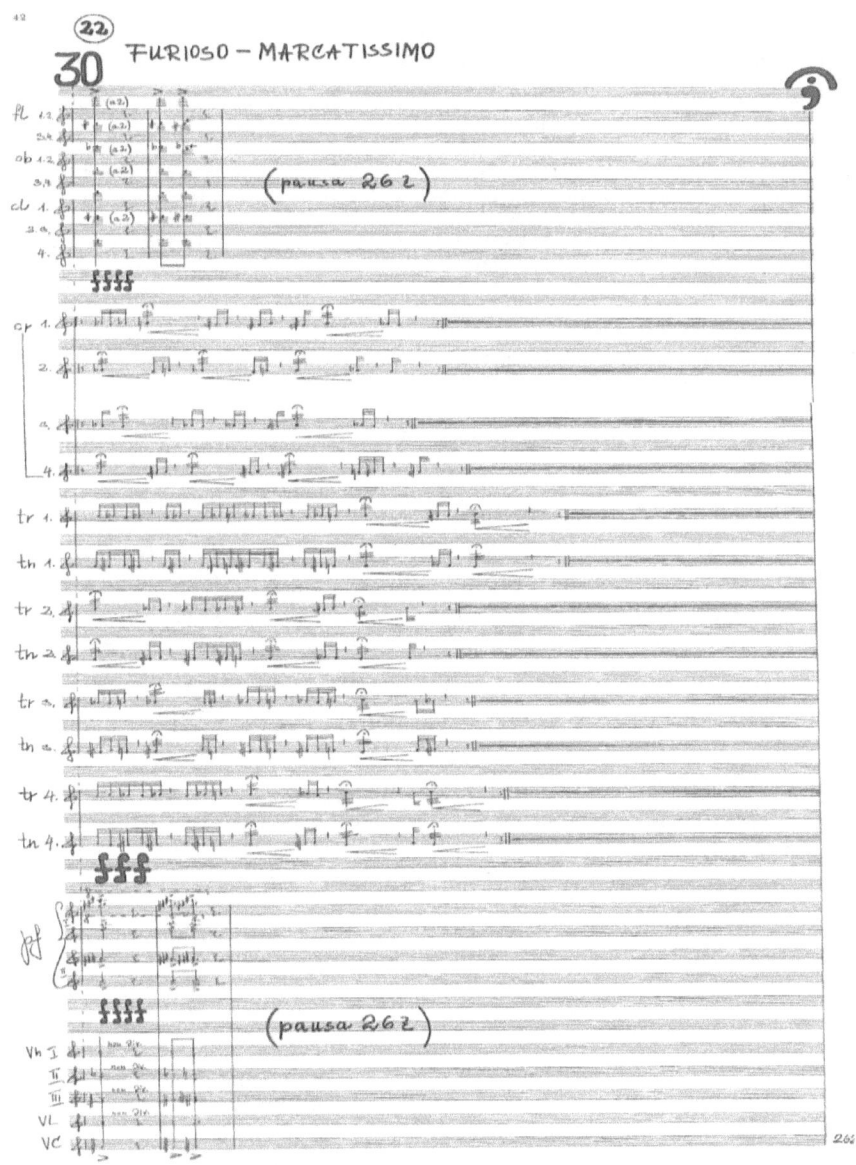

Figure 9-2: H. M. Górecki, Symphony No. 2, Op. 31, *Copernican*, first movement, 42. **H. M. Górecki,** *II Symfonia „Kopernikowska"* **na sopran solo, baryton solo, chór mieszany i wielką orkiestrę. © 1974 PWM Edition, Kraków, Poland. Extract Used by Kind Permission of Polskie Wydawnictwo Muzyczne, Kraków, Poland.**

According to Krzysztof Droba, the first movement of the Copernican Symphony may be located, along with the first movement of *The*

Symphony of Sorrowful Songs, among the most dramatic music ever composed by Górecki.[21] Dominated by radical expressive markings (*marcatissimo, con massima passione, con massima espressione, con grande tensione, ma ben tenuto*, all the way through *energico, ritmico* and *furioso*), this movement has evoked in its interpreters visual and „cosmic" associations. Teresa Malecka described it as an „enormous explosion" („wielki wybuch"), Mieczysław Tomaszewski as an „Apocaliptic chaos of the beginning" („apokaliptyczny chaos początku"), and Władysław Stróżewski wrote that it emits „the awe of the power of the Universe and the horror of the Apocalipse" („groza potęgi wszechświata i groza Apokalipsy").[22]

Bohdan Pociej interpreted this first movement of the Copernican Symphony as a kind of a „drama of creation" („dramat stwarzania").[23] In this context, it is significant to point out that the human voice appears only at the very end of this movement, to be fully developed in the diametrically different second movement. It is also important to emphasize that in Górecki's music from this period, singing plays a deeply significant function, associated with the element of subjectivity.[24] This general characteristics of his style allows us to interpret the vocal part in the Second Symphony simply as a voice of a concrete, individual person (a „creation"). This interpretation is convincing especially in reference to the contemplative second movement, where singing—this time mostly performed by the soloists, the baritone and the soprano—plays a formal-creative role.

---

[21] See Krzysztof Droba, *Górecki*, in *Encyklopedia*, op. cit., 431.
[22] See Bohdan Pociej, *Kosmos, tradycja i brzmienie*, op. cit., 4; Bohdan Pociej, *Bycie w muzyce. Próba opisania twórczości Henryka Mikołaja Góreckiego*, (Katowice, 2005), 131; Teresa Malecka, „Górecki's creative journeys between nature and culture. Around the 'Copernican' Symphony," in: *Interdyscyplinary Studies in Musicology* (Poznań, 2010); Władysław Stróżewski, „Recenzja w związku z nadaniem profesorowi Henrykowi Mikołajowi Góreckiemu tytułu doktora honoris causa Akademii Muzycznej w Krakowie;" in *Profesor Henryk Mikołaj Górecki, doktor honoris causa Akademii Muzycznej w Krakowie*, (an occasional publication, Kraków: Akademia Muzyczna, 2008); Mieczysław Tomaszewski, „Recenzja w związku z nadaniem profesorowi Henrykowi Mikołajowi Góreckiemu tytułu doktora honoris causa Akademii Muzycznej w Krakowie;" in *Profesor Henryk Mikołaj Górecki*, op. cit.
[23] Bohdan Pociej, *Kosmos, tradycja i brzmienie*, op. cit., 4.
[24] The composer discussed this issue in the context of *Beatus Vir*. See *Konwersatorium*, op. cit.

This movement is a meditation, filled both with delight and enchantment, but also with a sense of wonder evoked by the work of the Creator that goes far beyond the scope of knowledge of a human being. The music, full of internal focus, is defined by radically different dynamic and tempo markings than those that appeared in the first movement: *lento sostenuto contemplativo, largo tranquilissimo cantabilissimo,* and *molto lento semplice.* In interpretations of this movement of the Second Symphony the following expressions were used: „a meditation filled with delight" („pełna zachwytu medytacja"), „a religious adagio that magnifies spiritual elation" („religijne *adagio* potęgujące duchowe uniesienie")—by Bohdan Pociej; „the world of contemplation of beauty" („świat kontemplacji piękna")—by Teresa Malecka; or the „harmonious Divine Cosmos, that is contemplated and praised by the unified, at the end, duet of the baritone and the soprano" („harmonijny Kosmos Boży, kontemplowany i sławiony zgodnym na koniec dwugłosem barytonu i sopranu")—by Mieczysław Tomaszewski.[25]

This music brings to mind a comment by Pope John Paul II from his *Letter to the Artists* [*List do artystów*]: „In the face of miracles of the universe, delight is the only adequate stance." („W obliczu cudów wszechświata zachwyt jest jedyną adekwatną postawą.").[26] Krzysztof Droba writes: „in Górecki's music of the 1970s, the word starts where the music ends."[27] In reference to the Second Symphony, this sentence could be taken literally: the purely instrumental narrative in the first movement finds its completion and verbalization in the second movement.

As Górecki admitted, the verbal layer provided him with a point of departure for the music. He believed that, in a musical work, the connection of the word with the sound should be as natural as possible:[28]

---

[25] See Bohdan Pociej, *Kosmos, tradycja i brzmienie,op. cit.,* 4; Pociej, *Bycie w muzyce,op. cit,* 131; Teresa Malecka, *Górecki's creative journeys between nature and culture,op. cit*; Mieczysław. Tomaszewski, *Recenzja w związku z nadaniem, op. cit.*
[26] Jan Paweł II, *List do artystów,* Vatican (4 April 1999): 16.
[27] K. Droba, *Słowo w muzyce Góreckiego, op. cit.,* 4.
[28] H. M. Górecki's statement during the general discussion at the seminar on *Aktualna sytuacja muzyki religijnej i liturgicznej w Polsce,* in *Muzyka religijna w Polsce. Materiały i studia,*ed. ks. J. Pikulik, vol. 10 (Warsaw: ATK, 1988), 86.

> I believe that every word gives birth to a particular kind of sonority, this specific kind and not any other (...) We find a confirmation of this in the analysis of the pieces by Bach, Beethoven, Mozart and other great composers, where music complements the words and the words complement music. The content of the words is in this and no other sonority (...) You cannot compose music independently of its text.

In the Second Symphony, the composer pays particular attention to the words: „caelum" (heaven), „luminaria" (lights), and „solem"(the sun), while at the same time using characteristic melodic, harmonic, dynamic and textural gestures that are rooted in the tradition of musical symbolism. It is essential to note that the composer, by emphasizing the elements of the verbal layer through music, simultaneously conducts a particular „interpretation" of this text. Górecki's music is foreign to any convention and artificiality; all emphasized words are naturally blended into the flow of the musical narrative.

The fundamental way of emphasizing important textual expressions is their **repetitiveness.** This is an essential feature not only of the verbal layer of the Symphony, but also of other components, especially of the melody and harmony. It does not mean a „mechanical" repetition of melodic and harmonic patterns (similarly to *minimal music*), but rather provides the foundation for a particular, individual type of structuring the music, that serves to accomplish particular expressive goals. Repetitiveness assists in the emergence of a typical type of contrast, characteristics in Górecki's music and called by Krzysztof Droba a „nuanced" contrast. In the face of obsessive repetitiveness, the impact of every, even the smallest, change is magnified. In vocal-instrumental works, this contract is usually justified by semantics and expression; it has a great significance for the musical interpretation of the verbal text.

The repetitiveness of the words in the Second Symphony pertains only to the sections of the text that have been borrowed from the Psalms. The composer repeats whole verses of the Biblical text, and, at the same time, emphasizes (by repetition) individual words. In the foreground is the word „Deus"—an invocation that appears twice already in the psalm itself. It is magnified in the flow of the music by repeated recurrences. Thus, it becomes a kind of a reference point for the whole composition. The other repetitive words—„caelum",

„luminaria"—are connected to the „cosmological" and „light-related" layer, and related at the same time to the main idea of the composition. Significantly, the appearance of these words marks the main climaxes of the Symphony.

For the word „caelum" Górecki introduces an extensive, chromatic and oscillating melodic line that with great effort continually climbs upwards. It is accompanied by a gradual intensification of tension (*con sempre piu grande tensione et espressione*), expression (*stringendo*), and dynamics. Adrian Thomas proposed an interesting interpretation of this phrase: „Trying to comprehend the Lord's work, slowly and with great effort, the baritone aims towards higher sounds in the point of the climax..."[29] This first climax falls at the initial occurrence of the word „luminaria" in this movement. Here, the baritone ascends to the highest sound so far—E-flat4—and the dynamics reaches for the first time the level of *fff*. Nonetheless, it is the harmony that plays the most important role: the word „lights" is accompanied with the sonority of a pure A-flat major triad in the first inversion.

The impact of this effect, traditional since the oratorio *The Creation of the World* by Joseph Haydn, is magnified in Górecki's Symphony, because such a pure sonority appears for the first time since the beginning of this composition. From this moment on, it always accompanies the word „luminaria" and—what is significant—as the „sonority of light" it also closes the entire composition. Moreover, in the first climax, the composer uses yet another, important gesture: while the „luminaria" word resounds, the melodic line continues its ascent but it is suddenly taken over by the soprano, in *subito p* dynamics. The melody follows the notes of the Dorian mode based on E-flat, all the way up to G-flat5. The clearly legible symbolism of this broad melodic line resembles the rhethorical figure of *ascensus*, that traditionally accompanied words associated with the ascent to heaven, and spiritual growth. In this context, it may also be associated with the spreading of the light.

A different interpretation of this segment is offered by Teresa Malecka:[30]

---

[29] A. Thomas, *op. cit.*, 106.
[30] Teresa Malecka, *Górecki's creative journeys...*, *op. cit.*

> This simple singing of the soprano and the baritone, an octave apart, expresses, as it were, the delight of human beings: man and woman express their delight over the created Universe made by God, as we read in the Genesis: 'And God saw everything that he made and it was very good.'

This climax at the word „luminaria"—while almost ecstatic—turns out to be merely the first climax in the whole composition. The second climax will emerge soon, and rather unexpectedly, just in a moment, on the word „solem." At this climax, the soloists reach the absolutely highest registers in the entire Symphony: the sounds of A-flat5 in the soprano part and of F4 in the part of the baritone. The orchestra plays here, for the first time, *tutti*, with a dynamic level of *subito fff*. Additionally, various instrumental means are used to „brighten" the texture—high register of strings, wind instruments and the piano, or the harp *glissando*. Both „light-filled" climaxes of this movement may be considered as parts of the same, extended though divided, climax.

It is important to point out that the musical symbolism of the light is not limited in Górecki's Second Symphony to the vocal-instrumental fragments. One of the most inspired musical images of „Cosmos" understood as the absolute harmony of elements may be found in the penultimate sonority of the Symphony. This is a pentatonic cluster that is born nearly from nothing, grows from the lowest to the highest registers, and is brightened by successive entries of the strings (multiplied divisi), as well as by other instruments. This long, static, but also opalescent sonority saturates the whole available pitch space to the maximum. Bohdan Pociej writes about „the light, the sublime and pure sonority" that come into being in these final measures of the Copernican Symphony. While listening to this luminous music, Immanuel Kant's words come to mind: „A starry sky above us..."

To sum up, the first movement of the Copernican Symphony may be considered as a *sui generis* „objective presentation of the universe" whereas the second movement is a person's subjective reaction to the universe. In accordance with the interpreation by Bohdan Pociej, the first movement portrays the creative act. In this context, is is not without significance that human voices appear only at the end of this movement—since in the Biblical description of creation, human beings appear as the final, most perfect creation of the Creator.

Leszek Polony interprets this issue differently, writing: [31]

> In Górecki's music, this aspect that could be called cosmic „ontophany" and „hierophany"—that is the revelation of existence and the sacred perception of the Universe—are integrally connected to the „theophany," a revelation of God in a human dimension, in the internal experience of a human being.

3.2. The Role of Quotations: Folk and Religious Tradition

In one of interviews concering, among other issues, the Second Symphony, Górecki stated: „I am fascinated by tradition; sometimes it is just one phrase that does not leave me alone."[32] The particular role of national roots, expecially of the folk and church music, is an extremely important aspect of Górecki's works composed after 1970s. According to Teresa Malecka,[33]

> Górecki's attachment to his homeland means not only being interested in the land, its landscapes, nature, people, but first and foremost reveals his profound roots in the history, religion, and Christian culture.

A proof of Górecki's return to the roots is his use of texts that are monuments of ancient Polish literature, as well as quotations from the Bible, translated in the 16th century by Father Jakub Wujek. Nonetheless, the living presence of tradition is revealed primarily by specific traits of Górecki's music itself: it is filled with gestures typical of Polish folklore. It is important to point out, however, that this is not an artificial stylization, but rather a „natural" trait of the composer's individual language. Another trait revealing Górecki's attachment to tradition is his habit of quoting ancient Polish folk and religious melodies.

---

[31] Leszek Polony,„„Jeszcze o nowym romantyzmie," in *W kręgu muzycznej wyobraźni. Eseje, artykuły, recenzje* (Kraków: PWM, 1980), 220.
[32] H. M. Górecki, *Powiem Państwu szczerze...*, op. cit., 45.
[33] Teresa Malecka, „Między symfonią a pieśnią. Próba analizy integralnej *Symfonii pieśni żałosnych* H. M. Góreckiego," in *Muzyka w kontekście kultury*, ed. M. Janicka – Słysz, T. Malecka, K. Szwajgier (Kraków: Akademia Muzyczna, 2001), 798.

While introducing a quotation from a fifteenth-century chorale, *Laude digna prole* in the Copernican Symphony, Górecki preserved not only its original melody but also its setting in a four-part texture, *nota contra notam*. He merely replaced the original text with the words by Copernicus. It is important to point out that the composer had earlier used this chorale in an orchestral fanfare, *Wratislaviae gloria*. Thus, we can conclude that the *Laude digna prole* chorale is among the most significant melodies of lasting fascination for the composer. (See Figures 9-3 and 9-4).

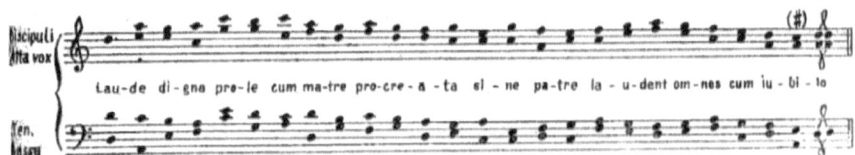

Figure 9-3: Chorale *Laude digna prole* from the Antiphonal by Bożogrobcy from Miechów (15th century).

A quotation may play different roles in Górecki's Copernican Symphony— architectural, semantic or symbolic. While appearing in the „golden mean" point of the second movement, the chorale also serves as a summary and the arrival point for the musical action of the whole composition. Thus, it becomes the conceptual culmination of the entire Copernican Symphony.

Musicological studies about musical quotations often emphasize that quotations of a foreign piece of music are not accidental and that they are designed to awaken particular associations. Zofia Lissa points out that quotations may serve as Leitmotifs, symbols or extramusical allusions,[34] while Mieczysław Tomaszewski states that quotations are meant to „evoke particular association of a sentimental or symbolic character, of an ideological or a patriotic nature."[35] It is important to note that the chorale cited by Górecki is not particularly easy to be recognized; on the contrary, even in the 1950s it was completely unknown.[36]

---

[34] Zofia Lissa, „O cytacie w muzyce," in: Lissa, *Szkice z estetyki muzycznej* (Kraków: PWM, 1965), 271.
[35] Mieczysław Tomaszewski, *Muzyka Chopina na nowo odczytana. Studia i interpretacje* (Kraków: Akademia Muzyczna, 1996), 117.
[36] See Adam Sutkowski, „Nieznane zabytki muzyki wielogłosowej z polskich rękopisów chorałowych XIII i XV wieku" in *Muzyka* 3 (1958), 28-36; Adam

Figure 9-4a. H. M. Górecki, Symphony No. 2 *Copernican*, 2nd mvt., p. 78.
Extract Used by Kind Permission of Polskie Wydawnictwo Muzyczne,
Kraków, Poland.

Sutkowski, "Organum 'Surrexit Christus hodie' i inne zabytki średniowiecznej muzyki wielogłosowej," *Ruch Muzyczny* 19 (1958), 2-6. Górecki probably found this chorale in one of these articles. As cited by Thomas, *op. cit.*, 106.

Figure 9-4b. H. M. Górecki, Second Symphony *Copernican*, 2nd movement, pp. 78-79. Extract Used by Kind Permission of Polskie Wydawnictwo Muzyczne, Kraków, Poland.

However, because of its complex features that are characteristic of early church music, it is easy to grasp its general „religious idiom." In the context of the Symphony's theme and its symbolism, to introduce such a quotation means to confirm the sacral references of this music.

The chorale that accompanies the words of Copernicus „about „the heavens that encompasses everything that is beautiful" is both focused to the highest degree and filled with noble simplicity. Simultaneously, it appears to praise the type of beauty that is understood in medieval terms as the *consonatia et claritas* (harmony and brightness)—this fact again, may evoke cosmological associations in the Symphony.

A significant issue pertains to the relationship of the musical material of this quotation to the „original" music of the Second Symphony. According to Mieczysław Tomaszewski, „a quotation by its very nature functions as a 'foreign' text that is cited in quotations marks; that is not one's own."[37] However, in Górecki's Symphony the chorale—while bringing in a new sound quality—seems to be, to use the phrase from Kazimierz Nowacki, „ideally melded with the atmosphere of this movement of the Symphony."[38] Similarly, Bohdan Pociej writes:[39]

> Here (...) the genius and the sonic imagination of the composer celebrates the greatest triumph over the historical time. The transition from the contemporary sound world to a sound world from four centuries earlier, and then a return to the contemporary world, is not any kind of a „leap;" it is not a transition, or retrograde motion. This chorus is the „echo of a respected past," while simultaneously, the tradition that it symbolizes appears to us as a great, marvellous **now.**

Therefore, the early music quotation in Górecki's Copernican Symphony does not function as a „foreign body" but it is perceived—to cite Mieczysław Tomaszewski again—as „an unexpected sonority that is simultaneously subconsciously expected."[40] This quotation is

---

[37] Mieczysław Tomaszewski, *Krzysztof Penderecki i jego muzyka. Cztery eseje* (Kraków: Akademia Muzyczna, 1994), note to p. 43.
[38] K. Nowacki, „H. M. Górecki. II Symfonia," *in Program Festiwalu „Warszawska Jesień" 1993*, 136.
[39] Pociej, *Kosmos, tradycja, brzmienie... op. cit.*, 4.
[40] Tomaszewski, *Krzysztof Penderecki i jego muzyka, op. cit.*, 64.

organically connected with the flow of the music that precedes and follows its appearance. We can assign to it a similar meaning that quotations play in the oeuvre of Krzysztof Penderecki. Tomaszewski points out that quotations in Penderecki's music „constitute an organic part of a work, its kernel rather than an addition; a kind of a *cantus prius factus*, that carry content „the meaning of which may be defined as a return to values that were recklessly lost."[41] The scholar names such „revelation" in music endowed with symbolic meanings „a moment of an epiphany" („moment epifaniczny").[42] Such moments most often evoke „religious, transcendental climate" and their characteristic features are: the limitation of musical means, contrast with the music that precedes their appearance, and a reference to a certain, characteristic sacral idiom.[43] In Górecki's Symphony, the quotation, even though its introduction appears to logically stem from the flow of the music, also has an impact of such a „moment of an epiphany." It is hard to find, however, the contrast of material, because the technique of reductionism is a characteristic feature of the entire composition.

In the Second Symphony contrast consists primarily in a particular, limited, difference of the expressive tone. In most of the second movement, the narrative is conducted from a subjective point of view—as it were—it is a meditation of a human being about the beauty of creation, at times a meditation filled with contemplative reflection, and at other times a meditation that reaches the level of ecstasy. This feature is underscored by suggestive markings for expression used by the composer—*sostenuto contemplativo, con massima espressione*, etc.

While the chorus sings the ancient chorale, the music is tinged with pentatonic elements in the strings, the chanting of brass instruments, and the "unreal" strikes of the tam-tam. Thus, the entire chorale quotation seems to come "from the outside," constituting an objective, universal "commentary" on the whole Symphony. While presenting Copernicus' words, this music simultaneously answers doubts and "glances" into the transcendent, eternal perspective.

---

[41] *Ibidem*, 17.
[42] See „'Sacrum i profanum w muzyce' - Z prof. M. Tomaszewskim rozmawia M. Janicka-Słysz," *Maszkaron* (January-March 2000), 3.
[43] *Ibidem*.

The presence of tradition in Górecki's Second Symphony is not limited to the use of quotation. The entire work is penetrated by the spirit of folk and church music. This is the situation that Teresa Malecka writes about: [44]

> Material from all sources may come into the work to be manifest in it, while preserving a different type of relationship with the original. This association with the concrete material is close and direct—in the case of quotations and variants. It may also be freer and concerned with a set of characteristics typical of a particular musical composition.

This distinctive "set of features" includes Górecki's oscillating melodic line, which can be associated with the chorale; melodies that often refer to modality and diatonicity; as well as some harmonic solutions. Typical in the piece, especially in its second movement, is tonal instability. Despite its dominance in the second movement, the Symphony's tonal center of E-flat, which constitutes a certain "sonic axis," oscillates between tonal and modal functioning. In the tonal sense, it refers to the harmonic E Minor; in the modal sense, it is a Dorian mode on E-flat. Similarly, at the culmination of the word "luminaria," the composer uses several chords related to each other through traditional, quasi-functional relationships. These tonal allusions are greatly weakened, however, by avoiding the leading tone and introducing the apparent dominant instead of the traditional dominant (E-flat and A-flat chords). In addition, the chords are usually not placed in a root position, but rather appear in inversions, in parallel motion. They also may be replaced by chords in parallel keys (E-flat minor replaced by G-flat major). This further emphasizes the tonal instability, obscures and hinders the unambiguous definition of the dominant key. These characteristics, typical of folk music, endow Górecki's Symphony with a special stamp of authenticity. Antonin Sychra writes:[45]

---

[44] Teresa Malecka, „Rosyjska muzyka ludowa w muzyce Mikołaja A. Rimskiego – Korsakowa," in *Spotkania muzyczne w Baranowie*, ed. T. Malecka, L. Polony, (Kraków: PWM, 1980), 110.
[45] Antoni Sychra, *Antonin Dvořak. Zur Ästhetik seines sinfonischen Schaffens* (Leipzig: VEB Deutscher Verlag für Musik, 1973), 37.

> The composer can adapt to the melodious, harmonic and rhythmic qualities of folk songs. His music will then bear a distinctive, appealing stamp, but in no case will it become folklore. The true connection with folklore and national character can only be identified when the composer captures the thinking and musical perception of the people, their experiences, and their spiritual condition.

It seems that Górecki's Symphony fits in with such national, folklore-based music, deeply rooted in the spirituality and traditions of the nation.

3.3. The Copernican Symphony and the „Sublime"

The aesthetic category of sublimity—organically melded with the notion of sacrum—is attributed to Górecki's music in almost all writings dealing with his works from the seventies and eighties of the twentieth century. Krzysztof Droba explicitly states that Górecki's compositions from that period, beginning with *Ad Matrem* (1971), pursue "the idea of sacred music, the sacrum."[46]

Before attempting to interpret Górecki's Symphony No. 2 in the light of the category of sublimity, it is worthwhile to focus on this concept itself and trace its understanding in the history of **aesthetics.**

Modernity owes the revival and the re-imagining of the category of the sublime to Immanuel Kant. While this notion was present in the philosophical thought (not only in aesthetics) already in the antiquity, until the eighteenth century, loftiness/sublimity was not a separate aesthetic category. Usually, it was treated as a desirable aspect, or a kind of a "modification," of beauty. The beauty of sublimity, typical of the „great" or „high" art, contrasted beauty with lightness, at least according to Plato. For Horace—as Władysław Tatarkiewicz reminds us—*pulcher* always meant the same as "sublime."[47] The first theoretical study of the „sublime" in literary language was presented in the first century BC. Pseudo-Longinos distinguished five features of the "noble style:" 1. the idealizing way of thinking, 2. an intense and

---

[46] Droba, *Górecki*, in: *Encyklopedia, op. cit.*, 424.
[47] See Władysław Tatarkiewicz, *Historia estetyki*, vol. I. (Wrocław-Kraków: Ossolineum, 1960), 19, 142.

inspired pathos, 3. the application of rhetorical figures, 4. a noble expression, 5. the arrangement of words and sentences that's full of dignity and inspiration.[48] In ancient belief, sublimity is the peak of expression: it enchants and captivates. It is also no accident that in ancient times two literary genres were born, which, in a sense, are dedicated to expressing the category of the sublime: an ode and a hymn.

An intuitive understanding that emerged among the thinkers of antiquity distinguishes loftiness from beauty. It found its theoretical expression in eighteenth-century philosophy in the reflections of Edmund Burke and Immanuel Kant. The time in which this reflection developed was not accidental—the Enlightenment resurrected the interest in the category of the sublime, observed among other aesthetic categories. The sublime could be found in nature, but it was desirable above all in the arts.[49] This concept was henceforth most often associated with the value of **greatness.**

Burke, according to his subjectivist axiological orientation, defined sublimity not as an objective phenomenon, but as a feeling, or a special state of the soul.[50] This is—reminds us Maria Gołaszewska—a kind of horror that creates satisfaction; in other words, a kind of serenity marked with a sense of horror that is born of astonishment resulting from an encounter with something great.[51] Interestingly, the philosopher listed factors that had the power to produce such a feeling: mystery, darkness, infinity, glamor, light, uncertainty, suddenness, difficulty and pain, but above all the imagination of power (in its peak form—the majesty of God), and the physical magnitude (understood primarily as height and depth).[52]

---

[48] See Maria Gołaszewska, *Istota i istnienie wartości* (Warszawa, 1990), 231.
[49] See Mieczysław Tomaszewski, „Romantyczna pieśń religijna: od 'credo' po 'confiteor'" [Romantic religious song: from „credo" to „confiteor"] in *Od wyznania do wołania. Studia nad pieśnią romantyczną. [From Confession to Calling: Studies in Romantic Song]* Kraków: Akademia Muzyczna, 1997), 164.
[50] See Edmund Burke, *Dociekania filozoficzne o pochodzeniu naszych idei wzniosłości i piękna*, Polish translation by P. Graff (Warszawa 1968), 63.
[51] See Gołaszewska, *Istota i istnienie wartości*, op. cit., 232.
[52] See Władysław Stróżewski, *O wielkości. Szkice z filozofii człowieka* (Kraków, 2002), 291-292.

The concept of "size" provided another source for Kant's reflections." „We call that sublime which is absolutely great," writes the philosopher in the *Critique of Judgment*, adding, "it is the size equal to only itself."[53] The so-called sublime, referring to the notion of infinity, is not to be found in this world, but only in the ideas of our intellect. What is significant, Kant does not exclude the possibility of encountering the sublime while facing harsh and dynamic nature (such as the raging sea) that would give the impression of infinity to a person endowed with sensitivity and imagination. It is significant that—like Burke—Kant also considers the sublime in a dialectical sense. It is[54]

> a feeling of displeasure, arising from the inadequacy of imagination in the aesthetic estimation of magnitude to attain to its estimation by reason, and a simultaneously awakened pleasure, arising from this very judgement of the inadequacy of the greatest faculty of sense being in accord with ideas of reason, so far as the effort to attain to these is for us a law.

In the twentieth century the reflection on the sublime was found, among others in the writings of phenomenologists, and—what is also notable, and even paradoxical—in the texts by postmodern philosophers. From the first group, Nicolai Hartmann, when analyzing this aesthetic category, draws attention to the difficulty of specifying what it is. The philosopher distinguishes a number of variations in this aesthetic value without going through—as Maria Gołaszewska points out—to the final view that would synthesize these different aspects into a unified whole.[55] Hartmann distinguishes the sublime appearing in human life, from the sublime nature (understood as an aesthetic category), and from the artistic sublimity. This value occurs everywhere when we encounter something large and powerful: the heights of the mountains, but also the miraculous life of the cell viewed through the microscope.

These examples demonstrate the assocation of sublimity with "raising something" above the normal level. The philosopher's essential

---

[53] Immanuel Kant, *Krytyka władzy sądzenia*, transl. J. Gałecki (Warszawa, 1964), 136. Cited from English translation, *Critique of Judgment* (Oxford University Press, 2007), 88.
[54] Ibidem, 152.
[55] See Gołaszewska, *Istota i istnienie wartości, op. cit*, 233.

statement is that the "substance" of aesthetics is the moral sublime, occurring in human life. In order for aesthetic loftiness to emerge, there is a need for distance and tranquility that would allow its perception. This kind of the sublime occurs, for example, in the phenomena of nature. In contrast, in the arts, we are dealing with artistic sublimity. In order for the sublime to be constituted here, certain essential features must be present in the artwork: magnitude, magnificence, seriousness, celebration, mystery, depth, violence, monumentalism, and so forth. It can be said that the appearance of the sublime as a certain aesthetic value in a work of art depends on the occurrence of other related values.[56]

A philosopher of postmodernism, Francois Lyotard, considered the aesthetic loftiness in association with postmodern criticism of the *mimesis* category. In his conception, this philosopher reached a certain limit, which is possibly symptomatic of postmodernism in general. According to Lyotard, the loftiness „extinguishes" representation. The sublime is what is not presentable. The author writes:[57]

> The sublime (...) takes place...when the imagination fails to present an object which might, if only in principle, come to match a concept. We have the Idea of the world (the totality of what is), but we do not have the capacity to show an example of it. (....) We can conceive the infinitely great, the infinitely powerful, but every presentation of an object destined to "make visible" this absolute greatness or power appear to us painfully inadequate.

The inexpressible can not be presented: it is. The absolute cannot be presented: it is. Exaggerated artworks may depict it negatively and thus attest to the impossibility of presentation. So, according to Lyotard, the art of experimentation is exalted by rejecting the beauty of the form that allowed the consensus of taste. *Here, now, it happens that ...* and this is the whole picture. The fact that *here and now* the image exists, rather than nothing—is just lofty, writes Lyotard.[58]

---

[56]See N. Hartmann, *Ästetik*, 2nd edition (Berlin 1966), 363ff.
[57] Francis Lyotard, *Postmodernizm dla dzieci* [Postmodernism for children] transl. J. Migasiński (Warszawa, 1998), 20-21.
[58] Francis Lyotard, „Wzniosłość i awangarda" in *Teksty drugie* 2/3 (1996), 181, cited after M. Matysek, „Nowa aisthesis," *Magazyn sztuki* 28 (2001). English

Maria Gołaszewska's summary of contemporary ideas of the sublime emphasizes that the element of absoluteness is being highlighted in this category. Here, artworks come closer to the limits of possibility. According to Gołaszewska, loftiness in the arts involves the explication of distinctive elements using appropriate means, such as monumentalization, or the high level of saturation of color (in painting, using saturated colors, or expanses of white). However, she warns that the actualization of sublimity in the arts is connected with the danger of exaggeration and unnaturalness.[59]

It appears that the greatest impact on the aesthetic-**musical** reflection had the classic understanding of the category of the sublime that originated in antiquity. In this concept, the sublime is tantamount to the "high" style, typical of certain literary and musical genres, such as an ode or a hymn. This way of reasoning refers to a certain, sanctified tradition, or the convention. Following this trajectory, Mieczysław Tomaszewski, in his analysis of Robert Schumann's *Dedication*, emphasized that musical determinants of a high, sublime style can include: transparency and architectural clarity, focused texture, as well as balanced and well-structured harmony and metre.[60] An attempt to capture the musical idiom of the sublime appears in studies of specific musical genres for which sublimity constitutes an essential quality. Father Karol Mrowiec states that for the musical „hymnity" (as a synonym of lofty style) to emerge, the characteristic "use of slow movement and steady rhythmic pattern" should be present. Stanisław Czajkowski adds that typical for the hymn is a "solemn, elevated, dignified tone." Musical means used to evoke the aesthetic category of the sublime include a noble stylistic-musical simplicity. These means are primarily concerned with forms, texture, and the subordination of melody and rhythm to the prosody of the text.[61]

The rich philosophical and aesthetic reflection on the sublime leads to searching for different possibilities of representing this category in all the arts, not just in the music. It does not necessarily have to be

---

translation cited after Patsy Duncan, *The Emotional Life of Postmodern Film* (New York: Routledge, 2015), 66.
[59] See Gołaszewska, *Istota i istnienie wartości, op. cit.*, 234-236.
[60] See Tomaszewski, *'Dedykacja' Schumanna do słów Rückerta: dźwiękowy „kształt miłości"*, in *Od wyznania do wołania, op. cit.*, 87.
[61] *Ibidem*, 34.

confined to the conventions of the so-called "high style." Instead, the sublime may be approached more directly. It seems that the most important musical works combine diffferent possible ways of evoking the quality of the sublime. This is exactly what Górecki does in the Copernican Symphony.

As Carl Dalhaus reminisces, from the second half of the eighteenth century onwards, the symphony was considered a "distinguished" musical genre, particularly strongly marked by the presence of the sublime.[62] E.T.A. Hoffmann carried out his analysis of Beethoven's Symphony No. 5 in the light of this category, admiring—and here I quote Maria Piotrowska—a „great" style of this composition, in which monumentality and diversity permeate rather than exclude each other.[63] However, the sheer majesty of the Copernican Symphony seems to endow it with a special individual character. The Symphony does not close-in within itself, but it is the means of expressing some 'more'—it connects with the sacred, the sacramental. The presence of the sublime in Górecki's music is confirmed by the words of Rudolf Otto, the servant of the loftiness of the *numinosum*, and the intuition of Roman Ingarden, who sought to identify the so-called metaphysical qualities in a musical work.[64]

The sublime arises from greatness; it is at the same time terrifying and fascinating. Simultaneously, this quality has been most closely associated with the idea of beauty, as shown in the usage of this word, where the only adjectives are the expressions "great" and "beautiful." It is worth emphasizing that the creation of the category of the sublime within the text itself may be influenced not only by its content and hymn-like quality, but by the very use of the Latin language. Igor

---

[62] See Carl Dalhaus, „E. T. A Hoffmanns Beethoven-Kritik und die Ästhetik des Erhabenen," in *Archiv für Musikwissenschaft* 38, no 2; 84-85; cited after Maria Piotrowska, „Paradygmat europejskiej muzyki klasycznej," in *Dziedzictwo europejskie a polska kultura muzyczna w dobie przemian. Studia pod redakcją Anny Czekanowskiej* (Kraków: Musica Iagiellonnica, 1995), 93.
[63] Piotrowska, *op. cit.* 93.
[64] See Roman Ingarden, *O dziele literackim. Badania z pogranicza ontologii, teorii języka i filozofii literatury,* M. Turowicz, transl. (Warszawa, 1988), 370.

Stravinsky, commenting on the introduction of this language in the *Symphony of Psalms* and *King Oedipus*, wrote:[65]

> I always thought that the sublime thing was to use a special, not everyday, language, so I selected Latin. This choice still had the added advantage that I was dealing with the language that was not as much dead as it was petrified, monumental and inaccessible to any trivialization.

The music of the Second Symphony is permeated by lyricism inspired by its text. The "feeling of magnitude" underlies this category, not only literally, by "pulsing" in its power in the first movement. It also appears, in a veiled way, in the second movement where it is associated with meditation on great things, well beyond the cognitive abilities of human beings. Precisely in the context of its second movement, Górecki's Symphony asks the question: can this composition be considered in its verbal-musical whole (or at least its final part) as a hymn? It seems that, indeed, yes, it can. The majority of qualities and typical characteristics of musical hymns are present in this music.

What is important, these features do not stem from any attempt at stylization or imitation, but rather from the application of Górecki's unique compositional technique. This is evidenced by, among others, the introduction at the end of the Symphony of a quotation from the solemn chorale. As Krzysztof Droba and Bohdan Pociej emphasize (among others) this quotation can not be treated as a "foreign body," since it naturally flows and co-mingles with the music of the Symphony.[66] According to Droba, in Górecki's oeuvre, "the basis and means of building the category of sublimity (sacral) is a specific, very individual compositional technique, that is the constructivist reductionism." The solemnity of Górecki's work has its origin in the technique itself: in the sound material, where, with its limitations, expression intensifies. As Droba writes,[67]

---

[65] Igor Strawiński, *Kroniki mego życia*, J. Kydryński, transl. (Kraków, 1974), 120-121, cited after Alicja Jarzębska, „Inspiracja religijna w utworach serialnych Igora Strawińskiego," in *Inspiracje w muzyce XX w.* (Warszawa: ZKP, 1993), 161.
[66] See Droba, *Górecki*, in *Encyklopedia, op. cit.,* 431; Pociej, *Kosmos, tradycja i brzmienie, op. cit.,* 4.
[67] *Ibidem,* 97.

Where the technique becomes a direct source of expression, one can not fail to notice this organic technical connection with its function. So it will not be any abuse to describe Górecki's constructivist reductivity as a sublime, sacred technique.

However, to return to the interpretation of the second movement of the Copernican Symphony, we intuitively grasp that this Symphony is a hymn. Yet, despite all external similarities and convergences with the conventions of the genre, there is a particular, personal tone that is not fully coherent with the principal idea of the religious hymn understood as, as Czajkowski writes, „praise, with elements of prayer of supplication."[68] This music carries the tone of existential fear resulting from human contact with something beyond human cognitive ability, a tone originating in the composer's emphasis on the dialectic response to Copernicus's discovery—turning upside down the "cosmos" in which humanity lived. In the musical layer of the Symphony, this tone appears in the echoes of the initial invocations of "Deus;" in the opposition between the dark tone of the harmonics, typical of the baritone, the brightening of the Dorian mode on E-flat in the part of the soprano, or in darker colors of the orchestra.

Fragments marked by this expressive "tone" occur in Górecki's Copernican Symphony next to moments full of brightness and glory. It is impossible not to refer here to the quoted definitions of sublime, in which the Kantian belief in the dialectics of fear and fascination is placed at the root and the source of this aesthetic value. It seems that Górecki's "hymn" is all the more sublime, as it is authentic, as it shows the state of human beings in the face of—to repeat Pascal—"infinite space, the eternal silence of fear."[69] It is important to note, however, that the last word in the Symphony No. 2 is hope (the A-major as a chord of light), which the composer endows with a profoundly Christian confidence in Providence that watches over humans lost in infinite space of the Universe.

In the light of the philosophical concepts of the sublime discussed above one can also attempt an interpretation of purely instrumental fragments of the Copernican Symphony—especially the first

---

[68] S. Czajkowski, op. cit., 219.
[69] Blaise Pascal, *Myśli*, transl. Tadeusz Boy-Żeleński (Warszawa, 1977), 185; cited after: W. Stróżewski, *O wielkości., op. cit.*, 286.

movement. Filling space with the power of sound and reaching the limits of dynamics may be associated not only with the sublime conceived by Edmund Burke as a physical (in terms of height and depth) immensity, as well as the with the Kantian feeling of a person on a collision course with the dynamic forces of nature, but also—as Hartmann pointed out—with a phenomenon that is both monumental and violent. It is impossible not to notice the analogy with the specific postmodern category posed by Lyotard, defining the sublime as an act, "the happening" of reality and the representation of what cannot be represented at all. While listening to the first movement of Górecki Copernican Symphony, that—in the words of the composer—captures a powerful "mechanism of the world," we are somehow transferred into the center of the creation, one might say, in an act of devotion that is impossible except by its own dynamism.

Finally, let us refer to Rudolf Otto again, to his definition of the *sacrum:* the aspect of mystery, the status of being fascinated and frightened at the same time—the *misterium tremendum et fascinosum*. This definition appears to be an expanded version of the definition of the sublime by Kant, Burke, and a number of other thinkers. It seems that in Górecki's music the sublime is organically linked with the sacred.

However, when we focus on the sacred, we are doomed to remain in the circle of analogies and distant comparisons. As Władysław Stróżewski writes,[70]

> The Sacrum, if the work of art really came to his realization, fascinates more than pure beauty, and at the same time is more distant, transcendent and lofty than all aesthetic **loftiness.**

While experiencing Górecki's music we can be filled with this fascination, as far as we are able to have (with Kant) the necessary imagination and sensitivity.

---

[70] Władysław Stróżewski, „O możliwości sacrum w sztuce," in *Wokół piękna, op. cit.*, 226.

CHAPTER 10

Mothers and Motherhood in Górecki's Third Symphony and Other Works

Maja Trochimczyk

1. Outlining the Terrain[1]

In a recent interview, when answering a question about his links to the country of his origin, Górecki compared a personal connection to one's homeland with the power of maternal bonding:

> Even though a child is cut off from the umbilical cord, it is a child of its mother, and, this is, perhaps, the strongest tie... There are not many 'renegade' children, 'renegade' mothers who would not admit their kinship, who would reject what is theirs by birth... Nobody chooses their time and place of birth.[2]

These words evoke the primordial, archetypal metaphor: the earth (land, country, or region) is the mother; the human person is the child; the two are connected by the "strongest tie."[3] The composer's choice of the maternal metaphor as a final argument in his discussion of cultural belonging, as an image of national, regional, and personal

---

[1] The first version of this paper, "Górecki and the Paradigm of the 'Maternal'," was presented during a symposium, "The Górecki Phenomenon," held on 5 October 1997 at USC within the *Górecki Autumn* festival. Revised and expanded as "Górecki and the Paradigm of the 'Maternal'" in *Musical Quarterly* 82, no. 1 (Spring 1998): 82-130; expanded in another version, "*Mater Dolorosa* and Maternal Love in the Music of Henryk Górecki".*Polish Music Journal*, 6/1 (2003). http://pmc.usc.edu/PMJ/issue/6.2.03/Trochimczykmater.html.
[2] See the interview in Chapter 3.
[3] For studies of maternal bonding and maternal love see Władysław Sluckin, Martin Herbert and Alice Sluckin: *Maternal Bonding* (Oxford: Blackwell, 1983); or Elisabeth Badinter, *Mother Love: Myth and Reality. Motherhood in Modern History* (New York: Macmillan, 1981).

identity, opens an avenue for the study of his music: an examination of his use of "maternal" imagery, subjects, and myths.

An annotated catalogue of Górecki's works in Adrian Thomas's monograph enumerates all of the composer's dedications.[4] There are two works dedicated "to the memory of my dear mother:" *Three Songs*, Op. 3, for medium voice and piano (composed in January 1956) and *Do Matki/Ad Matrem*, Op. 29, for soprano solo, mixed choir, and orchestra, composed over five days in June 1971. These two compositions, and the differences between the images of the maternal love arising from their texts and their musical settings, are an obvious choice for study. However, Górecki's output includes many other pieces connected to the idea of the maternal. There are three groups of works celebrating the heavenly motherhood of the Blessed Virgin Mary, the Mother of God:
(1) pieces with prayerful texts addressed to Mary,
(2) Marian songs, and
(3) works with references to *Bogurodzica* [Mother of God], a 13th-century Marian hymn, the first written document of Polish literature.

Ad Matrem appears on the list of Marian works under the first of these subheadings (prayers to Mary), and it is accompanied by Symphony No. 3, *Symphony of Sorrowful Songs*, Op. 36, for soprano and orchestra (1976), *O Domina Nostra* (*Meditations on Our Lady of Jasna Góra*), Op. 55, for soprano and organ (1982, 1985), and *Totus Tuus*, Op. 60, for mixed chorus a cappella (1987). The second group of the choral songs are a testimony to a sincere private devotion and strongly contrast with these monumental testimonials of a public religious commitment. This group consists of the *Marian Songs*, Op. 54, for unaccompanied mixed choir (1985), *Pod Twoją Obronę* [Under Your Protection], Op. 56, for eight-part mixed choir (1985), and some of the twenty-one unpublished *Pieśni Kościelne* [Church Songs] for mixed choir (1986), based on texts and melodies from Jan Siedlecki's *Church Songbook*,

---

[4] Adrian Thomas: *Górecki*. Series: Oxford Studies of Composers (Oxford and New York: Clarendon Press, 1997).

first published in 1878.⁵ References to *Bogurodzica* permeate Górecki's output from the 1960s onwards (See Figure 10-1: The first line of *Bogurodzica*). Some *Bogurodzica* allusions reduce the ancient anthem to the iconic ascending leap of the fourth followed by stepwise descent. A "motto" motive based on the incipit of this anthem (e.g. D—E—F—E) is used in such diverse works as *Songs of Joy and Rhythm* (version of 1960); Symphony No. 1, *1959*; *Miserere*, Op. 44 for unaccompanied mixed choir (1981); the Harpsichord Concerto, Op. 40 (1980; first movement), to the Fourth Symphony, *Tansman Episodes* (composed in piano score in 2006).⁶

Figure 10-1: *Bogurodzica*, as published in Jan Siedlecki, ed., *Śpiewnik kościelny*[Church Songbook] (Lwów: Wyd. Ks. Misjonarzy, 1928), 167.

---

⁵ Jan Siedlecki: *Śpiewnik kościelny z melodjami na 2 głosy* [Church Songbook with Melodies for 2 Voices] (Lwów, Kraków, Paris: Ks. Misjonarze, 1928). This is the 50th anniversary edition of a volume first published in 1878 and initially designed for Catholic school-children.
⁶ . See the composer's discussion of this issue in Chapter 4. See also Thomas, *op. cit.*, 9, 87. He lists also *Muzyczka IV*, *Two Little Songs*, Op. 33/1, and *Three Lullabies*, No. 3 as containing references to *Bogurodzica*. See Hieronim Feicht: "Bogurodzica" in *Studia nad muzyką polskiego średniowiecza* [Studies in Polish music of the Middle Ages] (Kraków: PWM Edition, 1975), 131-185.

After a further review of Górecki's topics and titles, one could add his lullabies to the list of mother-related compositions: *Kołysanka* [Lullaby] for piano, Op. 9 (November 1956, rev. June 1980) dedicated "to Jadwiga" (the composer's wife since 1959), *Kołysanki i Tańce* [Lullabies and Dances], Op. 47, for violin and piano (1982; dedicated to the composer's son, Mikołaj), and *Trzy Kołysanki/Three Lullabies*, Op. 49 for unaccompanied mixed choir (1984). Lullabies are a particularly maternal form of music, existing in every culture; moreover, as will be shown later, their expressive and structural characteristics are significant for Górecki's musical portrayals of motherhood.

A range of questions arises about Górecki's images of the maternal. What features of the music are used in his musical representations of motherhood, and to what effects? How is the mother portrayed? Is she an active subject, a person that develops and transforms over the duration of the work? Is she a "good" and happy mother? Do the images of motherhood have stable features in Górecki's output, or do they evolve over the course of his career? Does he accept the models and myths of motherhood that permeate his culture? What could be said about these myths?

2. The Maternal Archetype and Its Meanings

Western studies of cultural representations, models and myths of motherhood are associated with religious myths, cultural archetypes and the feminist ideologies. According to Carl Jung, the mother is among the key archetypes shared by humanity in the collective unconscious. These archetypes include also rebirth, the spirit and the trickster, or, in a longer list, "the shadow, the animal, the wise old man, the anima, the animus, the mother, the child."[7] As Jung writes, the archetype of the mother can manifest itself in an extensive number of related concepts, from mothers in the family, to „mothers" who take care of others such as a teacher or a nurse, to mothers in a

---

[7] See Carl Gustav Jung, *Four Archetypes: Mother, Rebirth, Spirit, Trickster* edited by Richard Francis Carrington Hull (Princeton: Princeton University Press, 2011); Carl G. Jung, *Two Essays on Analytical Psychology* (London 1953), 108.

figurative sense." Jung writes: „To this category belongs the goddess, and especially the Mother of God, the Virgin, and Sophia." He believes that the concept of the Mother is associated with „things arousing devotion or feelings of awe, as for instance the Church, university, city or country, heaven, earth, the woods, the sea or any still waters, matter even, the underworld and the moon."[8] These maternal symbols may have a positive or negative meaning, or may be ambivalent, as is the case of the goddesses of fate. Furthermore, according to Jung, mothers may be associated with the „maternal solicitude and sympathy; the magic authority of the female; the wisdom and spiritual exaltation that transcend reason; any helpful instinct or impulse; all that is benign, all that cherishes and sustains, that fosters growth and fertility."[9] According to Jung, the places of magic transformation and rebirth, together with the underworld and its inhabitants, are presided over by the mother. In spiritual terms, this „mother" is raised to the level of Divine Motherhood of the Goddess, such as Gaia, the spirit of the Earth, our Mother.

A more limited, socially and culturally, concept of motherhood attracted the attention of radical feminist writers that have been very critical of construing motherhood as a woman's main or sole vocation. These interpretations of „motherhood" are of limited significance for the study of Górecki's music, however, since he neither knew nor approved of feminist theories that place motherhood in the context of oppression at the level of individual identity or social functioning, leaving all the mystery of creation aside. When hearing the first version of my paper at the University of Southern California in 1997, the composer was surprised by the virulence of the feminists' critique of the maternal and by my locating of his work in this context. Let us review some feminist interpretations of motherhood.

Simone de Beauvoir, for instance, described women's capacity for bearing children as a liability when she stated that "woman's misfortune is to have been biologically destined for the repetition of

---

[8] *Ibidem.*
[9] Carl Jung, "The Mother Archetype," summarizing ambivalence of mother-symbols; https://www.scribd.com/document/202302142/Carl-Jung-The-Mother-Archetype.

life."[10] Shulamith Firestone wrote that "the heart of woman's oppression is her childbearing and childrearing roles."[11] According to Shari Thurer, who traced the convoluted cultural history of this myth, in the traditional Western embodiment the perfect mother is "properly married, faithful, subservient, modest, a woman who puts aside her own desires to rear and inspire her children. She is part of our mental furniture: the doormat."[12] Mary Jakobus defined the "maternal imaginary" as focused on "the fantasmatic mother who [...] exists chiefly in the realm of images and imagos (whether perceived or imagined), mirroring and identifications, icons and figures; who is associated sometimes with feminist nostalgia, sometimes with ideological mystification..."[13]

Of more interest for the concepts of motherhood permeating Górecki's sound world is the theory of „maternal thinking" developed by feminist philosopher, Sara Ruddick. She defined "maternal thinking" as an important type of philosophical thought, differing from all abstract systems by being "holistic, field-dependent, open-ended, not because of any innate sex differences but because that is the kind of thinking her [mother's] work calls for."[14] Ruddick's maternal thinking is the "capacity for attentive love" which serves to "invigorate preservation and enable growth" of individual persons; she borrows the concept of "attention" from the philosophy of Simone Weil.[15]

---

[10] Simone de Beauvoir, *The Second Sex*, trans. H.M. Parshley (New York: Vintage Books, 1974), 72. Quoted from *The Second Sex*, trans. H.M. Parshley (New York: Vintage Books, 1974), 72.

[11] Shulamit Firestone, *The Dialectic of Sex* (New York: Bantham Books, 1971), 72.

[12] Shari L. Thurer, *The Myths of Motherhood. How Culture Reinvents the Good Mother* (Boston, New York: Houghton Mifflin Co., 1994), 141.

[13] Mary Jakobus, *First Things: The Maternal Imaginary in Literature, Art, and Psychoanalysis* (New York: Routledge, 1995), iii.

[14] Quoted from Sara Ruddick: "Preservative Love and Military Destruction: Some Reflections on Mothering and Peace," in Trebicot, *op. cit.*, 231—262; cited from p. 250; see also Ruddick: "Maternal Thinking," in Trebicot, Op. *cit.*, 213-230; and a full-scale treatment of both themes in Sara Ruddick: *Maternal Thinking: Toward a Politics of Peace* (Boston: Beacon Press, 1989).

[15] Ruddick quotes Simone Weil: "Human Personality," in Weil's *Collected Essays*, selected and transl. by Richard and Rees (London: Oxford University Press, 1962).

Attentive love is "the supreme respect and concern for all life, the fostering of the development and growth of all human beings." Both men and women may practice this form of thinking; it arises from the existential experience of motherhood. We will find traces of such an affirmative approach in some of Górecki's texts and his interpretations of these texts.

Of greater importance, though, is his involvement in and relationship to images of the maternal permeating Polish culture. These myths and stereotypes differ considerably from notions put forward by the Western feminists, because motherhood is a culture-based institution. As Shari Thurer explains:[16].

> Motherhood—the way we perform mothering—is culturally derived. Each society has its own mythology, complete with rituals, beliefs, expectations, norms and symbols. Our received models of motherhood are not necessarily better or worse than many others [...] The good mother is reinvented as each age or society defines her anew, in its own terms, according to its own mythology.

Understanding the ideals of motherhood prevalent in Polish culture is vital for the study of Górecki's representations of the maternal. Paradoxically, this is still a neglected area; in Poland the maternal mythology has not yet attracted much critical attention.

3. Maternal Imagery in Polish Culture

My thoughts on the subject of maternal imagery are partly rooted in my personal experience: I view the Polish concept of motherhood from the double perspective of an "in/outsider," that is, as an heir to this cultural tradition and a mother, but also as a scholar who now observes Polish culture from North America.[17] From this vantage

---

[16] Thurer, Op. *cit.*, xv.
[17] I have examined some of these issues in my postdoctoral research project, "Women Composers in the Polish People's Republic (1945-1989)" conducted in 1995 at McGill University, Montreal (in association with the University of Warsaw, Poland) and supported by a postdoctoral fellowship from the Social Sciences and Humanities Research Council of Canada. Some findings of this project have been reported in "The 'Woman Composer' Debate from a Polish

point, it is clear that Polish women, in general, are not perturbed by their obvious linguistic invisibility: Polish language uses masculine generics.[18] According to a study by Adam Jaworski, in Polish, the male form of the generic "man" („człowiek") stands both for the male and for the whole human kind. The noun itself is „male"—and there is another noun used for „man" („mężczyzna") coupled with woman („kobieta"). (Interestingly, the plural of „człowiek" is „ludzie" – an entirely different noun denoting people). In addition, the traditional English practice of referring to "a baby" as a "he" in older child-rearing manuals does not have a Polish counterpart: "niemowlę" (infant) and "dziecko" (child) are both neuter nouns, the counterparts of "it." Nonetheless, Jaworski believes that the use of masculine „człowiek" for all human beings is a linguistic practice reflecting "the traditional way of treating male as the norm and female as a deviation." He observes: "Despite often seen and heard clichés that females have attained full equality (educational, professional, legal, etc.) the average Pole remains Jan Kowalski ('John Doe')."[19]

Leaving the language aside, the dominant myth of motherhood in Poland is that of the heroic figure of "Matka Polka" [Mother—Polish woman], whose work for the country is as vital as her importance for the family. The esteem for motherhood is connected with the emphasis on the mother's achievements in preserving the Polish language and culture. This gender-paradigm arose during the years of partitions (1795-1918), when the country lost its independence and the family became the stronghold of national identity. A nineteenth-

---

Perspective" at the Annual Meeting of the Canadian University Music Society (Brock University, St. Catharines, May 31, 1996). A brief summary, entitled "Notes on Polish Women Composers" has been published in the *Bulletin of the Polish Institute of Arts and Sciences in Canada and the Polish Library* 13 (1996): 36-40); reprinted in *IAWM Journal* 2, no. 2 (June 1996): 13-15

[18] Nonetheless, it is worth noting that discriminatory features of Polish, which is a language with grammatical gender, are much weaker than those of the English language. Moreover, it is worth noting that the word "słońce" (sun) is neuter and "księżyc" (moon) is masculine in Polish. Therefore, the stereotypical association of maleness with sun-light-day-rationality and femaleness with moon-darkness-night-irrationality (as in Mozart's *Magic Flute*), common in German, French or English, does not exist in Polish.

[19] Adam Jaworski, *A Linguistic Picture of Women's Position in Society. A Polish-English Contrastive Study* (Frankfurt am Main: Verlag Peter Lang, 1986), 38.

century allegorical postcard of a woman holding the torch of light for her small children, with an explanatory caption, "Let the survivors not lose hope and let them carry the light of education for the nation," provides the best visual interpretation of this tendency to link the maternal with the patriotic (see Figure 10-2 below). Thus, the maternal element in Polish culture became particularly prominent through the emphasis on the survival and transmission of Polish cultural values in the homes.

Figure 10-2: A vintage postcard "Niechaj żywi nie tracą nadziei i przed Narodem niosą oświaty kaganiec"[Let the survivors not lose hope and let them carry the light of education for the nation] issued by Towarzystwo Szkoły Ludowej [Folk School Society] in Kraków, n.d., c. 1880.

During the nineteenth century, the dividing lines in Polish society did not separate the public and the private domain into spheres of fixed gender (male and female); rather, the borderlines were drawn between the family and the community on the one hand (Polish), and the foreign state on the other (the three parts of the divided country were ruled by Russia, Prussia, and Austria).[20] Polish culture was affirmed through an allegiance to, and knowledge of, Polish language, literature, poetry, and music—all of which had a precarious status in public life and thrived in the homes. Thus, national identity was cultivated in the families; women's special role in that process has been widely recognized. At the same time, the women's presence in the public spheres of higher education, journalism, publishing, etc. was gradually increasing, on a par with their political emancipation.[21]

There is also a strong religious factor in the Polish vision of motherhood, based on the predominant position of Mary in the Polish form of Roman Catholicism Thus, the notion of „motherhood" has been shaped by the presence of the idealized „mother"—the „Mother of God" in the Catholic tradition. She is the perfect, Divine Mother of all; she grants graces and favors to her devotees. This powerful, benign, generous, and compassionate figure, permeating popular religious culture or „folk religiosity" of Polish villages, carries the remnants of the ancient Slavic worship of the Goddess of fertility and rebirth, visible in the dedication of the entire month of May to Mary (celebrating the rebirth of spring), or in the August harvest celebrations to Matka Boska Zielna (The God Mother of the Herbs, or Vegetation), celebrated in Poland on the Feast of the Assumption of Mary on August 15. In these devotions, Mother Mary is linked to

---

[20] The loss of statehood has simultaneously aggravated the relations of Poles to ethnic and linguistic minorities living on Poland's territory. See Norman Davies: *God's Playground* (New York: Columbia University Press, 1982)

[21] For detailed studies of the role of women in the various strata of Polish society of the 16-20th centuries see the special issue of *Acta Poloniae Historica* 74 (1996). The volume contains articles on peasant women, women of the landowning class, working-class women, the emancipation of women in Polish territories in the nineteenth century, women in Polish towns, women and politics. See also R. M. Ponichtera: "Feminists, Nationalists, and Soldiers: Women in the Fight for Polish Independence," *International History Review* 19, no. 1 (February 1997): 16-31, and A. Zarnowska: "Social Change, Women and the Family in the Era of Industrialization — Recent Polish Research," *Journal of Family History* 22, no. 2 (1997): 191-203.

agricultural celebrations of the fertility of nature and the cycle of life. Incidentally, this „Goddess"-like Mother resembles in her universal kindness and serenity the Buddhist Quan Yin, the Chinese version of the Avalokiteshvara Bodhisattva, the Bodhisattva of Great Compassion.

The other source of Marian cult and ideals stems from the profound and centuries-old cultural influence of the dogma of the Catholic Church, created and furthered by a male-dominated and masculinist hierarchy.[22] Unlike the Catholic churches of North America, however, where, under the influence of competing Protestant churches, faith in Jesus is often the sole focus of the liturgy, it is hard to find a single Mass celebrated in Poland without any Marian hymns or prayers. The religious calendar is filled with Marian holidays; as mentioned above, she is the dedicatee of the months of May ("May services" in honor of Mary), October (the Rosary month), and December (*Roraty*, services on the theme of waiting with the pregnant Mary for the birth of Jesus). In addition, there are sixteen Marian feasts scattered throughout theChurch calendar, including the Feast of the Queen of Poland which coincides with the state celebration of the May Third Constitution. In the Polish version of the popular *Loreto Litany*, Mary is named the Queen of Poland. Her images proliferate; she is the subject of songs, poems, and popular devotions.[23]

These two models of motherhood, the Heroic Polish Mother [*Matka-Polka*], and the Mother of God are the most important elements in the Polish concept of the maternal.

---

[22] The exclusion is revealed by the scarcity of women's voices in Church-sponsored publications, such as a collection of essays about the future of the Catholic Church in Poland, published in 1987 with a preface by Card. Józef Glemp (the leader of the Church in Poland). Forty authors were invited to contribute to this volume, including five priests and only three women. See *Kościół polski na przełomie 2000 roku* [Polish Church at the Turn of the 2000th Year] (Warsaw: Wydawnictwo Pallottinum, 1987).

[23] See Mieczysław Gogacz: *Dzień z Matką Bożą* [A Day with the Mother of God] (Warsaw: Wydawnictwo Sióstr Loretanek, 1986). This tiny book contains prayers, meditations on the Rosary, the Way of the Cross, and a "Litany of Flowers" praising the Mother of God. The author is a well-known professor of theology at the Catholic University in Lublin (KUL).

Figure 10-3: Our Lady of Jasna Góra – Matka Boska Częstochowska - icon housed at the Pauline monastery in Częstochowa, Poland (the wooden icon is here covered by a „crown and cloak" made of precious gems and gold).

The venerated image of Our Lady of the Bright Mount (Jasna Góra is a Pauline Monastery located in Częstochowa, the destination of pilgrimages and a site of worship) presents Mary as powerful and intensely serious. This Heavenly Mother has captured the Polish collective imagination so completely that various copies of her image are present in most Polish homes (see Figure 10-3).[24] The frontal position of Mary, confronting the viewer with an unflinching gaze,

---

[24] For a popular account of the history of the icon, as well as the history and treasures of the Pauline Monastery in which it is held see *The Cultural Heritage of Jasna Góra* (Warszawa: Interpress, 1974).

commands feelings of awe and respect; the scars on her cheek are a sign of suffering, that she shares with her worshippers.

The 13th-century Byzantine icon is very distant from the 19th-century representations of the Blessed Virgin as a charming and subservient child-mother, looking up to the heavenly Father. However, Mary's portrayals as silent, humble, obedient, and patiently waiting for grace frequently appear in the vast mariological literature, written almost exclusively by priests and male theologians.[25] The title of a book by a Polish theologian is quite telling in its gender dynamics: *He Looked at the Nothingness of His Handmaid.*[26]

This Mary, "the Mother of God, but not God, the Mother" has been the subject of much criticism from the Western feminists. Shari Thurer, for instance, pointed out the emphasis on Mary's perfect humility and warned that "there is an underside to Mary's selflessness: if we consider that Mary has no self, she has no needs of her own."[27] This selfless Mary is "a perfect canvas for our projections;" not a real woman, but an imaginary ideal construed as a model for all mothers. Thurer suggests that while Mary is worshipped, real mothers are often

---

[25] See Auguste Nicolas and Eugeniusz Dąbrowski, *Życie Maryi Matki Bożej* [The Life of Mary, the Mother of God] (Poznań, Warszawa, Lublin: Księgarnia Św. Wojciecha, 1963); Joseph Pohle, *Mariology. A Dogmatic Treatise on the Blessed Virgin Mary, Mother of God* (St. Louis, Mo., London: B. Herder Book Co., 1914, 1935, 1943); Gabriele Maria Roschini, *La Mariologia di San Tommaso* (Roma: Angelo Bellardetti Editore, 1950); St. Bernard of Clairvaux, *L'Oeuvre mariale de Saint Bernard* (Juvisy, France: Editions du Cerf). An online search of book catalogs reveals that only about 5% of mariological texts are written by women, and even these discuss the "mariology" created by male theologians and saints. See also the collection of *Women's Voices* cited above, esp. Sarah Coakley's "Mariology and 'Romantic Feminism': A Critique."

[26] Krzysztof Kowalik, *Wejrzał na nicość swojej służebnicy* [He Looked at the Nothingness of His Handmaid] (Lublin: Wydawnictwo Katolickiego Uniwersytetu Lubelskiego, 1995).

[27] Thurer, *op. cit.*, 81, 107-109. See also Teresa Elwes, ed., *Women's Voices: Essays in Contemporary Feminist Theology* (London: Marshall Pickering, 1992) and Maurice Hamington, *The Re-negotiation of Religious Imagery: Mary and Catholic Feminist Ethics* (Ph.D. Dissertation, Los Angeles: University of Southern California, 1994).

objects of contempt; [28] this duality informs the main problem with the maternal, that is its distance from, and the influence upon, real human life.[29]

Nonetheless, in Poland, such ambivalence towards Mary is uncommon. Her image juxtaposes several ideals of womanhood: a powerful, heavenly queen, a suffering mother, a perfect nurturer, an innocent virgin, a humble servant, and a superhuman being excluded from the common fate of all humans—the birthmark of original sin—by virtue of her Immaculate Conception. What aspects of this complex mosaic have captured the imagination of Henryk Górecki?

4. Górecki's Catholicism and Madonnas

While the equation of Polishness with Catholicism is an oft-repeated, though strongly contentious statement, the cultural uniformity of post-war Poland, with seriously limited minority populations of Jews, Ukrainians, Byelorussians, and Germans, has led to a prominence of Catholic symbols in the country's social life: 90 percent of contemporary Poles define themselves as Catholic. (Piotr Taras reports that already in the 1970s 93.4% of Poles belonged to the Roman Catholic Church by virtue of baptism; but 21% of Poles had serious doubts about faith and did not participate in religious services

---

[28] Carmel Elizabeth McEnroy, *Guests in Their Own House: The Women of Vatican II* (New York, Crossroad Pub. Co., 1996); M.J. Nunes, "The nineteenth-Century—A Turning Point for the Catholic Church and for the Lives of Women in Brazil," *Social Compass* 43, no. 4 (December 1996): 503-513; C. E. Gudorf, "Women and Catholic Church Politics in Eastern Europe," *Journal of Feminist Studies in Religion* 11, no. 2 (Fall 1995): 101-116. In addition, sociological research suggests that, in general, Catholics are less supportive of gender equity than non-Catholics; C. Wilcox and T. G. Jelen, "Catholicism and Opposition to Gender Equality in Western Europe," *International Journal of Public Opinion Research* 5, no. 1 (Spring 1993): 40-57

[29] The fact that the cult of Mary does not lead to the acceptance of gender equity may be seen in the discriminatory hierarchical structure of the Catholic Church: women cannot be priests and, as such, are excluded from the decision-making processes. Despite frequent petitions, all recent Popes, from John Paul II to Francis, consistently rejected the idea of admitting women to priesthood.

of any kind.³⁰) Sociological studies have found that a nation's dominant and unified religious environment affects the religious beliefs of its citizens to a much greater extent than their personal background and parental influences.³¹ Therefore, the traits of the Polish brand of Roman Catholicism could be a significant factor in the formation of Górecki's understanding of the maternal: he is a deeply devout man whose profound attachment to his faith has often been commented upon.³² The strong adherence to Catholicism and a high degree of personal religiosity is apparent in Górecki's public statements and aesthetic beliefs, in the choice of his texts, and occasions for which he has composed music. One could mention here the commission of *Beatus Vir* dedicated to Pope John Paul II, or the circumstances of *Miserere* written after clashes between Solidarity supporters and security police in Bydgoszcz.³³

Górecki's home in Katowice was filled with a multitude of folk paintings and sculptures on religious themes, including several reproductions of the Madonna of Częstochowa and folk sculptures of the "sorrowful Christ" [Chrystus frasobliwy].³⁴ His library was stocked with texts by Polish poets who expressed strong religious sentiments in their writings, for instance, Juliusz Słowacki, Cyprian Kamil Norwid,

---

[30] Piotr Taras,: "ProblemyOceny Polskiego Katolicyzmu" [Problems of Evaluation of Polish Catholicism], in *Kościół polski, op. cit.*, p. 175-200.
[31] J. Kelley and N. D. Degraaf, "National Context, Parental Socialization, and Religious Belief—Results from 15 Nations," *American Sociological Review* 62, no. 4 (August 1997): 639-659
[32] Tadeusz Marek and David Drew, "Górecki in Interview (1968) - and 20 Years After" *Tempo* no. 168 (March 1989): 25-29. See also Thomas, *op. cit.* (99-100, 106-107); as well as the composer's statements and images from his studio filled with religious folk art captured in cover photo and in a Dutch TV documentary, *Master Composers: Henryk Mikołaj Górecki* (VPRO, 1994).
[33] The composer discusses this issue with Adrian Thomas, *op. cit.*, 94. See also his words in Bernard Jakobson, *op. cit.*, 184. For an analysis of religious symbols in *Beatus Vir* see Dorota Dywańska, "I wszystko jest zawsze teraz: Archetyp-symbol-sacrum w *Beatus vir* Henryka Mikołaja Góreckiego" [And everything is always now: Archetype-symbol-sacrum in *Beatus vir* by Heryk Mikołaj Górecki], in *Inspiracjew muzyce XX wieku: Filozoficzno-literackie, religijne, folklorem* [Inspirations in Twentieth-Century Music] (Warszawa: Związek Kompozytorów Polskich, 1993), 177-183.
[34] See photos in Chapter 4 and the cover.

and Maria Konopnicka. The composer's Christian faith was closely connected to his aesthetic creed and he was particularly fond of Andrei Tarkovski's statement that "art is prayer."[35] In his acceptance speech upon being awarded an honorary doctorate at the Catholic University of America in Washinton, DC, 28 February 1995, Górecki stated that authentic artists know that their art is nothing else "but the reflection of God's beauty."[36] Many of his works explicitly focused on the sacred subject matter, particularly the devotion to Mary.

Let us first review the texts of his choral songs, including *Marian Songs* (1985), *Church Songs* (1986), and *Under Your Protection* (1985). The last work on this list is a setting of a popular prayer addressed to Mary, the "Holy Mother of God" who is the Mediatrix between the people and her divine Child. This prayer, and the remaining Marian songs, present an image of Mary as a Mediatrix, Protectrix, and Queen of a status equal to her Son. In Siedlecki's *Songbook*, the source material for many of Górecki's choral songs, Mary is the addressee of 80 songs; she also appears in 20 other chants constituting parts of specific services and eight texts without melodies. In comparison, the *Songbook* includes 40 songs addressed to the Most Holy Sacrament (Eucharist), 27 Lenten songs, 16 Easter songs, 15 Advent songs, and only four songs each for the Pentecost and for the Holy Trinity.

Two songs from Górecki's Marian collection (Op. 54) are addressed to "Mother of God, the Refuge of Sinners" in Siedlecki's *Songbook*. The third song is a version of "Hail Mary;" the fourth expresses the pilgrim's sorrow at leaving the sanctuary in Częstochowa; and the last one is a contemplation of Mary's Immaculate Conception. The twenty one *Church Songs* include seven texts to and about Mary who should "be praised a thousand times" (No. 11) as the "Lady of the World" (No. 6) and the "merciful Mother" of all the faithful (No. 10, No. 2). She is "all-powerful in heaven and on earth" (*Marian Songs*, No. 1); she is worshipped for her purity exemplified in her Immaculate Conception, and for her assumption to heaven (*Marian Songs*, No. 5). Her maternal genealogy extends to the previous generation; Górecki's *Church Songs* also include a setting of the only song in praise of St. Anne included in

---

[35] Quoted in the interview with Maja Trochimczyk, Chapter 3 of this volume.
[36] Quoted in Thomas, *op. cit.*, 107.

Siedlecki's Songbook, "Welcome Lady, Mother of the Mother of Lord Jesus" (No. 5).[37] The images of Mary appearing in these texts fuse into the figure of a powerful Queen-Mother. The maternal success of both women is the source of their power. It is interesting to note that there are no songs addressed to Anna's husband, Mary's father, and that there are few songs directed to St. Joseph, Mary's husband, and the Holy Family in Siedlecki's *Songbook* (11 and 2 respectively). According to Shari Thurer, the Blessed Virgin Mary may be described as "one of few female characters to have attained the position of archetype . . . the perfect nurturer. She stands for maternity itself."[38]

Górecki's *Church Songs* begin with an Advent song[39] from Siedlecki's collection (an expanded version of *Hail Mary*; No. 1) and continue with an explicit celebration of Mary's motherhood which is extended, after the death of Jesus, to all believers (No. 2, "Let us go hugging, like children"). The latter song, addressed to Mary's "heart, goodness itself" enumerates the features of her perfect motherhood: her concern for all her children, her unbounded love and forgiveness, her patience and sweet gentleness. While focusing their attention on the Divine Mother, the believers express a child-like simplicity and trust in Mary's all-embracing protection. Similar feelings of child-like trust underlie another of Górecki's favourite religious songs, *Already It Is Dusk*.[40]

The victorious Lady of the Bright Mount is a subject of one of Górecki's important "public" works: *O Domina Nostra (Meditations on Our Lady of Jasna Góra)*, Op. 55, for soprano and organ (1982, 1985). This composition was conceived as a celebration of the 600th anniversary of the Black Madonna Shrine in Częstochowa. The 35-minute work is

---

[37] Anna (Anne) is the patron saint of married people, mothers and miners. She receives prayers of intercession especially for women in labor.

[38] Thurer, *op. cit.*, 82-3.

[39] Advent services focus on waiting with pregnant Mary for the delivery of her heavenly baby; the faithful are waiting with her for the "Sun of salvation" – she is "the morning star" in the pre-redemptive darkness.

[40] This 16th-century hymn by Wacław z Szamotuł is properly entitled "Prayer. When Children are Going to Sleep;" Górecki quotes it in *Old Polish Music*, Op. 24, for brass and strings (1969) and in *Already it is Dusk, Music for String Quartet* No. 1, Op. 62 (1988).

an enormous supplication and mantra-like recitation of her holy names (see Figure 10-4: Text of *O Domina Nostra* with all the repetitions).

The three-part piece begins with a quiet invocation to "Our Lady" whose immense power and transcendent glory provide inspiration for the revelatory climax of the central section ("Claromontana Victoriosa Regina nostra MARIA"). The vocal part begins after a lengthy organ introduction lasting for eight minutes. The overall formal outline could be described as a symmetric ABA' form which includes an abbreviated return of the initial segment of the piece; there are eight repetitions of "Domina" in section A and five in section A'.

The musical setting highlights the text by repetition: eight successive occurrences of "Domina" in the first section are followed by two repetitions of "Maria," five of "Domina" and fifteen of "nostra." The composer affirms the sovereign authority of Mary before naming her "our" Lady." This „Domina" is the full equivalent of „Dominus"—but the term's translation by the word „Lady" is somewhat misleading, since in English the „Lady" does not have the same connotations of sovereignty and power as the „Lord."

After the outburst of exultant joy in the dramatic center of the piece, the music features a prayer-like section of monotone quasi-recitation ("Sancta Maria—ora pro nobis") followed by a tranquil, plaintive invocation, a repeated call upon the "Domina." By its insistent recurrences, the last word becomes less an assertion of the fact, than a humble request to Mary to be truly "ours" and to extend her maternal protection to all of her children. Górecki's spelling of MARIA with upper case lettering (used in the central, dramatic section of the piece), places a special emphasis on her name; he uses similar differentiation of upper and lower case in other works, such as *Totus Tuus*. In this extended meditation on the mystery of the Black Madonna, her principal attribute is that of the victorious Queen.

It is interesting to note that this attribute appears in twelve invocations in the closing segment of the *Loreto Litany*, the textual model for *O Domina Nostra*. In Górecki's work, she is described neither as a mother (twelve invocations in the Litany), nor as a virgin (seven invocations). Yet the final phrases of his text quote the *Loreto Litany* and allude to its Polish version which includes a petition to the Queen of Poland. The connection to the Litany is established by the use of a direct quotation ("Sancta Maria—ora pro nobis" appearing twice) and the symmetrical layout of the text mirroring the responsorial form of the Litany. In the composer's original text, printed on the first page of the score, Mary's royal attributes are paired: "Claromontana—Victoriosa."

What is the victory that the composer celebrates here? The long, narrative dedication, written "in gratitude for a 'dangerous journey' which had—once more—a happy ending" and mentioning specifically two doctors, Prof. Stanisław Rudnick and Prof. Donat Tylman, makes it clear that this work is, in essence, a *Heiliger Dankgesang*, a hymn of gratitude for recovery from a serious illness.

As in other works with brief repeated texts, especially *Totus Tuus* and *Ad Matrem*, the many symmetries in the textual source are obbliterated in the musical setting. Here, the composer highlights Mary's sovereign ladyship, her royal power, her strength. Our childlike dependence on her protection is suggested through the quiet, melodic repetitions of the word "nostra." Interstingly, by stretching out the repetitions of the divine names of Mary over enormous spans Górecki mirrors devotional practices from Eastern spiritual traditions, that transform ordinary time of daily life into a time of Divine Presence by, for instance, the invocations of holy names in Hinduism and the practice of chanting mantras in Hinduism and Buddhism.[41] The repetitions cast a spell on the audience; this is a white magic of faith...

---

[41]Robert A. F. Thurman, *Essential Tibetan Buddhism* (San Francisco: Harper, 1995); Klaus Klostermaier, *A Survey of Hinduism* (3rd ed.). State University of New York Press (2007); Julius J. Lipner, *Hindus: Their Religious Beliefs And Practices (*New York: Routledge, 2010, second edition).

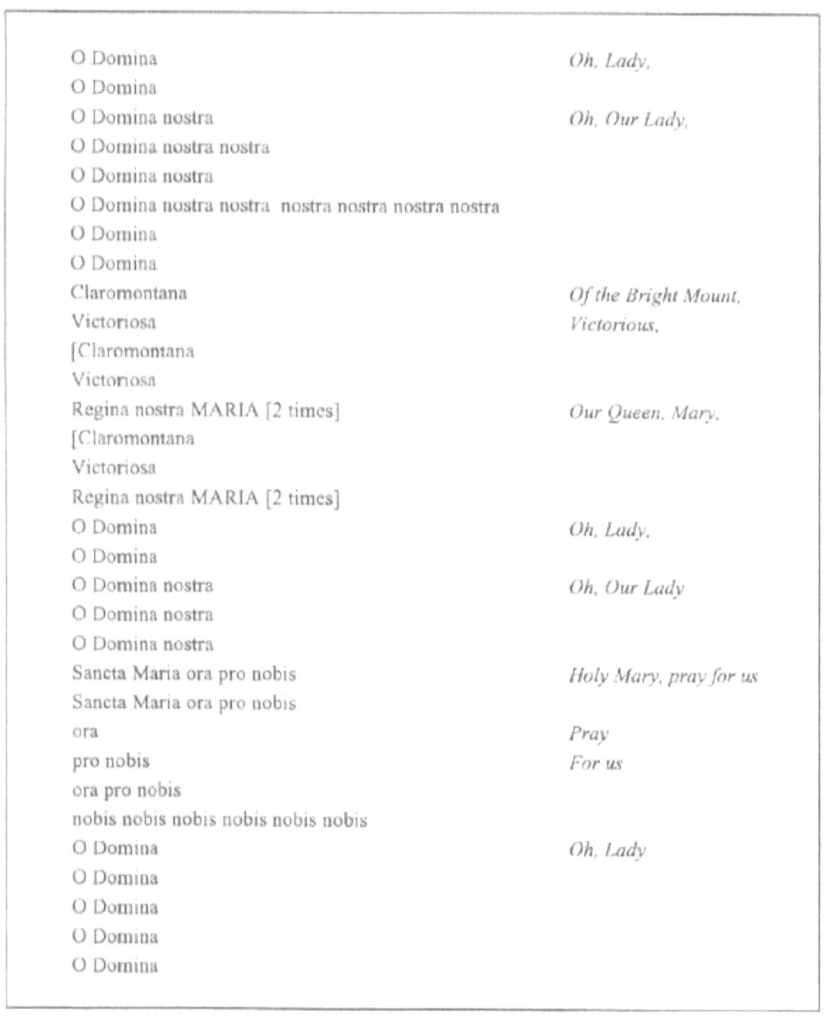

Figure 10-4: Text of Górecki's *O Domina nostra* with all the repetitions. Henryk Mikołaj Górecki, *O Domina Nostra, Meditation on the Black Madonna*, Op. 55 for soprano and organ (1982-855, revised 1990). © Copyright 1994 by PWM Edition, Kraków, Poland. Extract Used by Kind Permission of the Polskie Wydawnictwo Muzyczne, Kraków, Poland.

Mary, our Queen, becomes Mary, the Mother of the World, in another "public" choral work, *Totus Tuus* [All Yours], Op. 60, for mixed chorus *a cappella* (1987), dedicated to Pope John II on the occasion of "his third pilgrimage to his homeland." The text consists of a five-line Latin miniature by Maria Bogusławska:

Text	Translation
Totus Tuus sum, Maria,	I'm all Yours, Maria,
Mater nostri Redemptoris.	Mother of our Redeemer.
Virgo Dei, Virgo pia.	Virgin of God, Pious Virgin.
Mater mundi Salvatoris.	Mother of the world's Saviour.
Totus Tuus sum, Maria!	I'm all Yours, Maria!

The phrase *Totus Tuus* is the motto of Pope John Paul II to whom this work was dedicated. Górecki focuses attention on "the Name of the Mother"—to paraphrase Julia Kristeva—that is, the dyad Maria/Mater (see Figure 10-5: Textual repetitions in *Totus Tuus*). The forty repetitions of "Maria" and twenty of "Mater" are irregularly distributed through the piece.[42] The remaining words assure her of the caller's complete, unconditional devotion: "Totus Tuus Sum."

Górecki tellingly alternates dramatic exclamations of the name MARIA (in upper case letters; see Figure 10-6: Invocations to Mother/Mary in *Totus Tuus* and *Ad Matrem*), with tender settings of descriptive phrases, defining her characteristics: "Mater nostri, Virgo Dei." The Pope's motto, *Totus Tuus*, appears in slow rhythmic figures, with the pace evocative of relaxed breathing, and with consonant harmonies of traditional hymn settings.[43] The block chords of these tranquil, pensive episodes contrast with folk-inspired incantations of the holy name of MARIA that begin both sections of the work.

The textual repetitions highlight her maternal rather than her virginal features: she is the "Mother of our Redeemer," but primarily the

---

[42] There are 5 repetitions of "Maria," followed by 7 of "Mater," then 20 of "Maria," then 1 of "Maria," and 13 of "Mater," then, at the end, 14 of "Maria."
[43] The expression "Totus Tuus" is used on the title page of a Polish edition of a mariological treatise by St. Louis Marie Grignion de Montfort, adorned by the picture of the Black Madonna in full regalia: *Królowa Polski, Totus Tuus* [The Queen of Poland. Totus Tuus]. De Motfort's original title was *Treatise on the True Devotion to the Blessed Virgin Mary* (Turin: Centro Mater Divinae Gratiae, 1982).

"Mother of the World." Górecki's choice of repeated phrases pointedly focuses the listener's attention on Mary's universal motherhood. In each appearance of the phrase "Mater mundi Salvatoris" [Mother of the world's Savior], "Mater mundi" is repeated three times before the word "Salvatoris" shifts the meaning from „the World" to „the World's Savior."

MARIA MARIA!	Virgo Dei, Virgo pia,
MARIA MARIA!	Mater mundi
	Mater mundi
/pause/	Mater mundi Salvatoris.
	Mater mundi
Totus Tuus sum, Maria,	Mater mundi
Mater nostri Redemptoris,	Mater mundi Salvatoris.
Virgo Dei, Virgo pia,	Mater mundi
Mater mundi	Mater mundi
Mater mundi	Mater mundi Salvatoris.
Mater mundi Salvatoris.	Mater mundi
Mater mundi	Mater mundi
Mater mundi	Mater
Mater mundi Salvatoris.	
Totus Tuus	/pause/
Totus Tuus sum, Maria!	
Maria!	Totus Tuus sum, Maria!
	Totus Tuus sum, Maria!
Maria Maria Maria Maria Maria Maria	Maria!
Maria Maria Maria Maria Maria Maria	Maria!
Maria	Maria Maria!
	Maria!
/pause/	Maria Maria!
	Maria!
MARIA MARIA!	Maria!
MARIA MARIA MARIA!	Maria!
	Maria!
/pause/	Maria!
Totus Tuus sum, Maria,	/pause/
Mater nostri Redemptoris,	

Figure 10-5: Text of Górecki's *Totus Tuus* with all the repetitions. *Totus Tuus*, Op. 60 by Henryk Górecki © Copyright 1988 by Boosey & Hawkes Music Publishers Ltd. for the World except Poland, Albania, Bulgaria, China, Yugoslavia, Cuba, North Korea, Vietnam, Roumania, Hungary, Czechoslovakia, and the former territories of the USSR. Reprinted by permission of Boosey & Hawkes, Inc.

The musical interpretation of Bogusławska's text changes this line to: "Mother of the world, Mother of the world, Mother of the world's Savior." The maternal appeal of Mary, who is the surrogate, perfect mother of all the faithful, knows no bounds. The music disappears into silence with twelve repetitions of her name: "Maria, Maria, Maria...". She truly is a Divine Mother, worshipped by her children.

Figure 10-6a: Invocation to Mother/Mary in *Ad Matrem*, Op. 29. *Ad Matrem*, Op. 29 by Henryk Górecki. © Copyright 1972 by PWM Edition, Kraków, Poland. U.S. Renewal Rights assigned to Boosey & Hawkes, Inc. Reprinted by permission of Boosey & Hawkes, Inc.

Figure 10-6b (next page): Invocation to Mother/Mary in *Totus Tuus*, Op. 60. *Totus Tuus*, Op. 60 by Henryk Górecki. © Copyright 1988 by Boosey & Hawkes Music Publishers Ltd. for the World except Poland, Albania, Bulgaria, China, Yugoslavia, Cuba, North Korea, Vietnam, Roumania, Hungary, Czechoslovakia, and the former territories of the USSR. Reprinted by Permission of Boosey & Hawkes Music Publishers Ltd.

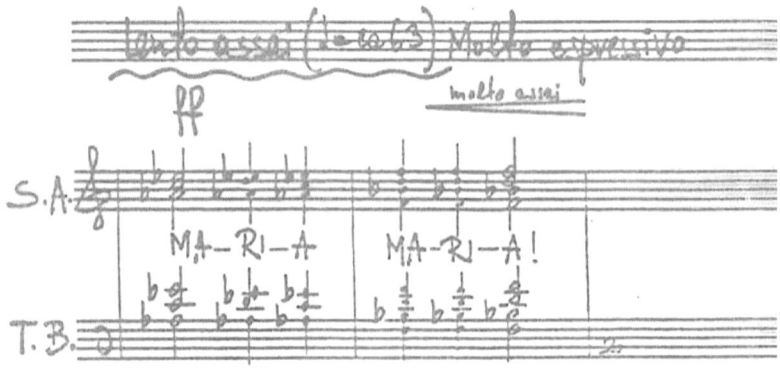

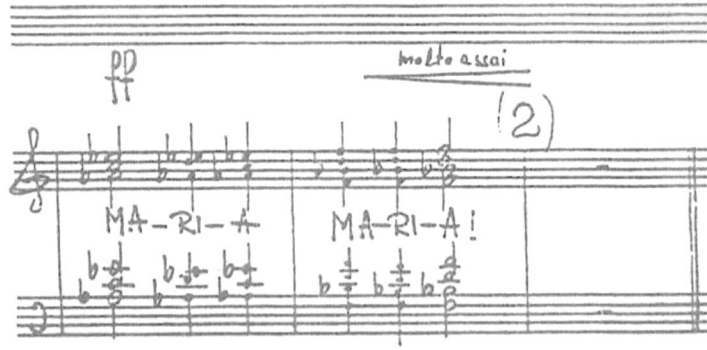

These recurrences of the holy name in both works, *Totus Tuus* and *O Domina Nostra*, bring existential associations of a two-fold nature, connected to religion and maternal behavior. The first type of gestural similarity relates the two works on "sacred" subject matter to their cultural context, that is, the use of repeated textual patterns in prayer, including the Litanies (especially the *Loreto Litany* as mentioned above, but also the Rosary), and the mantra-like "Prayer of Jesus" recited in the breathing rhythm of "IN—Jesus Christ, Son of God" and "OUT—Have mercy on me, a sinner." The recitation of prayers on one tone, as in plainchant's psalmody, is directly quoted in the section "Sancta Maria—ora pro nobis" in *O Domina Nostra* and with the words of *Hail Mary* ("Zdrowaś Mario, Łaskiś Pełna") in the second movement of Symphony No. 3.

The second layer of cultural association present in *O Domina Nostra* and *Totus Tuus* refers to the use of repetition in the linguistic practice of very young children and in the childhood genre, the lullaby. There is an urgent need for the reassurance of love in a child's repeated calls on mother's name; there is a soothing tranquility in the redundancy of the excessive recurrences of the same word, nonsense syllable, or phrase in her responses, which include comforting gestures and the singing of the lullaby. It is the repetitiveness and simplicity of lullabies, noted by researchers, that distinguishes them from other types of songs.[44] Górecki's repetitions share certain traits with the genre of the lullaby, and serve to evoke similar emotional responses. I will elaborate on this point at the end of this paper.

5. "To My Dear Mother:" *Three Songs* and *Ad Matrem*

So far, we have examined some of Górecki's music with religious themes, addressed to the heavenly Queen and divine Mother. These works arise from the composer's commitment as a religious man, a son of the Catholic Church—the Mother of all the faithful. His basic existential position, that of a son of a human mother, is reflected in two compositions that will be examined next, and connected to another „archetype" of Mother Mary, *Mater Dolorosa*.

Górecki's representations of motherhood in general have much to do with his relationship to his mother, Otylia Górecka (née Słota, 1909-1935): he was exactly two years old when she died at the young age of twenty-six. Adrian Thomas considers it such an important fact in Górecki's biography that the first sentence of his book reads: "Otylia Górecka died on 6 December 1935; it was her son's second

---

[44] Anna M. Unyk, Sandra E. Trehub and Laurel J. Trainor, "Lullabies and Simplicity: A Cross-Cultural Perspective," *Psychology of Music* 20, no. 1 (1992): 15-28; Sandra E. Trehub, Anna M. Unyk, Laurel J. Trainor, "Adults Identify Infant-directed Music," op. cit., Bernard Lortat-Jacob, "La berceuse et l'epopee: Questions de genre" [Lullaby and epic song: Questions of genre], *Revue de Musicologie* 78, no. 1 (1992): 5-25.

birthday."⁴⁵ The composer kept an old photograph of his mother next to his writing desk and for years refused to repaint the studio because there was a stain on the wall right under the mother's portrait that looked to him like the image of the heart, that miraculously appeared where it should be.

Figure 10-7a: Portraits of Górecki's parents in his Katowice studio, to the left of his desk, with two crucifixes, and two „ryngraf" metal plates with Mother Mary. Photo by Maja Trochimczyk, April 1998.

According to psychological studies, an early loss of a parent, mother or father, has an irrevocable effect on the child, causing life-long suffering but also giving rise to profound insights.⁴⁶ The research of Hope

---

⁴⁵ Thomas, *op. cit.*, xiii. See also the interviews with the composer's widow Jadwiga and daughter Anna by Beata Bolesławska-Lewandowska, *Górecki: Portret w Pamięci* [Górecki: A Portrait in Memory] (Kraków: PWM, 2013).

⁴⁶ Maxine Harris examines the irreparable changes in the psyche of children who have lost their parents; a deep attachment to the mother, and a symbiotic relationship of unity with her, gives way to anxiety and anger when separation is experienced, and to sadness and depression when the loss becomes final. See

Edelman suggest that, even if the mother died in labor and the child never knew her, there is a feeling of loss, emptiness, and longing, often not for the real person but for the idealized, perfect parent.[47] It appears that such feelings underlie the texts of Górecki's works dedicated to the memory of his mother.

Figure 10-7b: Portrait of Górecki's mother, detail.

The early *Three Songs*, Op. 3, for medium voice and piano (composed in January 1956), express filial grief in a straightforward manner. Górecki selected two mournful texts by a Romantic poet, Juliusz Słowacki (1809-1849), "Do Matki" [To Mother] and "Jakiż to dzwon grobowy" [What was this funereal bell], and concluded the cycle with "Ptak" [The Bird], by Julian Tuwim (1894-1953). It is a surprising choice of texts, juuxtaposing the darkest despair of Słowacki's fragments with the whimsical joy of Tuwim's charming miniature.

Harris: *The Loss that is Forever: The Lifelong Impact of the Early Death of a Mother or Father* (New York: Penguin, 1995). See also John Bowlby: *Attachment and Loss* (New York: Viking Penguin, 1991).
[47] Hope Edelman: *Letters from Motherless Daughters: Words of Courage, Grief, and Healing* (Redding, Mass.: Addison Wesley Publishing, 1995).

Two excerpts from Słowacki's poetry, written after the death of the poet's mother, Salomea Słowacka, describe the son's ominous dreams of being left alone, his nightmare of a last farewell fixed in the memory (No. 1), and the horrid reality of the funeral, when the son carrying the coffin is "tormented by black despair; covered by black mourning" (No. 2). In contrast, Tuwim's "The Bird" portrays a fleeting moment of nature's capricious beauty: a bird alighting on a twig, then flying away with song—"the swinging twig / still shudders with joy / that the bird made her dance so." (See the texts in the Appendix).

Figure 10-8: A descending "death" motive in the second song from *Three Songs*, Op. 3. Three Songs, Op. 3 by Henryk Górecki © Copyright 1977 by PWM Edition, Kraków, Poland U.S. Renewal Rights assigned to Boosey & Hawkes, Inc. Reprinted by permission of Boosey & Hawkes, Inc.

The Słowacki songs are filled with traditional musical gestures of sorrow and mourning. These symbols of grief include slow tempi, low registers, descending melodic patterns, and a preponderance of minor chords, dissonances, and, especially, "weeping" motives of descending minor seconds. One of the sorrowful gestures in the second song is of particular interest because of its subsequent prominence in the oeuvre of Górecki's older colleague, Witold Lutosławski. While researching Lutosławski's portrayals of the topos of death, I have noticed that, from the *Funeral Music* onwards (1956-58), the motive of a descending minor second coupled with a tritone can be understood as Lutosławski's preferred musical symbol of death and mourning.⁴⁸ Górecki's song, "Jakiż to dzwon," presents an unequivocal association of the descending tritonal motive with the mournful subject matter, made obvious in the work's opening measures. (Fig 10-8: Descending "death" motive in *Three Songs*, No. 2).

According to Elisabeth Kübler-Ross, the emotional state of someone who lost their loved one (or someone facing their own death) evolves through the stages of disbelief, anger and rejection, grief and despair, and, finally, reconciliation with the inevitability of this personal loss.⁴⁹ A similar trajectory towards a sublimation of grief and acceptance of life "as it is" underlies the emotional framework in several of Górecki's works, beginning with the *Three Songs*. After the heavy chords, slow tempi, and descending patterns in the first two of these songs, portraying the moment of the mother's death, the finality of her departure, and the despair felt during the funeral, the delicate textures and faster tempi of "The Bird" bring a fleeting moment of comfort.

Tuwim's lighthearted poem is well-known in Polish elementary schools, since it is a required reading in the course of Polish literature, and students have to memorize it and recite it in class. As such it may serve as a symbol of a happy childhood and the development of a child's abilities. However, since in Christian iconography the bird is a common symbol of the soul,⁵⁰ it is not difficult to interpret the protagonists of Tuwim's poem as symbols of the beloved mother (the bird) and her abandoned child (the twig). The contagious excitement of the little bird made the bush dance and swing with joy long after the bird flew away. Similarly, the young, happy mother shared the joy of

---

⁴⁸ Maja Trochimczyk, "'Dans la Nuit:' The Themes of Night and Death in Lutosławski's Oeuvre," chapter in *Lutosławski Studies*, Zbigniew Skowron, ed. (London: Oxford University Press, 2001): 96-124.
⁴⁹ Elisabeth Kübler-Ross,: *On Death and Dying* (New York: Macmillan, 1970); *Death: The Final Stage of Growth* (Englewood Cliffs, N.J.: Prentice-Hall, 1975); *Living with Death and Dying* (New York : Macmillan, c1981); *Death is of Vital Importance: On Life, Death and Life after Death*, ed. Göran Grip (New York: Talman Co., 1995).
⁵⁰ See Andre Grabar, *Christian Iconography: A Study of Its Origins*, trans. Terry Grabar (Princeton: Princeton University Press, 1969).

living with her child until she disappeared. The sudden end of her brief, intensely-felt presence left a gaping wound in the child's psyche. The orphaned child's loss will never be reversed, but it is possible to find comfort in remembering past joys.

This absent, beloved, mother is Górecki's main image of motherhood, associated with sorrow. The conceptual connections between the maternal imagery and the sorrowful subject matter are an important element in Górecki's music, especially in two works I would like to turn attention next to, that is *Ad Matrem* and the Symphony No. 3. Both concepts intersect in the image of the suffering mother, *Mater Dolorosa*. This image represents a darker side to Mother Mary's power, since her right to universal motherhood is based on her suffering at the bottom of the Cross where her "heart has been pierced by the sword of sorrow" (*Marian Songs*, No. 2, "Most holy Mother!"; a similar phrase appears in *Church Songs*, No. 2, "Idźmy, tulmy się, jak dziatki"). It is her grief and co-suffering with Jesus that endows her with her redemptive powers. This important image of *Mater Dolorosa* emerged in the Middle Ages; the phrase itself comes from a Latin sequence, *Stabat Mater*, describing the suffering of Mary at the foot of the cross. This sequence has been set to music by many composers, including one of Górecki's favorites, Karol Szymanowski.

Ad Matrem/Do Matki, Op. 29, for soprano solo, mixed choir, and orchestra was composed very quickly over a period of five days in June 1971. While its dedication to the memory of the composer's mother resembles that of the *Three Songs*, a brief comparison of the two pieces reveals Górecki's growing capability to sublimate and transcend his painful experiences, his ability to transform sorrow into art. In the *Three Songs*, Górecki relied on the conventional, rhetorical means of musical expression; the textual repetition is scant and the texts are not yet pared down to the essentials. Two decades later, the composer is able to reach the level of archetypes with simplicity and stark sonic contours of *Ad Matrem*—a work using extremely brief textual excerpts from the medieval sequence *Stabat Mater*.

Górecki selected only two attributes of Mary from the first lines of the sequence, framing them with invocations addressed to his mother: "MATER MEA LACRIMOSA DOLOROSA LACRIMOSA MATER MEA" [My mother, full of tears, full of pain, full of tears, my mother]. All the words are in upper case lettering, without punctuation signs; this typographic choice suggests the vocal mode of calling or screaming, loudly and breathlessly, without end.

The written out textual repetitons of "MATER MEA" emphasize the axial symmetry in the layout of this sparse text (See Fig. 10-9: The text and voices in *Ad Matrem*). This perfectly symmetrical text resembles the ternary design of the *Kyrie* of the Pre-Vatican-II Latin liturgy: "Kyrie eleison—Christe eleison—Kyrie eleison," each section having three repetitions. In both texts, the frame of calling upon the omnipotent power surrounds the invocation of suffering.

In the text of the *Kyrie*, the opening prayer of "Lord, have mercy" is addressed to *Kyrios* [The Lord]; similarly, *Ad Matrem* begins by calling upon the maternal power of "MATER MEA." The central position in the *Kyrie* is taken by the prayer for mercy to the anointed *Christos*, who was chosen to undergo the redemptive experience of passion, death, and resurrection. In a close analogy, the central portion of Górecki's text for *Ad Matrem* consists of two adjectives describing the suffering mother's unique features, her "oil of anointment." She is tearful and filled with pain, she is the *Mater Dolorosa* of the medieval *Stabat Mater* sequence; the "sorrowful Benedictrix" portrayed in medieval paintings with the sword of sorrow piercing her heart.

It is a stroke of Górecki's genius that his musical setting does not mirror this tripartite symmetry of the text. Instead, the composer divides the work into two main parts, based on the expressive modes of what could be dubbed *invocation* and *contemplation*. The short, repeated choral cry of anguish, suggestive of the extreme intensity of pain ("MATER MEA"), that appears in the first part of the work gives way to a quietly recited prayer in the conclusion. Górecki articulates this contrast by means of vocal setting and dynamics: in the first part the full choir sings massive chords *forte fortissimo* (*ffff*); in the second, the delicate voice of the solo soprano dissolves into silence (see Figure 10-10).

/percussion, with pauses/

/ffff, choir/
MATER MEA   My Mother
/pause/
/orchestra,
percussion/

/ffff, choir/
MATER MEA

/pause/
/orchestra/
/p, solo soprano/
MATER MEA   My Mother
LACRIMOSA   Tearful
DOLOROSA   Sorrowful
LACRIMOSA   Tearful
MATER MEA   My Mother
MATER MEA
MATER MEA

/orchestra/
/pause/

Figure 10-9: The text, its repetitive presentation and translation in *Ad Matrem*, Op. 29 (1971).

It would be easy to categorize this work as yet another religious composition on a Marian theme, a piece of interest solely for Catholics and historians of the music of the Catholic Church. Yet, the startling instrumental textures of this work create images reaching beyond

Catholic dogma, into the realm of universal archetypes, the core of human experience.

What are we to make of the work's opening, with its extended, fast-paced bass drum beats culminating in a brutal dissonance of "screaming" woodwind and brass (see Fig. 10-10: Fragment of *Ad Matrem*, rehearsal No. 5)? We know that the composer coded the dates of his mothers birth and death in the numbers of beats, chords, and lenghts of measures in this initial, dramatic fragment. The harsh tritone sonorities are repeated four times before a moment of silence. Soon, the relentless drumming resumes its steady pulse of ca. 264-288 beats per minute. The sixteenth-note pattern could easily be misread for a tremolo, but the score contains an explanatory note about its clearly rhythmic character. Again, two momentary silences punctuate the unidimensional texture of pulsating *crescendi* which lead to startling explosions of nightmarish, dissonant sonorities (See Ex. 10-11: Sectional formal outline of *Ad Matrem*). The loudest instrumental paroxysm is transformed into words: with one voice, with one anguished outburst, the choir calls upon "MATER MEA" (rehearsal No. 12).

All the voices in unison, at the maximum dynamic level, sing a plaintive motive based on the mournful interval of the minor second (E—F—E); this outcry is startling and almost too short to be fully grasped and appreciated. As it is heard against the tritone-based brass interjections, the coupling of the semitone and the tritone (that I pointed out in the *Three Songs*) again suggests the presence of the archetypal musical symbolism of death and suffering. This exclamation is followed by silence (a general pause of three successive fermatas) from which a new texture soon arises, permeated by the gentle sonorities of the flute, harp and strings (rehearsal No. 13). The tenderness and tranquillity of the new material is captured in the justly famous extreme markings of *tranquilissimo—cantabilissimo—dolcissimo—affettuoso e ben tenuto e LEGATISSIMO*, which provide a polar opposition to the *ritmico—marcatissimo—energico—furioso—con massima passione e grande tension*e assigned to the opening drum patterns.

This is not the only expressive contrast in *Ad Matrem*. Throughout the central segment of the work, gentle moments of respite alternate with sombre sections marked *molto lento*. In the latter fragments, voluminous, dark sound masses (based on a sustained harmonic interval of a major second, D-flat—E-flat, in the double basses) support a sinuous, lamenting cello melody. The emotive textures shift between these two modes of tranquility and sorrow until the reappearance of the drum pulsation with dramatic brass tritones at the climax of the work. As before, the drumming leads to the poignant choral exclamation; this expressive apex is followed by a pause of five consecutive fermatas.

In the final segment of *Ad Matrem* a sustained pitch C slowly arises from nothingness, first at the dynamic level of *ppppp*, then *pppp*, *ppp*, *pp*, to become truly audible when the solo soprano intones her plea. The vocal part seems to be very easy since the melody is built from only one rhythmic value, the half note, and it circulates in the narrow range of just three distinct pitches, A-flat—G—F. However, this simple melodic recitation calls for a touch of magic to be truly effective in performance.[51]

The text of *Ad Matrem* articulates the existential position of the child addressing the mother. This mother, though, is simultaneously "my mother" and "the Mother of God" described in the *Stabat Mater*, the Latin source of Górecki's text. Both images, of the human and the heavenly motherhood, blend: is the tearful mother the one that suffered and died? Is she the one at the bottom of the Cross?

The expressive power of *Ad Matrem* relies, in part, on this ambiguity. I will take this polyvalency of meaning one step further by interpreting the opening, startling instrumental and vocal gestures of *Ad Matrem* in the light of several maternal metaphors, all linked to suffering.

---

[51] Stefania Woytowicz's histrionic interpretation of this part (on the Olympia CD), replete with huge *portamenti* and vibrato, completely ruins the effect envisioned by the composer, who preferred more delicate sopranos, with clear tone and little or no vibrato.

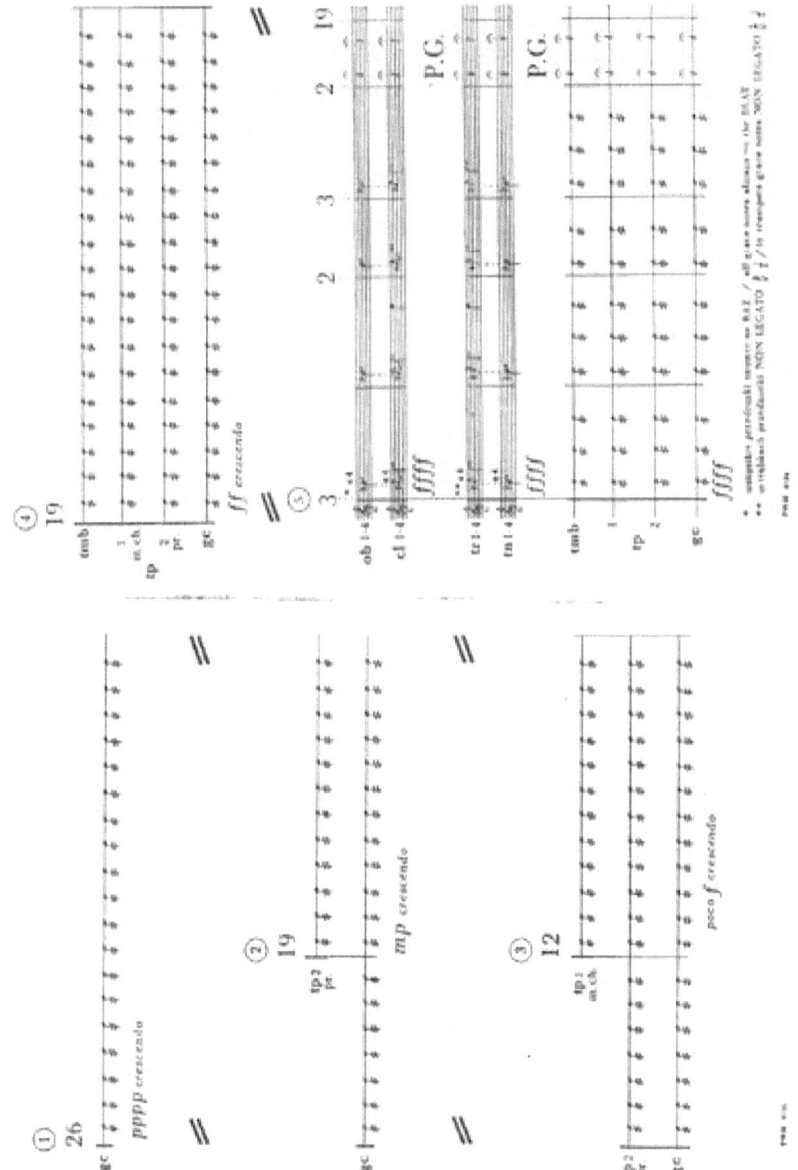

Figure 10-10: *Ad Matrem*, Op. 29, rehearsal no. 5.
Ad Matrem, Op. 29 by Henryk Górecki. © Copyright 1972 by PWM Edition, Kraków, Poland. U.S. Renewal Rights assigned to Boosey & Hawkes, Inc. Reprinted by permission of Boosey & Hawkes, Inc.

The first of these images is the representation of the birth process. The quick pulsation of the bass drum evokes a rapid heartbeat, the sudden tritone interventions—with their high levels of sensory dissonance—mirror stabbing pain, the overall temporal envelope of successive waves of sound interrupted by moments of silence resembles the pattern of pain and rest experienced in labor. A mother while giving birth alternates between feelings of an unbearable, throbbing pain of contractions which overwhelm her whole body, and moments of relief where the pain recedes into the background and she gathers strength for another onslaught of suffering. She rests and experiences the ultimate release mixed with joy only after the birth of the child.

But what about the drum pattern of over 260 beats per minute? This rapid pulsation can be interpreted as a homology to the terrible, pulsating pain in the woman's body, and to the intense fluttering of the baby's tiny heart, at birth highly exceeding its normal rate of 140-160 beats. The introductory instrumental passage of *Ad Matrem* would then suggest the qualitative elements of the experience of the birth process by the newborn child, whose stressful emergence into consciousness is a birth into language. It is hard not to hear the choral exclamation "MATER MEA" as an image of the first cry of a newborn child, of *every* human child. This is a collective cry coming from all of "us." Simultaneously, yet another metaphor arises from this simple sequence of stark percussive sounds. The fast-paced, heavy pounding of the bass drum may be heard as suggestive of the stifling breathlessness of a nightmare. The dramatic outcry, "MATER MEA," could then express the painful shock at the realization of the mother's death, a cry of despair followed by a silence pregnant with meaning, filled with tender memories and tearful recollections of the past...

Ad Matrem's expressive power rests on its simultaneous reference to birth and death; the work celebrates the sorrowful confluence of both ultimate events of human life. The experience of motherhood is here suspended between the extremes of stabbing pain and tranquil joy, the poles of agony and internal gladness. The melody of the solo soprano in the final segment of the piece arises from the silence "after the pain," and dissipates into the tranquillity of motionlessness. (The final annotation in the score reads "Absolutely no movement in the orchestra"). The composer interlocks all these images in one sequence of linearly juxtaposed sound blocks, carving their contours with utmost care.

OVERALL OUTLINE:							
A	B			A'		C	
a	b	a'	b'	a"			

DETAILS (measured in quarternotes):A							
Tempo 66-69-72							
Percussion	Pause	Percussion	Percussion and Winds	Pause	Percussion	Percussion and Winds	Pause
19 + 16	4	26+19+12+19	11	2	19+12+6+12	12	5

Continued: A			B				
Tempo 66-69-72			Lo stesso Tempo	Molto lento 40-42		Tempo 66-69-72	
Percussion and Winds	Percussion and Winds	Pause	Flute/Strings and Harp	Basson/ Strings/Piano	Pause	Flute/Strings and Piano	
11	5	3 (fer.)	25	24	2	25 +26+31	

Continued: B				A'			
Molto lento 40-42	Tempo 66-69-72	Lo stesso tempo marcatissimo					
Bassoon/Piano Strings	Flute/Strings Harp	Percussion and Winds	Pause	Percussion and Winds	Percussion and Winds and Choir	Tutta forza (No voices)	Pause
30	29	15 +6	2	17	5	12\	5 (fer)

Continued: C							
Lento e largo 46-48			rall.				
Strings and piano	Strings and Piano And Soprano		Strings, cont.	Pause			
32 + 2	32 + 12 + 12 + 10		10	6 (fer)			

Figure 10-11: Sectional formal outline of *Ad Matrem*, Op. 29 (details measured in quarter notes).

~ 211 ~

Górecki's works suggest, as no other music composed in Poland after World War II, a profound understanding of motherhood and its archetypes that draws upon the basic, universal experiences of human life. His emphasis on sorrow more closely approximates the real-life experiences of mothers than the flowery descriptions of blessed motherhood encountered in so many texts.

6. *Mater Dolorosa* and Maternal Thinking in the Symphony No. 3

The best-known appearance of the image of the *Mater Dolorosa* in Górecki's music occurs in Symphony No. 3, *Symphony of Sorrowful Songs*, Op. 36 (1976).[52] This work is Górecki's most powerful essay combining the themes of motherhood and death, images of human and heavenly motherhood. The texts of the Symphony juxtapose the image of eternal suffering of crucified Jesus and His Mother (the first movement) with two embodiments of this transcendental Passion in human history: the torment of a young prisoner during World War II (the second movement), and the lament of a mother grieving the death of her son (the third movement). The temporal framework of during—before—after death, coupled with the symmetrical design of the suffering mother—child—mother, unites the work beyond the superficial similarity of slow tempi and quietly sorrowful expression of the three movements.

In the first movement, a frame of two monumental canons for strings surrounds the plea of the *Mater Dolorosa* addressed to her dying Son[53]

---

[52] See Luke B. Howard, *"A Reluctant Requiem:" The History and Reception of Henryk M. Górecki's Symphony no. 3 in Britain and the United States.* (Ph.D. Diss., Ann Arbor: University of Michigan, 1997), 45-47. Howard further articulates his point in "Motherhood, Billboard and the Holocaust: Perceptions and Receptions of Górecki's Symphony no. 3" *Polish Music Journal* 6/1 (2003). See also Luke B. Howard, "Henryk M. Górecki's Symphony No. 3 (1976) as a Symbol of Polish Political History," *Polish Review* vol. 52 (2007): 215-222.

[53] For a multi-layer analysis of the structure of these two canons, see Ivan Jimenez, *Textural Depth, Structural Depth, Expressive Depth: Ladders From Line To Sonority In Arvo Pärt And Henryk Mikołaj Górecki*, Ph.D. Dissertation (University of Pittsburgh, 2007).

(see Figure 8-12 in Chapter 8 above). She reminds him of her love, of their closeness in the past, and breaks off with the words "you are leaving me now, my dearest hope"—set to a slowly ascending melodic line in the Phrygian mode, a mode traditionally associated with grief. Her text comes from a fifteenth-century Polish Lenten poem belonging to the textual tradition of *Stabat Mater*, the locus classicus of the "dolorosa" imagery.[54] A Polish poet, Halina Poświatowska, described this sorrowful image of Mary in her *Lenten Legend*, concluding with the words: [55]

> then—it is said— she ascended into heaven
> but equally well she could have descended into pain
> it was so deep.

The direct relationship to another famous *Stabat Mater*, that is the choral masterpiece by Karol Szymanowski (Op. 53, composed in 1925-26) points to Górecki's awareness of the widespread embedding of this archetype of *Mater Dolorosa* in Polish culture.[56] The profundity of Mary's pain is suggested in Górecki's Symphony by musical means—quietly intense sonorities, relentless pulsation of slow meters, huge dimensions of repetitive material. Her voice appears in the music in a monumental frame of two instrumental canons, the sheer span of which suggests the abyss of eternity.

The enormous scope of the design, the persistent repetitiveness and austere restraint of the music—arising from silence and darkness, then receding again, after the brief and sorrowful apparition—point beyond the realm of temporality. Although the representation of eternity in time is, strictly speaking, impossible—for, to quote St.

---

[54] The *Stabat Mate*" sequence names the "suffering mother" in its first strophe: "Stabat Mater dolorósa / Juxta Crucem lacrimósa, / Dum pendébat Filius" [At the cross her station keeping, / Mary stood in sorrow weeping / When her Son was crucified].
[55] Halina Poświatowska: "Wielkopostna Legenda," in *Wiersze Wybrane* [Selected Poems], ed. Jan Zych (Kraków: Wydawnictwo Literackie, 1997).
[56] See the essay by Teresa Malecka on Górecki and Polish culture in Chapter 11 in the present volume. *Stabat Mater* by Szymanowski is cited throughout Górecki's career, from Variations Op. 4 for violin and piano of 1956, to the Fourth Symphony, *Tansman Episodes* of 2006 (See Chapter 14 by Andrzej Wendland).

Augustine, in eternity "all is at once present, whereas no time is all at once present" (*Confessions*, Book 11, Chapter 11)—musical portrayals of timelessness often feature vast dimensions, extreme slowness of tempo, repetitiveness, canonic designs, and so forth.

Here, Górecki's Symphony No. 3 draws from the rich Western heritage of musical symbolism. [57] His objective is to create a sphere of "sacred time"—as he explained to student musicians during rehearsals for the first North American performance of the Third Symphony that he conducted during the *Górecki Autumn* at the University of Southern California in October 1997.[58] As the composer said, he would like to take his listeners from "the basement of everyday life, filled with noises, distractions and anxieties, to the tenth floor, or even to the sky of timelessness." This sacred sphere is dedicated, in the Catholic universe, to the contemplation of the divine mysteries, a prime position among which is taken by the suffering and glory of Jesus and his holy Mother.

The means of this transformation is a deceptively simple, meandering canon theme, that's multiplied into layers, stacked upon layers while ascending in a monumental climax. Ivan Jimenez describes the theme that "spans an octave which is completed through a gradual process. The melodic apex is reached in m. 13, exactly half way through the theme's total length. This melodic apex is followed by a gradual registral descent which completes a symmetric melodic arch."[59]

---

[57] See Thomas, *op. cit.*, 81-94; Luke Howard's dissertation provides a detailed overview, including additional source materials and analytical insights, as well as a richly illustrated reception history. For an overview of mystical aspects of the Symphony (confluence of suffering and love in "passion," human and Divine union), see Maria Anna Harley [Maja Trochimczyk], "To be God with God: Catholic Composers and the Mystical Experience," *Contemporary Music Review* 12, part 2, ed. Ivan Moody (1995): 125-145.

[58] Henryk Mikołaj Górecki, "Remarks on Performing the Third Symphony," 3 October 1997, translated by Maja Trochimczyk, Polish Music Journal 6, no. 2 (2003), http://pmc.usc.edu/PMJ/issue/6.2.03/GoreckiThird.html.

[59] Ivan Jimenez, in *Textural Depth, Structural Depth, Expressive Depth: Ladders From Line To Sonority In Arvo Pärt And Henryk Mikołaj Górecki*, Ph.D. Dissertation (University of Pittsburgh, 2007): 11.

Other analysts write about the way the theme itself is fashioned from core material of Polish religious folk songs, *Oto Jezus umiera* [*Here Jesus dies*] from Lent, and a Kurpie song *Niechaj będzie pochwalony* [*Let Him be Praised*]. The arch is then multiplied, by successive entrances of the strings—spanning six octaves.

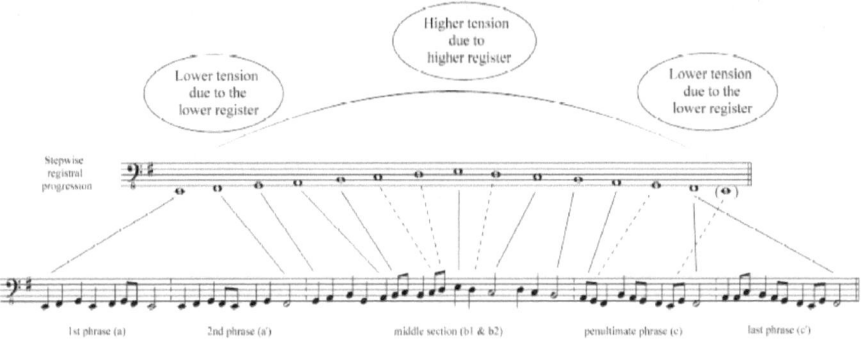

Figure 10-12, a: Arch-structure of the canon theme; b: The pitch span of the theme (below) and all canonic voices (above). analyzed by Ivan Jimenez, in *Textural Depth, Structural Depth, Expressive Depth: Ladders From Line To Sonority In Arvo Pärt And Henryk Mikołaj Górecki*, Ph.D. Dissertation (University of Pittsburgh, 2007).

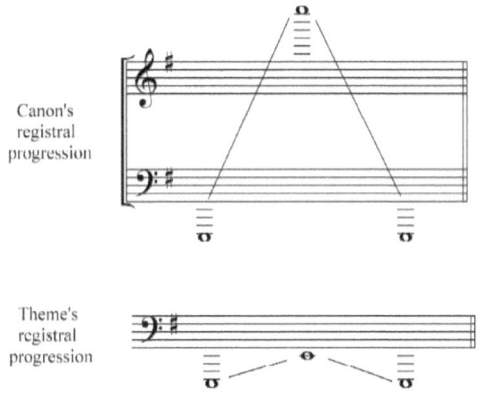

The second movement of the Symphony No. 3 brings the spiritual matter down to Earth; the text reverses the dialogic orientation, as it is directed from the child to the mother. After much searching, the composer selected an inscription scribbled on the prison wall in 1944 by the eighteen-year old Helena Wanda Błażusiak, a young Gestapo prisoner from Zakopane. During rehearsals at the University of Southern California the composer explained to the soprano, Elizabeth Hynes:[60]

---

[60] I served as translator for these interactions, and transcribed the recording, Henryk Mikołaj Górecki, "Remarks on Performing the Third Symphony," *op. cit.*

I would like to add something here about this inscription. In prison, the whole wall was covered with inscriptions screaming out loud: "I'm innocent" "Murderers" "Executioners" "Free me" "You have to save me"—it was all so loud, so banal. Adults were writing this, while here it is an 18-year-old girl, almost a child. And she is so different. She does not despair, does not cry, does not scream for revenge. She does not think about herself; whether she deserves her fate or not. Instead, she only thinks about her mother: because it is her mother who will experience true despair. This inscription was something extraordinary. And it really fascinated me: "Mother, do not cry, no. The purest Queen of Heaven, you always support me. Hail Mary." Here the inscription ended and I added: "You are full of grace." Not "Full of grace" as it is in the prayer, but "You are full of..."

Two aspects of this explanation merit comments: (1) Górecki's sensitivity to the young girl's "maternal thinking," and (2) his emphasis on Mary's maternal perfection, her "fullness of grace." Helena's words are a testimony to the maturity of her "attentive love" reflected in her concern for the well-being of others. The maternal thinking of the young daughter makes her share the pain suffered by her mother; she is mature enough, maternal enough to be that compassionate.

The inscription on the wall included only the first phrase of *Hail Mary*. Górecki's addition continues the prayer with "Full of grace." There is one difference between this phrase in the original prayer and in the Górecki quote: the composer makes the text more symmetrical by adding "ś" to the ending of the word "Łaski" [grace, second case]. This one-letter change, an archaism and an abbreviation, is of great significance for Górecki representation of Mary as the source of existence, a Divine Mother of all:

| Zdrowa(jeste)ś Mario | Healthy you **are**, Mary |
| Łaski(jeste)ś pełna | Grace, you **are** full of |

This condensed play on words emphasizes "the fullness of being" as an important attribute of Mary. The musical setting focuses on the

---

It is interesting that he told the same anecdote to Małgorzata and Marcin Gmys during the interview in 2002, see Chapter 5.

contemplation of this mystery by the prayerful girl: this is why the text is divided into individual words, separated by pauses in the vocal part. By doing so, explains Górecki, the music mirrors the inwardness, the hesitation of someone lost in thought, of someone hoping to receive at least a little of Mary's "fullness" in order to survive the ordeal.[61]

Helena's initial words, "Mamo, nie płacz" [Mama, don't cry], seem to supply Christ's response to the unanswered plea of Mary at the bottom of the Cross. Yet, the girl's beseeching is initially addressed to her own mother, not Mary. After calling upon her mother several times, Helena shifts her attention to the heavenly Queen. The closeness of the natural and the heavenly motherhood is articulated by the music. The singer makes the transition from "Mamo" [Mommy] to "Niebios przeczysta Królowo" [The purest Queen of Heaven] on the same pitch, as smoothly as possible. Only the shift of the underlying harmony highlights the change.

The repeated invocations constitute gentler variants of the calling motives ["wołanie"] addressed to Mother/Maria in *O Domina Nostra, Ad Matrem,* and *Totus Tuus*. In all these works the calling is followed not by an answer from the being that has been called, but by a shift in the mode of utterance, from invocation to contemplation, from an expression of an urgent need to a tranquil prayer. The model for these dialogic formal designs can be seen in the responsorial dialogues of actual Church prayers and litanies. I have already pointed out that the text of *O Domina Nostra* is designed as such a dialogue, though the symmetries are destroyed by the musical setting.

I have also compared the distinction between "MARIA"—"Maria" phrases in *Totus Tuus* (1985) to responsorial forms of litanies, and to the breath-based, mantra-like "Prayer of Jesus." It is remarkable, in the latter choral work, that the dramatic "MARIA" does not return in the final segment: there is no reason to return to its emotional intensity after reaching the equilibrium amidst the repetitions of the same name, uttered quietly, fading away into stillness. In *Totus Tuus,* the invocation serves to introduce both parts of the work, which then

---

[61] In his conversation with Elisabeth Hynes during the break in the rehearsal, USC School of Music, October 2, 1998, ibidem.

concludes in prayer. *Beatus Vir*, Op. 38 (1979) has a similar dramatic opening addressed to "Domine," but its form is much more complicated. In *O Domina Nostra* (1982), the prayerful call upon "Domina" permeates the whole work, with dramatic exclamations of "Claramontana—Victoriosa" and prayer fragments "Sancta Maria—ora pro nobis" embedded in this layer of beseeching.

All the mature "maternal" works by Górecki (excluding the *Three Songs*) contain versions of similar, paired gestures of calling out—contemplating within, of an invocation answered by a prayer. Górecki also uses this bipartite model as a basis for large-scale form, starting with *Ad Matrem* (1971). Here, the "invocation" appears in the first, massive part of the work while the "contemplation/prayer" is assigned to its smaller concluding section. In the *Symphony of Sorrowful Songs* this asymmetric design appears in the second movement, with its textual transition from the calling to the mother to reciting a prayer, intended to heal the pain and anxiety felt by the young prisoner. This model of invocation and prayer carries emotive associations with a shift from tension and longing to rest. As such it can also be seen as underlying the general outline of the large-scale form in Górecki's Symphony No. 2, *Copernican*, Op. 31 (1972). Its two movements outline a trajectory from maximum dissonance in the initial sections of the work, permeated with violent outcries, towards a resolution of tension in the lengthy consonant chords of the coda.[62]

It would not be out of place to mention here that thanks to the efforts of a British playwright Bob Bibby, we know that the young girl immortalized as a Nazi victim in the second movement of the *Symphony of Sorrowful Songs* actually survived the war to marry, have children, and die of old age in her hometown of Szczawnik. Bibby's one-hour play about her imprisonment, entitled *Lena*, was performed in March 2001 at a small theater in Bridgenorth, Shropshire, UK.[63] Incidentally (and synchronistically), the composer found out about the fate of Helena Błażusiak around the same time. As he reported to

---

[62] I discuss the Symphony's transition from a maximum of sensory dissonance to a consonant conclusion, paralleled by a change in spatial sound location, in "Spatiality of Sound and Stream Segregation in Twentieth-Century Instrumental Music," *Organized Sound* 3, no. 2 (1998): 147-166.

[63] Personal email from Bob Bibby to Maja Trochimczyk, fall 2001.

Małgorzata and Marcin Gmys, Helena survived the war, married and lived a quiet life with her family in Wadowice, a small town that Górecki passed through every time he went to visit the mountains, sometimes as often as twice per week (see Chapter 5). Clearly, Helena's prayer was answered.

To return to the *Symphony of Sorrowful Songs*, the text of the final movement in Górecki's Symphony No. 3 is a strophic folk song from Poland's south-western Opole region, written during the Silesian Uprisings against the Germans (1920s). The song, "Kajze mi sie podzioł mój synocek miły" [Where did he go, my dear little son] describes the feelings of a sorrowful mother, as Górecki says, in "terse, simple words. It is not sorrow, despair or resignation or the wringing of hands: it is just the great grief and lamenting of a mother who has lost her son."[64] Embittered accusations are followed by expressions of the mother's profound sadness at her loss leading to a resigned acceptance of her fate (see the Appendix: Texts of Symphony No. 3). However, Górecki understands this text as the image of an unchanging grief; to strengthen this interpretation he repeats one reproachful strophe at the end: "Oh, you evil people... why did you kill my son?"

After the loss of her child, the sorrowful mother becomes an altogether different person: she now belongs to a group which was recently called "the mothers of the disappeared" (*desaparecido*). According to Jean Bethke Elshtain, this existential category came into being and was given a distinct name as a group in Argentina after the 1976 military coup, when many young people, especially young men, were kidnaped and murdered by the agents of the secret service.[65] Alejandro Iglesias Rossi, an Argentinian composer, testified how frightening it was for him to go to school in Buenos Aires: every week, every day, another friend was missing, another seat was

---

[64] Henryk Mikołaj Górecki: "Powiem Państwu szczerze..." [I will tell you honestly. . .]. Tape transcript of Górecki's talk on his music given in 1977 in Baranów, Poland; *Vivo* 1 (1994). Cited in Thomas, *op. cit.*, 81.

[65] Jean Bethke Elshtain: "The Mothers of the Disappeared: Passion and Protest in Maternal Action," in Donna Bassin, Margaret Honey, and MeryleMahrer Kaplan, eds., *Representations of Motherhood* (New Haven and London: Yale University Press, 1994), 75-91

empty.⁶⁶ And one could not talk about it, one could not mention their names for fear of sharing their fate. Only the mothers could do that. That was the sole privilege of hundreds of mothers who kept walking around the main plaza of Buenos Aires sporting white scarves or strings with attached photographs of their lost ones. "They wore necklaces of despair and grief as others might wear pearls or brooches" writes Elshtain.⁶⁷ A silent circle, walking along very slowly: lost in grief, lost in memories, lost in thought.

Figure 10-13: Symphony No. 3, Op. 36, third movement, 79. Symphony No. 3, Op. 36 by Henryk Górecki © Copyright 1977 by PWM Edition, Kraków, Poland U.S. Renewal Rights assigned to Boosey & Hawkes, Inc. English, French and German translation: © Copyright 1992 by Boosey & Hawkes Music Publishers Ltd. Reprinted by permission of Boosey & Hawkes, Inc.

This painful dragging of feet appears to be the source of the pulsating slow tempo in the third movement of Górecki's Symphony. The main orchestral gesture of two alternating chords originates in the introduction to Chopin's Mazurka Op. 17, No. 4 (Figure 10-13: Symphony No. 3, third movement, 79). The chords have to be repeated

---

⁶⁶ Private conversation, Kazimierz Dolny (Summer Courses for Young Composers), September 1986.
⁶⁷ Bethke Elshtain, *op. cit.*, 77.

with a broad bow, with a stubborn relentlessness and a quiet intensity.

"Play it rhythmically, very slowly but rhythmically" said the composer during the rehearsal at the University of Southern California (on 2 October 1997). "It's like rocking a baby in your arms" added the singer, Elizabeth Hynes, illustrating her words with a silent gesture. It is like that, but it is also like rocking back and forth, back and forth, without end, without a pause for thought, after receiving a terrible blow, recoiling from the shock in a trance of sorrow.

That is the essence of this movement: the slow walking, the rocking slowness of pain, mirrored in the repeated gesture of comfort—"there, there, there. . ." The Polish equivalent of these "comfort" phrases—"cicho, cicho, cicho" [quiet, quiet, quiet]—is pronounced on a fixed intonation level. There is a slight descent and *decrescendo* at the end of each word which may be shortened to a softly whispered sonority of "ćśśś" [soft version of "chshshshsh"]. These comforting words and sounds may be addressed to a child, but also to the sorrowful mother and to every suffering person.

Anne Fernald's cross-cultural research into the prosody of exaggerated speech patterns of mothers or fathers addressing their small children, (commonly known as "motherese") suggests that the patterns carrying simple emotional connotations, such as approval, prohibition, attention, and comfort have similar pitch contours in five Western languages (British and American English, German, French, Italian; See Figure 10-14:). In her diagram, the "comfort" phrases consist of repeated words with narrow intonational range and descending direction. The steady pitch and slow tempo of these repeated expressions of compassionate, maternal love (representative of "maternal thinking" in general, not just in reference to children) are echoed in repeated sequences of chords which end the *Symphony of Sorrowful Songs*.

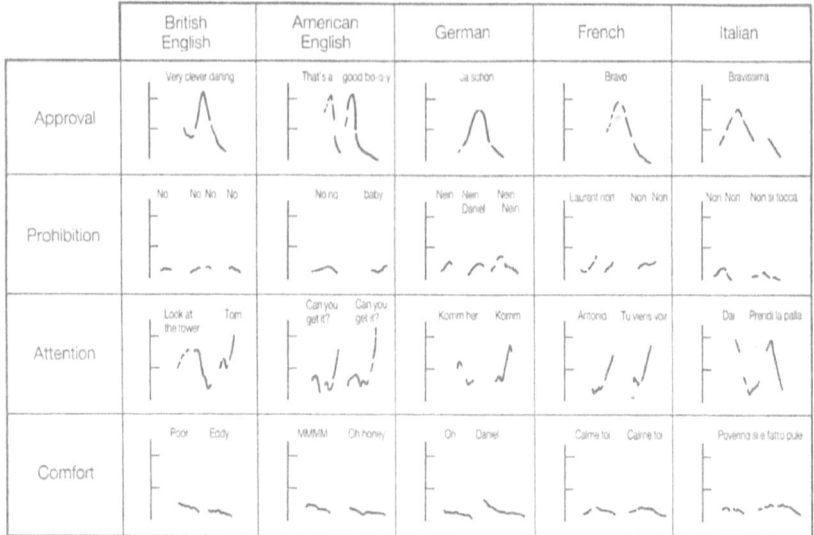

Figure 10-14: Examples of pitch contours from Anne Fernald, „Approval, Prohibition, Attention, and Comfort Vocalizations in British, American, German, French and Italian Mothers' Speech to Twelve-month-old Infants." 63. From *The Adapted Mind: Evolutionary Psychology and the Generation of Culture*, ed. James H. Barkow, L. Cosmides et al. Copyright 1992 by Oxford University Press. Used by permission of Oxford University Press, Inc.

Again, as in *Ad Matrem*, a basic musical gesture carries multiple connotations that imbue the music with layers of meaning. The slow rhythm of the two paired chord˙ is a homology to the slow walking pace of a suffering mother who contemplates her memories and her fate as "a mother of the disappeared" which has transformed the realities of her daily life. The composer himself used and imitated this physical image when explaining the interpretative changes needed to be made by the student orchestra at USC.

Moreover, his own conducting technique, described by Mark Swed in the review of the 3 October 1997 concert in Los Angeles, was very physical, with gestures of his whole body expressing the music and inciting the performers to follow:[68]

---

[68] Mark Swed: "Górecki's Third Is All His Own: Music Review," *Los Angeles Times*, 6 October 1997.

> He conducted without baton and without guile. An open right palm gently marked the meter until he approached climaxes. But then it was as if he roared. His whole body would tense up to the breaking point. With shaking fists, he exhorted the players to dig deeper into the sound of their instruments than they ever had before, but he seemed also to entreat God with the same gesture.

This comment captures primarily the gestural aspects of the first movement, featuring powerful, prayerful climaxes. The repeated chordal segments of Górecki's Symphony No. 3 allude simultaneously to three interlocking gestural patterns. The first gesture is the slow walking pace discussed above; the second pattern stems from the vocal utterances of comforting words and phrases. The narrow pitch range and oscillating, flattened contours of the repeated chords throughout the third movement resemble the repetitive vocal intonations associated with expressions of comfort. Finally, the steady repetitive patterns also evoke the rocking motions, the swaying of the body while putting a child to sleep. This soothing repetition of movement is meant to induce a numbing, comforting feeling in the baby, safely resting in the mother's arms.

These maternal gestures, the third type of motion alluded to in Górecki's Symphony, are the source for the steady rhythms of the **lullaby**, a domestic art form that has inspired an art-music genre practiced by many composers, including Górecki's favorites, Franz Schubert (*Wiegendlied*)[69] and Fryderyk Chopin, whose *Berceuse*, Op. 57 (1845) is often considered the paradigmatic musical lullaby.[70] Its compound duple meter, 6/8, with the rising and falling *arpeggio* figure serves as an image of the rocking cradle. As Górecki said in 1998, the actual rhythmic pattern is not that important: „It is a lullaby whether it is in 3/4 or 4/4 or 6/8 or even 9/8. A lullaby is not the rhythm by

---

[69] Susan Youens: "Metamorphoses of a melody: Schubert's Wiegenlied, D. 498, in twentieth-century opera," *Opera Quarterly* 2, no. 2 (summer 1984): 35-48
[70] The "lullaby" entry in the *New Grove Dictionary of Music and Musicians* defines the genre as associated with triple meter. For a study of lullabies in opera see Gerard Loubinoux: "Le chant dans le chant: A la recherche d'une memoire mythique" [Songs within songs: In search of a mythical memory], in *Opera, theatre, une memoire imaginaire* (Paris: Herne, 1990), p. 77-89.

itself, a lullaby is the emotional quality that the rhythm and melody create with the words."[71]

The repetitiveness and slowness of the real lullaby has a soothing effect on the listeners; according to one psychological experiment, listening to lullabies over extended periods of time induces a slower breath and heart rate in subjects (no doubt, a similar effect is desired for these songs's primary addressees, little children).[72] Some researchers claim that a remnant of ancient pagan magic incantations survives in the lullabies to "charm away" the evils roaming in the night.[73] The texts of lullabies range from soothing to frightening, the lullaby's incantations serves to alleviate fears as well as calm and appease the „horrors" of darkness.[74]

Again, to let the composer speak (from the interview in Chapter 4):

> It is not what is outside, but what is inside What is a lullaby? It starts from a relationship between the mother and the child, could be the father and a child. . . There is always a child and a parent, male or female. And what else? These are, if one were to define them, the most wonderful, tranquil moments of human life. When singing the lullaby, there is no teaching, no discipline. . . It is the most happy, blissful moment between the parent and the child.

Interestingly, the lullabies' repetitive patterns and their sing-song monotone recitation are also of importance in the process of language

---

[71] See the interview in Chapter 4.
[72] Johannes Kneutgen: "Eine Musikform und ihre biologische Funktion. Über die Wirkungsweise der Wiegenlieder" [A musical form and its biological function. Concerning the effects of the lullaby], *Zeitschrift für Experimentelle und Angewandte Psychologie* 17, no. 2 (1970): 245-65.
[73] Breandan O Madagain: "Echoes of Magic in the Gaelic Song Tradition," *Celtic Languages and Celtic Peoples* (Nova Scotia, Canada: St. Mary's University, 1992), 125-140; Yoshihiko Ikegami: "The Lullaby as Magic: A Textual Analysis of Traditional Japanese Children's Songs" in *The Oral and the Literate in Music* (Tokyo: Academia, 1986), 96-109.
[74] Yael Nov: "Trost und Schrecken im jiddischen und hebraischen Wiegenlied" [Consolation and terror in Yiddish and Hebrew lullabies], *Polyaisthesis* 3, no. 2 (1988): 120-130; Ana Lucia Cavani Jorge: *O acalanto e o horror* [Lullaby and horror] (Sao Paulo: Escuta, 1988).

acquisition.[75] The lullabies are sung/recited by mothers who, thus, provide sources of human identity for the newborn child and play an indispensable role in teaching children to speak. By listening to repeated strains of initially strange sounds that through repetition acquire meaning, infants enter the world of human language. Their linguistic skills grow from their mother's voices. Studies reveal that in teaching children their language mothers use a range of cross-culturally identical patterns, which join expressions of emotions and meaning.[76] It is through their "maternal thinking," through their attentive love and focus on the children's needs that the mothers create conditions for their children to grow mentally and emotionally. Thus, lullabies are one example of "motherese"—that is infant-directed speech patterns, as well as maternal vocalizations that are crucial aspects of acquiring language.

Górecki's published lullabies ("Uśnij, że mi uśnij" [Sleep, Sleep, For Me], "Kołysz-że się kołysz" [Rock, Rock], and "Nie piej, kurku, nie piej" [Rooster, do not Crow], from *Three Lullabies*, Op. 49 for choir) preserve the rhythmic features of folk lullabies serving as their models. In this short collection, the composer sets two songs in duple meters and one in triple meter. Anna Czekanowska's study of Polish folk music cites one of the songs used by Górecki, "Uśnij, że mi uśnij" (it is in duple meter), as an instance of a typical Polish lullaby.[77] The *Mazowsze* volume of the Oskar Kolberg collection of Polish folklore

---

[75] Luisa Del Giudice: "Ninna-nanna nonsense? Fears, dreams, and falling in the Italian lullaby," *Oral Tradition* 3, no. 3 (October 1988): 270-293; see also Anne Fernald: "Vocalizations," op. cit.

[76] See Anne Fernald: "Human Maternal Vocalizations to Infants as Biologically Relevant Signals: An Evolutionary Perspective," in Paul Bloom, ed., *Language Acquisition: Core Readings* (Cambridge, Mass.: The MIT Press, 1994), 51-94. See also Sandra E. Trehub, Anna M. Unyk and Laurel J. Trainor: "Adults Identify Infant-directed Music Across Cultures," *Infant Behavior and Development* 16, no. 2: 193-211; and, by the same authors, "Maternal Singing in Cross-cultural Perspective," *Infant Behavior and Development* 16, no. 3 (July-September 1993): 285-295.

[77] Anna Czekanowska: *Polish Folk Music: Slavonic Heritage—Polish Tradition—Contemporary Trends* (Cambridge and New York: Cambridge University Press, 1992), p. 136-137.

(vol. 26) shows a similar distribution of patterns and includes an equal number of lullabies in duple and triple meters.[78]

Ah, two little cats,
Greyish-brownish, both of them
They will do nothing else
But take care of you (*or:* entertain you)

Bzi bzi bzibziana,
zjedli wilcy barana,
a owieczkę psi, psi, psi,
ty, dzieciuchno, śpi, śpi, śpi.

Figure 11-15; a: A traditional Polish lullaby, *Aaa, kotki dwa;* b: A lullaby from the Kurpie region, "Bzi, bzi, bzibziana" no. 147 from Oskar Kolberg, *Dzieła wszystkie*, vol. 39, "Pomorze." (Warszawa: Ludowa Spółdzielnia Wydawnicza and Kraków: PWM Edition), 1965). Arranged by Górecki in *Ah, My Lavender Garland*, Op. 50 (1984) for mixed chorus *a capella*.

The chordal repetitions in Górecki's Symphony No. 3 do not share the conventional compound triple meters with the "artistic" instrumental lullabies; instead, they have more in common with the repetitiveness of the actual bedtime songs, such as "Uśnij, że mi uśnij" or a popular Polish lullaby, "Aaa, kotki dwa . . ." [Ah, Two Little Cats] (See Figure 10-15: Traditional Polish Lullabies). These lulling chants hover between speech and song, and are intoned in a tender, humming voice.

---

[78] Oskar Kolberg: *Dzieła Wszystkie* [Collected Works] 26, "Mazowsze," Part III (Warszawa: LudowaSpółdzielniaWydawnicza and PWM Edition), 1963. Reprint, orig. publ. 1887, p. 336-337

The *Aaa, kotki dwa* is sung with the melody of two interlocking minor thirds, G—E—G, F—D—F, without any cadences or closures. The melody is gradually flattened out and transformed into rhythmic humming which accompanies the sleep-inducing rocking motion. The song disappears into silence when the child falls asleep. The lullaby's duple meter and simplicity of rhythmic patterns consisting of alternating quarter notes and paired eight notes are mirrored on many pages of Górecki's Symphony No. 3, for instance in the rhythms of the canonic subject in the first movement of the work.[79]

More importantly, the rhythms of the lullaby contribute to the mosaics of comforting gestures evoked in the Symphony's final movement. The repeated chordal patterns simultaneously allude to the slow walking of someone lost in thought, to the rocking movement of pain-stricken people, to the comforting gestures that soothe this pain. It is the peculiar simplicity of this work, a simplicity marked by an abundance of musical references that distinguishes this work from many other compositions of "Holy Minimalism."

The significance of the repetitions and lullabies goes beyond the *Symphony of Sorrowful Songs*. The repeated rhythms in all of Górecki's „maternal" works draw simultaneously from cultural modes of expression of grief (slow walking, crying, lamenting), comfort (lullaby, repeated vocal phrases and gestures), and religious belief (invocations and prayers, and responsorial patterns).

7. Conclusions

The subjects of motherhood or birth are rare in contemporary Polish art music: such prominent composers as Witold Lutosławski, Krzysztof Penderecki, Grażyna Bacewicz and Marta Ptaszyńska have very few, if any, "maternal" works in their outputs. Some of Górecki's younger colleagues have focused on the darker and more disturbing aspects of motherhood, such as, for instance, those explored in Hanna

---

[79] The theme of the canon is derived from two religious songs, "Oto Jezus umiera" from Jan Siedlecki's *Śpiewnik Kościelny* (in triple meter) and "Niechaj bendzie pochwalony" from Władysław Skierkowski's *Puszcza kurpiowska w pieśni* (in duple meter). See Thomas, *op. cit.*, 84-85.

Kulenty's critically-acclaimed opera *The Mother of Black-Winged Dreams* (1996). Among Eastern European religious works, Arvo Pärt's *Stabat Mater* (1985) with its vivid representations of weeping portrayed by "streams" of descending violin melodies, is the closest counterpart to Górecki's sorrowful meditations. Pärt's work shares with Górecki's music an absence of irony and distance.

Górecki's imagery of motherhood juxtaposes poignant representations of maternal sorrow, captured in the symbolic icon of *Mater Dolorosa* with subtle representations of maternal power, as in the glorious *O Domina Nostra*, and the echoes of the humble genre of the lullaby. His maternal imagery stems from the intensity of attachment of mother and child, in an archetypal bond that results in intense suffering when broken.[80] This bond links the "mother/child dyad" so strongly that it overwhelms the mother's separate personal identity; by becoming a mother every woman is irreversibly transformed and all her aspirations are submerged in her "primary maternal preoccupation."[81] Feminist Meryle Mahrer Kaplan writes: "Social studies literature, practical child-rearing manuals provide an image of the mother who is submerged in the mother/child dyad, and lost to the world."[82]

The suffering human mother is tearful (the Symphony No. 3, third movement and *Ad Matrem*) and full of sadness (*Three Songs*, and the Symphony No. 3, second movement). In contrast, the heavenly Mother Mary is an all-powerful Queen, the Mother of the World (*Totus Tuus*) and the Mother of the faithful (the Symphony No. 3, first and second movements and *O Domina Nostra*). She is defined by being a mother of the Savior (*Totus Tuus*), but also a suffering mother at the bottom of the Cross, *Mater Dolorosa* (*Ad Matrem* and the Symphony No. 3, first and second movements). References to the absence of the natural mother and to the eternal source of maternal grace in the suffering *Mater Dolorosa* are often juxtaposed (*Ad Matrem* and Symphony No. 3, second movement).

---

[80] See John Bowbly, *The Making & Breaking Of Affectional Bonds* (New York: Routledge, 1992, 1979).
[81] Thurer, *op. cit.*
[82] See Meryle Mahrer Kaplan, *Mothers' Images of Motherhood: Case Studies of Twelve Mothers* (New York: Routlege, 1992), p. 5).

In conclusion, it must be said that Górecki's portrayals of sorrowful motherhood have nothing in common with the national myth of the heroic Polish Mother, *Matka-Polka*. Instead, he draws upon certain topoi from the Catholic tradition—Mary as victorious Queen and *Mater Dolorosa* from the *Stabat Mater* sequence—and alludes to the universal archetypes rooted in basic emotive behavioral patterns as his contexts and inspirations. Notice that, by filling his music with expressions of longing for the perfect mother, by constructing passages of maximum drama juxtaposed with total tranquillity, Górecki disruptively places into one category ideas traditionally associated with contrasting emotive realms: "suffering" has a negative valence while "mother" is mostly associated with total goodness.[83]

The tension arising from this mixture of negative and positive emotive values (that is,"suffering" and "mother") adds a layer of expressive richness to his works. The exploration of the theme of motherhood in the Polish composer's output suggests that close readings of well-known pieces such as Symphony No. 3 can benefit from unconventional methodologies and from situating these works in their broad cultural and conceptual contexts.

---

[83] See Rozsika Parker, *Mother Love/Mother Hate: The Power of Maternal Ambivalence* (New York: Basic Books, 1995).

APPENDIX

A. Texts to Górecki's Three Songs Op. 3 for medium voice and piano, with translations by Maja Trochimczyk.

Three Songs, Op. 3 by Henryk Górecki
© Copyright 1977 by PWM Edition, Kraków, Poland
U.S. Renewal Rights assigned to Boosey & Hawkes, Inc.
Reprinted by permission of Boosey & Hawkes, Inc.

<u>1. Juliusz Słowacki, *Do Matki/To Mother*</u>

W ciemnościach postać mi stoi matczyna
Niby idąca ku tęczowej bramie
Jej odwrócona twarz patrzy przez ramię
I w oczach widać, że patrzy na syna.

> *In the darkness I see mother's figure:*
> *She seems to walk towards the rainbow gate –*
> *Her face, turned away, looks over her shoulder*
> *And in her eyes I see that she looks at her son.*

<u>2. Juliusz Słowacki, *Jakiż to dzwon grobowy/The Funereal Bell*</u>

Jakiż to dzwon grobowy	*What sepulchral bells*
Z wiejskiego zabrzmiał kościoła?	*Resounded from the village church*
Idzie tłum pogrzebowy –	*The funeral crowd approaches –*
Schylone do ziemi czoła:	*Their heads bowed down to the earth;*
Trumna – za trumną dzieci	*The coffin – children behind it,*
Smutna przyjaciół drużyna	*A sorrowful group of friends*
Blada gromnica świeci	*Carrying their pale candles*
Ciche modlitwy powtarza.	*Repeating their quiet prayers. They*
Weszli we wrota cmentarza	*entered the cemetery gates*
Pd trumną ramię syna.	*The son's arm under the coffin.*
Czarną dręczeni rozpaczą	*Tormented by black despair,*
Czarną okryci żałobą...	*Covered by black mourning...*

3. Julian Tuwim, *Ptak/The Bird*

Na gałązce usiadł ptak:	*A bird alighted on a twig:*
Zaszczebiotał, zatrzepotał	*How it twittered, how it flutteredi*
Ostry dzióbek w piórka otarł,	*It wiped his sharp beak in feathers.*
Rozkołysał cały krzak.	*It made the whole bush swing.*
Potem z świrem frunął w lot!	*Then it flew away with song!*
A gałązka rozhuśtana	*And the swinging twig*
Jeszcze drży uradowana	*Still trembles with joy*
Że ją tak rozpląsał trzpiot.	*That the bird made her dance so.*

B. Texts for Górecki's Third Symphony, *The Symphony of Sorrowful Songs*, Op. 36 (1976) With translations by Maja Trochimczyk.

Symphony No. 3, Op. 36 by Henryk Górecki
© Copyright 1977 by PWM Edition, Kraków, Poland
U.S. Renewal Rights assigned to Boosey & Hawkes, Inc.
English, French and German translation:
© Copyright 1992 by Boosey & Hawkes Music Publishers Ltd.
Reprinted by permission of Boosey & Hawkes, Inc.

1. *Lento—Sostenuto tranquillo ma cantabile* – fragment of the Lament Swiętokrzyski / Lamentation of the Holy Cross Monastery, 15th century.

Synku miły i wybrany,	My son, chosen and beloved,
rozdziel z matka swoje rany;	share your wounds
A wszakom Cię, Synku miły	with your mother;
w swem sercu nosiła,	Because, dear son,
A takież Tobie wiernie służyła.	I have carried you in my heart
Przemów k(u) matce	and always served you faithfully.
bych się ucieszyła,	Speak to your mother
Bo juz jidziesz ode mnie,	to make her happy;
moja nadzieja miła.	As you are already leaving me,
	my cherished hope.

2. *Lento e largo—Tranquillissimo* — Inscription from Zakopane, „Pałace" Prison, Cell No. 3, Helena Wanda Błażusiakówna [young, unmarried woman with the family name Błażusiak], 18 years old, jailed since 25 September 1944.

Mamo, nie płacz nie.	Mother, do not weep, no.
Niebios Przeczysta Krolowo,	The purest Queen of Heaven
Ty zawsze wspieraj mnie.	Support me always.
Zdrowaś Mario, łaskiś pełna.	Hail Mary, full of grace.

3. *Lento—Cantabile-semplice* —A folk song from the Opole region.

Kajze mi sie podzioł	Where have I lost him
Mój synocek miły?	My beloved son?
Pewnie go w powstaniu	Perhaps in the uprising
Złe wrogi zabiły.	The evil foes killed him.
Wy niedobrzy ludzie,	Ah, you evil people,
Dlo Boga świętego	in the name of God
cemuście zabili	why did you murder
synocka mojego?	my little son?
Zodnej jo podpory	Never again
juz nie byda miała	will I have any help
choćbych moje stary	even if I cry
ocy wypłakała.	my old eyes out.
Choćby z mych łez gorzkich	Even if my tears
drugo Odra była,	flowed like the Oder river
jesce by synocka	they would not have revived
mi nie ozywiła.	my lttle son.
Lezy on tam w grobie	He lies in his grave
a ja nie wiemkandy,	and I don't know where
choć sie opytuja	though I keep asking
między ludźmi wsandy.	people everywhere.
Moze nieborocek	Perhaps the poor lad
Lezy kaj w dołecku,	lies somewhere in a ditch
A mógłby se lygać	while he could have been
Na swoim przypiecku.	resting in his warm bed.

Ej ćwierkejcie mu ta wy ptosecki boze kiedy mamulicka znaleźć go nie moze. A ty boze kwiecie, kwitnijze wokoło, niech sie synockowi choć lezy wesoło. Wy niedobrzy ludzie, Dlo Boga świętego cemuście zabili synocka mojego?	Oh, sing for him God's little birds, since his mommy cannot find him. And you, God's flowers bloom all around so my little son rests in joy, at least. Ah, you evil people, in the name of God, why did you kill my little son?

CHAPTER 11

Górecki and the Polish Musical Tradition: Wacław of Szamotuły, Chopin, Szymanowski, Polish Folk and Church Music

Teresa Malecka

> I dwell deeply rooted in tradition and that is where I search for the key to the present. A key that would help me convey what I am in now, what surrounds me.[1]

When Henryk Mikołaj Górecki made this statement in 1977, he was separating the present from tradition. In 2008, however, he stated that tradition "is all that we have of the most valuable." And, significantly: "This is not the case of simple allusion... It is a historical progression."[2] The composer also knew how to be more specific: "All traditions will die, yet Beethoven will live. So will Chopin, Szymanowski."[3]

Polish Musical Sources in the Works by Górecki	
Chorale in the Form of a Canon for string quartet, 1961/81	Wacław of Szamotuły, *Already it is Dusk*, 1556[4]

---

[1] Henryk Mikołaj Górecki, "Powiem Państwu szczerze. Konwersatorium kompozytora w ramach II Spotkań Muzycznych w Baranowie Sandomierskim," [I will tell you frankly...Lecture at the Second Musical Encounters in Baranów Sandomierski] ed. W. Widłak, *Vivo* 1 (1994), 44.

[2] Students of the Academy of Music in Kraków, Anna Satyła and Krzysztof Cyran, in conversation with the composer, May 2008, *Jubinalia*.

[3] Henryk Mikołaj Górecki, "Już taki jestem zimny drań. Rozmowa z W. Widłakiem," [I am such a bastard. A conversation with W. Widłak] *Vivo* 1 (1994), 39.

[4] See Wacław z Szamotuł, *Modlitwa, gdy dziatki spać idą* [Prayer when children go to sleep] in: *Pieśni, per chorum quattuor vocum*, ed. by Zygmunt M. Szweykowski (Kraków: Wydawnictwo Dawnej Muzyki Polskiej / Early Polish Music, vol. 28, 1973, 14.

Old Polish Music, 1969	Wacław of Szamotuły, *Already it is Dusk*, 1556 Medieval organum *Benedicamus Domine* ca.1300, Poor Clares' Antiphonary, Stary Sącz
String Quartet No. 1, *Already it is Dusk*, 1988	Wacław of Szamotuły, *Already it is Dusk*, 1556
Symphony No. 2 *Copernican*, 1972, movement 2	Anonymous song *Laude digna prole*, 15th c., Antiphonary of the Brothers of the Holy Sepulchre, Miechów
Symphony No. 3 *Symphony of Sorrowful Songs*, 1976, movement 1	Beggars' Lenten song *Jesus is Dying* (church songbook by Rev. Jan Siedlecki) The song *Praised be Jesus Christ* from a collection of folk songs by Władysław Skierkowski
The same, movement 2	"a *Podhale* character" (Henryk Górecki)
The same, movement 3	Folk song from the Opole region, *Kajże mi się podział mój synocek miły / Where have I lost my lovely son* Mazurka in A minor, Op. 17, No. 4 by Fryderyk Chopin
Broad Waters for *a capella* choir, 1979	From a collection of folk songs by Jadwiga Gorzechowska and Maria Kaczurbina [5]
Dark Evening is Falling, 1981	From the same collection
My Vistula, Grey Vistula, 1981	From a collection by Jadwiga Gorzechowska[6]

---

[5] Jadwiga Gorzechowska and Maria Kaczurbina, *Jak to dawniej na Kurpiachbywało* [*How it was once in Kurpie*] (Warsaw: Nasza Księgarnia, 1969).
[6] Jadwiga Gorzechowska, *Szeroka woda* [*Broad waters*] (Warsaw: Ruch, 1967).

O, My Garland of Lavender, 1984	From a collection by Oskar Kolberg[7]
Cloud Comes, Rain Falls, 1984	From the same collection
Marian Songs, 1985	From Jan Siedlecki's Church Songbook
Church Songs, 1986	From the same songbook

Bohdan Pociej describes the composer's relationship to other artists as "transforming impulses, processing quotations, their incorporation into his very own style. Górecki makes his choice in full consciousness of artistic freedom."[8]

Of the three areas associated with placing a work of music in an intertextual perspective proposed by Mieczysław Tomaszewski—"inspiration, context, and resonance"—it is the category of inspiration that proves to be crucial here. I understand "inspiration" as an evocation of the "work's intertextual roots in the heritage of the past."[9]

Exactly: Górecki's music—individual and original— is visibly rooted in the European and Polish traditions. The most important sources of inspiration include an attachment to the native country, complete with an interest in its nature, landscape, and people; and, above all—a deep rootedness in Polish history, art (poetry, literature, music), but also in a simple and almost folk-like religiousness—i.e., in Christian culture in general.

In fact, it could be claimed that Górecki draws from two basic spheres of Polish inspirations: folk music and church music, understood both as original folk or church song and as artistic music based on or inspired by folklore or church music.[10] Thus, the sources might

---

[7] Oskar Kolberg, *Dzieła wszystkie* [*Complete works*], ed. Jan Burszta (1961-87), Bogusław Linette, 1988- (Kraków/Warszawa, 1961-1989, Poznań, 1990-).
[8] Bohdan Pociej, *Bycie w muzyce. Próba opisania twórczości H. M. Góreckiego* (Katowice: Akademia Muzyczna im. K. Szymanowskiego, 2005), 26.
[9] Mieczysław Tomaszewski, *O muzyce polskiej perspektywie intertekstualnej. Studia i szkice* (Kraków: Akademia Muzyczna, 2005), 15-16.
[10] For a different interpretation of this topic see Violetta Kostka, „Elementy narodowe w muzyce Henryka Mikołaja Góreckiego / National Elements in the

include a 16th-century song by Wacław of Szamotuły, a Chopin Mazurka, Szymanowski's music, and an old, medieval organum.

Many works by Górecki, starting with *Old Polish Music* (1969), relate specifically and significantly to a more or less remote past. This relationship has multiple facets: stylisations and archaisations as well as allusions, reminiscences and quotations. We should not forget that in Górecki's oeuvre, there are also simple adaptations for chorus *a capella* of Polish folk and church songs.

1. Around *Already It Is Dusk*

Certain spheres of inspiration are particularly intense in their impact on the music of Henryk Mikołaj Górecki; some of his works are particularly strongly rooted in Polish tradition. One notable example is the 16th-century song by Wacław of Szamotuły, *Already it is Dusk*, present in three pieces by the composer: the *Old Polish Music*, the *Symphony of Sorrowful Songs* and the String Quartet No. 1. In the *Old Polish Music* it appears in a combination of two significant early music quotations: *Already It Is Dusk* itself and the medieval organum *Benedicamus Domine* (ca. 1300) from the antiphonary of the Poor Clares in Stary Sącz. The Third Symphony, *Symphony of Sorrowful Songs* brings together an even greater variety of Polish inspirations.

The structure of *Old Polish Music* (written in a period in the composer's artistic biography that was defined by Krzysztof Droba as the phase of reductive constructivism) is based, among other elements, on a polarity of two types of sonority: brass instruments and

---

Music of Henryk Mikołaj Górecki (abridged), in: W*spółczesna muzyka estońska w kontekście muzyki europejskiej. Materiały z międzynarodowej sesji muzykologicznej towarzyszącej projektowi Nowa Estonia { Musica Nova, październik 2002 / Contemporary Estonian Music in the Context of European Music*. Materials from the international conference organised in the framework of the project New Estonia { Musica Nova, October 2002, ed. by Monika Bąkowska-Lajming, Gdańsk: Nadbałtyckie Centrum Kultury 2003, p. 39-50 (Polish version) and 51-58 (English version).

the strings.[11] Each layer has its individual source material: the brass that of the *Benedicamus Domine* (Figure 11-1, 11-2), the strings that of *Already It Is Dusk* (Figure No. 11-3, 11-4).

Figure 11-1: Organum *Benedicamus Domine*. Antiphonary of the Poor Clares in Stary Sącz.

---

[11] Krzysztof Droba, s.n. "Górecki Henryk Mikołaj," *Encyklopedia Muzyczna PWM. Część biograficzna*, ed. Elżbieta Dziębowska, vol. 3 (EFG), (Kraków: PWM, 1987), 428.

Figure 11-2: Title page of H.M. Górecki, *Old Polish Music/ Muzyka Staropolska*. Old Polish Music, Op. 24 by Henryk Górecki. © Copyright 1988 by Boosey & Hawkes Music Publishers Ltd. for the World except Poland, Albania, Bulgaria, China, Yugoslavia, Cuba, North Korea, Vietnam, Roumania, Hungary, Czechoslovakia, and the former territories of the USSR. Reprinted by Permission of Boosey & Hawkes, Inc.

Figure 11-3: Wacław of Szamotuły, *Already It Is Dusk* (*cantus firmus* only).

Figure 11-4: Rehearsal number 83 in H. M. Górecki, *Old Polish Music / Muzyka Staropolska. Old Polish Music,* Op. 24 by Henryk Górecki. © Copyright 1988 by Boosey & Hawkes Music Publishers Ltd. for the World except Poland, Albania, Bulgaria, China, Yugoslavia, Cuba, North Korea, Vietnam, Roumania, Hungary, Czechoslovakia, and the former territories of the USSR. Reprinted by Permission of Boosey & Hawkes, Inc.

The clarity of this structure also pertains to the way of developing texture—in a steady expansion of the number of voices in both instrument groups, with an almost constant growth of dynamics. The modal scales that provide the basis for the musical material of this work defy unequivocal definition due to their ambiguous centres— the more so as these centers differ for both melodies, occurring in their various guises: original, inverted, or otherwise transformed. Krzysztof Droba's statement about the presence of a Mixolydian mode in the *Benedicamus* chorale is probably based on a somewhat paradoxical situation: its initial phrase is absent from almost the entire piece and it only appears in the main climax and in the finale.

From then on, it is omnipresent: as the basis and the background for the part of trumpets and (in multiple octaves) as the lowest and highest notes in diatonic clusters in strings. Yet the essence of the climax consists, rather than in the melody itself, in its harmonisation with a quotation from the original *Benedicamus Domine* chorale that resounds in trumpets *sotto voce* (!) in a *piano* dynamics (!). It is one of these moments that Mieczysław Tomaszewski would describe as an epiphany.[12] (Figure 11-5).

---

[12] Mieczysław Tomaszewski, "Sacrum i profanum w muzyce. Z prof. M. Tomaszewskim rozmawia M. Janicka-Słysz,"*Maszkaron* 1-3 (2003), 30.

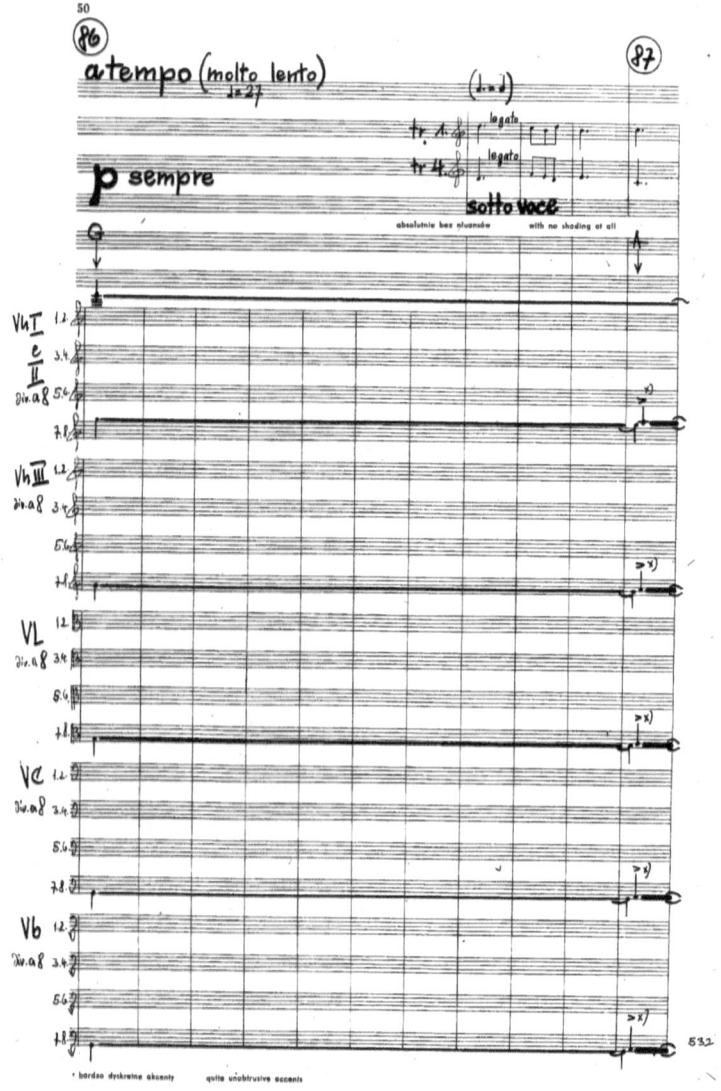

Figure 11-5: *Benedicamus Domine* cited in *Old Polish Music/Muzyka Staropolska. Old Polish Music*, Op. 24 by Henryk Górecki. © Copyright 1988 by Boosey & Hawkes Music Publishers Ltd. for the World except Poland, Albania, Bulgaria, China, Yugoslavia, Cuba, North Korea, Vietnam, Roumania, Hungary, Czechoslovakia, and the former territories of the USSR.

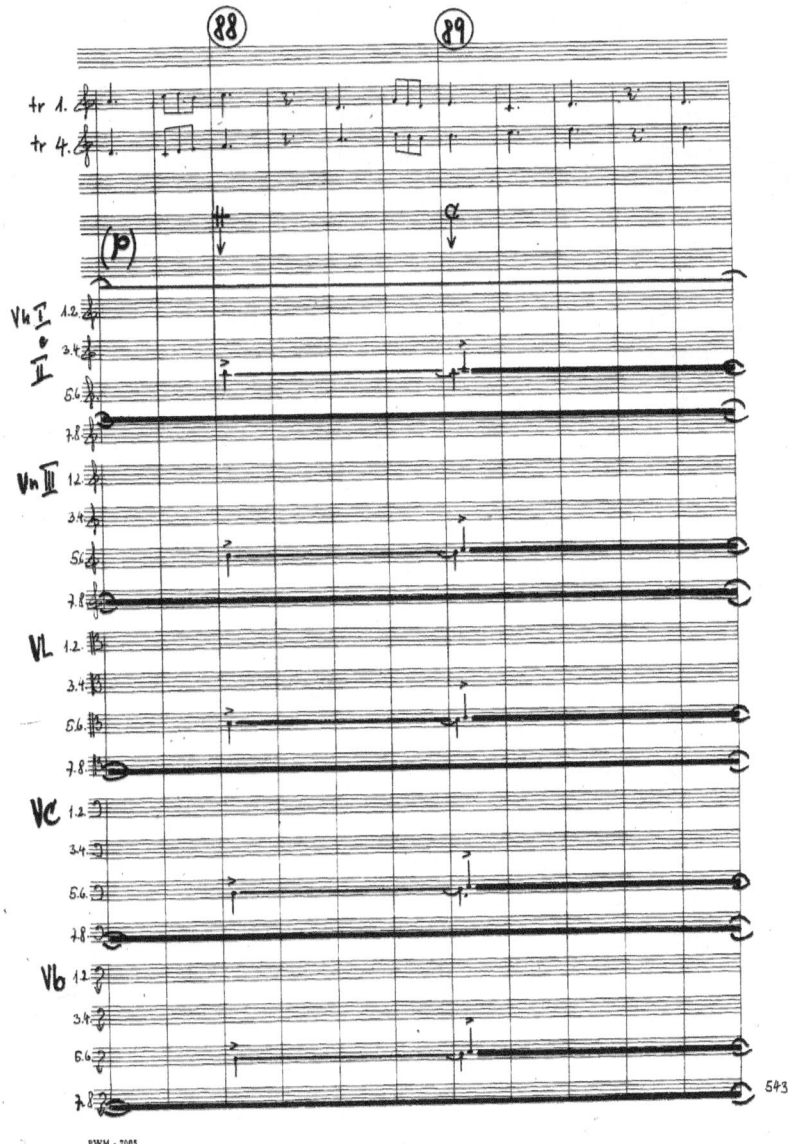

Figure 11-5, continued: *Old Polish Music*, Op. 24 by Henryk Górecki. © Copyright 1988 by Boosey & Hawkes Music Publishers Ltd. for the World except Poland, Albania, Bulgaria, China, Yugoslavia, Cuba, North Korea, Vietnam, Roumania, Hungary, Czechoslovakia, and the former territories of the USSR. Reprinted by Permission of Boosey & Hawkes, Inc.

~ 243 ~

The significance of this arguably paradoxical climax is additionally enhanced by the specific way of manipulating source material. Here, Górecki plays a game in which variants and modifications of both ancient melodies come ever closer to being straight quotations of the original form of the song. Adrian Thomas describes a similar situation in *Recitatives and Ariosos, Lerchenmusik*—where the material for "music within music" has been that of the first theme of Beethoven's Piano Concerto No. 4 in G major— as a gradual removal of "the fine layers of filter."[13]

Old Polish Music owes its ascetic character to modal, archaic melodies that have become its basic fabric and, on the other hand, to an iron consistency in constructing texture and form. It is not a coincidence that David Drew described this work as a "great cathedral," as opposed to the "small chapel" of the String Quartet No. 1 *Already It Is Dusk*.[14]

2. Górecki – Chopin

> "Chopin... God must have given him something so that he could see what he saw …."[15]

Górecki's utter fascination with Chopin is a characteristic of his since early youth.[16] Paradoxically, in the panorama of the impact of Chopin's music on later generations of composers described by Mieczysław Tomaszewski as "extraordinarily strong and unquestionable,"[17] its presence in Górecki's work can only be viewed as minimal. Adrian Thomas indicates a few cases of barely noticeable references to Chopin's harmonies, textures, rhythms, or with what he refers to as Chopin's "genteel world" in various pieces by Górecki. Some of these

---

[13] Adrian Thomas, *Górecki* (Kraków: PWM, 1998), 163.
[14] David Drew, CD notes, Elektra Nonesuch, 1991.
[15] Students in conversation…
[16] See the interview with Maja Trochimczyk in Chapter 4 of this volume.
[17] Mieczysław Tomaszewski, *Chopin. Człowiek. Dzieło. Rezonans* [Chopin. The Man, the Work, the Resonance]. (Poznań: Podsiedlik-Raniowski i Spólka), 790.

have been pointed out to him by the composer himself, and Thomas described this information as "surprising."[18]

CHOPIN	GÓRECKI
The finale of Piano Sonata No. 2 in B-flat minor, Op. 35	*Four Preludes,* Op. 1 (IV)
Mazurka in A minor Op. 17, No. 4 Introduction Middle section, A major chord	Symphony No. 3 (Movement 3) The beginning and the long *ostinato* The finale, A major chord
Polonaise in D minor (op. posth.)	String Quartet No. 2 *Quasi una fantasia*

The most obvious and possibly the most widely known case of a Chopin reference in Górecki's music is the appearance of the Mazurka in A minor Op. 17, No. 4 in the third movement of *The Symphony of Sorrowful Songs*. Interestingly, the A minor key and the two tonally-ambiguous chords (*ABF—ACF*) constitute the entirety of Górecki's allusive quotation from Chopin.[19] (See Figures No. 11-6, 11-7).

The sounds are the same, yet differences abound. In Chopin's work, the key seems to modally oscillate between A minor and D minor; in Górecki's Symphony, it resolves into A minor, somewhat paradoxically by an E note added to the chords, by a "stroke" in the harp and piano. It is noteworthy that Thomas cites Wilfrid Mellers who considered this combination of two chords with a dissonant E as an allusion to the "crunching" dissonance in the climax of the development in the first movement of Beethoven's Third Symphony.[20] In the Chopin Mazurka, a triple repetition of two chords and their resolution in D minor functions as the introduction; in the Symphony, two chords become

---

[18] Adrian Thomas, *Górecki* (Kraków:PWM, 1998), 179.
[19] M. Tomaszewski, *Muzyka Chopina na nowo odczytana* (Kraków: Akademia Muzyczna 1996), 116.
[20] Thomas, *Górecki, op. cit.,* 124-125.

the material of a long (50-measure) section providing the *ostinato* in irregularly-varying meter (2/4 – 3/4) and forming the background for a folksong from the Polish region of Opole.

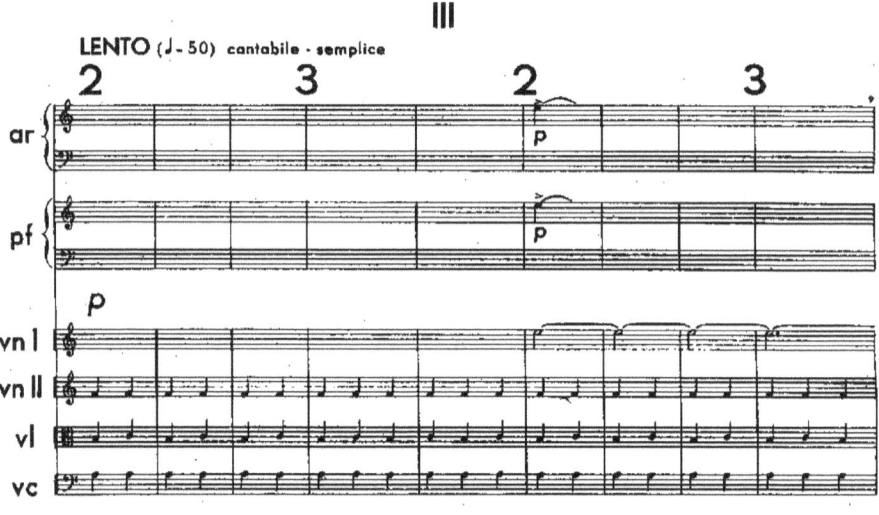

Figure 11-6: Chopin's Mazurka, Op. 17, No. 4, the beginning (above).

Figure 11-7: Górecki's Symphony No. 3, third movement (below). Symphony No. 3, Op. 36 by Henryk Górecki. © Copyright 1977 by PWM Edition, Kraków, Poland. U.S. Renewal Rights assigned to Boosey & Hawkes, Inc. English, French and German translation: © Copyright 1992 by Boosey & Hawkes Music Publishers Ltd. Reprinted by permission of Boosey & Hawkes, Inc.

It is the manifestation of pain—the lament being marked *espressivo* in the Mazurka and *cantabile semplice* in the Symphony's third movement—that provides an additional connection between the two compositions. Of some significance here might also be the shift of a minor second between the chords. In the Mazurka, Heinrich Leichtentritt can hear "a tone of lamentation ..." and Zdzisław Jachimecki "tearful expressions..."[21] Indeed, in Third Symphony, a mother is lamenting and mourning her son, and the *Songs* themselves are *Sorrowful*.

Adrian Thomas also notices the presence of Chopin sources in the finale of the Third Symphony.[22] He is of the opinion that the repeated A major chords there have been derived from the characteristic A major drone in the *Trio* of the Mazurka. Yet this coincidence can be explained by laws of a more general nature. As a rule, the trio of a dance piece in any minor key is set in its major counterpart (the Mazurka), nor is it a rarity to find a major-key finale in a minor-key piece (the Symphony).

3. Górecki - Szymanowski

"Where Szymanowski went, I went too."[23]

It would be difficult to find a greater contrast of personalities, personal histories, worldviews, and lifestyle than that of Karol Szymanowski and Henryk Mikołaj Górecki. And yet, their many similarities, and closeness, kinship even, are only matched by Górecki's veritable fascination with Szymanowski, dating back to his earliest youth. The two composers are united by their love for the region of Podhale, its foothill landscape, its nature and culture. Both embraced this region as their second home. They are also alike in their friendship with the *górale* (highlander) families, in their shared fondness for the folk music of the region, and in their music-making with the Podhale mountainfolk.

---

[21] Tomaszewski, *Chopin, op. cit.*, 603.
[22] Thomas, *op. cit.*
[23] Thomas, *op. cit.*, 117.

Szymanowski, enthralled with the music of Podhale in its pure and unadulterated form, wrote in 1924: [24]

> Musical *'beaux esprits'* and the so-called 'subtle natures' recoil from this 'cacophonic music' and only see it as primitive barbarity. ... Yet how life-giving it is ... in its closeness to nature, in its power and directness of temperament, and even in the untainted purity of race...

Seventy years later, Górecki said of the folk music of Podhale: [25]

> Some could say this is highly primitive musical material. The harmonic-rhythmical structure is very limited: quarter-notes in simple D major and G major harmonies, occasionally also in A major... In the music of Podhale, apart from its tangible features, there is something else that you either discover—hear, feel—or you don't. You have to have your antennae attuned to that; otherwise, all you see is the external and primitive structure.

It seems that both composers have grown similarly-attuned antennae. Adrian Thomas shows numerous affinities, extending even to the musical material and themes, in the works by both composers. He also points out that they both derived their material from common sources, such as the song collection of Rev. Władysław Skierkowski.

SZYMANOWSKI'S COMPOSITIONS	GÓRECKI'S REFERENCES IN
Stabat Mater	Symphony No. 3, *The Symphony of Sorrowful Songs*
Violin Concerto No. 2	*Beatus Vir*

The Szymanowski context for Górecki's oeuvre makes itself felt at its strongest in the relationships between the two masterpieces of sacred music: *Stabat Mater* and the Symphony No. 3. Both works are

---

[24] Quoted in Tadeusz A. Zieliński, *Szymanowski. Liryka i ekstaza* [Szymanowski: The Lyricism and the Ecstasy] (Kraków: PWM, 1997), 226.
[25] Henryk Mikołaj Górecki, "Zawsze jestem sobą, Z Henrykiem Mikołajem Góreckim rozmawia Mieczysław Kominek," *Studio* 8 (1993), 9. See Chapter 2.

dominated by modal thinking—what is more, this modal thinking understood as a reference to folklore as well as religious music. (Figures 11-8, 11-9).

Figure 11-8: Karol Szymanowski, *Stabat Mater* (1925-26). © 2000 by PWM Edition, Kraków. Poland. Extracts are Used by Kind Permission of Polskie Wydawnictwo Muzyczne, Kraków. Poland.

of the Polskie Wydawnictwo Muzyczne, Kraków, Poland. In both pieces, the melodic layer plays a significant role in creating a lyrical type of expression, obviously saturated with sorrow. Some affinity can also be observed in certain compositional gestures, such as the instrumentation—to mention only the special role of the harp in both pieces. Another similarity, pointed out by Adrian Thomas, is a melodic motive appearing in many of Górecki's works that he calls a "turn," or a "Skierkowski turn."[26] This motive appears in the initial soprano part

---

[26] Thomas, *op. cit.*, 118.

in the climax of the final movement of *Stabat Mater* and in the second movement of *The Symphony of Sorrowful Songs*. (Figures 11-8, 11-9).

Figure 11-9: Górecki, Symphony No. 3, Second Movement. Symphony No. 3, Op. 36 by Henryk Górecki. © Copyright 1977 by PWM Edition, Kraków, Poland. U.S. Renewal Rights assigned to Boosey & Hawkes, Inc. English, French and German translation: © Copyright 1992 by Boosey & Hawkes Music Publishers Ltd. Reprinted by permission of Boosey & Hawkes, Inc.

Figure 11-10: Karol Szymanowski, *Stabat Mater* © 2000 by PWM Edition, Kraków, Poland. Extracts are Used by Kind Permission of Polskie Wydawnictwo Muzyczne, Kraków. Poland.

Figure 11-11: Górecki, Symphony No. 3, beginning of second movement. Symphony No. 3, Op. 36 by Henryk Górecki.

Symphony No. 3, Op. 36 by Henryk Górecki. © Copyright 1977 by PWM Edition, Kraków, Poland. U.S. Renewal Rights assigned to Boosey & Hawkes, Inc. English, French and German translation: © Copyright 1992 by Boosey & Hawkes Music Publishers Ltd. Reprinted by permission of Boosey & Hawkes, Inc.

A slightly different version of this motive—in fact, one that has an entirely different function within the composition—may be found in Szymanowski's Violin Concerto No. 2 and in Górecki's *Beatus Vir*. In the Concerto, the initial motive (E-G-F sharp) seems to permeate almost the entire first movement; in *Beatus Vir*, it appears as the material for the religious finale (with bells), replete with symbolic associations. Repeated eleven times, it precedes a quadruple repetition of a chord— thus representing an encoded date of birth of St. Stanislaus (11 and 4 for the 11th of April), who is celebrated by Górecki in this work, commissioned by Cardinal Karol Wojtyła in 1977 and ultimately composed for the Polish Pope, after his ascension to this position in 1978.

The references to the music by Chopin and Szymanowski in the Symphony No. 3, *The Symphony of Sorrowful Songs* are accompanied by other quotations and allusions to Polish music. In fact, this Symphony exemplifies the greatest emphasis on tradition in the whole oeuvre of Henryk Mikołaj Górecki. In this work, many more or less distant allusions to the music of his great predecessors may be identified, together with references to and quotations of Polish folk songs (of the Opole region), church songs (Lenten songs and *Praised be Jesus Christ*), and, finally, references to the musical idiom of the Tatra foothills, Podhale.

The composer's masterpiece, the apogee of his output is, at the same time, his most past-oriented piece. This is a characteristic of the worldwide history of reception of the Symphony No. 3, paradoxically described by the composer as his "most avant-garde work:" it has also been affected by the strongest impact of the past. To use the words by poet Joseph Brodsky ("It is one of the aims of a work of art to produce debtors; the paradox is that the deeper the debt, the richer the artist"[27]), one could say that the Symphony No. 3 is the "deepest in debt:" it has the deepest roots in tradition, that provides both the greatest inspiration for the music and the means for coping with the work's pregnant message.

Bohdan Pociej wrote: "Górecki is deeply rooted in Polishness, in Polish spiritual (and material) culture and its inherently Christian—not solely Catholic—traditions. He is solidly grounded in what is usually referred to as the native country in the full sense of the phrase, a sense that brings together language, faith and religious customs, time and

---

[27] Josip Brodski, *W cieniu Dantego* [In Dante's Shadow] quoted in Stanisław Balbus, *Między stylami* [Between Styles] (Kraków: 1996), 11.

space, history, tradition, heritage and the feeling of community, of solidarity, that derives thereof."[28]

4. Folk Songs and Patriotic Songs

Simple Polish folk songs manifest themselves with the greatest intensity in Górecki's pieces for choir *a capella* written over a period of almost 20 years (1975-2004). Yet their majority, composed in 1979-1988, is the creation of an artist burdened with the weight of events in his nation's history. In those difficult Polish years, the composer found two enclaves of peace: folk wisdom, with its strong associations with nature, and religious spirituality.

The notion of water, Polish rivers Narew and Vistula, dew, but also the region of Powiśle, as well as the elements of Slavic Midsummer Day rituals, are the concepts permeating the six folk songs *Broad Waters* Op. 39 of December 1979, dedicated to Górecki's friends in Kraków. The cycle is based on traditional lyrics and melodies from the namesake collection by Jadwiga Gorzechowska and from *As It Was Long Ago in Kurpie* collected and edited by Jadwiga Gorzechowska and Maria Kaczurbina. It opens a series of works for *a capella* choir that is characteristic for the period of Górecki's retreat from monumental and diverse orchestral settings and, more importantly, from great, even grandiose subjects—yet without abandoning significant, profound messages. These works form an important part of his so-called "late style."[29]

In this context, the lyrics of the final song from the *Broad Waters* collection provide food for thought:

> Broad is the water in the Vistula
> And I'll tell you my thoughts now.
> As yesterday, likewise today,
> I must be with you forever.

---

[28] Pociej, *op. cit.*, 32.
[29] I discuss this problem at greater length in "Henryk Mikołaj Górecki. Late Style," in *Melos und Ethos: gestern, heute,...morgen?* (Music Centre Slovakia 2009), 160-168.

As early as 1979, the Vistula becomes a metaphor of Polishness; the artist's attachment to it is an expression of his position and views on his native land.

In the musical layer, the simplicity of form, together with a diversity of expressive types (defined in great detail by the composer), the repetitiveness of metro-rhythmic schemes, mostly derived from folk dances, such as the oberek or the mazurka; the tendency to "distort" the rhythmic regularity; the modal shaping of musical material, in turn associated with the instability of the modes (e.g. the oscillation of Aeolian and Doric mode in the first song); the simple diatonic melodies (though chromaticism may be at times combined with fluctuation between major and minor modes)—are all features that place the songs of the *Broad Waters* cycle among masterpieces, that is highly individual adaptations of folklore.

The title song, the cycle's finale, with its pregnant confession ("I must be with you forever") brings about a reduction and a simplification of metro-rhythmic form; a brightened aura of sonority and harmony (a crystallisation of the G major key); and a broadened phrase structure. Coupled with expression described as *maestoso espressivo* or *lento espressivo*, these traits impart to the song the character of a hymn. It seems that it was the composer's aim to express his attachment to his native land with optimism as well as solemnity.

My Vistula, Grey Vistula Op. 46 of 1981, with its lyrics and the melody taken from Jadwiga Gorzechowska's collection *Broad Waters,* can be perhaps seen as a manifestation of the situation thus described: a simple folk song expresses a profound idea. The Vistula, the quintessential Polish river, answers the question, "where have you gathered your waters?" with "in the Polish land / that beloved land / there is none like it." One could add: "against all odds."

This simple song, modal and tonal (F major), based on the metro-rhythmic model of a lullaby, and permeated, at the same time, with intense, yet beautiful, chords—also, with the repetitiveness of its motivic material and successions of rising and falling melodic lines—is an image of both a river's natural, regular flow and the calm, rolling movement of the waves. The flow and the waves of the river are symbols of the peaceful "beloved land."

These songs about Poland's natural landscape and its rivers form a separate, important category in Górecki's oeuvre. In contrast, songs that are clearly political in intention are a rarity. In 2004, Górecki composed a harrowing *Song of the Katyń Families* at the bidding of and to the lyrics by Tadeusz Lutoborski; the text is of a questionable literary value, yet highly patriotic. The work carries a dedication: "To Heroes: the Victims and their Descendants." This sombre song is filled with a gloomy atmosphere—dominated by low vocal registers, uniform steady rhythm of the quarter-notes, and the pervading minor key (A minor). Yet, brighter moments do appear. As the text speaks of the Polish Pope, the soprano's melodic line makes its single ascent (to A4) over a "serene" harmony of a dominant seventh chord. When the words described how one might become a Pole, the musical layer brings in a perfect cadence. The composer reverts to the sombreness of the beginning with "Poland is not yet lost" (a textual quotation from Poland's national anthem) and closes this song of tragic expression with an A-flat major tonic chord, as if he wanted to quote John Paul II: "there is no evil from which God cannot draw forth a greater good."[30]

5. Church Songs

Górecki's creative path, as few of his fellow composers,is intertwined with the rhythm of Poland's transformation, starting from 1956, the so-called Polish October, followed, a year later by the composer's debut at the Warsaw Autumn Contemporary Music Festival. The history of Poland in the second half of the 20th century was marked by breakthrough moments culminating in 1978 with the the election of the Polish Pope and in 1979,with the First Pilgrimage of John Paul II to his homeland. Then, through the events of the Martial Law (1981-83), this path eventually led to freedom (1989). At the same time, the composer's oeuvre expanded through the creation of some of the greatest masterpieces of music bearing a distinctly religious message—*The Symphony of Sorrowful Songs* (1976) and the Psalm *Beatus Vir* (1979).

---

[30] Jan Paweł II, *Pamięć i tożsamość* [Memory and Identity] (Kraków: Znak, 2005), 171.

After the time of „Solidarity" and enthusiasm for freedom (1980) in contemporary Polish history came the time of the imposition of martial law upon the nation (1981-1983). Similarly, in Górecki's work, after the culmination of the idea of the sacred, one can talk about the limitation, the reduction of resources, the withdrawal of the creator into the realms of modest simplicity, that is into the domain of folk and church songs for choir *a capella* as well as chamber music. This is the phase of „late style," which, according to Mieczysław Tomaszewski, presents a feeling of existential danger to many creators, as a "shadow of the shadow" appears. In Henryk Mikołaj Górecki's output, church songs for chorus *a cappella* are a testimony of these times.

Most of Górecki's religious music contains a typically Polish element, the veneration of Mother Mary. It permeates *Totus Tuus*, a work dedicated to John Paul II as mentioned above, and before that, in 1985, the *Marian Songs*. Górecki arranged five church songs, all Marian in character, and dedicated the collection to the successor of Karol Wojtyła at the post of the Cardinal of Kraków, Franciszek Macharski. In the composer's hands, *Marian Songs,* while retaining the simple lyrics and melodies of the original church songs, have acquired features characteristic of his own style (the beauty of chordal structure, repetitiveness, ostinato, and modality) with a somewhat ennobling effect. I see the lively rhythm of these songs and the cheerful major keys as the composer's allusion to religious songs performed during the month of May at popular devotions to the Blessed Virgin Mary. The enhanced effects of repetition and *ostinato* transport them from the sphere of singing into that of contemplation with a prayerful focus (this is especially evident in *Hail Mary*).

Choral religious songs, among which Marian songs are the largest group, were composed primarily in May and June of 1986 (though one of the songs comes from February, and two do not have a date). The creative process in May was intense; the composition of individual songs was sometimes divided between one or two days: on the Feast of Our Lady of Fatima on 13 May two songs were composed. In June, the composer returned to work on these *Church Songs* less often.

Thanks to the help of Father Wojciech Kalamarz, I managed to determine the textual and musical source for these works. Most of the original, ancient melodies (sometimes reaching as far back as the 14th century) come from the *Church Songbook* by Father Jan Siedlecki (originally collected in 1878 and reprinted throughout the 20th century, in 1928, 1987, 2001, etc.). The song collections gathered by priests Michał Marcin Mioduszewski, Józef Mazurowski, Szczepan Keller and Jan Żmijka were also helpful.

Among the songs for the Blessed Virgin Mary there is a great diversity: an Advent song, a fragment of the *Hours* (*Godzinki*), and finally songs typical of the traditional May devotions. From Lenten songs, Górecki chose the well-known *People, my People / Ludu mój ludu* as well as a fragment of *Bitter Sorrows—Lament of the Soul over the Suffering Christ/ Gorzkie Żale—Lament duszy nad cierpiącym Chrystusem*. Three songs are related to the worship of saints; their choice is significant. St. Anna—referred to in the text as the Lady, Mother of of the Mother of Jesus (in the hymn *Hello Lady, Mother of the Virgin; Witaj Pani, Matko Matki*) and St. Joseph (in the song *Happy, who has a patron... /Szczęśliwy, kto sobie patrona....*), are two characters closest to the Mother of God. These songs may also be interpreted as belonging in the Marian circle.

The third saint is St. Nicholas (Mikołaj)—this is the patron saint of the composer, commemorated in his middle name (St. Nicholas's feast day is on 6 December, the composer's birthday), and also the patron saint of his son (the song *Let's shout everyone / Krzyknijmy wszyscy*). Among religious songs arranged by Górecki in the *Church Songs* collection are also songs for Easter, in honor of the Holy Trinity, and in praise of the Blessed Sacrament.

While working on the arrangements, the composer cited the lyrics of the original songs with few, minor changes. They were primarily shortened. In most cases, only the first few phrases and the original opening stanzas were left. An extreme example is provided by the song *Father, God Almighty / Ojcze, Boże Wszechmogący* in which out of seventeen verses merely the first three and the last one remained in Górecki's arrangement.

Some *Church Songs* are based on short texts, e.g. consisting of only two verses. These songs resemble a type of an invocation repeated several times, which brings them closer to the category of prayer. The songs *Holy, Holy, Holy/Święty, Święty, Święty*, or *We Greet and Praise / Pozdrawiajmy, wychwalajmy* may serve here as examples. In some songs, the composer repeats single verses or verbal passages. The most significant changes appeared in a Marian song from the *Catholic Songbook / Katolicki Kancjonał*, entitled *Be Greeted a Thousand Times /Tysiąckroć bądź pozdrowiona*. In making this arrangement, the composer skipped many stanzas and added a new one. The description characterizing the Virgin Mary was expanded by adding a significant word: "Calvary." What's more, the verse where this word has been inserted, "The Queen of Heaven, Lady of Angels, Mary of Calvary" became the refrain for the whole song. This is a fact of great significance.

In this context, it is worth mentioning the shared fascination of the composer and of Karol Wojtyła—John Paul II with Calvary (Kalwaria, understood as both the site of Christ's passion and a pilgrimage site in Poland). This fascination lasted from the Pope's childhood to the moment of his election as the Pope, and was expressed later, during his visits to Poland. Kalwaria Zebrzydowska, with its sanctuary dating back to 1600, was a frequent place of pilgrimage, a place of contemplation and prayer, associated with the most difficult of intentions.

Of great interest in musical arrangements of *Church Songs*, is also the relationship between the original melodies and their settings in the composer's unique style. A strong connection between Górecki's version and the original is clearly noticeable in melodies, metro-rhythmic features, and formal shapes. The mark of the composer's individual style is most evident in the particular, characteristic harmonies and choral textures.

Essentially, the melodies were taken from the original church songs with few alterations, although there are significant changes in some individual cases, the extreme example of which is the song of *God Father Almighty / Ojcze Boże Wszechmogący*. Numerous changes in the metro-rhythmic layer, sometimes linked to the slowing down or the acceleration of tempo, lead to a dramatic change in the song's narrative character.

The characteristic feature of the original songs with their main principle of repetition of musical material is found in the *Church Songs / Pieśni Kościelne* enhanced by Górecki's use of repetition as the basis of shaping the form. However, numerous "interventions" break the regularity or even the formal schemes of originals; these interventions may include: the use of short introductions preceding the basic texts and harmony of the songs; the heightened atmosphere of prayer; and the irregular repetition of individual musical or textual phrases (or just their endings).

In most cases, the composer retained original keys in his arrangements. The few changes that occurred were generally of a technical nature (due to the ambitus of individual voices), but sometimes they also affected the expression and articulation. In the song about St. Anna—the mother of the mother of Christ—the transposition from the original key of G major to A-flat major may have had an additional symbolic significance. The A-flat major is the key used to set the main word in the Copernican Symphony—"light." At the same time, in interpretations by some nineteenth-century theorists, this key is associated with the aesthetic categories of infinity, piety and nobility. It is difficult to have a more accurate alignment with the qualities of the figure of the Holy Mother.

The composer's harmonic language crystallized in the 1970s is easily recognizable in these songs. Modal-tonal shaping of the polyphonic choral texture (ranging from two to ten voices) is a constant feature here. In many cases, polyphonic chords are enriched with numerous foreign notes, most of which are dissonant. This factor, associated with the instability and alteration of the scales of folk music, creates an effect of shakiness and ambiguity of sonority, while simultaneously building the extraordinary atmosphere of the Lent in the song *People, my People / Ludu mój ludu*.[31] On the other hand, there are also songs

---

[31] The composer's fondness for this melody may be noted by his citation from *Ludu, mój ludu* in the Harpsichord Concerto, see Teresa Malecka, „O koncercie

that are dominated by simple chords (sometimes just in fifths), giving them an archaic character (for instance, *Chryste Panie / Lord Christ*). The sonorous and harmonious aura of a song may grow clearly from the composer's experience with his greatest sacred music masterpieces. For instance, a series of chords resembling those from *Beatus Vir* appear in *Hail Mary/ Zdrowaś bądź Maryja*.

In Górecki's oeuvre, a constant motive is conveyed through his favorite concept. The idea of "motherhood" followed by a "Marian quality," occupies a significant, even central, place in his universe. [32]This fact in a sense also manifests itself in *Church Songs / Pieśni kościelne*. The theme of the mother, his own early loss (he was two years old when his mother died), enriched with references to the Mother of God, is constantly present in the composer's works: from the earliest songs (*To Mother*, from the Three Songs, Op.3) to *Ad Matrem, Symphony of Sorrowful Songs*, and *Totus Tuus* (1987). Thus, we may consider the *Church Songs*, due to the characteristics of the composer's style (sonoristic language, harmony, texture, and the narrative style), and to the predominance of Marian themes, as belonging in the main portion of the composer's oeuvre: for him music was the "result of religious concentration and meditation."Górecki said, "See the Creator of everything—and write for him."

---

klawesynowym Góreckiego," in *Mieczysławowi Tomaszewskiemu w 60-lecie urodzin*, ed. Teresa Malecka (Kraków, 1984), 111.

[32] Maja Trochimczyk first discussed the topic of the "maternal" in Górecki's music in 1997, during the Górecki Autumn symposium in Los Angeles; a paper published in various versions, in 1998 in *Musical Quarterly*, in 2003 in *Polish Music Journal*, and as Chapter 8 above. See the Bibliography for details.

CHAPTER 12

Górecki at the Keyboard: The Piano in his Compositional Output

Teresa Malecka

> "I used the first money I'd saved to buy Chopin's *Impromptu* and Szymanowski's *Mazurkas*... I still have the scores, and this is how my strange story begins: with Beethoven's *Symphony No. 9*, Szymanowski's *Mazurkas*, and Chopin's *Impromptu*."
> ~ Henryk. M. Górecki[1]

The piano plays a particular role in Górecki's *oeuvre*, and this is neither because his catalogue includes a Concerto for Harpsichord or Piano and String Orchestra, nor because thirty of the composer's eighty-one opuses include the piano in their orchestration—usually one, but sometimes two. The special role of the piano in Górecki's music consists in the fact that the instrument has a key function in very different pieces, and that this function can be very different as well; also, in most cases, the piano part is deprived of any virtuoso aspects and articulates a peculiar understanding of the expressive effect or of the work's message.

A question arises whether the variety of the piano's functions within this music runs parallel to stylistic changes in the successive phases in the composer's life and work, or whether other factors come into play —such as categories of genre or the type of expression.

---

[1] Henryk Mikołaj Górecki, "Powiem Państwu szczerze" [I will tell you frankly...] Lecture at the 2nd Musical Meeting in Baranów Sandomierski, 1977, *Vivo*, 1 (1994): 43-44.

1. The Piano and Stylistic Periods

Significantly, Górecki's first opuses include pieces for piano (*Four Preludes* and Toccata for two pianos) or with piano accompaniment (*Three Songs* and Variations for violin and piano). This instrument is almost always present in his early works up to Op. 13. This is probably a consequence of the simple fact that the piano can be described as Górecki's first and foremost instrument. In their early youth, composers usually write for their "first" instrument.

The period of crystallization of the composer's individual language—the time of his early and mature output, described as the phases of serialism, sonorism and reductionist constructivism in his oeuvre—could be said to have no need, or even no use, for the piano. This was more of an era for prepared piano, something outside his interests at the time—despite the strongly avant-garde-like character of Górecki's oeuvre. In the 1970s, things change. The apogee of the composer's creative path (*Ad Matrem*, Symphony No. 2, Symphony No. 3, and *Beatus Vir*) features the sound of the piano as a necessary element of the music, as a major contribution to its peculiar tonal aura, even to its peculiar beauty.

In Górecki's output, the Harpsichord Concerto of 1980 occupies a place of its own, a place of significance, too, since the composer has made provisions for a piano version as well. Yet it is not the piano or the pianistic aspect that comes to the fore; it seems that this Concerto opens a new period in the composer's output and, at the same time and in a certain sense, it foreshadows a "new piano" in Górecki's music.

For it is in the 1980s that his oeuvre begins to exhibit symptoms of the so-called late style: the tell-tale limitation of instrumentation, and the concentration of his music around two modes of compositional utterance: choruses *a capella* and chamber music. And again—if quite differently than in the previous phases—the piano acquires a particular significance, becoming (obviously, apart from the string quartets) an essential element of the sound world in his instrumental chamber pieces.

2. The Piano in the Apogee Phase

Górecki's instrumentation in the 1970s is a feature of his then-crystallized style, represented in his masterpieces of music-with-text filled with a clearly religious message. Beginning with *Ad Matrem*, and then in the Second and Third Symphonies—and then again in *Beatus Vir*—Górecki's great works for the symphony orchestra include the piano (often in four-hand parts or as two instruments) as well as the harp, both instruments often performing simultaneously or interchangeably, in similar roles. Both instruments are entrusted with single chords of differentiated intervallic structure, or even with single notes: pedal notes in the piano, open strings in the harp.

Ad Matrem presents a struggle between two contrasting universes of expression: dramatic calls to a lost (earthly) mother, *Mater mea*, interspersed with an idyllic image of the Mother of God. The work ends in a prayer to Mother Mary, keenly aware of the Mother's pain under the cross. While the piano participates in both types of expression, its role is truly fundamental in the creation of the musical aura of the image of the Virgin and of the prayer addressed to her—the semantic and expressive culmination of the work: *Mater mea dolorosa lacrimosa.* The piano part is limited to several repetitions of highly dissonant chords arrested at a pedal note, creating a peculiar tonal aura.

The Second Symphony, *Copernican* features a prominent part of the piano in the bipartite work, where the first movement is a musical image of the chaos of the universe and its underlying mechanisms, and the second movement contemplates the beauty of nature. In the first movement, the two pianos collaborate to create dominating repeated or shifted *ffff* tutti chords of full-note structure and extensive ambitus. Chords are doubled in octaves from a subcontra E to E4 (the limits of the ambitus of vertical chords is defined by the scope of the piano keyboard). These chords shift towards the centre over chords built from augmented major seconds. They are separated or amplified with interventions of ever-recurring sudden and dramatic strikes in the timpani and the bass drum, forming an image—clear to all familiar with the composer's "cosmic" fascinations—of a Big Bang explosion.

The second movement brings a certain "easing" and the release of tension. The two pianos participate in creating a tonal universe appropriate for an aura of contemplation of nature understood as a work of God. This music ushers us into the sphere of transcendence. The baritone solo, in a melodic line typical of the later Górecki style, anchored in a falling minor second, serves as a necessary vehicle for humanity's fundamental call to God (*Deus*); this progression gradually ascends from E-flat to E-flat 2.

The simple, calm melody of the voice in a slow tempo and with a long if varying metric pattern seems immersed in the sonorities of the orchestra, deprived of its high-pitched instruments and enriched with peculiar chords in both pianos that are sharply struck and resound with the pedal. The musical material of this fragment is dominated by pentatonic chords (D-flat, E-flat, E-flat, G-flat, A-flat, B-flat: a half-tone-free pentatonic scale). The same material appears in piano chords, which, as the solo vocal reaches the top pitch, are resolved in a brightened harmony of an A-flat major triad at the entire's Symphony crucial word, *light*. The piano chords accompany sections that follow: a soprano solo, an octave-attuned duet of the soprano and baritone seemingly expressing human delight—that of a man and a woman—in God's created universe.

The piece ends in a long-standing, yet dynamically-pulsating, chords performed by the massive forces of the full orchestra (winds and strings, no piano, no harp and percussion) in a pentatonic intervallic structure, "purified" and once again resolving into a triad in A-flat, a key associated with the emotions of fear and horror (c.f. Zanussi's tragic reading of the Copernican revolution) as well as the immobility or the silence of the night in the tradition of Baroque rhetoric, and, in a late-Romantic perspective, an expression of a completeness of emotions both mild and solemn. The triple repetition of the final chord (*p—pp*), placed in the second inversion, with the fifth as its foundation, i.e. with a clearly weakened center, is once again coloured with the sonorities of the two pianos.

It seems that Górecki's works from this period feature the piano in a somewhat symbolic function of creating color: the chords struck and sustained by the pedal resound in an ever-broadening space. It seems, finally, that the part of the piano or pianos has become essential to create a tonal aura necessary to convey a transcendent dimension.

The role of the piano is different in the individual movements of the Symphony No. 3, *Symphony of Sorrowful Songs*. In the vocal-instrumental section of the first movement (between the canons in the strings), this role is the closest to the one already discussed in other compositions. In the second movement, the piano part, clearly audible over the strings and the harp, has been enriched with a melodic element that is of importance for the rendering of the song of the incarcerated girl from Podhale (with its Lydian fourths, a typical Podhalean interval)—even though it is limited to multiple repetitions of the so-called Górecki's turn.[2]

The girl's simple request addressed at her weeping mother is accompanied by chords in the first inversion (with augmented thirds) resounding with the pedal. As the girl's song changes into a prayer: "Niebios przeczysta Królowo..." [Immaculate Queen of Heavens], the piano falls silent and only reappears in the movement's final moments, at the text of one of the most universal prayers inserted there by the composer: "Zdrowaś Mario, łaskiś pełna..." [Hail Mary, full of Grace], which forms—at the same time because and despite of its simplified means of expression and its *piano* dynamics (or possibly for these reasons exactly)—the unique climax of the piece.

In the third movement, the composer derives his material for the initially-orchestral introduction, and then for the accompaniment to a folksong from Poland's Opole region, from the initial motif in Chopin's Mazurka in A minor, Op. 17, No. 4. Thus, it would seem that the part of the piano could have been more significant in a traditional sense. Nothing could be more wrong. Two chords of indefinite tonality: A—B—F—A—C—F constitute the entirety of the allusive quotation from Chopin's Mazurka (possibly, this was a case of a single phrase that, as the composer reminisced, "sometimes cannot leave him alone"), that is entrusted to the strings and not the piano.[3] In Chopin's work, the key

---

[2] Adrian Thomas, *Górecki*, (Oxford: Clarendon Press 1997), 85.
[3] Mieczysław Tomaszewski, *Muzyka Chopina na nowo odczytana* (Kraków: Akademia Muzyczna, 1998), 116.

seems to modally oscillate between A minor and D minor; in Górecki's Symphony, it crystallizes into A minor thanks to the dissonances in the piano part itself.

Therefore, the role of a single note in the piano acquires a great significance. It is interesting to note here that Adrian Thomas quotes Wilfrid Mellers's interpretation of the combination of the two chords with the dissonant E as an allusion to the "crunching" dissonance in the climax of the development in the first movement of Beethoven's Third Symphony.[4] The *ostinato* chords quoted from Chopin that accompany the song of the mother longing for her son is further coloured with piano's dissonant "jolts," described by Thomas as a "crunching dissonance."[5] In the movement's final section, that is simultaneously the finale of the entire *Symphony of Sorrowful Songs*, the meaningful A major chord appears again. Since the mother has lost all hope of finding her lost son, she sings for him:

> "Ej ćwierkajcie mu tam, wy ptosecki boze....
> A ty boze kwiecie kwitnijze wokoło..."
>
> [Oh, sing for him, God's little birds...
> And you, God's flowers, bloom all around him].

Here, sorrow is transformed into hope. Wilfrid Mellers emphasizes the multiple and "obstinate" repetitions of the A major chords which, in his opinion, "are, in their very different way, as remarkable as the infinitely repeated C major triads at the end of Beethoven's Fifth. In both cases there is neither a chord too many nor too few."[6]

And, last but not least, the *Beatus Vir.* A single sentence to the effect that the piano part has been constructed according to the described model would have sufficed—were it not for the fact that the piano becomes essential to express something of remarkable import. A motive built from the Górecki "turn" orchestrated with the strings, bells, two harps, piano and flute, is repeated eleven times. It is preceded by four repetitions of a chord: together the repeated

---

[4] Thomas, *Górecki*, 92-93.
[5] *Ibidem*.
[6] Wilfrid Mellers, *Round and About*, 24, quoted in Thomas, 93n.

elements articulate the encrypted date of birth (the 11th of April) of St. Stanislaus, in whose honor the work was commissioned by Cardinal Karol Wojtyła in 1977 (it was completed for and dedicated to the Polish Pope, after Wojtyła's election to papacy). The piano helps build the clearly sacred tonal aura of the work's finale and thus participates in the articulation of a date crucial to the circumstances of its composition and its subsequent performance.

3. The Piano of the Late Style

In the 1980s, Górecki's *oeuvre* culminates in the idea of the sacrum in its apogee phase. What follows can be described as his *late style*—as understood by Mieczysław Wallis and Mieczysław Tomaszewski.[7] The composer abandons rich and varied orchestration and complicated messages, pregnant with meaning for the simplicity of choral music *a capella*, with inspirations drawn from folklore and church culture, and for the intimacy of chamber music and its cryptic content (as evidenced in Third String Quartet "*...songs are sung*"). Górecki's situation is not unlike that described by Tomaszewski: here we witness the appearance of a sense of endangerment, of a Conradian "shadow line."[8]

The Concerto for Harpsichord (or Piano) and String Orchestra (1980), in which Thomas finds affinities with the aesthetics of *Les Six* group of composers, and with Poulenc's *Concert champêtre* in particular, is a piece of critical significance in many ways. The great vocal-instrumental works, sacred, solemn even—are now replaced by a short instrumental concerto that presents as its main features the aesthetic categories of *play* and *playfulness*. Its treatment of the genre's tradition—despite the visible associations with Bach and Scarlatti pointed out by David Drew—is quite free, if not perverse. It is possible that this piece foreshadows a new mode of treating the piano,

---

[7] Mieczysław Wallis, *Późna twórczość wielkich artystów* (Warszawa: Państwowy Instytut Wydawniczy, 1975). I discuss the concept of the late style in "Henryk Mikołaj Górecki. Styl późny," [H.M. Górecki. The Late Style], *Res Facta Nova*, 2010, 11 (20), 135-150.
[8] Mieczysław Tomaszewski, *Życia twórcy punkty węzłowe, op. cit.*

still a prominent item in the composer's instrumentation—especially in chamber music from the new period of his *oeuvre*.

The various types of contrasts and oppositions characteristic for the concerto genre, such as the rivalry between the solo instrument and the orchestra or the thematic contrast, seem highly condensed in Górecki's piece. Indeed, in the first movement, the solo instrument and the orchestra play together—which does not signify that they have not preserved their own identities. Quite the contrary: these distinct identities have been emphasized by imparting to the two planes (the soloist and the orchestra) quite different character, thus combining the solo/tutti relationship with that derived from thematic dualism. It appears that the solo instrument presented the first theme—motoric, figurative and rapid—while the orchestra played the second theme—lyrical and cantilena-like—all at the same time.

Another opposition emerges between the first and the second movements on the level of tonality, switching the keys from D minor to D major, and on the level of expression. The work comes out of the sorrow and the tearfulness of a Lenten song (in the orchestra, in the first movement, there appears a reminiscence, a quasi-quotation of *Ludu mój ludu* [*People, oh my people*]. It is accidental. Or, knowing Górecki—is it?). In the first movement's final section, comes a sudden resolution into a D major chord that leads into a transition—*subito, attaca, assoluto, senza cesura*—to the second movement. For a while, the dialogue between the parts of the soloist and the orchestra becomes conventional, but it soon reverts to simultaneous play. This time, however, the two protagonists present a synthesis of the material from the two planes articulated earlier.

The basic constitutive categories/qualities of the Concerto for Harpsichord/Piano, and especially those of its solo part, such as figurativeness, motoric quality, rapid tempo, *quasi*-movement, and vivacity, are typical features of solo parts in any instrumental concerto. The qualities that are construed over this foundation—the play and playfulness combined with the melancholy, the *quasi*-quotation of the popular church song, the mixture of high and low style—presage in a way the puzzling *Little Requiem for a Polka* for piano and 13 instruments (1993). Were it not for the fact that, in the meantime, another major work has been written for piano, clarinet and cello—*Recitativos and Ariosos, Lerchenmusik* (1984-86)—one could come to the erroneous conclusion that this is Górecki embarking on the road of postmodernism, and that the piano is to become the medium for this postmodernism in his music. Yet *Lerchenmusik* features an allusion to Beethoven's Piano Concerto in G major, and this allusion to the past is made in a *seria* convention.[9]

The third movement of the Harpsichord Concerto seems a catalogue of the possible ways of combining two different piano "musics," and, at the same time, a gradual transition from allusion to quotation.

The beginning relates to the Beethovenian theme present, from one point of view, in its incomplete version. From another perspective, it has been enriched with a dissonant-sounding part of clarinets and celli, and its successive entries are extended by single chords and seemingly "purified" of dissonance, only to display the complete theme of Concerto in G major in the key of A-flat major. The composer's persistent and gradual advance to the quotation has been described by Thomas as "removing the fine layers of filter."[10]

Recitativos and Ariosos, Lerchenmusik are, in a way, a culmination of the presence of Beethoven's music in Górecki; it should be noted that the role of the piano is crucial here. It is, in fact, the source of inspiration: after all, the first theme of Beethoven's Concerto for Piano in G major appears in the piano part. The piano is also the lead instrument in Górecki's piece and it is in this instrument that Beethoven's presence manifests itself.

Little Requiem for a Polka (1993) for piano and 13 instruments (piano, winds, strings, and bells) is set for flute, oboe, clarinet in B-flat, bassoon, trumpet in C, horn in F, trombone, tubular bells, and strings. The work was commissioned by the Holland Festival and the Schoenberg Ensemble, originally entitled *Night Serenade* and premiered as *Kleine Requiem für eine Polka* in Amsterdam in 1993. In this composition, as indicated by the title, the piano plays a leading

---

[9] Teresa Malecka, *On the Role of Tradition*, Chapter 11 in the present volume.
[10] Thomas, *op. cit.*, 125.

part, a constant and, at the same, a multifaceted one. The change of the title from *Night Serenade* is one of the many riddles in the life and work of this composer and a challenge to cryptologists—and, in the opinion of David Drew, a challenge that has little chance of a solution. The author leaves the question unanswered: "As with the title, so with the music: it is what it has to be and could not be otherwise," writes David Drew.[11] The piano plays almost continually through the four-movement piece (with only occasional pauses). It constitutes the musical axis of the whole; its part is both quasi-thematic, singing and melodic, and serves as the accompaniment; it either measures out the pulse or produces its distortions... It is fundamental in shaping the sharp contrasts between the mood, the character and the expression of the individual parts.

The remaining instruments might play or not—the piano is a constant. At first, it works with bells to create a remarkable atmosphere of peace and mystery (*Tranquillo*), playing a little tune that is in fact a variant—in a minor key this time—of the Górecki turn (A-C-B-C). Only a while later, it starts to sing a progression of mainly descending fourths and fifths, with strings (*Tranquilissimo*). Then, the piano changes from the melancholy A minor into a brightened A major, where an extended version of the "turn" has been harmonized in major sixths and coloured with strikes of mildly dissonant notes from the key of E major (*dolce, sereno*). And thus back and forth... In the middle sections of this work, the piano participates significantly in the madness of orchestra's motoric textures.

In the second movement, in its changing metres and interventions of syncopated motives, the piano provides a "pedal" or an "ostinato" by striking eight-note minor or major chords (spanning from the contra to the three-lined octave)—always at the downbeat, at "one"—to emphasize the prevailing mood of chaos and anxiety derived from the variability of the metre. The third movement—that "certain polka" for which this requiem has been written—is a manic, spinning and, at the same time, trivial dance built over a piano *ostinato*—and it is the piano

---

[11] David Drew, CD liner notes for *Kleines Requiem fur eine Polka*, Nonesuch CD with *Kleines Requiem für eine Polka*, Op. 66; Concerto for Harpsichord & String Orchestra, Op. 40; and *Good Night*, Op. 63. Nonesuch 9 79362-2, 1996.

that is responsible for the triviality. The chords' unisons and fifths are played in turn in the left hand in a constant quarter-note rhythm; the full chord falls on the second quarter-note, and the chord is partly a tonic, and partly a dominant (in relation to the key of the moment). The woodwind part brings sharply accented repetitions of individual notes, a "grotesque" material in a Lydian scale, remaining in a tritone relationship to the key of the piano. Adrian Thomas describes this movement as "popular music-making, be it from the village hall or the circus."[12]

The final movement is a return to the atmosphere of calm, meditation and, possibly, sorrow. The choral-sounding strings and horn, in long values and slow tempo, seem to be remaining in a dialogue with single and dissonant notes in piano and bells. In moments of silence, repeated and dense dominant chords appear in the part of the piano, and the finale boils down to the piano's D-flat major chord over its drone in strings. The last word belongs to the piano.

In his quest for an interpretation of this work, David Drew states that Górecki is not the kind of person who would use the word *requiem* with no consequence, or who could ignore the effect of its combination with the merry associations of the Czech dance popular in 19th-century Europe. The composer's single comment on this piece does not explain anything; more likely it enhances the mystery: "the clown is, underneath the greasepaint, ineffably sad."[13]

4. Towards an Interpretation

In the apogee phase, the simplicity and the modesty of performance means in piano technique are out of proportion to the import and the significance assigned to the instrument by the composer. The piano part has nothing to do with the mastery of performance, with great displays of pianistic technique.

---

[12] Thomas, *Górecki, op. cit.*, 146.
[13] *Ibidem*, 145.

The single, repeated, pedal-held, long-lasting, multi-voiced chords in a broad, many-octave ambitus—"resounding and co-resounding" in the terms of Irena Poniatowska[14]—produce a peculiar tonal aura in a seeming broadening of space that could be described as "a secondary illusion of space."[15]

Simultaneously, the very same chords through their multiplied repetitiveness produce an effect of slowing-down time, almost stopping down time—in a "distortion" of the quasi-temporal structure of the music. One could repeat Tomaszewski's comments on the Franciscan idiom in Szymanowski that the great resounding chords "voice a symbolic aspect" that these tones "open to evocations of transcendent associations."[16]

In the output of the so-called "late style," the significance of the piano manifests itself in a more direct way; it becomes a dominant, a concertizing instrument. It is omnipresent in the works described above; however, the composer only rarely uses virtuosic effects in these orchestral or chamber compositions. Still, the piano plays a form-making, a "mood-making", an "expression-making" role; it shapes the expressive basis of these works. In the Concerto and the *Little Requiem for a Polka*, the piano evokes an expressive mood of play, of playful yet not merry madness, somewhat along the lines of Johan Huizinga: play is a discrete category, play cannot be described as an opposite to seriousness, play can be serious.[17] In *Recitativos and Ariosos*, the piano does exactly that: it conducts a serious, *serio*, dialogue with the past. The past whose name is Beethoven.

---

[14] Irena Poniatowska, *Faktura fortepianowa Beethovena* [Beethoven's Piano Texture] (Warszawa: PWN, 1972), 231 - 232
[15] Suzanne Langer, *The Problems of Art.......*, quoted in J. Makota, *O klasyfikacji sztuk...*, 35.
[16] Mieczysław Tomaszewski, *Nad pieśniami Karola Szymanowskiego. Cztery studia* (Kraków: Akademia Muzyczna 1998), 97.
[17] Johan Hiuzinga, *Homo Ludens*. (Switzerland: Routledge and Kegan Paul Ltd., 1944); PDF Edition:
http://art.yale.edu/file_columns/0000/1474/homo_ludens_johan_huizinga_routledge_1949_.pdf.

The peculiar role of the piano in the oeuvre of Henryk Mikołaj Górecki could be described as symbolic in Leszek Polony's understanding of the term. Polony stated that "alongside those sanctioned by habit, symbols exist of indefinite meanings, ambiguous, mood-evocative ..." What is meant here is the "unspecified and allusive character of the symbol..." the meaning of which is exposed "in a flash of intuition rather than in logical-analytical discourse."[18]

---

[18] Leszek Polony, "Muzyczne ikony niewidzialnego" [Musical icons of the invisible], in *Ikony Niewidzialnego,* K. M. Lis, Z. W. Solski eds. (Opole, 2003), 106.

CHAPTER 13

Górecki Conducts Górecki in Los Angeles, 1997

Maja Trochimczyk

> Everyone has to create their own process of creation; there are no recipes for this. Each great composer had a different way: Mozart, Chopin, Beethoven... I think that there is not one way that people create in. I truly respect people who are systematic like Tchaikovsky who had to compose for several hours daily. Schubert also got up at 4 or 5 every morning and composed until nine. And I? I waste five months and then go crazy and compose for thirty hours daily, but I am happy that I have so many ideas, so many projects that I would like to work on. This fills me with joy: I do not have to search; I have music in my head. ~ *Henryk Mikołaj Górecki, October 1997*

That is just one of the secrets of his way of composing that Górecki shared with the composition students of the University of Southern California in Los Angeles in October 1997.[1] The lecture, or rather an extended QA session with young composers and performers was one of the events of the *Górecki Autumn: A Residency* at the USC School of Music, co-sponsored by the Polish Music Center, and filled with lectures, seminars, concerts, and celebrations. A performance of the Third Symphony, *Symphony of Sorrowful Songs* conducted by the composer and played by the USC student orchestra was one of the highlights not only of the Residency, but also of the entire musical year in Los Angeles, if one were to believe Mark Swed of the *Los Angeles Times*.[2] In 1997, Górecki was at the apex of his worldwide fame that followed the incredible popular success of his Third Symphony among Western audiences—growing exponentially since 1992, the release of its recording by the London Sinfonietta under David Zinman, with soprano Dawn Upshaw.

---

[1] Henryk Mikołaj Górecki, "Conversation with USC Music Students," *Polish Music Journal*, 6 no 2 (2003), English translation by Maja Trochimczyk. http://pmc.usc.edu/PMJ/issue/6.2.03/GoreckiStudents.html

[2] Mark Swed, "Falling into Place: Year in Review, 1997" (*Los Angeles Times*, 21 December 1997).

Interestingly, the composer had already attended a performance of the Third Symphony in Los Angeles, albeit he did not conduct it. The previous concert, given by the Los Angeles Philharmonic Orchestra on 17 September 1993, was conducted at the Hollywood Bowl by David Alan Miller, with soprano Christine Brewer. The West Coast premiere of the work was scheduled, incidentally or not, on the anniversary of the attack on Poland by Soviet troops, assisting the Nazi Germany in defeating the country, abandoned by all its allies (17 September 1939). During the 1993 travel to California, the composer also attended various performances in New York.

In the late 1990s, Górecki was receiving countless invitations from the best orchestras of the world, yet he chose to come to Los Angeles and conduct students. Why? His visit to America was a response to two invitations, from Prof. Thaddeus Gromada, the Executive Director of the Polish Institute of Arts and Sciences in America (PIASA) and editor of the *Tatra Eagle* and from the University of Southern California's School of Music in Los Angeles. As a result of extended discussions with the representatives of the University (of which more below), Górecki agreed to come. In this way he could participate in two distinct events on both coasts of the U.S., both very much to his liking.

Figure 13-1: Header of the *Tatra Eagle*. Courtesy of Thaddeus Gromada.

A lifelong admirer of the Tatra Mountains and its folklore, Górecki stayed in the village of Chochołów as often as he could, and the last decade of his life was spent in the Tatra Foothills village of Ząb, where he built his dream home to compose, read, and enjoy the crisp mountain air, awe-inspiring beauty of nature, and the intense, rough beauty of the *górale* [*highlander*] music. His love for the Tatra Mountains and their folklore was expressed in the textures, dissonances, and vigor of many of his works, especially the three String Quartets. He also dabbled in playing the second fiddle with the *góralska kapela* [highlander ensemble] and relished the opportunity to return to America to celebrate the Podhale and the Tatra Mountains culture.

The composer also developed a passion for performance; in 1996, he accompanied the Polish jazz singer Wanda Warska in his songs performed on tour through small towns of Poland. In the same year, he conducted his Third Symphony the way he really liked this work to be played (extremely slow and intense) at the First Festival of Polish Composers in Bielsko-Biała.

Figure 13-2: Górecki plays the second fiddle in "góralska kapela" with Thaddeus Gromada, and Jane Kedron. The 50th anniversary of the *Tatra Eagle*, New Jersey. Reproduced from the *Tatra Eagle*, courtesy of Thaddeus Gromada.

On 28 September 1997 the composer participated in the celebrations of the golden jubilee of the periodical *Tatra Eagle* as a guest of honor. The *Tatra Eagle* has been published by Polish Americans who came from the Tatra Foothills to the East Coast. These publishers were not just *górale* émigrés: Prof. Thaddeus Gromada was the Executive Director of PIASA, where his sister, Janina/Jane Gromada Kedroń worked as Administrative Manager. During the *Tatra Eagle* festivities, Górecki was the home guest of Jane and Henry Kedroń in Hasbrouck Heights, New Jersey, not far from New York.

That visit also included home music making: the composer played the second fiddle in an ad hoc *góralska kapela*. In this musical endeavor, he joined the *Tatra Eagle's* editors, Gromada and Kedroń, as well as singer Andrzej Bachleda (see Fig 13-1 and a photograph in Chapter 3). The composer was happy among friends, but anxious about the second part of his American adventure. As Dr. Gromada described it,[3]

> a day before the planned departure for Los Angeles, the composer became very agitated and filled with anxiety, he categorically stated that he was not going to get on the plane and continue on with his travel. Nothing worked, neither a visit to the doctor, nor the beseeching and begging by friends. There were repeated efforts to persuade Górecki how important is this festival of his in California. Gradually, after a while, he started making his demands. Finally, the extremely emotional composer stated that he would go on condition that he would be accompanied by all three friends—both the Kedrońs and Andrzej Bachleda—to provide him with moral support.

And this is what had happened. As Director of the USC Polish Music Center, I had only lived in the U.S. for a year, having been brought to Los Angeles by the late Dr. Stefan Wilk and his wife, Mrs. Wanda Wilk, the founders of PMC in 1996. In my position, I played a key role in the preparation of Górecki's visit: it was my job to persuade the notoriously publicity-averse composer to come to Los Angeles.[4]

Up to that time, despite repeated invitations by the Wilks and the Dean of the USC School of Music, conductor Larry Livingston, he had refused every invitation. Dean Livingston was interested in bringing Górecki to Los Angeles because, among other factors, as a conductor, he often traveled to Poland and liked the country's musicians. He invited many Polish students to enroll at USC, picking the best performers to bolster the USC School of Music's Symphony Orchestra. Over the years, his choices included cellist Alicja Dutkiewicz, flautist Adrianna Lis, bassoon player Marzena Nabours, clarinetist Jan Jakub Bokun, and many other talented young musicians.

---

[3] Email from Thaddeus Gromada to Maja Trochimczyk, 26 October 2011.
[4] Elaine Dutka wrote about the composer's lack of interest in travel and my role in bringing him here in "How USC Nabbed the Great Górecki" (*Los Angeles Times*, 21 September 1997.

Figure 13-3: Górecki with Janina Kedroń and Ms. Gromada in the home of Andrzej Bachleda in Zakopane, July 1997. Photo by Maja Trochimczyk.

After the Wilks' phone invitation, I called and wrote to the composer. I had corresponded with him earlier, in 1993, while working on my doctoral dissertation at McGill University.[5] I was seeking to interview him about the topics of "space and spatialization in music"—the subject of my dissertation—and mystical experiences and music, for an article I was working on at that time.[6] Back in 1993, though, he admitted that he could not read the article I had sent him in English without the assistance of his daughter, and noted in a P.S.: "As for not liking interviews, etc.—I agree, except for a tiny detail—do you know **why** I do not like interviews? So there!!! However, as a rule, I do

---

[5] Maria Anna Harley, *Space and Spatialization in Contemporary Music: History and Analysis, Ideas and Implementations*. Ph. D. Dissertation, McGill University, Montreal, Canada, 1994.

[6] Maria Anna Harley, "*To be God with God:* Catholic Composers and the Mystical Experience." *Contemporary Music Review,* vol. 12, part 2; "Contemporary Music and Religion," ed. Ivan Moody, (1995): 125-145. "A Mystic in the Cathedral: Music, Image and Symbol in Andriessen's *Hadewijch.*" *The American Journal of Semiotics* 13, no. 1-4, (Fall 1996 [1998]): 249-275. Special issue, "Signs in Musical Hermeneutics," ed. Siglind Bruhn.

answer letters. H.M.G."⁷ The noted profound dislike of interviews has also impacted his travel to Los Angeles.

Nonetheless, due to this history and the composer's satisfaction with my work as a musicologist, I was invited to visit him in Poland and conduct further negotiations about his potential travel to Los Angeles. On 18 July 1997, I visited Górecki in Zakopane, in the foothills of the Tatra Mountains, at the home of his friend, a noted classical baritone, Andrzej Bachleda. The visit turned out to be an exam of sorts: if I passed, Górecki would come to L.A., if not—there would be no festival. He wanted to know what kind of people would be hosting him and who would be his translator in California. I was surprised by the size of the "examination committee" that welcomed me in Bachleda's home: at the table, besides Górecki, I found Mrs. and Mrs. Bachleda; Dr. Gromada; his wife, Theresa; his sister Janina/Jane Kedroń, the Deputy Director of PIASA; and her husband, Henryk. The Gromadas and Kedrońs were not strangers to me—several months earlier I became a member of the Institute, one of the most distinguished Polish organizations in America.

What was the topic of discussion in Zakopane? Primarily, the purpose and conditions of the visit: Why do we need Górecki so much? What kind of a Polish Music Center is that? Would our guest be treated with respect? Would we be able to guarantee that he would not be harassed by journalists? The Polish Music Center at the USC School of Music was established in 1985 by Dr. and Mrs. Stefan and Wanda Wilk and grew in stature thanks to the dedicated support by Witold Lutosławski, who donated to USC for the fledging institution the manuscripts of five of his most important works (*Mi Parti, Preludia i Fuga, Mała Uwertura, Novelette*, and *Paroles tissées*). The Wilks did not have at their disposal the four millions of dollars, required to fully endow a new Center and continued to make annual donations. Mrs. Wanda Wilk, a USC graduate in music education became the first Director while working as a volunteer. Besides Dean Livingston, USC music faculty did not include any specialists in Polish music, while Polish Americans in Los Angeles were more interested in film festivals and folk dancing by local groups, Krakusy and Podhale, than in the music of the Polish

---

⁷ "Co do nie lubienia wywiadów itp. – to się zgadzam poza drobnostką – czy Pani wie **dlaczego** nie lubie wywiadów? Ano!!! Na listy z reguły jednak odpowiadam." Handwritten letter. Maja Trochimczyk Collection.

avant-garde. Górecki's visit was to be a public demonstration of support, showing that the Center is important; that it has a full backing of the Polish music world; and that its establishment is a great, shared success of the Wilks and the University.

This argument, to come to the rescue of the institution practically co-founded by Witold Lutosławski (who died just a few years earlier, in January 1994) was decisive and the composer agreed to become the star and the focal point of the festival. I do not doubt that his personal paternal feelings also played a role: while in Zakopane, he started to call me "Ania" because I reminded him of his daughter, a wonderful pianist Anna Górecka. After having been thus „adopted" by the famous composer, I returned to Los Angeles, to plan further course of action. We agreed to his request that that he would be accompanied by a friend, Andrzej Bachleda.

Figure 13-4: Andrzej Bachleda, Jane Kedron, Górecki and Henry Kedron on USC Campus in front of Bovard Auditorium, 3 October 1997. Photo by Maja Trochimczyk.

The additional magnet for the composer was being hosted at home not in a hotel; it was the home cooking of Mrs. Wilk and her heartfelt hospitality that he found so welcoming. That's where the guests were staying for the week-long festivities and that's where one of the concerts took place.

The festival *Górecki Autumn: A Residency* was a celebration in the honor of Dr. Stefan and Wanda Wilk, in gratitude for founding and funding of the Center and the establishment of the position of its professional director, that I assumed in August 1996. The Program included three concerts, a lecture by the composer's biographer Adrian Thomas,[8] and an academic conference about Górecki's music. It all started from a chamber music concert on October 1, unfortunately scheduled, as it turned out, on Yom Kippur—what was pointed out as USC's grave error by some of the reviewers, but that did not reduce the crowds in the audience.

The composer actively participated in rehearsals of the following pieces on the program: *Cztery Preludia* of 1955 (played by Wojciech Kocyan), Wariacje Op. 4 (1956) for violin and piano, Sonata Nr. 1, Op. 6 for piano (1956/1990; played by Robert Thies), *Valentine Piece*, Op. 70, *For You, Anne Lill*, Op. 58 (1986), played by Emily Lin, and an *Intermezzo* for piano (1990). Additionally, Linda Wand and Robert Thies also gave a secret, pre-premiere performance of *Kleine Fantasie*, just completed and scheduled for its official premiere in Germany.

Górecki also coached the USC Contemporary Music Ensemble conducted by Dave Crockett for the final concert on October 5, featuring *Good Night*, Op. 63, for soprano, alto flute and piano (1990) and *Kleines Requiem für eine Polka* for chamber ensemble (1995). He clearly enjoyed teaching young musicians and sharing insights into understanding and performing his works; he enjoyed the colorful richness of the Preludes interpreted by Wojciech Kocyan, then doctoral student at USC, now professor at Loyola Marymount University. The composer was particularly thrilled by the performance of his Sonata by another eminent, prize-winning pianist, Robert Thies.

---

[8]Adrian Thomas, *Górecki* (Oxford University Press, 1996). His lecture on "Intense Joy and Profound Rhythm: Introduction to the Music of Henryk Mikołaj Górecki" is published in the *Polish Music Journal*, 6 nr 2 (2003), http://www.usc.edu/dept/polish_music/PMJ/issue/6.2.03/ThomasIntro.html

Figure 13-5: Press clippings about Górecki's visit to Los Angeles, 1997. Maja Trochimczyk Collection. Used by Permission.

The apex of the festival was an unforgettable concert *Górecki Conducts Górecki*, with the composer leading the USC Symphony Orchestra of young students in his Symphony No. 3, *Symphony of Sorrowful Songs*. With USC School of Music professor, soprano Elizabeth Hynes, this extremely slow, intense, and serene performance of maternal grief became such a triumph that is was declared by the *Los Angeles Times* the event of the year 1997.[9]

The event was well-documented in the local and international press, with the chronological list of main news stories, as follows:[10]

---

[9] Mark Swed, "Falling into Place: Year in Review, 1997" (*Los Angeles Times*, 21 December 1997); Jon Regardie and Jack Skelley, "Culture and Controversy: A Top 12 of 1997 in the Arts" (*Los Angeles Times*, 29 December 1997). The first proclamation of the event's importance came in a review by Mark Swed: "Górecki's Third Is All His Own" (*Los Angeles Times*, 6 October 1997). Another important publication was by Richard Ginell in the *American Record Guide, January/February* 1998).

[10] The press coverage included 20 articles; in addition to the ones listed above there were previews and notices in the *USC Chronicle, the Daily Trojan (USC student paper), News of Polonia*, and *Los Angeles Times*. Fragments of these reviews were published in *Polish Music Journal*, 6 nr 2 (2003), ed. Maja Trochimczyk,

- Jack Skelley: "Górecki to Grace USC" (*Los Angeles Downtown News* 26, no. 39, 29 September 1997);
- Maria Anna Harley and James Harley: "Henryk Mikołaj Górecki" Musical Biography" (*News of Polonia* 3, no. 5, 22 September 1997);
- Greg Sandow: "Celebrating the Surprises That Are Górecki's Gift" (*Los Angeles Times*, 1 October 1997);
- Mark Swed: "Górecki Festival Begins with Searing Early, Late Works" (*Los Angeles Times*, 2 October 1997);
- Mark Swed: "Górecki's Third Is All His Own" (*Los Angeles Times*, 6 October 1997);
- Paul Gannon: "Polish Composer Directs USC Symphony" (*The Daily Trojan*, 6 October 1997);
- Alan Rich, "A Lot of Night Music — Ship of Foolishness" (*Los Angeles Weekly*, 10-16 October 1997);
- Danuta Derlińska-Pawlak, "Jesień Góreckiego w Los Angeles," (*Przegląd Polski, Nowy Dziennik*, 30 October 1997;
- Elaine Dutka: "How USC Nabbed the Great Górecki" (*Los Angeles Times*, 21 October 1997;
- Melissa Payton: "Górecki's Visit to USC Ends on a High Note" (*USC Chronicle*, 20 October 1997,
- Wanda Wilk: "Behind the Scenes" (*News of Polonia*, November 1997);
- Mark Alburger, "Górecki Autumn at USC" (*20th Century Music*, December 1997);
- James Harley: "Celebrating Górecki in California" (*Musicworks*, Spring 1998);
- Mark Swed, "Falling into Place: Year in Review, 1997" (*Los Angeles Times*, 21 December 1997); and
- Jon Regardie and Jack Skelley, "Culture and Controversy: A Top 12 of 1997 in the Arts" (*Los Angeles Times*, 29 December 1997)
- Richard Ginell: Los Angeles: USC Symphony: Górecki Symphony No. 3" (*American Record Guide, January/February* 1998).

For Górecki—an untrained conductor without much prior experience on the podium—conveying the exact emotional expression was of paramount importance. In order to articulate the mood of tranquility after the tragedy, students had to stop rushing, calm down and play every note with full intensity—the piece was to be all *"sostenuto* and very calm, *cantabile."*[11] Among the reviewers, Alan Rich noticed the hypnotic, incredibly slow tempo: the Symphony lasted for 65 minutes, as compared with the 53 minutes of the David Zinman recording that brought it international fame.[12]

Figure 13-6: Górecki rehearsing with USC student orchestra, with translator Maja Trochimczyk, 2 October 1997.

---

[11]Górecki, "Remarks on Performing the Third Symphony", *Polish Music Journal*, 6 nr 2 (2003), English translation by Maja Trochimczyk, http://www.usc.edu/dept/polish_music/PMJ/issue/6.2.03/GoreckiThird.html
[12]Alan Rich, "A Lot of Night Music — Ship of Foolishness" (*Los Angeles Weekly*, 10-16 October 1997). David Zinman conducted the London Sinfonietta and soprano Dawn Upshaw in a recording issued in 1992 by Nonesuch; it became the bestselling Classical CD of 1993, and was even listed on pop charts. See Luke B. Howard, "Motherhood, Billboard, and the Holocaust: Perceptions and Receptions of Górecki's Symphony No. 3," *The Musical Quarterly* 82, no. 1 (spring 1998): 131-159; and by the same author, "'Laying the Foundation:' The Reception of Górecki's Third Symphony, 1977-1992" *Polish Music Journal*, vol. 6 no. 2 (2003). http://www.usc.edu/dept/polish_music/PMJ/issue/6.2.03/Howard.html

As Górecki's personal translator and event organizer, I spent the week with him on campus, participating in all rehearsals, organizing concerts, making sure that every wish of the composer was fulfilled. At the orchestral rehearsals, I translated his remarks about performing the Third Symphony and reaching utmost intensity of expression, sustaining and saturating every note with emotion. It was easy to feel this acceptance, sense of connection, and positive emotions during the rehearsals for the symphonic concert on Friday, 3 October 1997. My job was to help the composer by translating his remarks to the students into English and by making sure he was comfortable and satisfied with his experience.

Even then, a day before, and on the way to the rehearsals, at the last minute Górecki wanted to withdraw. There was quite a crowd assembled to persuade him to perform—the whole group with Andrzej Bachleda and his other friends, whose travel from New Jersey was undertaken for this very purpose, to offer Górecki encouragement and ensure that he feels safe in a circle of friendly faces. Young musicians were well prepared; USC is one of the best music schools in the country. Yet, they knew the notes and did not understand the music. Resolving that issue was the composer's main focus during the rehearsals. Below are fragments of his directions to the students (that I translated during the rehearsal and for later publication):

Movement No. 1, *Lento sostenuto tranquillo ma cantabile* (34'53"):

> Górecki: Some general remarks: Please sustain the half notes, without diminuendo, in a contemplative mood. It should all be sostenuto and very tranquil, very cantabile. That is all [...] I have stage fright when I face you. I do not do this every day. Instead I listen to music and I'm more interested in playing myself than conducting. But I will improve before tomorrow if I live that long. Did you practice this section slower or faster?

> Students: - Faster!

> Górecki: - Nonetheless, I would like to play it slower. This is the whole problem. If we play it in a romantic fashion, then the canon stops being what I imagined it to be. It is based on a very long theme. It is so long that perhaps it would even find its way into the Guinness Book of Records! Therefore, the canon has to be "broader" - do not rush it. The most important problem for me at the end of the twentieth century is the continual lack of time. We are always in an

awful hurry and still we waste an incredible amount of time, for instance in front of the TV or in a car. While I do like some aspects of our "fast" civilization—I love to fly in airplanes, I am fascinated with cosmic adventures, trips to the moon or Mars—and we do live in astounding times, still, here, in this music, we have to surrender ourselves to this other dimension of time. We have to slow down.

Only then the sonority will be fantastic: the higher the music will go, the more distinctly it will sound. I dream of writing such tranquil music. I do not want to compose anything that echoes the modern "rush"—the cell phones, the telephones and faxes. It has to be calm. Life is too beautiful to be wasted in this way, by rushing things so much. How should I explain it to you? Perhaps you should think about an elevator: you leave behind the basement of everyday life, filled with noises, distractions and anxieties, and you take the elevator up to the tenth floor, or even into the sky of timelessness. When you are in this music, time slows down, it is as if you were in heaven, it is like eternity. Do you understand what I want to achieve there? Total calm... Let us play it again.

Górecki's comments about Movement No. 2 (Lento e Largo, 9'42" in performance) were few and did not contain any general comments about the expressive character of this work, so they are omitted.

Movement No. 3, *Lento cantabile – semplice* (21'16" in performance):

> Górecki: Here each sound has to be audible. I would like you to make sure that everything is audible at rehearsal number 3 and later at number 7. When the orchestra plays alone I ask you to please play it with a crescendo. However when Elizabeth sings we should go a little bit under, lower but still with full sonority and with crescendos. A final matter: at number 9 in D major you have to be very careful with shifts to F-sharp. Thank you.
>
> Here—four measures before number 12 we should make an allargando and later play a tempo. Let us now take a small "breathing space" so that you can understand my intentions. This is a mother's song. This song has to be expressed both by the orchestra and the soloist. It has to be contemplative in mood, but still maintain the tempo. It approximates the speed of slow walking, when one walks alone, lost in thought. We have to enter into this mood. It is as if we were walking, or even slowly dancing. You have to think about walking here.

> For me it is a very difficult movement because I do not usually engage in conducting and I do not know how to enchant you with my hand movements, but music carries me away and I may at some spots (and please forgive me if I do) make a wrong movement at a certain time, but you know the score and could play on. So then do not look at me, at what I am doing, but listen to each other, listen to what happens around you.

According to the composer, the most important thing students had to realize was that the Symphony was filled with "tranquility after the storm"—calm after the tragedy has already happened. Students had to stop rushing and play every half note with full saturation and intensity, without diminuendo—the piece was to be played all *"sostenuto* and very calm, *cantabile."*

To make it easier for the students to understand the spiritual quality of his music, Górecki compared the spiritual state achieved in the first movement of the Symphony (which had a very long and slow theme of a broad "breath" and vast scope) with the state of suspension and weightlessness beyond time, a state that may exists in a plane or in an elevator, suspended between the floors. The state of „suspension" of being "in-between" was extremely important—leaving the departure and arrival points behind.

After several examples, the young musicians understood his intent, and during the concert were up to the challenge, playing with extreme intensity, focus and saturation of sound.

In a conversation with the singer Elizabeth Hynes, during a break in the rehearsal, Górecki explained the back-story behind the Symphony, focusing on the meaning of the text in the Second Movement:

> Górecki: I would like to add something here about the inscription. In prison, the whole wall was covered with inscriptions screaming out loud: "I'm innocent," "Murderers," "Executioners," "Free me," "You have to save me"—it was all so loud, so banal. Adults were writing this, while here it is an eighteen-year-old girl, almost a child. And she is so different. She does not despair, does not cry, does not scream for revenge. She does not think about herself; whether she deserves her fate or not. Instead, she only thinks about her mother: because it is her mother who will experience true despair. This inscription was something extraordinary.

Figure 13-7: Górecki with pianist Robert Thies. Photo by Maja Trochimczyk.

The interpretation that composer taught to USC Student Orchestra was characterized by flat, organ-like dynamic layers; extreme steadiness of tempi; softness of a saturated tone created with broad bowing; clear articulation of dynamics; sustained emotional intensity; and a duration over ten minutes longer than any known recording (the Symphony clocked at one hour and five minutes according to reviewer Richard Ginell, and lasts 66 minutes on the documentary CD recordings by KUSC radio station).

The steadiness of repetitions in extremely slow tempi was apparent under Górecki's baton in Los Angeles, but it also characterized the version that Górecki conducted in October 1996 at the Festival of Polish Composers in Bielsko-Biała, a mid-sized town in the foothill area of the mountains of Beskid Śląski in south-western Poland. The composer was the co-founder and artistic director of the festival, initiated in 1996 and now bearing his name. It was very important for Górecki to spend time among the "common people" who needed music in their life journey, and could listen with more devotion and gratitude than the jaded crowd in large metropolitan centers of the world.[13]

---

[13] See "Composing is a Personal Matter" – interview in Chapter 4 of this volume.

Given a choice of London or Bielsko-Biała, without hesitation, he would opt the latter.

The Bielsko-Biała Festival brought together a group of professional musicians who came specifically to perform with Górecki.[14] The soprano part was performed by Zofia Kilanowicz, a classical singer of górale ancestry, who added some folk inflections to the solo part. In interviews with Beata Bolesławska-Lewandowska,[15] Kilanowicz discussed the enormous impact of the Third Symphony on her entire life (it allowed her to return to performing after the onset of MS), and stated that the 1996 performance lasted for one hour and ten minutes, longer than any other interpretation on record.

Even in Los Angeles, Górecki refused to conduct the professional L.A. Philharmonic Orchestra, but agreed to work with students. The concert was sold out with long lines of potential listeners waiting to get inside Bovard Auditorium. The atmosphere was electric before the concert and enthusiastic afterwards. Polish actress and artist based in Los Angeles, Beata Poźniak, thus describes her encounter with the composer:[16]

> My encounter was lovely but brief. I remember joking to Henryk Górecki: "My Mom is thrilled that you dedicated "Beatus Vir" to me! He laughed back and said: "that is why my journey in life will always be blessed, have a sacred path. And since your name IS Beata it is destined to be that way too. Creating is a spiritual experience. Unexplainable." I shared with him that when I create a character I channel energy. I said to him, please, don't laugh, it's personal: When I make a sculpture I it's not me , it's my hands doing (creating) it for

---

[14] The festivals under Górecki's patronage were dedicated to a single composer each year, with Górecki's music serving as the theme in 1996 and in 2003, and other composers including his favorites: Chopin, Szymanowski, Karłowicz, Moniuszko, Wieniawski, Bacewicz, jazz composers (Kurylewicz, Konieczny). See http://www.fkpbb.pl/ for more details. After Górecki's death the festivals bear his name.
[15] Beata Bolesławska-Lewandowska, *Górecki: Portret w Pamięci* [Górecki: A Portrait in Memory] (Kraków: PWM, 2013). In the same volume, the genesis of the Festival of Polish Composers is recalled by its three main "actors" – Władysław Szczotka, the organizer, harpsichordist Ewa Stojek-Lupin – the initiator; and Jacek Krywult, City Mayor, who ensures the festival's continuity.
[16] Email from Beata Poźniak to Maja Trochimczyk, November 26, 2017.

me. "Exactly" - he said - "when my ears hear something from the Above then I share or channel that."

Figure 13-8: Górecki after the concert with a listener, actress Beata Poźniak. Used by Permission.

Let Mark Swed of the *Los Angeles Times* describe this "unlikely appearance:"[17]

> Unlikely is an understatement. No one was sure if the temperamental composer, who was said to be trying to worm out of the performance up until the last minute, would really show. After a suspenseful late start to the concert, there he was, the 63-year-old composer limping on stage (a hip injury in childhood received improper medical attention) and looking slightly impish. He conducted without baton and without guile. An open right palm gently marked the meter until he approached climaxes. But then it was as if he roared. His whole body would tense up to the breaking point. With shaking fists, he

---

[17] Mark Swed: "Górecki's Third Is All His Own (*Los Angeles Times*, 6 October 1997).

exhorted the players to dig deeper into the sound of their instruments than they ever had before, but he seemed also to entreat God with the same gesture.

The tempos were unprecedented; Górecki added a full 11 minutes to the suggested timing of 54 minutes printed in the score. And the performance was simply extraordinary, practically unfathomable under the circumstances. Górecki is not a very experienced conductor. He had little more than a single rehearsal. The orchestra, consisting of university students, has been together only the few weeks of the new school year. But Górecki's personality is like a force of nature, and he achieved an intensity that I have never heard equaled in this music from far more accomplished orchestras.

Figure 13-9: *Górecki Conducts Górecki* with USC Student Orchestra; 3 October 1997, Bovard Auditorium. Photo by Anacleto Rapping from *Los Angeles Times* archives. Used by Permission.

Richard Ginell in the *American Record Guide* thus described this unique and magical performance:[18]

---

[18] Richard S. Ginell, "Los Angeles: USC Symphony: Górecki Symphony No. 3." (*American Record Guide*, January/February 1998).

A short, somewhat stocky man wearing a purple bowtie, walking to the podium with a pronounced limp (stemming from childhood), the 63-year old Górecki appeared like a stern, strong spiritual figure, waving his arms sans baton in graceful, imploring, breaststroke-like motions. At the great emotional first movement climax after the soprano's solo, his gestures became jerky and punchy, urging the young musicians to pour it on.

Górecki took his first movement at a glacially slow tempo, slower than anyone (35 minutes, as opposed to the usual 25-30 minute range), allowing the mournful, overlapping canons to emerge with aching deliberation, while the remaining two movements were closer in tempo to other interpreters. Clearly Górecki takes his subtitle, *Symphony of Sorrowful Songs*, very seriously—and his passionate, lingering conception would sober any New Age dabblers who might want to use this music as passive, meditative background.

Figure 13-10: Górecki after the concert with USC Student Orchestra; 3 October 1997, Bovard Auditorium. Photo by Anacleto Rapping from *Los Angeles Times* archives. Used by Permission.

At the end of the year, the *Górecki Conducts Górecki* concert at USC was named No. 1 classical music event in Los Angeles by Mark Swed, the

Los Angeles Times' principal classical music critic, and listed as No. 5 of all music events by his colleagues:

> **Mark Swed — No. 1: Górecki's Grooves.** "Górecki Autumn" at USC came, seemingly, out of the blue, not unlike the way the Polish composer's Third Symphony did when it hit the classical charts a couple of years ago. A fussy and unpredictable character, Górecki had only once before conducted his symphony, and that was in Poland. But there he was, in front of the USC orchestra and an overflow audience that paid a mere $5 a ticket, digging deep into profound music and getting the student players to give what had to be the most committed, probing, intense performance of their young lives. A lot of grandchildren will be hearing about this someday.

> **John Regardie and Jack Skelley**[19]**— No. 5. The Great Górecki:** The classical coup of the year went to USC School of Music, who persuaded Polish composer/hermit Henryk Górecki to make his American conducting debut with his popular Symphony No. 3 during October's five-day "Górecki Autumn." The somber minimalist work came off as deeply passionate. It sold out instantly but not just because the tickets were only $5.

John Regardie Jack Skelley placed the concert on the fifth place among 12 most important cultural events of Los Angeles and in the first place among classical music events. This was an incredible distinction because there are hundreds of concerts in Los Angeles every year. The magic of the Symphony and its hypnotic interpretation under the baton of its creator resulted in a miracle of sorts. Mark Alburger in *20th Century Music* wrote of "ideal sense of tempo, space and balance." Alan Rich noticed the hypnotized public and incredibly slow tempo: under Górecki, the Symphony lasted for 65 min while in Zinman's recording it was only 53 min. Mark Swed stated that the participants in this event would be telling stories about it to their grandchildren, because for young musician to experience such intense and profound interpretation of music was practically unheard of during their school work.

The radio broadcast was repeated several times but was not issued on a CD; the composer did not want to give his permission because of language and diction mistakes of the soloist, Elizabeth Hynes who,

---

[19] "Culture and Controversy: A Top 12 of 1997 in the Arts" by Jon Regardie and Jack Skelley (*Los Angeles Times*, 29 December 1997).

despite having been coached by a Polish singer Beata Bałon, mixed up her vowels in several places, distorting the meaning of the text. In addition, the composer had reservation about her grand, operatic voice, resembling the style of the first interpreter of this part, Stefania Woytowicz, with a broad vibrato and heavy portamento. He did not discuss this issue publicly, but repeatedly refused to grant permission for the release of the CD. The performance remained as a documentary recording, with few copies given to the main participants and kept in the KUSC radio archives where it was found and broadcast after the composer's death on November 12, 2010. Mark Swed again remembered the event as completely magical:[20]

> The concert was quite an occasion. Once agreeing to conduct, Górecki did everything he could to worm out of the assignment. When none of his tactics worked, he then delayed the performance by nervously fiddling with his tux for ages. He slowly and sheepishly limped on stage (he had a childhood leg injury). But once he began, he entered into what could only be described as a cosmic trance. He led an unbelievably slow, 65-minute performance of extra-ordinary depth and passion. Conducting without a baton, he carefully beat time, allowing the power to build with infinite patience. At the climaxes, he erupted, shaking his fists with terrifying intensity. Górecki wasn't a practiced conductor, but he was a pianist able to make the piano resound as though its strings were the size of the Golden Gate Bridge cables. That he could get that same unfathomable sound after a single rehearsal from a student orchestra and soprano Elizabeth Hynes felt at the time like a feat of magic.

It is interesting to compare the timings of this version, the "authoritative" interpretation of the work by its author, with several important recordings that he either did, or did not approve of. His favorite two sopranos, Dawn Upshaw and Zofia Kilanowicz shared the "crystalline" pure quality with little vibrato. The following recordings are compared in the table below:

1. Great Symphony Orchestra of the Polish Radio in Katowice, with Stefania Woytowicz, soprano, Jerzy Katlewicz, conducting, version performed at the Warsaw Autumn Festival in September 1977, not approved by the composer; recorded in 1978 for Polskie Nagrania, released in 1993.

---

[20] Mark Swed, "Rare performance at USC of Górecki-led Third Symphony will be broadcast," (*Los Angeles Times*, 18 November 2010).

Movement	Symphony Orchestra of the Polish Radio in Katowice, Stefania Woytowicz, cond. Jerzy Katlewicz (1978/1993)	The London Sinfonietta, Nonesuch Recording, with Dawn Upshaw, cond. David Zinman (1992) Nonesuch	Silesian Philharmonic Orchestra, with Zofia Kilanowicz, cond. Jerzy Swoboda (1994), Fryderyk Phillips et co.	USC Student Orchestra, Elizabeth Hynes, Cond. Henryk Górecki, Los Angeles (1997)	National Symphony Orchestra of the Polish Radio in Katowice, with Zofia Kilanowicz, cond. Antoni Wit (2001) TVP1/Naxos	Szymanowski Symphony Orchestra in Kraków, Zofia Kilanowicz, cond. Jacek Kaspszyk (2003) EMI Classics
1 - Lento sostenuto tranquillo ma cantabile	25 minutes 33 seconds	23 minutes 48 seconds	28 minutes, 48 seconds	34 minutes 53 seconds	27 minutes 18 seconds/ 27 minutes 11 seconds	30 minutes 14 seconds
2 - Lento e Largo	10 minutes 18 seconds	13 minutes 40 seconds	9 minutes 26 seconds	9 minutes 42 seconds	10 minutes 37 seconds/ 10 minutes 17 seconds	8 minutes 56 seconds
3 - Lento cantabile - semplice	16 minutes 21 seconds	17 minutes	18 minutes	21 minutes 16 seconds	17 minutes 55 seconds/ 18 minutes 36 seconds	17 minutes 38 seconds
TOTAL time (some pauses between movements)	52 minutes 15 seconds	53 minutes 50 seconds	56 minutes 15 seconds	65 minutes 56 seconds	58 minutes 26 seconds/ 56 minutes 4 seconds	56 minutes 48 seconds

Table 13-1: Comparison of Timing in the Third Symphony.

2. National Symphony Orchestra of the Polish Radio in Katowice, with Zofia Kilanowicz, soprano, Antoni Wit, conducting, performing with the composer in attendance at the Archikatedra Chrystusa Króla in Katowice and recorded for broadcast by TVP-1 (2001); the recording issued by Naxos

3. The London Sinfonietta, with Dawn Upshaw, soprano, David Zinman, conducting. Released by Nonesuch in 1992.

4. The Silesian Philharmonic Orchestra, in Katowice, with Zofia Kilanowicz, cond. Jerzy Swoboda (1994), Fryderyk Award; Phillips and other labels release.

5. USC Symphony Orchestra with Elizabeth Hynes, soprano, Henryk Górecki, conducting. Bovard Auditorium, USC Campus, Los Angeles (1997), documentary recording not publicly released.

6. Karol Szymanowski Symphony Orchestra in Kraków, Zofia Kilanowicz, cond. Jacek Kaspszyk (2003) EMI Classics.

The greatest differences in timing are in the first movement, that's taken way beyond slow by Górecki himself. However, the aesthetic preference of the composer also includes extending and slowing down the last movement, five minutes longer in his interpretation than by Jerzy Katlewicz. Similarly, the last movement was at least three minutes longer than either of his preferred recordings. It is also interesting that the expressive and intensely sorrowful second movement in the Zinman/Upshaw recording lasted full four minutes more than Górecki's own interpretation! It is due to the radio broadcasts of this movement that the Symphony so quickly rose in popularity in the 1990s.

It is very interesting to note, that over the years, it was Zofia Kilanowicz, born in Podhale (Nowy Targ) and singing with a folk górale inflection, that became THE soprano for the Third Symphony, appearing in a multitude of concerts in Europe, Asia and North America; starting from a 1993 performance in Kraków under Jacek Kaspszyk. Kilanowicz recorded the Symphony multiple times: in 1994 with Silesian Philharmonic, conducted by Jerzy Swoboda; in 2001 with the National Symphony Orchestra of the Polish Radio in Katowice (NOSPR) with Antoni Wit; in 2003 with NOSPR and Jacek Kasprzyk; and in December 2003 with NOSPR and Henryk Górecki conducting at the Holy Cross Church in Zakopane. This exceptional recording was honored by the 2006 Fryderyk Award for the best contemporary music recording of the year (the 1994 interpretation by Swoboda earlier also received this Award). Kilanowicz also sung the Third Symphony with Górecki conducting in Rome and in Germany. The composer wrote the following in her score: "Dear Zosia, a hundred thanks for miraculous singing. I thank you very, very much. Let heavenly angels watch over your voice."[21] As she reported, the composer[22]

> accepted my interpretation, with my *górale* intonation (*zaśpiew*) [...] He lived for a long time in Chochołów, then in Ząb, and I come from Nowy Targ. This *górale* intonation was mine, he never told me how to sing this; I sung myself this way, but he accepted it fully. This is mine and nobody can copy that.

Figure 13-11: Górecki and USC Symphony Orchestra. *USC Chronicle.* Used by Permission.

◎ ◎ ◎

Górecki Conducts Górecki was not the only concert "conducted" by the composer during the 1997 Festival. He participated in chamber music and solo rehearsals by standing in the back of the auditorium and conducting the music to himself, while singing the main melodies. He was particularly preoccupied with maximizing the expressive contrasts of the *Kleines Requiem für eine Polka* for chamber ensemble (1995), performed by the USC Contemporary Music Ensemble on 5 October 1997. During the rehearsals for this and other concerts of the

---

[21] Zofia Kilanowicz, interviewed by Beata Boleslawska-Lewandowska, op. cit. p. 240.
[22] She described his personality as similar to his music - a deep, distinct, sometimes melancholy, not joyous, broad and tranquil (p. 243). He was a good conductor, who conducted almost without the score. She also credited this symphony with inspiring her to return to performing in 2007 after a hiatus caused by serious illness (MS).

Górecki Autumn, young musicians crowded around the composer when he was showing them how to sharpen the rhythms and intensify the expression. He was mobbed by crowds of young students also during the intermissions and after the concerts.

Eager to talk to them both in Polish and German, as well as using my assistance as his personal interpreter, he was very friendly and welcoming to everyone. He refused to be interviewed by professional journalists, or give a press conference, yet, he cherished a personal response of listeners to his music.

In Górecki's works we are thrown into a world of sharply-chiseled colors and emotions; joy after suffering, tranquility and calm after pain and dramatic struggle. The overall expressive tone is unique and this is what the composer was pointing to while „conducting" the music in an empty concert hall. He asked the musicians to intensify the expression, deepen the contrasts. He was not very happy with the version of his music he heard at the rehearsal, but the musicians understood his intent and at the concerts were able to convey what he intended. The festival ended with the composers' triumph.

Long after he left the academic world in 1979 when he resigned from the position of the President of the Academy of Music in Katowice, the composer enjoyed teaching students the core principles of his craft and aesthetic belief. USC students had an opportunity to learn a lot about Górecki's compositional aesthetics and fascinations during one of the nonpublic event of the Górecki Autumn, a composition and performance forum at Newman Hall filled with over a hundred of students.

The session was structured as a QA moderated by Adrian Thomas. Students asked about everything: how he composes, did the war and suffering impact his music, what composers he likes, does he like to listen to his own music, is Mozart better than Chopin, what is the role of melody in his music. The composer, dressed for the occasion in USC T-shirt, had two translators on hand, me and a doctoral student of comparative linguistics, Joanna Niżyńska.

The conversation immediately assumed a personal, direct tone and changed into a lesson of life wisdom. Górecki wanted to share with the young listener his intensity, passion, focus on doing one thing at a time. When asked about the past and the war, he responded by stating that it is pointless to dwell on the past: "What is interesting in wars, illness, persecutions? We have to deal with the future and with music."[23]

> In music, we have three elements: rhythm, harmony, and melody. But melody is the result of something else. Now let's think what distinguishes one person from another person, how can you tell one composer from another? Is this a difference in melody, in harmony, or maybe of rhythm? When we hear a fragment, perhaps just one measure of some music, sometimes even only one chord, already we are able to tell whose music it is. Do you agree with me? Naturally, this has to be done by a person who has some musical abilities and musical knowledge. This person has to be capable of distinguishing between such composers as Mahler, Bruckner, Wagner, or Stravinsky. This person has to know where this difference lies.

Figure 13-12: Górecki "conducts" the *Kleines Requiem* during the rehearsal at USC Newman Hall in Hancock Auditorium. Photo by Maja Trochimczyk.

---

[23]Górecki, "Conversation with USC Music Students," *Polish Music Journal*, 6 no. 2 (2003), English translation by Maja Trochimczyk, http://www.usc.edu/dept/polish_music/PMJ/issue/6.2.03/GoreckiStudents.html

Melody is built from harmony. I do not at first create a melody and then harmonize it. Each composer built his own melodic structures in accordance with his harmony. Thus, we can tell if the music was composed by Vivaldi, Schubert, or Brahms, whether it is a chord by Brahms or Mahler, a minor third by Mozart or Chopin. Do you have to hear Chopin's whole melody to recognize that the music was composed by Chopin? No. At times it is sufficient to have just one or two chords and you are home...

The beginning, when the conscious work on harmony and melody begins, is very mysterious. The whole conscious process of constructing the music is always subservient to the inspiration, to whatever passes through my mind. It is not a mechanical matter, though naturally there are many combinations that you could examine in order to recognize all the different possibilities latent in a given structure. I have to figure out what can I make from my material.

I do not like listening to recordings of my music, because I get very upset about things that are not done the way I want them to be done. However, I do like, quite a lot, the London recording of the Third Symphony, with Dawn Upshaw. She has the perfect voice for the part; she is the perfect soprano. I like this recording even though there are some technical faults with it, even though I heard a lot of critical opinions about it.

Could music exist without spirit at all? Without any spiritual inspiration? Why would anyone say that Schubert's music is non-spiritual? In the past, all the composers, all the Mozarts, Schuberts, Haydns, Beethovens, and many others until the times of Bartók and Stravinsky, did not talk about these issues, because they could not imagine that music could be composed without this spiritual inspiration. Each man, each person, as we sit here, consists of two elements: body and soul. We all know what body is: that many liters of water, that much minerals of this kind and that. . . What truly distinguishes us from each other, what makes us distinct individuals, is the spirit. This spirit works in us, we are not robots, as yet.

In 1905, a French poet said to his friend some very simple truths about life: "If you are reading, do read, and do not just turn pages. If you are listening to music, really listen." Nadia Boulanger used to say: "If you are washing the window, wash it for real, if you are writing, write, and if you are playing, play and do not think about what you will be doing the next day." Someone who is very young and lives in Los Angeles will tell me: "And when I drive my car, I can eat my sandwich and talk on my cell phone at the same time." I say:

"Yes, you can, but what for? Then you have no pleasure in eating your sandwich, and no pleasure in driving your car. If you do not focus, you do not enjoy life." This is my attitude to these things. Let us not waste time, because life is too short.

Górecki encouraged the students to be creative and inventive; to find their own path and to work really hard: „In Poland we have a saying that genius is 90 % work and 10% talent but I do not agree with that. I think that genius is 99% work and 1% talent... For me black and white keys are enough. Progress is your challenge, you are the young composers and the future of music belongs to you." It is not surprising that after such a warm and heartfelt conversation, students felt connected to the composer and liked him.

Figure 13-13: Górecki discusses his music with USC composition students; with translators Maja Trochimczyk and Joanna Niżyńska, 3 October 1997.

During the entire festival in Los Angeles, the composer spent a lot of time discussing "life and music" with his friends, listening to scholars talking about his work during a symposium *The Górecki Phenomenon*.[24] He was very impressed and interested in the

---

[24] The program of the October 5 event was as follows: Prof. Adrian Thomas (Cardiff, Wales, UK): "A Comparison of Early and Late Styles in the Music of

statements of scholars who researched his music.²⁵ The topic of interpretation and performance inspired the composer to a long digression; he was also deeply moved by my study of the concept of motherhood in music.²⁶ He admitted that it was a very painful topic for him and that I „hit the nail on the head." He lost his mother at the tender age of two and his childhood was filled with illness; so he sublimated his suffering in a series of pieces of profound intensity. The Third Symphony is the best known of these works, but his songs, religious works and *Ad Matrem* are also important (see Chapter 10 for more details).

At the end of the Los Angeles celebrations, on 4 October 1997, Górecki gave a lecture on the importance of promoting Polish music to the Friends of Polish Music, an organization supporting the Polish Music Center.²⁷ The event was held at the Wilks residence in Studio City. He made a speech about promoting Polish music abroad, or rather the absence of this promotion by the government during the communist era, when the State Folk Song and Dance Ensemble Mazowsze was sent on expensive and expansive tours, while serious composers languished in obscurity.²⁸ The lecture was accompanied by a mini-concert planned to include songs to Maria Konopnicka's poems and some songs by Szymanowski, but not all were performed. Górecki

---

Górecki" Dr. James Harley, Los Angeles: "Performance Difficulties in Górecki's Music" David Kopplin, Los Angeles: "The Concept of Time in Górecki's String Quartets" Maja Trochimczyk: "Górecki and the Paradigm of the 'Maternal'"Luke B. Howard: "Laying the Foundation: The Reception of Górecki's Third Symphony, 1977-1992"Mark Swed (*L.A. Times*, Los Angeles), respondent at the Arnold Schoenberg Institute. Mark Swed was the respondent. The composer was present to participate in the discussion.included papers published six years later in the *Polish Music Journal* http://pmc.usc.edu/PMJ/issue/6.2.03/contents.html. http://pmc.usc.edu/PMJ/issue/6.2.03/Goreckiprogram.html

[25] The symposium *The Górecki Phenomenon* featured, in addition to Adrian Thomas also David Kopplin, Mark Swed, and James Harley.

[26] See Chapter 10 of this volume.

[27] Henryk Mikołaj Górecki, "Promoting Polish Music (Speech to the Friends of Polish Music, 7 October 1997)," transl. Maja Trochimczyk, *Polish Music Journal* 6/2 (2003),http://pmc.usc.edu/PMJ/issue/6.2.03/GoreckiAMP.html

[28] See Henryk Mikolaj Gorecki, "Promoting Polish Music," translated by Maja Trochimczyk, *Polish Music Journal* 6/2 (2003), http://pmc.usc.edu/PMJ/issue/6.2.03/GoreckiAMP.html.

accompanied Andrzej Bachleda on the piano and did not like his interpretation, so he cut the recital short.

Figure 13-14: Górecki plays the piano with Adrian Thomas, Los Angeles, 4 October 1997, Photo by Vladek Juszkiewicz. Used by Permission.

Instead, he played the world premiere of the *Intermezzo* dedicated to Stefan and Wanda Wilk. The manuscript of this work belongs to the Wilk family and is one of the lasting effects of the composer's visit to Los Angeles (not included on his work lists).

In this piano miniature, the composer portrayed the nervous energy of Dr. Wilk (right hand) and the contrasting, lyrical melody in low register representing the positive and friendly demeanor of Mrs. Wilk (left hand). At the end he wrote their last name "W I L K" under a series of "Beethovenian-style" chords, all resonant major triads: F – B – A – F sharp – B; with B major (Si) standing for Stefan and A major (La) standing for Wanda.

This coding of names into the music, by letter names or solfège was one of Górecki's favorite ways of honoring individuals connected to his works, to mention only the name of Louise Lerche-Lerchenborg coded in *Lerchenmusik* (1984-1986) in notes E-C-B (E-C-H in Polish) and B-flat-G (B-G in Polish), or the name of Carol Wincenc, American flutist, close friend and the dedicatee of the *Concerto Cantata* op. 65, for flute and orchestra (1993), in the *Valentine Piece* for flute and bell (1996), with her name coded as A-C-E.[29]

As it turned out during the week in Los Angeles, Górecki was not hard to entertain. He was not interested in the traditional tourist attractions, such as visiting Hollywood's stars, or Rodeo Drive. He wanted to see California mountains and visit JPL/NASA to see the vessels sent to Mars and other spacecraft. He got both wishes fulfilled.

Since I lived in a little house in our "Podhale" (Foothills) area, the composer visited my home and drove through the local mountains, quite different from the Tatras. The walks on the grounds of USC were a replacement to sightseeing because the program of his visit was so intense that there was no time for field trips, except for a drive to San Diego, where he was hosted by the Polish Club of San Diego (directed by Jerzy Barankiewicz). and gave a lecture about his music.[30]

Heartfelt letters I received from the composer include the following note written on the frontispiece of the score of the Symphony (see the end of Chapter 3, p. 43-44 above):

> Dear Maja! My heartfelt thanks for the perfect preparation of my "Autumn." It is somehow turning out very official - but I would like to thank you from the bottom of my heart, for your wonderful work, for your understanding my music, for addressing very important problems (again, too official) — God damn it! Thank you and Jim for all that you have done for me. Lots of hugs. With best wishes that both of you will "make it" in L.A. ~ Devoted H.M. Górecki

A year later I received another note:

---

[29] Another notable example is the monumental Fourth Symphony, Tansman Episodes where Aleksander Tansman's name was coded using letter-names of notes, solfège and the Latin for C (ut), e.g., A-E-Eflat-D for the first name Aleksander. See Andrzej Wendland, *Górecki. IV Symfonia. Tansman Epizody. Fenomen. Żywioł. Tajemnica.*(Łódź: Tansman Association and Institute of Polish Music, 2016): 166.

[30] As reported by Danuta Derlińska-Pawlak, a member of the club, in "Jesień Góreckiego w Los Angeles," (*Przegląd Polski, Nowy Dziennik*, 30 October 1997.

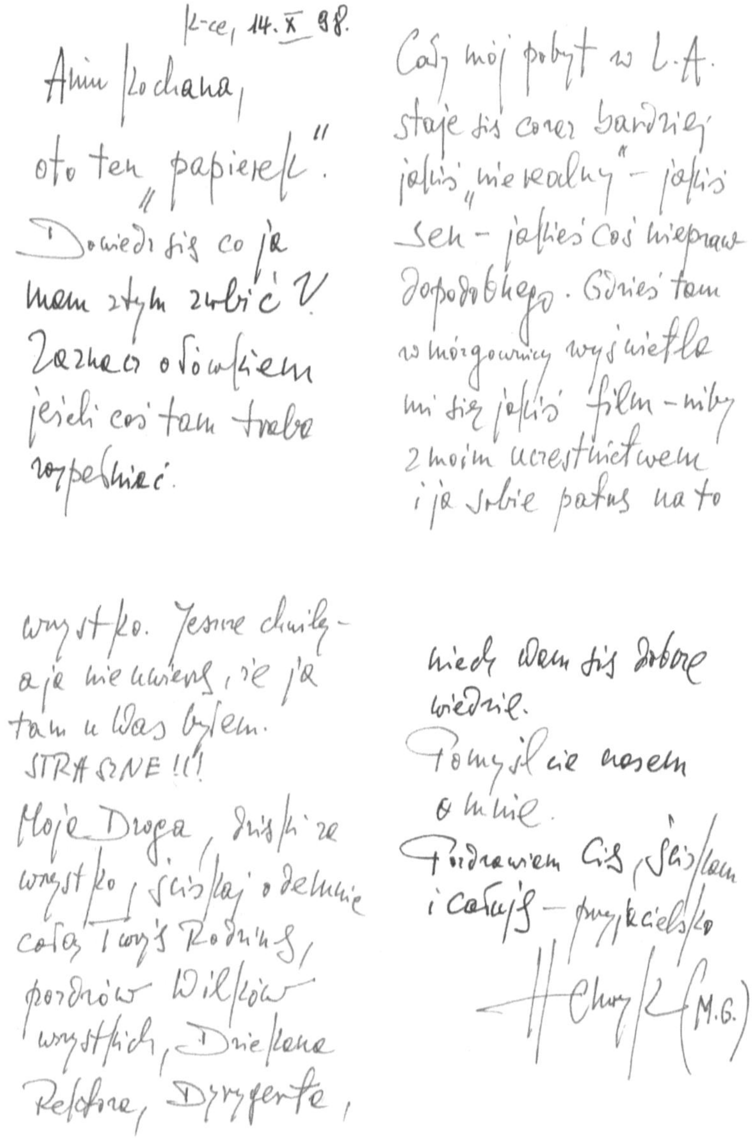

K-ce, 14.X.98.

Aniu Kochana,

oto ten papierek.
Dowiedz się co ja
mam z tym zrobić ?
Zaznacz ołówkiem
jeśli coś tam trzeba
uzupełnić.

Cały mój pobyt w L.A.
staje się coraz bardziej
jakiś "nierealny" – jakiś
sen – jakieś coś niepraw
dopodobnego. Gdzieś tam
w mózgownicy wyświetla
mi się jakiś film – niby
z moim uczestnictwem
i ja sobie patrzę na to

wszystko. Jeszcze chwilę –
a ja nie uwierzę, że ja
tam u Was byłem.
STRASZNE !!!

Moja Droga, ściśnij ze
wszystko, ściskaj odemnie
całą Twoją Rodzinę,
pozdrów Wilków
wszystkich, Dziekana,
Rektora, Dyrygenta,

niech Wam się dobrze
wiedzie.
Pomyślcie nosem
o mnie.
Pozdrawiam Cię ściskam
i całuję – przyjacielsko

Henryk (M.G.)

Figure 13-15: Note from Górecki to Maja Trochimczyk
(misnamed Ania), October 14, 1998.

Katowice, 14 October 1998

My dear Ania,

Here's the "paper." Find out what I should do with that. Mark with a pencil if anything has to be filled out.

My whole stay in L.A. becomes more and more "unreal"—as if a dream—as something completely improbable. Somewhere in my big brain [*mózgownica*] a film is being played back—as if with my participation and I watch all this myself.

One more moment and I will not be able to believe that I actually was there with you. HORRIBLE!

My dear, thanks for everything. Hug from me your whole family, send greetings to all the Wilks, to the Dean, to the Professors, the Conductor. May things go smoothly for all of you.

Think about me, sometimes.

I greet you, hug you, and kiss you – as a friend [*przyjacielsko*]

Henryk (M.G.)

◎ ◎ ◎

The 1997 event was Górecki's last visit to Los Angeles. He later travelled to North America to receive honorary doctorates from three American institutions: Catholic University of America, University of Victoria, British Columbia, Canada (2000); and Concordia University, Montreal, Quebec, Canada. Each event included public appearances, lectures, and interviews. He also enjoyed conducting in other countries: most notably in Third Symphony performances with Zofia Kilanowicz held in Italy, Germany, and Poland.

He returned to conducting at "his" Festival of Polish Composers in Bielsko-Biała in 2003, when his music was celebrated on the occasion of his 70th birthday. At that time Górecki became the honorary citizen of the town and conducted the gala concert, presenting his *Salve Sidus Polonorum*, the cantata about St. Adalbert (Wojciech), the patron of Poland, and *Beatus Vir*. It is interesting to note that *Beatus Vir* was the first work he conducted in public, in front of the newly elected Pope John Paul II back in 1979 (this composition was commissioned by the then Cardinal Wojtyła).

After 1997 however, Górecki's music was rarely heard in Los Angeles while John Adams and the American minimalists Phillip Glass and Steve Reich became the "kings." Only the Los Angeles Master Chorale included Górecki's music in several concerts, most notably giving the American premiere of Górecki's *Lobgesang* Op. 76 in 2008,[31] and paying a "Tribute to Górecki" after his death in 2010. This 2012 concert of Brahms and Górecki presented *Miserere*, later released on a critically acclaimed CD. The Tribute concert ended with a luminous rendition of *Five Marian Songs*, a work of serene piety that truly deserves its label of "mystic minimalism."

Another notable Górecki event in Los Angeles was the Jacaranda New Music Ensemble's all-Górecki concert of 19 November 2011, co-organized with the Helena Modjeska Polish Arts and Culture Club (that I was the president of at the time), and the Consulate General of the Republic of Poland. Entitled *Songs of Stones: Music of Henryk Górecki*, the concert presented Four Preludes Op. 1 (1955); String Quartets No. 1 and 2; and *Kleines Requiem für eine Polka* Op. 66 (1993). The performers featured Mark Robson, piano; the Calder Quartet, the Lyris Quartet, and the Jacaranda Chamber Orchestra, with Mark Alan Hilt, conductor. Patrick Scott, Artistic Director of the Jacaranda, wrote in the program notes:[32]

> One year after his death, this evocative program brings together early piano music with two strikingly different string quartets. The first is a one-movement tone poem, the second a four-part journey. A unique instrumental requiem closes the celebration with the haunted serenity that is Górecki's trademark, as well as brash drama, a sense of absurdity and his fervent spirit of consolation.

The Los Angeles Philharmonic was one of the commissioning entities for the composer's *Fourth Symphony, Tansman Episodes*, but did not succeed in performing the *Symphony* before the composer's death.[33] The orchestra co-commissioned this work with the London Philharmonic Orchestra and the London group gave the world premiere in 2014. With the piano score ready since 2006, the

---

[31] https://www.youtube.com/watch?v=QJbHaVJMjEw
[32] Patrick Scott, Program notes for all-Górecki concert, "Songs of Stones" by Jacaranda: Music on the Edge, Santa Monica, November 19-20, 2011.
[33] See Chapter 14 by Andrzej Wendland for the genesis and compositional history of the Fourth Symphony.

Symphony was orchestrated after Górecki's death by his son Mikołaj. Its California premiere took place in January 2015, and the work was welcomed by Mark Swed as "quirky, final, major musical statement:"[34]

> The four movements go through weird changes. Strings repeat the motifs over and over, punctuated by a pummeling of syncopated bass drums, the only percussion. When trumpets and horns join in, they are oracular. The piano, placed in the center of the orchestra, adds emphasis. The organ is used for its weight. Many of the repetitions are exact, but a whack on a drum is sometimes slightly off the beat, or a dissonance is added, or there is a long silence. The symphony begins like a beating healthy heart, but terrifying episodes of arrhythmia come out of nowhere. [...] The scherzo-like third movement, which sets off with cantankerous horns and trombones stuck in pugnacious grooves, is interrupted by an extended slow, decisively Minimalist section for solo cello and piano (with a solo violin and piccolo) eventually joining in for an episode of hypnotic chamber music. The last movement hints at a folk-like character, but the thumping propulsion is never far away. The symphony closes with a 30-second crescendo by the three bass drums and then a shuddering crash.

And so, with a "shuddering crash" ended Górecki's affair with Los Angeles. His premature death at 77 put an end to a transcendent streak of creativity of unparalleled intensity and impact. Here in California, we were truly lucky to able to witness this supernova of pure musical talent and we are all the better for it.

---

[34] Mark Swed, "Henryk Górecki's Quirky, Final Major Musical Statement," *Los Angeles Times*, 18 January 2015, http://www.latimes.com/entertainment/la-et-cm-la-phil-review-20150119-column.html.

CHAPTER 14

Henryk Mikołaj Górecki
The Phenomenon, Element, and Mystery:
The Fourth Symphony, *Tansman Episodes*

Andrzej Wendland

Henryk Mikołaj Górecki (1933—2010) was an icon of the contemporary world, one of the most original composers of our time. His work, considered an extraordinary phenomenon, is distinct from all other music; "nobly separate." He did not yield to fashions; instead, he consistently created his own musical world that paralyzed his listeners with the power of expression. The composer's output is extremely diverse, lavishly blossoming, both in terms of forms and genres. It is only subject to the laws of personal invention of its creator, immersed, as he was, in the **elemental matter of music**. He shaped this element according to its principles, using his imagination, inventiveness, artistic conceptions, and the ideas of sound.

His compositions are built from contrasting blocks of sounds and textures. "It was not about the aesthetisation of reality, but about the elemental elements of this reality." (Andrzej Chłopecki) The composer worked in a space—time created by himself; an individual space—time. This **phenomenon** is not subjected to analyses and classifications; this phenomenon "eludes the grid of concepts."

Has Górecki embarked on a search for mystery through "revealing the naked essence of things"? Is there a deeper dimension of reality hidden beneath the naked "body of sound," musical themes presented directly? A mystery? After all, sounds only partially express what is inexpressible. Górecki as a believer teaches us the respect for the underlying Mystery, which is not subject to being discovered or interpreted, but instead reveals its inexhaustible nature. His music points to the dual nature of the Mystery: revealing and obscuring, expressing and penetrating. Thus, the Mystery becomes accessible to all but perceived by few. "The sacred, if it really came to its realization in a work of art, fascinates more than pure beauty, and, at the same time, it is more remote, transcendent, and sublime than all the sublime." (Władysław Stróżewski). As Stéphane Mallarmé wrote, "everything that is sacred and holy and desires to remain so must refrain from secrecy." The work of Henryk Mikołaj Górecki can thus be seen on the triple axes of the "**Phenomenon, Element, and Mystery**." My first contact with Górecki's music, in the 1970s, made a profound impression on me. I heard the Songs of Joy and Rhythm for two pianos and orchestra. This music you cannot pass by indifferently, this music leaves a lasting and profound imprint. If today I would attempt to describe these feelings in depth, I would have had to use Górecki's own words, which come from his 1961-62 notebook:

> Something put into motion produces energy.
> Energy, energy and energy again.
> Dynamite! I like the mass and grind. [*zgrzyt*]

The amazing rhythmic scope. Bravado and a humble, rough vitality from the very beginning of the work. Irregular chords of piano and strings. The music seems to be hurried; it is hard to keep up with it. Only the third movement brings calm and a more contemplative atmosphere, evoking and reflecting the meaning of the poem by Julian Tuwim, entitled *A Song of Joy and Rhythm*, which inspired Górecki to write this composition.

> When I am in myself, I rest happily
>   Enveloped with great silence all around
> Then, my heart beats to the beat of everything
>   That surrounds me.

My first meeting with Henryk Mikołaj Górecki took place on December 18, 1998 at the Silesian Philharmonic in Katowice, during the celebration of the 65th birthday of the composer. It was then that I had a conversation during which I asked about the possibility of writing a symphony for the Tansman Festival 2000 in Łódź. Górecki expressed an interest and gave an initial consent. However, after a few months of discussions, in November 1999, I received the following letter:

Dear Professor,
[...] Unfortunately, I have to decline composing a work for the next year's Tansman Festival. The most common cause: lack of time—I cannot do it.
*   I'm sorry for the trouble.*
*   Yours faithfully,*
*   H. M. Górecki*

Nonetheless, I did not give up. After all, I thought there would be more festivals and I realized how much patience, humility and work I needed, and how difficult was the task facing me. Probably also facing the composer. I maintained a good relationship with Górecki; I went to important festivals and concerts with his participation. We held meetings and conversations. An opportunity to meet in person was the bestowing on Górecki of the Tansman Award 2002 for "outstanding musical individuality and uncompromising creativity." This was a very important event. The laureate received a sculpture with an image of Tansman; the presentation of the award took place during a gala concert at the Teatr Wielki, honoring the composer and his music. The concert was broadcast by Polish Television and Polish Radio and became a great success.

In a letter of 10 November, 2012, Górecki wrote:

Dear Professor,
I would like to once again very warmly thank you for this wonderful stay in Łódź,
    For ALL THAT YOU HAVE DONE for me.
    It was all wonderful and touching.
    Thanks a hundred times. [...]

With very cordial greetings,
    And a handshake,
    H. M. Górecki

However, as it turned out later, the key moment in the genesis of the Fourth Symphony, *Tansman Episodes* was the longest conversation I have ever held in my life, that took place with the composer the day after the Tansman 2002 Award concert at the Grand Hotel in Łódź. This conversation spanned many topics. We talked about life, about music, about creativity. Time after time, Górecki asked important questions, and over and over again I tried to find out what the composer was thinking about. I was interested, for example, in discovering where the composer's inspiration comes from.

Inspiration / Tradition

An inspiration or a breath of something into something, *creatio ex nihilo*, creation of something from nothing. Where to find sources of inspiration in the works of Henryk Mikołaj Górecki? How does the transformation of the creative impulses occur, processing and adapting so many borrowings into his own compositions?

First of all—***spirituality*** itself. The religious inspiration, natural and simple, reaching to the deepest experiences, into the sphere of intimate, personal spirituality of the creator, is ubiquitous in Górecki's works. Hence, the inclination toward contemplation, the penetration of spiritual depths, that would consequently lead him toward simplicity and the restoration of the "melodiousness and a singing quality" in his later works. Sometimes the titles of compositions themselves, the purpose and the texts used in them, speak for themselves: *Beatus Vir, Miserere, Marian Songs, O Domina Nostra, Under Your Defense, The Angelus, Holy Spirit, Salve Sidus Polonorum, Kyrie*, or *Sanctus Adalbertus*.

We find in this music a prayerful concentration, sublimity and a hymn—like quality, but also a note of simple folk religiosity. These elements may be found also in works not belonging to religious genres, such as the symphonies: Symphony No. 2, *Copernican;* Symphony No. 3, *Symphony of Sorrowful Songs*, especially the first movement; and Symphony No. 4, *Tansman Episodes*, especially the second movement. In all these compositions we notice a clear, spiritual, and religious inspiration.

Secondly—***nature***. The natural world fascinated the composer through its original sources, its elements, its beauty accessible to our cognition, and the cyclical nature of passing. He was fascinated by the individual accident and the overall necessity; by nature's purpose and pointlessness; by its order and chaos; by life and death—by nature's dreaded secrets, obscuring the element of the Mystery. It is in relation to nature, to its poetics, sincerity and simplicity of expression that the composer found answers to questions about the existential experience or human fate. As Górecki stated:

> Since we are walking this land ... something in this earth is in us. Milosz, Szymanowski, Chopin—they are so, because they come from somewhere! [1]

---

[1] Henryk Mikołaj Górecki, „Już taki jestem zimny drań..." [I am such a bastard], H.M. Górecki talks to W. Widłak, *Vivo*, 1 (1994): 38.

> I'm searching for something that allows me to look at photographs or paintings and say: here are Kurpie, here Masuria, and this is Podhale. These are the qualities that distinguish a region. The same happens with me, in my music.[2]

Profound connections to nature and admiration of Polish landscape are particularly apparent in the "Silesian climates," in the unforgettable landscapes from the composer's childhood and youth, but, especially, in the composer's love of Podhale and the mountains. Górecki was associated with the Podhale region since 1959, when he and his wife Jadwiga discovered the Chochołów village. This personal connection lasted until his final days in the village of Ząb near Zakopane in the Tatra Mountains, where he had built a house, lived and composed.

A new approach to the use of folk tradition may be perceived in the treatment of the musical space, and in the treatment of what we call the character of *górale* [highland] music. In Górecki's works, more so than in the music by other Polish composers, this tradition appears directly, deeply, in its original form, and—simultaneously—in a form that is very modern, but at the same time atavistic, even "wild." Here, it suffices to cite examples from the three String Quartets. It must be added that the composer not only admired the natural world of the mountains. He also participated in the region's culture—by playing the folk fiddle [*gęśle*] with the musicians of highland *kapelas*.

Sensors on "Something"

> [...] But in Podhale music, besides what is tangible, there is something else that one may either discover—hear and feel it—or not. You need to have sensors that focus on this something; without them you may only observe this outer, primitive structure.[3]

What is in the words of Górecki this "something," that you need to set your sensors to? How should we understand this? Let's reflect for a moment and let's try to name that "something" and bring it closer. It

---

[2] Henryk Mikołaj Górecki, „Powiem Państwu szczerze..." [I will tell you frankly...], *Vivo*, 1 (1994): 46.

[3] Henryk Mikołaj Górecki, "Zawsze jestem sobą" [I am always myself], a conversation with Mieczysław Kominek, *Studio* 8 (1993): 9. Reprinted above as Chapter 2.

seems that it may be essential to follow the composer's thought in an attempt to discover his ways of perceiving, understanding and combining all of these elements that would allow Górecki to transform "what he sees and experiences" and to find that personal tone, that source of sound that identifies his deep roots in nature, in tradition, in culture, and in music.

> [...] All these impressions ... This music was heard without hearing it. It was not, ad yet it was ... That was important then! To be aware of what this music was made of. It did not emerge just to come into being, just to get something created. No. Music was in all this—only as a kind of a miracle, I do not know what, people started to sing and play... The roots are not in the music itself, they are in all of it.
>
> I would say that this music is secondary—a consequence of all the factors that contributed to the creation of such music. To write a piece without using things that seem to be well known—these tunes. And yet, so that it could be, damn it, Podhale! This augmented fourth, diminished fifth, and diminished seventh: whether you want it or do not want it—all this identifies.
>
> [...] And then, this original string instrument, plus some pipes. The singing and these strings are inseparable from the dance; they are inseparable from clothing; they are inseparable from playing the rhythms [*dylem po dylu*]. So that's how it goes, one with the other. I see all this as a whole.[4]

"I see all this as a whole..." "I was looking for these prototypes, I was looking for and I was interested in this transformation. The clash: the artistic music and its prototype" —said Górecki. These ideas lead to the emergence of basic elements in Górecki's music; elements that are distinct and primitive, is if they were naked. The composer strives in his thinking and creating for a reconstruction or a renewal of this most elemental material. He seeks to reach an archetypal form of expression. And he finds it! He creates it by himself; makes anew, by inventing these novel, bare "Górecki's elements," that become the sound source [*źródłodźwięk*], the essence of things. The relationship with nature is a key here. Górecki understood the folk quality in this way; it was a part of his music and of himself. He sought to attune himself to it, to become one with it: "I see all this as a whole!"

---

[4] *My Podhale, Gawęda,* interview with Henryk Mikołaj Górecki by Maria Baliszewska, excerpts from the recording of the Polish Radio Tatry, ed. Marcin Trzęsiok.

Let's return to the basic question. What is that "something"? It seems that this is a profound, inner wisdom of life that flows from folk tradition; a wisdom possessed by the highlanders, a wisdom that accompanied them all along the way.

> And wisdom has this feature in and of itself that brings out the" heart of the matter "in the most lapidary way possible! In folk culture, universal reflection is often sung. In one phrase you can express the whole human being and—what is even more important—if it is not expressed in this way it will not be expressed at all! [5]

These are the words of Prof. Józef Tischner, a Catholic priest and a philosopher who was also of highland origin. Górecki discovered this wisdom; he heard it, and felt it. He had his sensors attuned to this "wisdom" and, even more importantly, he had perfect pitch about these matters. "And if you drink from the source you will not want to drink from the pool anymore." (Leonardo da Vinci)

The third element—*culture.* Górecki was very firmly rooted in Polish spiritual culture. His work, but, importantly, also his attitude was profoundly Polish, supported by deep roots and a strong grounding in the spheres of faith, language, place, history, tradition, literature, art and, finally, music. His faith and worldview led him towards non-Marxist philosophers, and he was perhaps the most fascinated by works of the Polish philosopher Henryk Elzenberg, well-known for his attitude based on solid, ethical principles.[6]

Górecki was an eminent expert in Polish poetry; and this fact is also reflected in the composer's oeuvre, first in the sphere of poetic inspiration, for example Julian Tuwim's *Songs of Joy and Rhythm,* where the text is transformed into a musical form. Here we can talk about certain reflexivity and a poetic quality of Górecki's compositions. Secondly, his knowledge of poetry is apparent in his use of poetic texts directly, for instance the verse by Juliusz Słowacki, whom he

---

[5] Father Józef Tischner, *Myślenie w żywole piękna* [Thinking in the Element of Beauty] (Kraków: Znak, 2013): 97.

[6] The connection between Górecki and Henryk Elzenberg asserted by Wendland throughout this article has evaded the attention of the composer's other biographers, as well as his family and friends—and is not confirmed by the majority of scholars. It is possible, however, that they shared this interest in conversations and the composer did not disclose it to others. [*Editor's Note*].

considered to be the most outstanding Polish romantic poet. These compositions include Three Songs, Op. 3 *To Mother/ Do Matki, What Funeral Bells/Jakiż to dzwon pogrobowy* or *Songs to the Words of Juliusz Słowacki/śpiewy do słów Juliusza Słowackiego*. In addition, he used poems by Cyprian Kamil Norwid in *Blessed Raspberry Songs*, Op. 43 [*Błogosławione pieśni malinowe*]; the verse of Maria Konopnicka in *At my window* [*U okienka u mojego*] (1995); and excerpts from longer works by Stanisław Wyspiański in *Three Fragments by Stanisław Wyspiański* [*Trzy fragmenty do słów Stanisława Wyspiańskiego*] (1996). Finally a series of poetic texts came from folk traditions, such as *Broad Waters* [*Szeroka Woda*] or *Marian Songs*. Of course, we should not forget the spiritual poetry of Biblical texts: Psalms in *Beatus Vir, Euntes ibant et flebant*, etc.

One of the greatest Polish poets of the 20th century was Zbigniew Herbert. While Górecki did not use Herbert's poetry in his compositions, some convergence of their ideological attitudes and inspiration cannot be overlooked. Another important writer was Gustaw Herling-Grudziński (a writer, not a poet) whom Górecki particularly appreciated for his uncompromising attitude in searching for and presenting the truth about the world—the truth, drama and tragedy of human fate.

The final element is music. Here Górecki's distinctive "Polish idiom" (introduced in a specific, but heterogeneous way) is encoded in his musical phrases, at the level of the sound substance itself. This pertains to, as already mentioned above, his interest in tradition, Polish language, landscape, religion and people. This passion and grounding of music, however, manifests itself on two levels—the Polish tradition and the European tradition.

The Polish tradition. Here it should be mentioned that Górecki studied the writings by Oskar Kolberg in great detail; as he admitted "I consider Kolberg's works as the greatest 'Bible.' Everything is there!"[7] The composer profusely drew from early music and folk music of Poland. Let us recall numerous quotes and arrangements including examples mentioned above, such as the use of "Already It Is Dusk" by Wacław of Szamotuły in the First String Quartet, or numerous allusions to and transformations of the oldest Polish hymn,

---

[7] Henryk Mikołaj Górecki, „I'm such a bastard," *Vivo*, 1 (1994): 38.

Bogurodzica in the *Songs of Joy and Rhythm* and in the Fourth Symphony, *Tansman Episodes* (even though these transformation are intentional only at a certain level). Finally, another example is that of the *Songs of Kurpie* (2003).

The grounding in the Polish traditional church music is manifested in numerous works, scored mainly for the choir, such as *Marian Songs*, *Church Songs*, or *Amen*.

In the area of the so—called artistic Polish music, inspirations are very clear and encoded in his compositional thinking and the specific "Polish phrase," whose sources can be found in Fryderyk Chopin's music. The best known, spectacular reference to the Chopin tradition is the borrowing of the initial fragment one of the most melancholy mazurkas, Chopin's Op. 17, No. 4, that is the chord sequence (A—F) incorporated into the Third Symphony (1976). However, it must be added here that Górecki persistently used the first of these chords (A—B—F) much earlier, for instance seven years prior, in the coda to *Canticum graduum* (1969).

Another great Polish composer who influenced Henryk Mikołaj Górecki was Karol Szymanowski. One of Górecki's "identifying motives" important to his "brand" is the so—called "turn" —a rising third, followed by a falling semitone. Although this sequence of intervals has strong roots in the Polish folk tradition, and Górecki himself used this melody in the early Variations, Op. 4 (1956), it is important to notice the presence of this motive both in Górecki's Third Symphony and in Szymanowski's *Stabat Mater* (in the climax of the soprano part in the last movement). These affinities are too readable and, consequently, they became synonymous with Górecki's relationship with Szymanowski. In the end, Górecki himself said: "Where Szymanowski went, I went as well."[8] Finally, let us add that the "turn" is also present in a number of other works, including the second movement in the Symphony No. 4, *Tansman Episodes*.

The second level of Górecki's grounding in music refers to **the European tradition.** However, it should be noted at the outset that the so—called "Polish tradition" is really an illusion, because in this

---

[8] Henryk Mikołaj Górecki cited by Adrian Thomas in *Górecki* (Kraków: PWM, 1998): 117.

area we have always remained in constant connection with the development of European musical culture, to mention only the work of Chopin, Szymanowski, and Alexander Tansman.

> [...] I'm deeply rooted in the tradition and I'm looking for the key to the present. A key that would make it easier for me to pass on what I am now, what surrounds me. [...] Tradition is incredibly fascinating to me; sometimes it is one phrase that does not give me peace.[9]

Górecki greatly appreciated the accomplishments of many composers and knew their works well, with all the weight of tradition, starting from the Renaissance tradition of Claudio Monteverdi (whom he discussed only in the most positive terms), as well as the Baroque tradition of Johann Sebastian Bach, who often rescued Górecki from difficulties and helped him overcome compositional crises. Similarly, he knew and appreciated the classical tradition of Mozart and Beethoven. From the latter, he drew profusely, for instance using in his String Quartet the so-called "Beethoven chords."

Later came Romanticism, which the composer at first partly overlooked, but at the end of his life highly valued. Let us point to the work of Richard Wagner whose operas Górecki analyzed in depth. Among other results of this fascination is the appearance of a quote from *The Ring of the Nibelung* in the Fourth Symphony, *Tansman Episodes* as well as the composition of *Two Tristan Postludes and Chorale* for symphony orchestra.

◎ ◎ ◎

In 2003, I had another opportunity to meet Górecki and talk about the new composition for the Tansman Festival at the marathon of all of Górecki's works, organized by the director of NOSPR (National Polish Radio Symphony Orchestra), Joanna Wnuk-Nazarowa on the occasion of the seventieth birthday of the composer (6 December 2003 in Katowice). The concerts were held simultaneously in two concert halls: in the main hall, the symphonic pieces could be heard and in the other, smaller hall—chamber music and works for solo instruments. We usually do not have an opportunity to encounter all the works by Henryk Mikołaj Górecki (or any other composer) in one day. Such a

---

[99] Górecki, „Powiem Państwu szczerze...", *op. cit.*, 45.

unique situation leads to a thorough comparison and reflection. While sitting next to the composer, I spent several hours listening to successive performances. Here, certain processes of evolution and stylistic changes were evident; the path of his compositional development has become more readable. But there were also serious question marks. Why so? Why then? Issues appeared that were earlier unnoticed, or downplayed. It was during the marathon festival that I noticed the existence of two "different Góreckis"—even though the juxtaposed works came from the same time period.

Re—Evaluation

In the oeuvre of Henryk Mikołaj Górecki, the 1960s consist mainly in experimental, sonoristic works, such as the Genesis cycle (1962—63), in which the composer gave up even the use of musical notation, for the sake of graphic notation. In July 1962, Górecki, in an interview with Leon Markiewicz, said: "I stand on the ground of Boulez's statement: At last people have understood that melody, rhythm and harmony cannot make music." [10]

But the same period, the beginning of the sixties, brings to us also quite a different Górecki! Two works, *Chorale in the Form of a Canon* for string quartet (1961) and the more famous *Three Pieces in Old Style* for string orchestra (1963) fundamentally deviated from the parallel development of the avant-garde. [11] It is significant that the composer did not assigned opus numbers to these works! Perhaps, as Adrian Thomas wrote in his biography, it was a testimony to their "marginal significance for Górecki, although looking back now, it seems that they were as decisive for his long-term development as all other works of that period." Perhaps, at that time, the composer was not sure if he was going to follow this path and how he would have developed this music in the future.

---

[10] Leon Markiewicz, „Conversation with Henryk Górecki," *Ruch Muzyczny* 17 (1962):.7. Reprinted in this volume as its Chapter 1.
[11] Górecki's interest in Polish music dates back to the years of student life. But in these two works the composer turns for the first time so clearly to the sources, to his fascination with the early music and the church song. Soon it will bring some allusions also in other works, for example *Old Polish Music* (1969) or *Canticum graduum* (1969). By turning to sources related to early music, Górecki made yet another symbolic change, "a return to values"! See also Malecka's Chapter 11.

Górecki always seemed to be independent in his relationship with the outside world. Therefore, as Thomas writes, "without devoting himself to theoretical or philosophical considerations, he passionately deals with music and shapes it in a way that his own hearing will give him. Thus, the shift of attention of the composer in the seventies [...]"[12]

Let's try to re-trace this briefly: why exactly did he change at that time? Let us ask what were these "significant causes"? I believe that the sources of this "shift of attention", which we will call "re—evaluation," should be identified in the early 1960's, in the experiences, readings, and existential reflections of the composer.

This **re-evaluation took place at a completely different level than is usually believed: not only through cool analysis and reasoning in the intellectual process, but simultaneously by supporting their own observations and experiences with deep reflection and contemplation, which in turn led to transformation. The resulting artistic consciousness crystallized directly in the creative act and manifested itself through expression in distinct personal and musical compositions.**

All this is connected with Górecki's extensive readings of poetry published during this period and with his thoughts that influenced the formation of his worldview. Apart from the poetry by Zbigniew Herbert, Tadeusz Różewicz, the prose by Gustaw Herling-Grudziński and many others, exceptional importance should be assigned to the extraordinary and original work of the eminent Polish philosopher, Henryk Elzenberg—whom Górecki highly valued.[13] This is a book entitled, *Trouble with Existence. Aphorisms in the Order of Time* published in 1963.[14] It is here, in philosophical, ethical and aesthetic reflection, that we can find and perhaps explain and clarify how Górecki's thought has been "re-evaluated" at this time, how such concepts as beauty, the meaning of values in life and creativity have been constituted or conceived; and finally how he tried to comprehend and respond to questions: what is music?, what is

---

[12] Adrian Thomas, *Górecki*, op. cit., 9.

[13] Yet, the composer did not disclose this interest to his family, friends or biographers. Wendland's theory is not supported by others. [*Editor's note*].

[14] Henryk Elzenberg, *Kłopot z istnieniem. Aforyzmy w porządku czasu* (Kraków: Znak, 1963), 466.

beauty? I believe that through his thoughts, his attitude to life and through his works, Elzenberg became the mentor of Henryk Mikołaj Górecki, just as he was earlier a friend and guide of Zbigniew Herbert. The poet says: "What is beauty—but a vehicle of passion and virtue?" Górecki responds: "The art must be understood in the closest approximation to the fact of life," "one must suffer to create." Elzenberg adds: "the numerous forms of life are beautiful; life is a condition of the existence of all things of value that are a part of it; that exist in the consciousness of the living: things come into being, so they are valuable indeed." The philosopher continues: "Suffering is a fundamental experience, it connects with cognition, being a 'school of wisdom' [...] "Death is the condition for the existence of beauty. Only what is mortal can be beautiful. [...] And this is a tragic view of the world [...] Suffering and death are just; they bring forth the greatness of the great and the wickedness of the wicked."

The meaning of life, that is elusive on the level of history and on the level of nature, is objectively rooted in moral values. For Elzenberg, "artistic craftsmanship reflects moral fortitude." How to translate all this into a composer's creativity? Górecki admits: "Was I going to write ten of these first Symphonies? I could write them! *Scontri*—first, fifth, tenth, eighteenth. No! I'm done. I'm still looking." [15]

In the late 1960s, Górecki faced the problem that György Ligeti described a quarter of a century later:

> Being a contemporary composer has come to an end. To be more 'modern' is to cross the limits of the absurd. Go back to the past to admit defeat ... I'm trapped. One wall is the avant-garde, the other is the past. And I want to escape.

Recognizing the crisis, the exhaustion of the system's potential, and the contradictions between the directions in which the world and music were moving and the Reality, Górecki had to find a way out and make a turn. "It seems to me that we—taking all the composers, not just Polish—have lost something. We convinced ourselves that all music, that all art should look the same way," said the composer.[16]

---

[15] „I would not owe this land. Grzegorz Michalski talks with Henryk Mikołaj Górecki." *De Musica* vol. 7-8 (Kraków: Wydawnictwo Astraia, 2009), 16.
[16] *Ibidem.*

It was no longer possible to work for the "dust of phenomena." What should be done in such a situation? Nicolaus Copernicus in *De revolutionibus orbium coelestium* noted that if

> ... scholars do not agree with each other on issues related to their research, it is evident from the order of their evidence that either they have left the essential condition or, conversely, they have added something alien. Something that does not belong.

If dysfunctions, contradictions, or conflicts occur in the system, then you need to look at it "from the outside"— states the theorem of Kurt Gödel. You have to go to a higher level of logic, Bertrand Russell would have said. You have to, even—right away—"jump out of the system," concluded Douglas R. Hofstadter.[17] Thus, we should move on to the next level.

So, what was forgotten? What have we lost? What essential condition was omitted? What aspects have been overlooked and what needs to be restored? It is about restoring the phenomenon of Reality as unity, as an indivisible whole, taking into account not only the ratio [mind] but also the *spiritus*, and therefore the qualitative change? Creativity is, after all, a phenomenon of Reality. It concerns itself with deep structures. You have to include the "Spirit" (Teilhard de Chardin), "Depth" (Paul Tilich) and Transcendence. The human being is not just a rational mind.

Górecki "jumped out of the system" to a level of a higher order because he did not lose his intuition. He "jumped out of the system" to build "on the rock." On the way to the mountain peaks, he abandoned the sands of relativism, pragmatism, etc. This great talent generated a sound element charged with "Energy" and the eternal "Intelligence" (Edgar Varése) and with the "higher mathematics" in music, which is a function of an integral personality—according to Igor Stravinsky.

From now on, the music of Henryk Mikołaj Górecki assumes an elementary form, apparently well—known, stripped of all ornaments: not to bewilder with simplicity, but to expose the Truth of Being. This revelation of elementary, universal, archetypal qualities becomes its

---

[17] Douglas R. Hofstadter, *Gödel, Escher, Bach, An Eternal Golden Braid* (New York: Basic Books, 1979), 17.

essence and the source of its power. Górecki did not turn to some kind of an historical style, as musicologists tried to interpret his transformation. He "jumped out of the system" and overcame the "natural determinism" and the gravity of the world reduced to matter and its suggestive mechanistic illusion. (Roman Berger)

From then on, the anti-formalist work of Górecki will be a unique landmark in the history of music. The consequence of such a redefinition is to create a new direction, which I would symbolically refer to as "from Xenakis to Monteverdi." As a result, this path results in the need to change the paradigm. The full manifestation of this new form of expression, preceded by the *Refrain* and *Old Polish Music*, occurs in *Ad Matrem* for soprano, choir and symphony orchestra (1971). After the Second Symphony, *Copernican*, the culmination comes in the Symphony No. 3, *Symphony of Sorrowful Songs*. The Fourth Symphony, *Tansman Episodes* will be the grand finale.

In the 1970s, few scholars were aware of the full significance and importance of this re—evaluation, this transition that was not a stylistic change, but a qualitative change. The difficulty with understanding and accepting such a change was that it was not a "smooth" transition, but a jump—as Thomas Kuhn would say—from one paradigm to another.[18] The most spectacular example is the Third Symphony. The issue with acceptance of this Symphony is that critics and musicologists sought in this work something that cannot be understood only in terms of rationalistic thought and the application of musical theories. That is why Górecki did not try to explain anything, but he repeated: "I knew what I wrote," "This is my most avant-garde composition," "These are not just two chords crossed with each other, there is much, much more."

It took many years for the Third Symphony to be properly understood, but it was not the "subject matter experts" who understood it, but rather the audience: listeners instinctively felt and read the message of the *Symphony of Sorrowful Songs*. That explains such a great popularity of this work and its success all over the world. To sum up, in Elzenberg's words: "First comes the recognition of certain values, then the choice of worthy goals, and then the meaning." "A man simply

---

[18] Thomas S Kuhn, *The Structure Of Scientific Revolutions* (Chicago: University of Chicago Press, 1962).

knows the meaning by knowing values that are independent of us." And, the philosopher wrote, "knowing the values is linked to the moral imperative to realize them in one's own life." Finally:

> Music [...] gives a restorative bath by which the soul returns back to its emptiness, to the point of departure, so that it can take a new direction, free from the pressures of the past. Everything: just to work again starting from the elements. [19]

Three Symphonies

To speak of the Fourth Symphony, *Tansman Episodes,* one should give a brief account of the first three. After all, the four symphonies were created during 47 years of the composer's creative life (1959—2006), so they span his whole oeuvre. They document the artistic path, the stylistic changes, and the development of the composer's musical language. The popularity of Symphony No. 3, the incredible artistic and commercial success of this work, made the whole world, not just the music world; expect another symphony from the composer. Exactly 30 years later, the Fourth Symphony was created. However, it was set aside and it took several years for the public to learn about its existence. The world knew the Third, but the other two symphonies rarely appeared on the concert stages of the European, American or Asian symphony orchestras. Nonetheless, each of the symphonies is important, and each one is different, unlike the others.

The Symphony No. 1, *1959,* is based on the principles of serialism, abstract and without non-musical content. It consists of four parts: Invocation, Antiphon, Chorus and Lauda. The core of the instrumental ensemble is formed of strings and percussion instruments, as well as harps and keyboards. The only moment connecting the 1st and 4th Symphony through a certain analogy of thinking or references to the highland folklore occurs in the fourth movement of the Fourth Symphony, *Tansman Episodes* (measures 7-10, 16-19, and 22-25) and in Lauda at the end of the fourth movement of Symphony No. 1, *1959*. In both cases, the composer introduced a melody in the violin part, while using an accompaniment of an empty A string, thus imitating the sound of a highlander band.

---

[19] Elzenberg, *op. cit.*, 196.

The Second Symphony, *Copernican* (1972), with its symbolic and metaphoric expression of cosmological-theological themes, is a work in which the composer expressed his passion for contemplating the Cosmos. This "cosmic space" was already in an "instinctively musical way" created by Górecki in *Scontri* where it took the form of a spatial arrangement of instruments. The Second Symphony begins with a violent, percussive beat in the deafening dynamics of four *ffff*. A full six-octave chord is played by the *marcatissimo* orchestra, *con massima passione, massima espressione, grande tensione*. It is a symbol of cosmic matter, a dark element emanating with expansive energy, dissonant harmony, and a persistently repeated rhythm. At the end of the first movement, the composer slowly extends the harmony from low to high registers in an unbroken *crescendo,* as if embracing the Universe to catch the light.

In contrast, the second movement is a contemplative, mystical *Adagio* in which the brilliance of thought and spirit takes over. This movement illustrates the progressive transformation of Górecki's musical language towards modality and diatonicity. Some traits appear that result from his earlier compositional experience, in terms of sound, expression and form. Where a certain polarization of the musical material appears, the composer uses more than one tonal center. Such examples will also be found in the Symphony No. 4.

It is easy to see that the drama connected with Copernicus' coup, i.e., the replacement of the geocentric model with a heliocentric one, that was the theme of the Second Symphony has its reference and continuation in the Symphony No. 4 in the form of the symbolism of the human drama in general: the human condition and role in the universe. Comparing the initial measures of both symphonies leads us to unexpected associations:

- Symphony No. 2: drum beats and massive chords of the *marcatissimo* orchestra.
- Symphony No. 4: massive orchestra chords and strings with deciso *marcatissimo* drums.

The Third Symphony, *Symphony of Sorrowful Songs* (1976) is diametrically different from the other three. The name contains a specific concept, a contemplative idea deeply rooted in Polish tradition and language. The work uses texts referring to the trauma and affection in mother—child relationships. Symphony No. 3 is a synthesis of Górecki's compositional techniques and creative impulses, in which the imagination and intuition of the creator were the only guides. If one were to look for a "common" moment shared by the 3rd and 4th Symphonies, one would find it in the use of the "circuitry" in the main theme of the second movement of *Tansman Episodes* (although the sounds and rhythmic sequences appearing there resemble more closely those of *Miserere*). Nevertheless, the original source from which the "circulation" originated remains the same.

The extraordinary commercial success of the Symphony No. 3 made the world expect another symphony. The composer received many proposals and commissions:

> I denied dozens of times; I refused the biggest caliber of musicians: conductors, soloists. The representatives of great, prestigious philharmonic orchestras, operas, festivals came to me. Some, reading these words will roar with laughter. They will think, what an idiot, you have to go with the flow.... But I do not understand that. So, I would have 10 bags, each with a million dollars? And what? [...] Can I look in Bartók's eyes, or Messiaen's or Bach's? All of them could do business instead of art. And yet they did not do it. [20]

The Fourth Symphony, *Tansman Episodes*

Therefore, we had to wait thirty years for the next symphony. In the meantime, Górecki composed mainly chamber music, string quartets, and choral works—with notable exceptions of *Beatus Vir*, the Harpsichord Concerto, the *Concerto-Cantata* for flute and orchestra, and *The Little Requiem for a Polka*. The Fourth Symphony, *Tansman Episodes*, Op. 85 is an extensive, over 37-minute composition set for a large, ca. 100-person symphony orchestra with quadruple wood (flutes, clarinets, bassoon) and brass (trumpets, horns, trombones, and tuba). In addition, the instrumentation features kettledrums and other percussion instruments (glockenspiel, tubular bells, three bass drums, and cymbals); piano, organ and strings in the "16, 14, 12, 10, 8" setup. Many sections in the piano and organ parts are soloist in style.

---

[20] A. Malatyńska-Stankiewicz, „Zostanie dobroć i poezja," [Goodness and poetry will remain]. *Dziennik Polski*, 19 November 2010.

The Symphony consists of four non-titled movements—episodes played *attacca*, without interruption. The expressive markings of *deciso, marcatissimo* [decisive, with the greatest emphasis] predominate throughout this work. Górecki left the completed score of the Fourth Symphony in the format of a reduced piano score, written using two to five systems, depending on needs. Most often there are three systems. The composer used this notational convention since the 1960s, in order to be able to perform his works on the piano. The orchestration was done later. The entire Symphony is precisely described in terms of instrumentation, dynamics, articulation and metronome-labeled tempi. Sometimes also the duration of particular episodes is indicated. The manuscript also has very accurate, even meticulous—as never before—annotations with places and dates when subsequent fragments of the symphony were composed.

The score was prepared for release by Górecki's British publisher, Boosey & Hawkes, in October 2011; it was orchestrated by Mikołaj Górecki, the composer's son, also a composer living in the United States. Through exceptional knowledge of his father's compositional techniques and notation styles, the younger Górecki was the only person capable of fulfilling his father's will. Indeed, while playing the completed score for his son in the summer of 2006, Górecki often mentioned that completing the full orchestral score would be his son's task. The publisher released the score in 2013, with the catalog number 18855.

The *Tansman Episodes* appear to us as a summation of the whole oeuvre of Henryk Mikołaj Górecki. Could we then interpret the Fourth Symphony as a work illustrating the journey along the life's road? Following the way of life, which is the drama of the creator, but also the drama of man in general, in the universal sense of the word. This composition also provides the culmination for its author's artistic pathway. Górecki said of his music: "In fact, it is the expression of one idea, evolving in different ways." [21]

Regardless of the evolution of the musical language, the composer intended to use these means consistently for a purpose; that purpose remained unchanged. Composer Rafał Augustyn, a former student of Górecki, said: "Maybe it is that all the Master's creativity ... should be

---

[21] Górecki, "Powiem Państwu szczerze…," *op. cit.*, 43.

seen as a way of counterpointing composition—unlike Lutoslawski, where almost every piece is a microcosm of his music." [22]

This way, the passionate and awe—inspiring drama is emphasized in the first movement of the Fourth Symphony by the persistent chords and drum beats, with increasing dynamics. The second and third movement s portray the way of a person through life—through its episodes and moving existential experiences. In the fourth movement, through a mysterious return of the first theme, the cycle closes, returning like the spiral of time and leading into the finale in ecstatic rapture—Wagner's theme—to find the source and redemption, which is symbolized by the final luminous chord. In this sense, the entire Fourth Symphony could be read as a conscious summary of the composer's creative journey: "My life / should make a circle /close up with a well composed sonata. "[23]

The first notes of the score were written on music paper in the village of Ząb on **March 12, 2006.** In the manuscript, the composer left a cryptogram, which explains the way in which he built the theme for the Fourth Symphony, *Tansman Episodes,* namely the use of 'musical' letters from the first and last names of Aleksander Tansman.

---

[22] Beata Boleslawska-Lewandowska, *Górecki: Portret w Pamięci* (Kraków: PWM, 2013), 75.
[23] Zbigniew Herbert, a fragment of the *Breviary* poem from the volume *Epilogue of the Storm* [*Epilog burzy*] (Kraków: Wydawnictwo a5, 2011), 640.

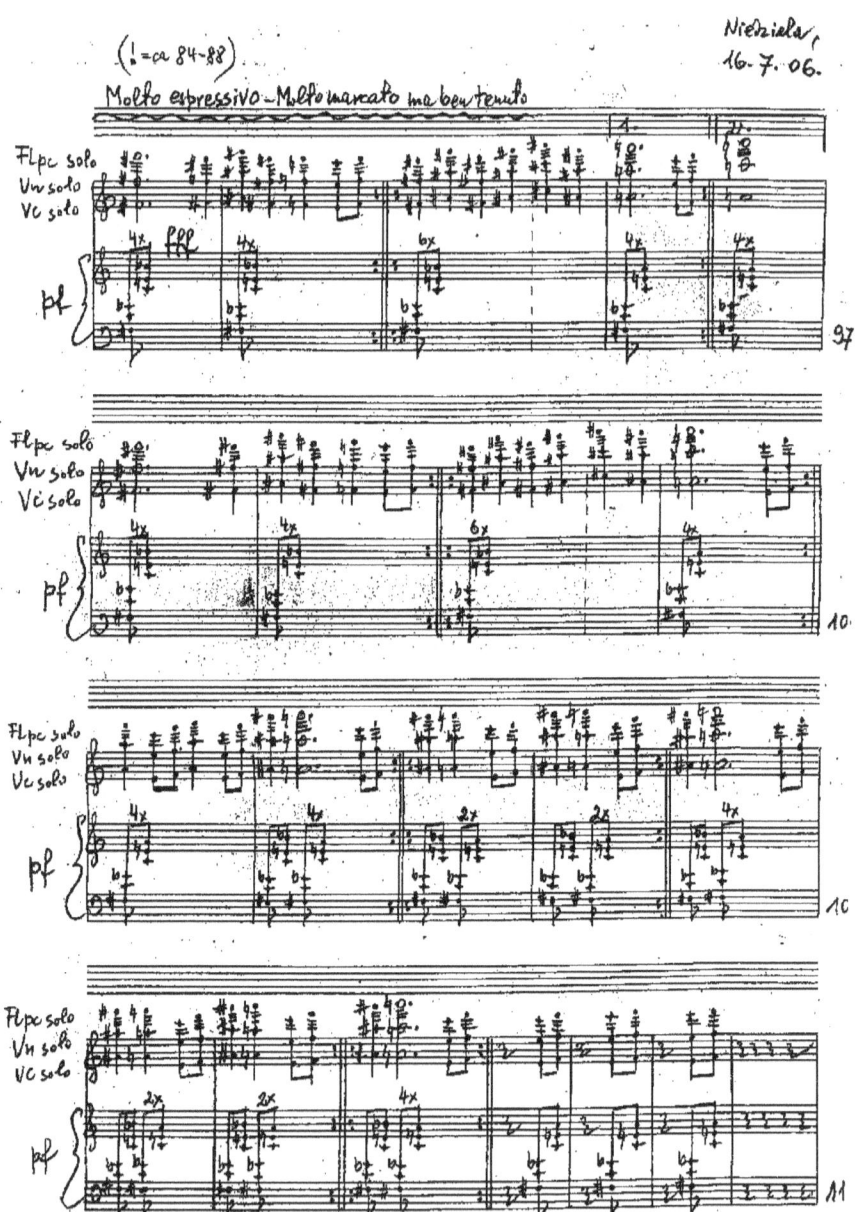

Figure 14—1: Górecki's Fourth Symphony, *Tansman Episodes*, a sample page from the piano score, with instrumentation indicated in notes, from the composer's manuscript (p. 160). Symphony No. 4 by Henryk Górecki. (c) Copyright 2013 by Boosey & Hawkes Music Publishers Ltd. Reprinted by permission of Boosey & Hawkes, Inc.

Figure 14—2: Górecki's Fourth Symphony, *Tansman Episodes*, the title page from the piano score, with the name of Aleksander Tansman transposed into musical notes. Symphony No. 4 by Henryk Górecki. (c) Copyright 2013 by Boosey & Hawkes Music Publishers Ltd. Reprinted by permission of Boosey & Hawkes, Inc.

Such cryptograms were introduced by other prominent composers before Górecki, to mention only Johann Sebastian Bach, Robert Schumann and Johannes Brahms. Górecki earlier used "musical" letters for the creation of motives and themes in the *Recitatives and Ariosos, Lerchenmusik* for clarinet, cello and piano (1984—1986), in which both themes are derived from the letters of the name of the person who commissioned this piece, Louise Lerche-Lerchenborg. Another example is the *Valentine Piece* for flute and bell (1996) written for the American flutist Carol Wincenc, with her initials coded in the music.

The Fourth Symphony begins with massive blocks of incomplete minor chords. They are incomplete because they are deprived of the fifth, although in such a resounding sonic mass, the formant of the fifth would reveal itself anyway. After that, there are strokes on three big bass drums in the *forte fortissimo* dynamics. Everything is played *deciso marcatissimo*, with intensity and the greatest emphasis.

As early as the 1960s, the element of sound stability became a characteristic feature of long-term planning in Górecki's compositions. In the Fourth Symphony, the stabilization of the selected type of sonority is obtained through parallel displacement of the same type of chords. This chordal parallelism (also characteristic for Tansman), is often found in Górecki's music—although the chords are less likely to remain in their principal forms, as it is the case in the first episode of the Fourth Symphony.

Repetitions of motives, so characteristic of Górecki, influence the attention of the listener and fix a specific mood, expression and sound color of the Symphony. When we invoke in memory the initial fragments from the First and Second Symphonies and compare them to the Fourth, we will notice—regardless of all the essential differences—numerous textural similarities in the opening sections of these compositions.

Now, after many repetitions of the second motive from the theme, the ominous sound of a cluster appears. When the orchestra tutti plays a chord in D minor, the organ and piano perform an E-flat minor chord (no fifth). This harmonic rift is an attempt to widen the harmonic field, combining several harmonic languages of different stylistic roots.

Here, Górecki clearly sought to confuse and obscure the patterns of structuring the musical material.

It is **Easter Sunday. April 16, 2006**. Slowing down, quieting down—contemplative, *allargando* and *diminuendo*. The composer changes the meter to 6/4 and proceeds to the first theme of the second episode, intoned very slowly and *cantabile* by the clarinets.

It was certainly an important time for Górecki, a time of concentration and prayer. This smooth transition from aggressive chordal textures in the first episode through a soft modulation, introducing the "G" tonal center in strings, took place on April 10-16, 2006, during Easter. In these chorale sections, Górecki presents himself to us as a person who recognizes the reality of the Mystery. A Mystery that remains beyond any means of expression, whether it be a word or a sound. This is the attitude of *apophatic* theology—contemplative silence as an attitude towards the Mystery. The composer seeks this mood, expressed in beauty and harmony, because after all, "this world needs beauty in order not to sink into despair." [24]

The entire second episode of the Fourth Symphony is a prayer. In prayer we look for support—this is provided by a constantly returning G major chord. For prayer, you need concentration, peace and quiet. To this purpose we have: piano dynamics and extensive, standing chords that seem to last forever. Then, there are pauses and fermatas. The tonal center, the harmonic and the symbolic core, to which "everything" is heading, is the chord of G major. This constant chord—symbol of "eternal existence," of realism and the truth of life, is the root and foundation. A solid foundation, because Górecki's "house of music" is not built on the sand, but on the rock. [25] It is firmly rooted, like the composer's faith; it is durable and inviolable.

---

[24] Henryk Mikołaj Górecki's quotation for Włodzimierz Siedlik, "Henryk Mikołaj Górecki and his music," *Pro Musica Sacra*, 10 (2012): 95.

[25] Robert Tyrała, „Kulturowy i religijny kontekst twórczości kompozytorskiej Henryka Mikołaja Góreckiego (zm.2010). Niebiańskie polany jako przesłanie jego kompozytorskiej twórczości." [The cultural and religious context of composer Henryk Mikołaj Górecki (zm. 2010). Heavenly glade as a message of his composer's work], *Pro Musica Sacra* 9 (2011): 12.

It is precisely in this type of elements, or whole works, that the lofty style, the high style of Henryk Mikołaj Górecki is revealed. What are the characteristics of this style? Mieczysław Tomaszewski, while researching the paradigm of the sublime style, pointed out that the musical determinants of this high style could be: architectural transparence and clarity, narrow texture, and the harmonization of the harmonic pulse with the metric pulse. [26]

It is Friday, June 16, 2006. Two fermatas on the last chords of the second movement and a general fermata above the last bar line. Suspension. Contemplation of silence. No sound or words would be able to express it. However, the tension before the arrival of "new" remains. We move attaca to the Scherzo, the third movement of the Fourth Symphony.

Wednesday and Thursday, 28 and 29 June 2006. The composer again sat down with the score. A definite change of the mood and the texture of the work. Here, in the accompaniment an aggressive harmonic *ostinato* emerges at the dynamic level of *fortissimo*; the expressive annotation of *deciso marcatissimo* returns. Based on the syncopated *ostinato*, the horns and trombones intone a new motive, in the musical style and instrumentation connected to the second movement of *Kleines Requiem für eine Polka*. Thus, Górecki starts his grotesque dance.

The whole sequence is the first example of the "second apparition of humor" in the Symphony No. 4. Through the so-called "higher humor," which is an attempt to find the right place in the all-encompassing unity —of this Divine Intention, or Albert Einstein's *The Mind of God*— and the connection between the paradoxical elements of reality, the composer discovers a higher harmony of spirit, that "higher level." And "the things that Górecki sees and experiences" appear in the form of "musical comedy."

Once again, the composer succeeds in surprising the listener. The recipient may be confused by such a commentary on reality. So let's

---

[26] Mieczysław Tomaszewski, *Od wyznania do wołania. Studia nad pieśnią romantyczą* [From confession to crying. Studies of romantic song]. (Kraków, 1997), 87.

reflect on, and let's investigate these, perhaps the least discussed, issues in recognizing Górecki's intentions and thoughts; hidden, because the composer wears a mask here to say things without doing so directly.

Mask, Humor, Irony

For many years, for musicologists and biographers writing about the work of Henryk Mikołaj Górecki, but also for performers and listeners, some segments or fragments of his compositions constituted an unsolved mystery. They are referred to as "circus music," composer's "excess," "clowning," or "a whirling carousel." This applies to such works as the Harpsichord Concerto, *Concerto-Cantata, Little Requiem for a Polka*, and the last two movements of the Fourth Symphony, *Tansman Episodes*. However, there has been no attempt to interpret the composer's attitude—for some unknown reason, scholars left this problem intact.

And yet there are many questions: What does Górecki want to say? Or maybe, what does he wish to avoid? Is it, for example, obscuring excessive pathos in direct references to the reality he experiences? Maybe, it is a defense against sentimentality? Or does the composer want to avoid categorical, unequivocal statements? Or maybe he seeks to reveal insurmountable contradictions in defense against didacticism and bias? So many questions.

Perhaps this is yet another form of communication (worked out by the composer) as an "ironist"—maybe it is a step towards the listener, maybe it is yet another "brand feature" of the composer, similar to the "turn" and the "motto?" A sign appealing to a system of values shared with the recipient; in an indirect, but simultaneously also refined and discreet way? For years, Górecki gave us his music directly and straightforwardly; but he actually never communicated with us, he did not speak to us directly. "An ordinary thing, but an extraordinary way." (Pope John XXIII) To say it to us, to express it, he puts on a mask. "All earthly affairs of human beings are hooked up with safety pins and buttons and held together by robes. [...] In these signs and symbols, people consciously or unconsciously live, work, realize their existence"—wrote Thomas Carlyle in *Sartor*.[27] This kind of philosophy is rooted in the present. What is sensual and concrete—let's say, in our case, the notes, sounds—constitutes but a starting point in the search for what is important, what is spiritual. The meaning of the philosophy of the mask relies on its conclusions—the transition away from the facts to deeper meanings; that finding a symbolic meaning even in what is seemingly ordinary, trivial. As Jacek Woźniakowski writes, "the symbolist throws away the data to find what is more real." And to quote Carlyle again: "It is more about directing attention to the spiritual reality, 'naked,' lying on the ground of sensual forms, showing that the 'naked world' is possible, and there is more hidden beneath the world of robes."

Thus, a deeper dimension of the directly inaccessible reality may be revealed. Humor and irony were the subjective ways of experiencing paradoxical manifestations of reality also during certain periods in Górecki's life: in the initial several dozen years, "that were the story of an idiot," and then in the period of "depravers," "engineers of visual debauchery," and "confused alchemists of hallucination." (phrases from poems by Zbigniew Herbert). Górecki stated: "I'm getting off this train, I do not understand this way of speaking at all. So much evil is happening in Poland. [...] Perhaps the purpose is to leave nothing here on this Earth, only desert and shields. [...]."

Let us add that humor, under certain circumstances, is able to combine ridiculousness with pathos, and that humor is sometimes considered as an aesthetic category, a subclass of comedy—sometimes even identified with it. Often it is humor that leads to harmony and beauty; it is a peculiar subversive way of experiencing and revealing these traits. Perhaps, it is also from this angle that one should look at the late works of Henryk Mikołaj Górecki. The dispute of goodness with despair, the turmoil of human drama, and thus "the world needs beauty not to plunge into despair." Then, doubt: "maybe I'm a clown?"

The philosopher Thomas Carlyle considered humor as one of "the highest marks of genius." Humor was also the externalization of this genius: "the highest emanation of a deep, noble and loving nature,"

---

[27] Thomas Carlyle, *Sartor* quoted after Anna Malecka, *The Philosophy of Robes, The Symbolism of Thomas Carlyle* (Krakow: Miniature Publishing, 1996), 36.

wrote Carlyle. Humor does not denounce directly, and therefore Górecki does not speak to us directly. A primary significance lies in a contradiction with a secondary, symbolic meaning. Such an understanding of humor in music also brings us closer to the irony in which the intended meaning is opposed to the literal meaning of the "expressive content" of the sound. "A clown hides under his lipstick unspeakable sadness," commented Górecki, while answering questions about grotesque fragments of his works.

Musical comedy is revealed when sound patterns are disproportionate in relation to representational patterns that underpin our perception and reception. What the intellect sees as very real turns out to be, in a momentary glimpse, a sudden flash of understanding, nothingness. Revelation is hidden under superficial reality: "through the utilitarian sound, thanks to humor one can reach a transcendental vision."[28]

The purpose of the so-called "higher humor" is not to show contradictions, but to find the right place in the universe, to find unity and connections between paradoxically different elements. Through humor, the more elevated, all-encompassing harmony of the spirit is discovered at a higher level. All this requires concentration and deep reflection: "music is the result of concentration and meditation. See clean water, green grass, healthy forests, fresh air. See the Creator of everything and write for him."[29]

As the result of this concentration and deep reflection, Górecki wears a mask in order to be able to refer to the paradoxical manifestation of reality and to transform it into sound matter. The role of seemingly straightforward, and sometimes apparently "literal," sensual themes—"straight from the circus"—is a way to find symbolic meaning. The symbolic vision of things distances one from the sensual and provides an indispensable starting point for the search for the essential, the spiritual. "The symbolist gives up the data to find something more real."

---

[28] Albert J. LaValley, *Carlyle and the Idea of the Modern* (New Haven, CT: Elliot's Books, 1968), 39.

[29] Quoted from Robert Tyrała, „Kulturowy i religijny kontekst twórczości kompozytorskiej Henryka Mikołaja Góreckiego." *Pro Musica Sacra* 9 (2011), 11.

In the case of Górecki, however, it is important to remember that we are not concerned with purely formal approaches to music. Using certain rhetorical and musical figures, surprising with their variability and contrasts, he also expresses his general attitude to life, his philosophy of life. The use of extreme contrasts points to the antithetical way of thinking and forming the musical material—which is consistent with the rest of his personal qualities and reveals a much higher level of compositional expression than is commonly believed.

We may observe two levels:
- direct, basic elements referring to tradition and folklore and
- higher, symbolic, spiritual, transcendental.

What is characteristic and important for Górecki is to create in the listener an effect of a surprise. You have to admit that he does it perfectly. Most often, however, this effect is received directly, straightforwardly; it is interpreted as an "excess" or "circus fun." However, the point is that by the contrasts the composer shows us the contradiction between two opposing worlds and two value systems, and expresses his attitude towards them. We have no doubt which side Górecki supports.

As in the poetry of Zbigniew Herbert, "a sober diagnosis of the situation of modern man stands in elementary contradiction to a dramatic gesture of disagreement over this situation."[30] The poet writes: "... but I raise my eyes and my hands raise the song"[31] Maybe? But Górecki was not optimistic; he did not see clear positives in the coming future. This "Tuwim—like" gaze at "truth, being, visible, unique, eternal" combined with the results of his own experiences, prompted him to reflect deeply, from the position of an outsider. He was aware of the irrevocable brokenness of the world, of the order of things submerged by the fall.

---

[30] Stanisław Barańczak, *Uciekiner z Utopii* (Kraków, 1985); cited from London edition (London: Polonia Book Fund, Literary Offices, 1985), 113. English version, *A Fugitive from Utopia: The Poetry of Zbigniew Herbert* (Cambridge, Mass. : Harvard University Press, 1987).

[31] Zbigniew Herbert, *Kapłan* from the volume *Struny Swiatła [Strings of Light]* (Kraków: Wydawnictwo a5, 2011), 27. English translation in *The Collected Poems 1956-1998* (New York: Atlantic Books Ltd, 2014).

What does this postmodern daily life offer today? It consists of discontinuities, the intertwining of various activities, starting from common existential and ending on professional or hobby—related. Life consists of interrupted threads of various activities not necessarily performed to the end. Thus: discontinuity, "fragmentation," lack of relationships, sometimes lack of linear logic. Perhaps the fragmentation and episodic character, the discontinuity of music, are rooted in these observations. We arrive at the core of disagreement over what the composer sees and experiences. As Hermann Hesse described it:[32]

> Inability to be liberated: the drama of existence. They suffer from suffering, in which their talents are consumed by fire, making them infertile (it is creativity). The few who can be liberated reach the absolute and die (this is a constant struggle). In front of others lies the opening of the third kingdom—the imaginary world, sovereign— humor. This is where the intricate, contradictory ideal—the bipolar— resides. Only humor—perhaps the most interesting and the most accomplished achievement of humanity—fulfills this inability, embraces and merges with the rays of its prisms all the domains of humanity.

Górecki did not protest, but rather retreated and looked from the periphery at what was happening. He wore a mask and, in a way known only to himself, he expressed his views through the ironic, grotesque, sarcastic laughter of the clown, laughter through tears. The most famous examples of Górecki's bitter ironic style are the Harpsichord Concerto (1980), Concerto—Cantata (1991—92), Kleines Requiem für eine Polka (1993) and the Fourth Symphony, *Tansman Episodes* (2006).

Someone could want to find traces of this ironic stance of Górecki only in his last works. Yet, the first composition with an unusually bitter and ironic expression was his *Epitafium*, Op. 12 of 1958 for mixed choir and an instrumental ensemble. The inspiration for this work came from a poetic aphorism by Julian Tuwim written on a napkin in a cafe in w Zakopane only an hour before his death:

---

[32] Hermann Hesse, *Der Steppenwolf* [*Wilk Stepowy*], first published in 1927, translated into English in 1929; *Steppenwolf*, 19th edition (New York: Henry Holt and Company, 1963); cited from pp. 59-60 of the Polish edition (Poznań: Wydawnictwo Poznańskie, 1977).

To save it, turn off the eternal light
If it ever were to shine for me.

This is a paraphrase of the last words by Goethe: "open the other curtain, let in more light."

◎ ◎ ◎

We return to the village of Ząb and the Symphony No. 4. It is **Sunday, July 9, 2006.** After stopping the narration, after all these pauses and fermatas, we are immersed in the section B, *Scherzo, Tranquillo e cantabile*, the third movement of the *Tansman Episodes*. Only the piano and cello remain from the entire 100—person orchestra.

In late compositions by Górecki, one can feel the ultimate things. The immediate impulse for the emergence of many works was the personal response of the composer to poignant crumbs of life, personal dramas, or stories he heard. This music comes from the deep interior of the human experience; it refers to those layers of human emotions that have always been related to eternal questions, seeking to get closer to the Truth. Górecki always used contrasts to free his emotions and magnify expression. Sometimes, it was a piercing scream, a maximum of musical expression, for example the *ffff* in *Ad Matrem*. Yet, it was never about throwing thunderbolts. As the composer said: "... I was always irritated by grand words, screams ..." [33]

> The scream evades form
> It is poorer than the voice
> which rises
> and drops ...
> ... it is brightly dark
> from the incapacity of articulation
> rejected the grace of humor
> because it does not know halftones [34]

---

[33] Henryk Mikołaj Górecki, „I will tell you frankly..." 47.
[34] Zbigniew Herbert, *Mr. Cogito and Pop*, from the volume *Pan Cogito* (Warsaw: Czytelnik, 1974), cited from (Kraków: Wydawnictwo a5, 2011), 407. English translation *Mr. Cogito*, by John Carpenter; Bogdana Carpenter (New York: The Ecco Press, 1993).

Therefore, more and more often, in the most dramatic, tragic, final cases, the composer speaks intently, as if in a whisper. We feel as if the entire composition was the way to what is to happen in this episode, B *Scherzo*, and what the composer would like to tell us—dramatically, tenderly, and cantabile. Every phrase is distinct and has its own internal drama. This movement is an exceptionally beautiful example of Górecki's lyricism, characterized by its overwhelmingly quiet intensity of expression.

August 5, 2006, Saturday. "One more time, again" *[Jeszcze raz od nowa]*—with these words written into the manuscript in the composer's hand begins the fourth movement of the Fourth Symphony, *Tansman Episodes*. Indeed, this episode in its melodic layer starts with a variation on the first motive of the theme from the Symphony's first movement. The marking of *Allegro marcato* now returns along with the dynamic level of *forte*. Again, a "spinning carousel" appears— this grotesque feature of Górecki's music, the manifestation of a specific kind of humor that "embraces cosmos in its reach, melting it through emotion into unity" (A. J. LaValley).

The fourth movement abounds in numerous quotations and self-quotations, specific codes to be deciphered by the recipient—as if Górecki wanted to tell us that the Fourth Symphony is a continuation, but also a summary of his whole creative journey and that he and his work are a part of the great European musical family. Let us mention several of these quotations—codes:

- folk traditions: imitation of a highland band [*kapela*] in the fourth episode,
- historical traditions: *Bogurodzica* in the second episode,
- Polish music:
  - cryptogram of the letters Alexander Tansman in the theme of the first movement of the symphony
  - Szymanowski's "turn" in the second episode
  - Sound complex G—C—sharp—D—sharp in the fourth episode
- European musical traditions—a quote from *Der Ring des Nibelungen* [*The Ring of the Nibelung*] by Richard Wagner in the fourth episode,
- Górecki's self-quotations:

- *Concerto-Cantata* and *Kleines Requiem für eine Polka* in the fourth episode
- formal solutions from *Lerchenmusik* in the third episode
- similarity of the first measures of the First, Second and Fourth Symphonies

It is the Sunday morning of August 20, 2006. Górecki, after many variational arrangements of the main theme and saturating it with a diversity of sonorities, now returns to the original version, albeit in a different harmonic setting. The orchestra is silenced and the solo piano presents the theme of the Fourth Symphony as majestic and decisive, in Górecki's favorite harmonic setting, using chords in first inversion.

Then, after a brilliantly simple modulation, in the last measure of *poco allargando*, Górecki will lead us to a surprising quote from Richard Wagner's *Der Ring des Nibelungen*. The fascination with Wagner's compositions and studying his scores coincided with the period of reflection about the Fourth Symphony, *Tansman Episodes*. What could have attracted Górecki to Wagner and, consequently, what was the reason not only to use this quote, but also to write another work for the symphony orchestra entitled *Two Tristan Postludes and a Chorale*?[35] "How is it with this Wagner? I open the tap and how his music flows..."—Górecki wondered.

The motif of Siegfried from *The Ring of the Nibelung* appears in maximal instrumentation, using the entire orchestra, with piano and organ, as the final stage of the cosmological passion of the composer, and an expression of the metaphysical meaning of music. Here, we follow Arthur Schopenhauer's dictum that "music becomes the sounding Will of the World." *Largo—deciso*, the orchestra's sonority fills completely, totally the whole space and in its ecstatic sublimity illuminates with a mystical light. It is pure, sublime, and beautiful.

---

[35] The world premiere of the *Two Tristan Postludes and Chorale* in Mikołaj Górecki's orchestration took place on October 16, 2016, as part of Tansman Festival 2016 in Warsaw. The Sinfonia Varsovia Orchestra was led by Maestro Jerzy Maksymiuk.

Górecki possessed here the mysterious ability to transform time into space. The same one about which old priest Gurnemanz speaks to young Parsifal, anticipating Einstein's theory of relativity: "My son, look, time has become space." The composer still needs this expanding space, this expansion and continual increase, as if he wanted to capture the passing. And it is just here that a true miracle takes place, marked by the brilliant imagination of the composer: the miracle of the symbolic passage. From the solo piano repetition of a stable, fixed chord, which is the echo of the first motive of the *Tansman Episodes*, to the ecstatic sublime sonority of Wagnerian *forte fortissimo*, as if the composer wanted to embrace and raise the whole universe, all within just four measures, within a seemingly static sequence of four whole—tone vertical chords!

As we started the Symphony, so will we finish it. In the form of a long stormy coda returns a segment from the first movement of the symphony, based on the second part of the theme. For a moment, a contemplative cadence returns. Tranquility. Fermatas. Calm. Here are three bass drums that start at an extremely quiet *piano* level with a long (lasting a few dozen seconds) *tremolo* and *crescendo* leading into the orchestral tutti. The 100-person ensemble ends the Fourth Symphony with a sudden *sforzato ffff*—a short pure chord of light, a chord in A major, as if the gate of the heavens slammed shut! THE END!

It is 11.30 am on Sunday, August 20, 2006. Henryk Mikołaj Górecki finishes his last symphony, the Fourth Symphony, *Tansman Episodes. Ad maiorem Dei gloriam.* Did the composer while writing the last note and word THE END think about a certain, sunny autumn morning? Rome, October 2003, Thursday 11:30 am, when, for the last time he shook the hand of Pope John Paul II while explaining why he has not been composing a Mass. "I only have a Kyrie. 25 minutes of music ... "

A Question About Form

In the music of Henryk Mikołaj Górecki we immediately hear the way of presentation of the sound matter. His simplicity of construction can be very misleading. The superficial glance at the score reveals so few sounds, diatonicity, tonality, modality, the limitation of material. Thus, it may result in hasty, often misleading conclusions.

Although the thought that organizes his unconstrained element is an unlimited fantasy, the form of the works is programmed in ways that are firmly embedded in traditions such as the arch form, the rondo, the refrain form, ostinato, variations, canon, or the *Barform*. This demonstrates the profound connections with the tradition as pertains to the structure of compositions: architecture and construction in a sense of proportion and form. The use of forms resulting from the heritage of tradition is absorbed by Górecki, as it were, naturally. In his music, all these great energies must be somehow organized, subdued, and disciplined; they must take the form based on proven models.

The composer thinks about the forms that the music should be "poured into." Thus, you could reverse the order between the structure and the music. On the one hand, you invent the form and the construction for the whole work; on the other hand, you begin with the music that could be written down and structured in different ways. What I am trying to say is that all music begins with sound. It is always based on some musical association, a musical theme or a structure. Now it is fashionable to say that there are no themes, but they continue to exist. At times I even treated a 12-tone series as a theme. When composing, I always begin with introducing some order. I have many things prepared much, much earlier when I actually begin to compose a piece. In this way I have researched and analyzed the possibilities provided by my materials. However, many pieces that I have worked on have never been finished. I only ordered the materials without composing them out into pieces. It is very important for composers to think these ideas through.[36]

In the beginning, these are classical, neoclassical, proportional and symmetrical patterns. This is **motoric constructivism**. Later **serialism** comes as a form of organization of sound material, which culminates in the First Symphony 1959 and in *Scontri* (1960). Górecki briefly turns to **punctualist textures**, highlighted by changes in the dynamics, rhythm and registers. In turn, after the "constraining" armor of serialism comes a **sonoristic period** in which energetic

---

[36] „Composing is a Terribly Personal Matter: Henryk Mikołaj Górecki in conversation with Maja Trochimczyk," *Polish Music Journal* 6 no. 1 (2003). pmc.usc.edu/PMJ/issue/6.2.03/GoreckiKatowice.html. See Chapter 4.

sonorities with the formative role of color reach the apogee of *Genesis* (1962—63). The period of **reductive constructivism**, in which the composer shows more discipline and reduction of the compositional means is crowned by the *Muzyczka IV. Trombone Concerto* (1970).

After 1971, there is a phase of creativity known as **religious creativity**. Of particular importance are vocal-instrumental works like the Symphonies No. 2 and No. 3 or *Beatus Vir* (1979). Finally, the **late period** to 1987 is dominated by choral religious music, folk and church songs, and chamber music, including string quartets. The last period of creativity includes *Concerto-Cantata, Kleines Requiem*, the Third String Quartet, and as yet unknown works such as *Kyrie, Sanctus Adalbertus, Two Tristan Postludes and Chorale* for orchestra or the Fourth Symphony. Mieczysław Tomaszewski wrote that the composer music acquires the character of a farewell, which sometimes results from the loneliness of the composer. It is characterized by a fragmentary quality of music, with cohesion built on a higher level. Elements shaping the forms of Górecki's compositions include sharply outlined expression, a wide range of tempi, as well as dynamic and expressive contrasts. Music arises on the axis of contrast between the sonic sharpness and the euphony, between tension and calm.

In the Fourth Symphony, the strong impact of expression and unrestrained imagination is held in check by formal solutions such as the repetition of the same motives, reminiscences, such as recurring themes, or sets of new musical thoughts organized as episodic sequences. The composer reaches the integration of form through the use of the same theme that is variationally developed in the extreme movements of the Symphony.

While considering the music of Henryk Mikołaj Górecki from a perspective of time and asking questions about the form, one may clearly observe the evolution of the composer's musical language. The fascination with avant-garde and searching for innovations (which the composer never denied) that had to be digested and absorbed at a higher level of synthesis, led the composer to a new kind of music, a music of an extraordinary power, expression and spiritual strength.

The Essential Quality of Henryk Mikołaj Górecki's Music

In the music of Western culture and in the history of the development of the compositional process, we can try to distinguish the substance that is the essential, the essence from the accidentals that is, what is added, and what stems from the substance itself. Regarding music, the substantial element is the melodic—harmonic—rhythmic structure, while the accidental elements are the tempo, volume, color, expression, and symbolism. One could ask what else in the 20th and 21st centuries has become essential in music after all the revolutions of change, breakthroughs, new directions, aleatoricism and transformations. However, to a large extent, an awareness of the substance, essence, and an intuition of substance remained.

In the 1970s, Górecki realized that it was time to return to the core of values, to the essentials of composition. He was not the only one, of course. You no longer had to invent new, sophisticated or complicated techniques, nor widen systems of dodecaphony, serialism, sonority, aleatoricism, or other "isms." Instead you needed to focus on substance, sound, and expression—in order to say what is important, universal; in order to give a testimony.

You have to think substantially, but not about the 'dust of phenomena,' only pure quality.[37] Simplifying musical language and giving it new meaning was the way to go. Due to the right of the antithesis, a return to the roots took place. Again what was a primarily and substantial emerged—the original substance—melody, harmony, rhythm, and chord. What is the essence, the material of Henryk Mikołaj Górecki's music and what makes us immediately perceive that incredible power of his music? Bohdan Pociej states, that it is[38]

> the concrete sound of the essential structure that gives music this extraordinary strength. Górecki's music is characterized by exceptional sound clarity, internal structural clarity, focused on the essence; it is substantial to the core.

---

[37] Henryk Elzenberg, *Problem with existence.*
[38] Bohdan Pociej, *Being in music, an attempt to describe the work of Henryk Mikołaj Górecki*, (Katowice: Karol Szymanowski Academy of Music. 2005), 82.

From here we will be able to immediately determine the character, the kind of this music. This will be:
- raw music, devoid of any ornamentation
- music expressive and expressive, very strong, even sensual
- music of extremes
- on the one hand, full of sonic aggressiveness and sharpness
- on the other hand, full of tenderness, an overwhelming lyrical expression

From a single sound, a sound group, a cluster, a melody and a chord will emerge. "In spite of the intentional poverty there is an extraordinary concentration of expression. Would anywhere else the sonority of one chord become so incredibly important?"[39]

The music is given directly. Immediately audible is the manner in which the composer presents the sound substance. While, Górecki does not address us either directly or indirectly, this sound specificity provides an extraordinary power of impact. The distinctive "clarity of sound and simple, clear structure of the work, focused on essence"—Górecki could be called the essentialist—are the distinguishing features of his music and allow us to recognize his works immediately. Since the composer gives us what is meaningful, in the simplest of possible ways—"an ordinary thing, but an extraordinary way" (Pope John XXIII)—it is very important that all markings, dynamic signs, tempo and meter signs are placed in the foreground. The music is "naked." If not properly read and performed, it will lose its power of interaction, it will become banal. That's why Henryk Mikołaj Górecki so refined these elements and was so demanding in this regard. And all this, so that the listeners of his works would be able to understand that "the power of being and sound energy comes directly from the sound substance, reveals the very essence of sound creation, so that the listening to and experiencing the work would show the interplay of sacredness with the secular, of heaven and earth."[40]

---

[39] Małgorzata Gąsiorowska, „The retention time of Henryk Mikołaj Górecki," *Ruch Muzyczny* 25 (1983), 4.
[40] Bohdan Pociej, *op. cit.*, 12.

The "Overtone" of Górecki's Music

Many scholars writing about the music of Henryk Mikołaj Górecki have tried to identify, separate and name the characteristic feature of the sound world of the composer, the feature that is particular only to him, that identifies and distinguishes him. Many musicologists have tried to describe this phenomenon. Bohdan Pociej captured it most accurately. However, the use of the term "chord" automatically implies associations with Chopin's "Chopin chord," the Tristan chord by Wagner, the Prometheus's chord by Scriabin, or the "Tansman chord." Here belongs also the sequence of consecutive chords (B-flat—E-flat—and A major chords—plus E-flat minor chord) that are often called the "Beethoven chords" by Górecki and appear in his Second String Quartet *Quasi una fantasia*. So what is this phenomenon? How to describe and name it?

This "Górecki's chord", described, among others by Bohdan Pociej, does not yield to classical harmonic analysis. This is not a structured sound construct that appears in the same form in different works. Furthermore, it is not even homogeneous, and not repetitive. And yet it is present, or rather encoded, in all of Górecki's works. The essence of this "sonority" evades rational, musicological analysis, since it belongs to the mystical world. It is a certain constant that is always present, but reveals itself only in certain circumstances, under certain conditions. Let us finally name it, say what it is.

This is a specific "state of sound" that is a characteristic, yet difficult to define "overtone," rooted in tradition, in faith. It is specifically Polish, and at the same time reaches deep down to the source, to the essence of things. This tone or the state of sound reveals "the sounding Will of the World" and it is perceptually only possible in such performances and interpretations, in which the music reaches the level of the transcendental.

Let us call this "tone" the **Górecki Overtone** [*Alikwot Góreckiego*], i.e., a state of sound that remains "beyond." Górecki's Overtone is something that is "beyond" and is not an integral part of the music matter itself. It is, as Bohdan Pociej, said an "absolute expression." It is a sign of Górecki's style. The Górecki Overtone, that elusive state of sound, is the first stage of sacred spirituality in the sound medium of music; it is a sonority that persists, always and forever. The composer expresses in this "Overtone" a longing for fullness, for "pleroma" that becomes ever more euphonious. Its light-dark symbolism combines the revealed light and the darkness of the Mystery. The Górecki Overtone is a musical symbol of God's existence.

John Sherba, one of the members of the famous Kronos Quartet sought to accurately describe this state when he said: [41]

> Górecki felt responsible for every note. And that makes his music difficult to play, because performers should also feel that responsibility, for every chord, for every note [...] These chords and notes have to be played perfectly, purely,[42] because when the chord is played perfectly, in tune, a special overtone appears — and when that happens, you can shake up the whole concert hall. I think this is what Górecki was trying to achieve and that he aimed to go even further [...]

What conditions must be met in order for the Górecki Overtone to appear? Under what circumstances does it reveal itself? What should the performer know (in particular, the conductor) to make Górecki's music not only professional in the sense of a quality performance, but also "real"? First and foremost, you need to be aware of the particular risk involved in performance. Musicians, performers must have, or create in themselves a kind of availability, which Krzysztof Droba calls "the orchestra's sense of transcendence." Let's add that it is not about the instrumental efficiency of the performers, because this must always be the starting point and remain high. What matters is a full opening up to the music and the intuition, the grasping of its extra-instrumental (extra-musical) essence. And then, perhaps the Górecki Overtone will emerge. Music will become transcendental.

Conclusion

Górecki said: "The beauty that is now so neglected, even ridiculed, came later."[43] And "this world needs beauty in order not to sink in despair."[44] His music functions on the axis of contrast between the

---

[41] John Sherba's excerpt from an interview in *Górecki: Portret z pamięci* edited by Beata Bolesławska-Lewandowska (Kraków: PWM, 2013), 330-331.
[42] Sherba does not think only of intonation here—*the author's note*.
[43] Cited from Agnieszka Malatyńska-Stankiewicz, *op. cit.*, 2010, 13.
[44] Quoted from Włodzimierz Siedlik, *op. cit.*, 2012, 95.

sonic focus and the euphony, between tension and calming, between explosive energy and contemplation, between the power of life and the power of the spirit. "The contrast between matter and spirit, profanum and sacrum, manifests itself through the means of material expression, but on the other side of that matter is the abolition of the material overcome by spirituality. Here exists the bipolar order of the matter and the spirit." (Bohdan Pociej). [45]

Górecki's music is permeated by an extraordinary simplicity, logic, and clarity of form. The essence of spirituality lies between the sounds in space, not where the sound starts, but where it ends: the greatest urgency of ardent expression is not captured by shouting, but in full silence. The traits of suffering, the experience of life, the tradition, folklore, the wisdom of faith, have always been present in the composer's life and also—fundamentally, substantially—present in the very sound of his music. The element of beauty is revealed by the clarity and transparency, and by the logic of the architectural flow, the logic of the melodic and metric phases.

"This organic association of technique with its function becomes the source of the explosive expression of Górecki's music." (Krzysztof Droba) The radical asceticism of sound is opposed to the incredible expression of the music. This means that Górecki tried to reach the level of an archetypal expression. Instead of remaining at the surface layer, he sought to find that "sound source." "It is a music that has been consistently engineered for its unique, masterly style, and at the same time that it is purged of everything that is expected, ordinary, mundane, or ordinary. Thus, it invites a focus on itself." (Mieczyslaw Tomaszewski).[46]

Henryk Mikołaj Górecki was one of the forerunners of the "new language" of the 20th century music, which he did not define verbally, but emphasized by transforming elements and giving them a new, original idiom, its proper meaning. There is a distinct feature of the artistic attitude of Górecki—present from the beginning to the end— he is inclined to bring ideas to their ultimate conclusions, in total exploitation, his materials reach the wall of inability to develop any further. As a creator, he was uncompromising. He demanded of

---

[45] Bohdan Pociej, *Being in music, op. cit.*, 86.
[46] Mieczyslaw Tomaszewski, "Sacrum i profanum..." *op. cit.*, 3-4.

himself the most, so that he was certain of every note he had written before he gave the manuscript to the publisher. He also demanded the most from performers: not just a professional technique, but a total commitment, to the limits of their capabilities. Finally, he required the most from the listeners: to be completely focused, attentive and full of concentration. He expected them to be attuned to that "other dimension." It is only at the intersection of these three factors that Górecki's music emerges. The expression becomes fully articulated and comprehensible; thus he Górecki's Overtone is revealed. Music reaches its fullness. It transcends.

However, the fundamental meaning is assigned to the aspect of the Mystery—fascinating, sublime, and beautiful at the same time. This Mystery is of fundamental importance. In this musical drama we see Górecki as a human being and as the creator of infinite spaces that awaken existential terror. "The eternal silence of these infinite spaces terrifies me" said Blaise Pascal.[47] And, we should add, the sacred, if a work of art really came to its realization, fascinates much more than pure beauty. At the same time it is more remote, transcendent, and sublime than all that is sublime.

Górecki's music conceals in itself something that can be called "the mystery of time." Time stops in Górecki's music. The composer needs this precise type of "extended time" to realize his compositional ideas. A slow pace predominates so that the "flow" of musical time becomes sacred. This sacrum "integrates the concepts of 'transfer' or 'relocation' that means removal from the constraints of time and space." (Mieczysław Tomaszewski) The sonority, time and space constitute the form of a work.

According to Bohdan Pociej, "time in Górecki's music appears dualistic:" 1. as dynamic, linear time; 2. as an a—dynamic time of self—contradiction, self—erasure. As Andrzej Chłopecki stated:[48]

> Górecki shakes up the category of time on the edges of its musical influence, stretching the perception of the listener to the limits of impossibility [...] To the limits of impossibility he stretches the

---

[47] Quoted from *Pascal's Pensées* (Lanham: Dancing Unicorn Books, 2016).
[48] Andrzej Chłopecki, *Muzyka wzwodzi. Diagnozy i portrety* (Kraków: PWM, 2014), 346-347.

simplest sound structures, extended over long periods of time to the limits of endurance, elongating the duration of their operation, throwing expression into the interior of sounds and harmony rather than in their motion. Górecki builds what is sometimes called sacral time in music.

The work of Henryk Mikołaj Górecki is a work combining "two worlds;" it is a work permeated by metaphysics through and through. "Why is there something rather than nothing?" There is no shorter, more lapidary, and perhaps more in—depth question in the core of metaphysics, like Leibniz's question, cited above. This question is not a about particulars, about individual causes. It is a fundamental question about the origin of all causes and all phenomena.

Music—"the sounding Will of the World" (Arthur Schopenhauer). "Music—a guest from another world" (Leszek Kołakowski). In his creative search, Górecki creates such music that could not have been written by a composer—intellectualist, or an aesthete. Such music could only be written by a man who, in his art, was facing the Mystery.

◎ THE END ◎

◎ HENRYK MIKOŁAJ GÓRECKI ◎

◎ LIST OF WORKS ◎

Ten Preludes for piano (1954-55)

Piano Concerto (1954-55)

String Quartet (1954-55)

Legend for orchestra (1954-55)

Obrazki Poetyckie / Poetic Pictures for piano (1954-55)

Five Mazurkas for piano (1954-55)

Prelude for Violin and Piano (1954-55)

Romance for piano (1954-55)

Terzetto quasi una fantasia for oboe, violin and piano (1954-55)

Two Songs to Texts by Maria Konopnicka for voice and piano (1954-55)
- Movements: I. Przez te łąki, przez te pola / Through these meadows, these fields. II. Kiedy Polska / When Poland
- World premiere: 5/28/1995, New York, Andrzej Bachleda, baritone, H. M. Górecki, piano

Four Preludes /Cztery Preludia, Op. 1 for piano (1955), 8'
- Publisher: Chester Music and PWM Edition for the world.
- Publisher: Boosey & Hawkes for the world (Synchronisation rights only).

Toccata, Op. 2 for two pianos (1955) 3'
- Publisher: Chester Music and PWM Edition for the world.
- Publisher: Boosey & Hawkes for the World (Synchronisation rights only).

Three Songs / Trzy Pieśni, Op. 3 for medium voice and piano (1956)
- Text: Juliusz Słowacki, Julian Tuwim (Polish)
- Dedicated "to the memory of my beloved Mother"

- Movements: I. Do Matki/To Mother; II. Jakiż to dzwon grobowy/ What a funereal bell, III. Ptak / The Bird.
- Publisher: Chester Music and PWM Edition for the world.

Variations / Variazioni / Wariacje, Op. 4 for violin and piano (1956) 10'
- Publisher: Chester Music and PWM Edition for the world.
- Publisher: Boosey & Hawkes for the world (Synchronisation rights only).

Quartettino, Op. 5 for two flutes, oboe, and violin (1956), 8'
- Movements: I Molto allegro, II Lento e molto espressivo III Presto. Publisher: Boosey & Hawkes for the USA, Canada and Mexico.
- Publisher: Chester Music and PWM Edition for the rest of the world.

Piano Sonata No.1, Op. 6 for piano (1956/84/90) 12'
- Movements: I Allegro molto, con fuoco. II Grave pesante e corale. III Allegro Vivace ma non troppo.
- Dedicated "J.R." to Jadwiga Rurańska (future wife)
- Publisher: Boosey & Hawkes for the world.
- World premiere complete: 3/17/1991 in Helsinki byPaul Crossley, piano

Songs of Joy and Rhythm / Pieśni o Radości i Rytmie, Op. 7 for two pianos and chamber orchestra (1956/59) 14'
- Scoring: picc.1.0.1.1-0.1.1.0-timp.perc(3):SD without snares/SD with snares/xyl-cel.2pft-strings(6.6.6.6.0).[1]
- Movements: I Prelude et Toccata, II Recitative – Study, III Lyrical Interlude, IV Little Piano Concerto.
- Publisher: Boosey & Hawkes for the World (excluding Poland, Albania, Bulgaria, China, Cuba, North Korea, Vietnam, Romania, Czech Republic, Slovakia, Hungary and the former territories of Yugoslavia and the USSR).
- Publisher: PWM Edition for the rest of the world.

Songs of Joy and Rhythm / Pieśni o Radości i Rytmie, Op. 7. Version II, for two pianos and chamber orchestra (1956/59 revised in 1990, Scott Stroman) 14'-16'
- Movements: I Marcato II con moto, III Non troppo, IV Ritmico.
- Publisher: Boosey & Hawkes for the World (excluding Poland, Albania, Bulgaria, China, Cuba, North Korea, Vietnam, Romania, Czech Republic, Slovakia, Hungary and the former territories of Yugoslavia and the USSR).

---

[1]Instrument abbreviations in the scoring from Boosey & Hawkes website: http://www.boosey.com/downloads/BH_StandardAbbreviations_New.pdf

- Publisher: PWM Edition for the rest of the world.
- World Premiere: 7/8/1990 Almeida Festival, London

Sonatina in One Movement, Op. 8 for violin and piano (1956) 3'
- Publisher: Chester Music and PWM Edition for the world.
- Publisher Boosey & Hawkes for the World (Synchronisation rights only).

Lullaby / Kołysanka, Op. 9 for piano (1956, 1980)

From the Bird's Nest / Z ptasiego gniazda, Op. 9a (1956), for piano:
- Movements: I March, II Folksong III Old Melody IV Scherzo, V Second Folk Song VI interludium VII Batagelle, VIII Second March IX finale a la danse
- Unpublished

Sonata for two Violins / Sonata na dwoje skrzypiec, Op. 10 (1957)
A transcription for two violas is also available.
- Movements: I Allegro molto, II Adagio sostenuto, III Andante con moto- Con anima a la danse
- Dedicated "to Jadwiga Rurańska"
- Publisher: Chester Music and PWM Edition for the world.

Concerto for Five Instruments and String Quartet/ Koncert na pięć instrumentów i kwartet smyczkowy,Op.11 (1957) 10'
- Scoring: fl.cl-tpt-xyl.mand-2vln.vla.vlc.
- Dedicated to Leon Markiewicz
- Movements: I Sostenuto, II Dolce, III Non troppo, IV marcato, ritmico
- Publisher: Boosey & Hawkes for the USA, Canada and Mexico.
- Movements: I Sostenuto, II Dolce, III Non troppo, IV marcato, ritmico
- Publisher: Chester Music and PWM Edition for the rest of the world.

Epitafium, Op. 12 for mixed choir and small ensemble (1958), 5'
- Text: Julian Tuwim (Polish), dedicated to the memory of Julian Tuwim
- Scoring: picc-Dtpt-perc(5):SD without snare/ SD/ 3susp.cym (sm,med,lg)-vla.
- Movements: I Preludium, II Chorale, III Antiphon, IV Postludium
- Publisher: Boosey & Hawkes for the USA, Canada and Mexico.
- Publisher: Chester Music and PWM Edition for the rest of the world.
- World premiere: 10/3/1958 2nd Warsaw Autumn Festival, Warsaw Philharmonic Choir, Silesian Philharmonic Orchestra, Andrzej Markowski, cond.

Five Pieces / Pięć utworów, Op. 13 for two pianos (1959), 7'
- Publisher: Chester Music and PWM Edition for the world.
- Publisher: Boosey & Hawkes for the world (Synchronisation rights only).

Symphony No.1 '1959' Op. 14 for string orchestra and percussion (1959) 20'
- Scoring: timp.perc(7):3SD without snares/SD/TD/3susp.cym /xyl/marimbaphone/vib-hpd-harp-strings(16.16.14.12.10).
- Movements: I Invocation, II Antiphon, III Chorale, IV Lauda
- Dedicated to Prof. Bolesław Szabelski
- Publisher: Boosey & Hawkes for the USA, Canada and Mexico.
- Publisher: Chester Music and PWM Edition for the rest of the world.

Three Diagrams / Trzy diagramy, Op. 15 for flute solo (1959)
- Publisher: Chester Music and PWM Edition for the world.

Monologhi, Op. 16 for soprano and three groups of instruments (1960), 17'
- Text: Henryk Mikołaj Górecki (Polish), dedicated "to my wife"
- Scoring: Group I: 2 harps-perc:glsp/vib/marimbaphone; Group II: perc(3):6susp.cym; Group III:perc(2):3tam-t.3gongs
- Publisher: Boosey & Hawkes for the USA, Canada and Mexico
- Publisher: Chester Music and PWM Edition for the rest of the world.

Scontri / Collisions, Op. 17 for orchestra (1960) 17'
- Scoring: 2.2picc.0.2.Ebcl.bcl.2.2dbn-4.4.3.1-perc(8)-2pft-2harps-strings (30.0.12.12.8) perc1:2bongos/glsp/2tam-t ; perc2:BD(lg)/3Chin.bl /2susp.cym perc3:2timbales/4susp.horseshoes/2susp.cym; perc4:2tom-t/4cowbells; perc5:2tom-t/3horseshoes; perc6:2SD/vib/2susp.cym; perc7:BD/5tpl.bl/2susp.cym; perc8:2SD/marimbaphone/2gongs. Dedicated to Jan Krenz
- Publisher: Boosey & Hawkes for the USA, Canada and Mexico.
- Publisher: Chester Music and PWM Edition for the rest of the world.
- World Premiere: 9/21/1960, the 4th Warsaw Autumn Festival, Polish Radio Symphony Orchestra from Katowice, Jan Krenz, cond.

Chorale in the Form of a Canon / Chorał w formie kanonu (WOO) (1961/1984) for string quartet

Diagram IV, Op. 18 for flute solo (1961)

Genesis I: Elementi, Op. 19/1 for string trio (1962), 13'
- Scoring: vln.vla.vlc.

- Publisher: Boosey & Hawkes for the USA, Canada and Mexico.
- Publisher: Chester Music and PWM Edition for the rest of the world.
- World Premiere: 5/29/1962, in Kraków, Poland, by Antoni Feliks, vla/Edward Wiertelosz, vlc

Genesis II: Canti Strumentali, Op. 19/2 for 15 players (1962), 8'
- Scoring: picc.fl-tpt-mand-gtr-pft(4hands)-perc(2): 5wdbl/2gongs/ BD/tam-t(lg)/4bongos/2large gongs/BD(lg)/tam-t-3vln.3vla.
- Publisher: Boosey & Hawkes for the USA, Canada and Mexico.
- Publisher: Chester Music and PWM Edition for the rest of the world.

Genesis III: Monodramma, Op. 19/3 for soprano, metal percussion and six double basses (1963) 10'
- Text: Henryk Mikolaj Górecki
- Scoring: perc(13):12blocks/8cyms/4gongs/12tgl/ 8susp.cym/4tam-t/t.bells-6db.
- Publisher: Boosey & Hawkes for the USA, Canada and Mexico.
- Publisher: Chester Music and PWM Edition for the rest of the world.

Three Pieces in Old Style / Trzy utwory w dawnym stylu (WOO) for string orchestra (1963) 10'
- Scoring: strings (min:12.10.8.6.4)
- Publisher: Boosey & Hawkes for the world (Synchronisation rights only).
- Publisher: Chester Music and PWM Edition for the world
- World Premiere: 4/30/1964 in Warsaw, Poland by Ensemble 'Con moto ma cantabile'

Choros I, Op. 20 for strings (1964), 18'
- Scoring: strings (24.0.12.12.8).
- Publisher: Boosey & Hawkes for the USA, Canada and Mexico
- Publisher: Chester Music and PWM Edition for the rest of the world.
- World Premiere: 9/22/1964 in Warsaw, Poland by the Silesian State Philharmonic Orchestra / Karol Stryja, cond.

Refrain / Refren, Op. 21 for orchestra (1965), 17'
- Scoring: 0.4.4.4-4.4.4.0-3timp.perc(1):tam-t-strings.
- Publisher: Boosey & Hawkes for the USA, Canada and Mexico.
- Publisher: Chester Music and PWM Edition for the rest of the world.
- World Premiere: 10/27/1965 in Geneva, Orchestre de la Suisse Romande, Pierre Colombo, cond.

Musiquette 1 / Muzyczka I, Op. 22 for two trumpets and guitar (1967) – withdrawn by the composer, dedicated to Szabelski for 70th birthday.

Musiquette 2 /Muzyczka II, Op. 23 for 4 trumpets, 4 trombones, 2 pianos and percussion (1967), 7'
- Dedicated to Andrzej Markowski
- Scoring: 4tpt.4trbn-perc(5):cyms/tam-t/3susp.cym/BD(lg)/tam-t(lg)/BD(lg)/cyms(lg)/tam-t(lg)-2pft.
- Publisher: Boosey & Hawkes for the USA, Canada and Mexico.
- Publisher: Chester Music and PWM Edition for the rest of the world.

Old Polish Music / Muzyka staropolska, Op. 24 for brass and strings (1967-69), 23'
- Scoring: 5hn.4tpt.4trbn-strings(min.8.8.8.8.8).
- Publisher: Boosey & Hawkes for the World (excluding Poland, Albania, Bulgaria, China, Cuba, North Korea, Vietnam, Romania, Czech Republic, Slovakia, Hungary and the former territories of Yugoslavia and the USSR).
- Publisher: PWM Edition for the rest of the world.
- World Premiere: 9/24/1969 in Warsaw, Poland, by the National Philharmonic Symphony Orchestra / Andrzej Markowski, cond.

Musiquette 3 / Muzyczka III, Op. 25 for viola ensemble (1967), 14'
- Scoring: (the work can be played by any multiple of the minimum number of three violas).
- Dedicated to: Anna and Zygmunt Lis
- Publisher: Boosey & Hawkes for the USA, Canada and Mexico.
- Publisher: Chester Music and PWM Edition for the rest of the world.

Cantata / Kantata, Op. 26 for organ (1968), 13'
- Publisher: Chester Music and PWM Edition for the world.

Wratislaviae gloria / Sygnały Wratislaviae Gloria, fanfare for brass and strings (WOO), unpublished

Canticum Graduum, Op. 27 for orchestra (1969), 12'
- Scoring: 4.0.4.4sax.4-8.4.4.0-strings (24.0.8.8.8).
- Dedicated to: "A Otto Tomek"
- Publisher: Boosey & Hawkes for the world (excluding Poland, Albania, Bulgaria, China, Cuba, North Korea, Vietnam, Romania, Czech Republic, Slovakia, Hungary and the former territories of Yugoslavia and the USSR).
- Publisher: PWM Edition for the rest of the world.
- World Premiere: 12/11/1969 in Dusseldorf, West German Radio Symphony Orchestra / Michael Gielen, cond.

Musiquette 4 – Trombone Concerto / Muzyczka IV, Koncert Puzonowy, Op. 28 for clarinet, trombone, cello and piano (1970), 9'
- Publisher: Boosey & Hawkes for the World (excluding Poland, Albania, Bulgaria, China, Cuba, North Korea, Vietnam, Romania, Czech Republic, Slovakia, Hungary and the former territories of Yugoslavia and the USSR).
- Publisher: PWM Edition for the rest of the world.
- World Premiere: 4/15/1970, in Vienna by Warsztat Muzyczny: Edward Borowiak,trbn/Witold Galazka,vlc/Czeslaw Palkowski, cl/Zygmunt Krauze,pft (ensemble the Music Workshop / Warsztat Muzyczny)

Ad Matrem / Do Matki, Op. 29 for soprano solo, mixed choir, and orchestra (1971), 10'
- Text: Henryk Mikolaj Górecki (Latin)
- Dedicated "In Memory of My Mother"
- Scoring: 4(III,IV=picc).4.4.4(III,IV=dbn)-4.4.4.0-timp(2). perc(2):SD/v.large BD-harp-pft-strings
- Publisher: Boosey & Hawkes for the USA, Canada and Mexico.
- Publisher: Chester Music and PWM Edition for the rest of the world.
- World Premiere: 9/24/1972 at the 16th Warsaw Autumn Festival by Stefania Woytowicz and Warsaw Philharmonic Symphony Orchestra and Chorus, Andrzej Markowski, cond.

Two Sacred Songs / Dwie pieśni sakralne, Op. 30 for baritone solo and orchestra(1971), 5 '
- Text: Marek Skwarnicki (Polish)
- Dedicated "to my Wife Jadwiga"
- Movements: I Lento sostenuto, II Maestozo
- Publisher: Chester Music and PWM Edition for the world
- World Premiere: 4/6/1976, 16th Poznan Musical Spring Festival, Jerzy Artysz, baritone, Polish Radio Symphony Orchestra, Kraków, Jacek Kaspszyk, cond.

Two Sacred Songs/ Dwie pieśni sakralne, Op. 30bis for baritone solo and orchestra (1971), 5'
- Text: Marek Skwarnicki (Polish)
- Dedicated "to my Wife Jadwiga"
- Movements: I Lento sostenuto, II Maestozo
- Publisher: Chester Music and PWM Edition for the world.

Symphony No.2 *Copernican*/ Symfonia nr 2 "Kopernikowska,"Op. 31 for soprano, baritone, mixed choir and large orchestra (1972), 35'

- Text: Psalm 145 (v.6), psalm 135 (verses 7-9), and excerpt from Book I "De revolutionibus orbium coelestium" by Nicolaus Copernicus (L)
- Scoring: 4(III,IV=picc).4.4(IV=bcl).4(III,IV=dbn)-4.4.4.1-timp(3).perc(3):BD/SD(sm)/tam-t(lg)/BD(lg)/SD(med)/BD(lg)/SD(lg)/tam.t(lg)-harp-pft(4hands)-strings(36.0.12.12.12)
- Dedicated: "to the Kosciuszko Foundation"
- Publisher: Chester Music and PWM Edition for the world.
- Publisher: Boosey & Hawkes for the world (Synchronisation rights only).
- World Premiere: 6/22/1973 in Warsaw, Stefania Woytowicz, sop / Andrzej Hiolski, bar / National Philharmonic Symphony Orchestra and chorus / Andrzej Markowski, cond.

Euntes Ibant et Flebant, Op. 32 for mixed chorus *a cappella* (1972), 9' ["They Walk and Cry..."]
- Text: Psalm 125 (verse 6) and Psalm 94 (verse 6) (L)
- Publisher: Boosey & Hawkes for the USA, Canada and Mexico.
- Publisher: Chester Music and PWM Edition for the rest of the world.
- World Premiere: 8/31/1975 in Wrocław by the National Philharmonic Choir of Warsaw / Andrzej Markowski, cond.

Two Little Songs of Tuwim /Dwie piosenki, Op. 33 for a choir of four equal voices (1972), 4'
- Text: Julian Tuwim (Polish)
- Dedicated to: "Kochanej Anusi" [To dear Ania]
- Publisher: Boosey & Hawkes for the USA, Canada and Mexico.
- Publisher: Chester Music and PWM Edition for the rest of the world.

Three Dances / Trzy tańce, Op. 34 for orchestra (1973) 12'
- Scoring: 2(II=picc).2.2.2-3.4.3.1-timp(2)-strings
- Dedicated to: Antoni Szafranek and the Rybnik Philharmonic
- Publisher: Boosey & Hawkes for the world (Synchronisation rights only).
- Publisher: Chester Music and PWM Edition for the world.
- World Premiere: 11/24/1973 in Rybnik, Poland by the Rybnik Philharmonic Symphony / Antoni Szafranek, cond.

Amen, Op. 35 for mixed chorus *a cappella* (1975), 8'
- Text: religious in Latin
- Dedicated to: " To the 15th Poznań Musical Spring Festival"
- Publisher: Boosey & Hawkes for the USA, Canada and Mexico.
- Publisher: Chester Music and PWM Edition for the rest of the world.
- World Premiere: 4/5/1975, 15h Poznan Musical Spring Festival, Poznan Boys Choir, Jerzy Kurczewski, cond.

Two Signals / Dwa hejnały for Woodwinds and Brass (WOO), for World Ice Hockey Championship, Katowice

Symphony No.3 'Symphony of Sorrowful Songs' / Symfonia pieśni żałosnych, Op. 36 for soprano solo and large orchestra (1976) 54'
- Text: Old Polish religious and folk texts, trans. in French by Jerzy Lisowski and in German by Wilhelm Szewczyk (P)
- Dedicated: "Mojej Zonie" [To my Wife]
- Scoring: 4(III,IV=picc).0.4.2.2dbn-4.0.4.0-harp-pft-strings(16.16.12.12.8).
- Publisher: Boosey & Hawkes for the USA, Canada and Mexico.
- Publisher: Chester Music and PWM Edition for the rest of the world.
- World Premiere: 4/4/1977, at the Royan Festival, Royan, France, Stefania Woytowicz, soprano / Symphony Orchestra of South German Radio Baden-Baden / Ernest Bour, cond.
- World stage premiere: 5/12/2007, at the Gilam Opera House, Brooklyn, NY, with Bill Morrison, filmaker / Robert McGrath, director / Brooklyn Philharmonic / Ridge Theater / Michael Christie
- World premiere of a version: 2/27/1993 in Winnipeg, Canada by The Dance Collective/Winnipeg Symphony Orchestra

Three Little Pieces /Trzy małe utworki, Op. 37 for violin & piano (1977) 3'
- Movements: I Allegro ma non tanto, II Lento, cantabile e dolce, III Animato, marcato
- Dedicated "Kochanemu Mikołajkowi" [To Dear Little Mikołaj]
- Publisher: Boosey & Hawkes for the World (excluding Poland, Albania, Bulgaria, China, Cuba, North Korea, Vietnam, Romania, Czech Republic, Slovakia, Hungary and the former territories of Yugoslavia and the USSR).
- Publisher: PWM Edition for the rest of the world.
- World Premiere: 1/5/1978 in Katowice, Poland by Mikolaj Gorecki, violin and Jadwiga Gorecka, piano

Beatus Vir, Op. 38 Psalm for baritone solo, mixed choir and large orchestra (1979) 35'
- Text : Psalms 142 (verses 1,6-8,10), 30 (verses 15-16), 37 (verse 23), 66 (verse 7), 33 (verse 9) (L)
- Scoring: 4.4.4.4(III,IV=dbn)-4.4.4.4*-perc(2):glsp/t.bells-2harp-pft(4 hands)-strings *if four tubas are not available, the 1st and 2nd tuba parts may be played by two (additional) trombones
- Dedicated "To Holy Father John Paul II"
- Publisher: Boosey & Hawkes for the world (Synchronisation rights only).
- Publisher: Chester Music and PWM Edition for the world.
- World Premiere: 6/9/1979, Kraków,Poland by Jerzy Mechlinski / Krakow Philharmonic Orchestra & Chorus / H.M. Górecki, cond.

Broad Waters / Szeroka Woda, Op. 39, five folksongs for unaccompanied mixed choir(1979), 16'
- Movements: I A ta nasza Narew [O our Narew], II Oj kiedy na Powislu [Oh, when in Powisle], II Oj, Janie, Janie, IV Polne róże rwała [She picked wild roses], V Szeroka woda[Broad waters]
- Text: Traditional (Polish)
- Dedication: "Przyjaciołom krakowskim" [To my Cracow Friends]
- Publisher: Boosey & Hawkes for the world.

Concerto for Harpsichord and String Orchestra, Op. 40 for harpsichord (or piano) and string orchestra (1980), 9'
- Scoring: if harpsichord solo: strings (6.6.4.4.2), if piano solo: strings (8.8.6.6.4)
- Dedication: "To Elżbieta Chojnacka"
- Publisher: Boosey & Hawkes for the world (Synchronisation rights only)
- Publisher: Chester Music and PWM Edition for the world.
- World Premiere: 3/2/1980 in Katowice, Poland, by Elżbieta Chojnacka, harpsichord / Polish Radio Symphony Orchestra / Stanisław Wisłocki, cond.

Mazurkas / Mazurki, Op. 41 for piano (1980), incomplete, unpublished

Dwie Pieśni do słów Lorki / Two Songs of Lorca, Op. 42 for medium voice and piano(composed in 1956, rev. 1980), 10'
- Text: Federico García Lorca, trans. Mikołaj Bieszczadowski (Polish)
- Movements: I. Nocturne, II. Malaguena.
- Publisher: Boosey & Hawkes for the world.

Blessed Raspberry Songs / Błogosławione Pieśni Malinowe, Op. 43 for voice and piano (1980), 20'
- Text: Cyprian Kamil Norwid (Polish)
- Movements: I Błogosławione pieśni malinowe [Blessed raspberry songs], II Co ranek, skoro ustępują cienie [Each moring when the shadow recede], II Litość [Compassion], IV O! Boże... jeden, który JESTEŚ [Oh, God... the one who IS]
- Publisher: Boosey & Hawkes for the world.
- World Premiere: 10/2/2001 in Poznan, Adam Kruszewski, voice, Henryk Mikołaj Górecki, piano

Miserere, Op. 44 for unaccompanied mixed chorus (1981), 37'
- Text: Religious (Latin)
- Scoring: SATB Chorus
- Dedicated "Bydgoszczy poświęcam" [I dedicate this to Bydgoszcz]

- Publisher: Chester Music and PWM Edition for the world.
- Publisher: Boosey & Hawkes for the world (Synchronisation rights only).
- World Premiere: 9/10/1987 in Włocławek. Poland by the Kraków Philharmonic Chorus, members of Bydgoszcz 'Arion' Choir

Dark Evening is Falling / Wieczór ciemny się uniża, Op. 45, five folk songs for mixed chorus *a cappella* (1981)
- Text: Traditional (Polish)
- Movements: I Pytają sięludzie [People ask], II Uwiją, wianuszki [They will pleat small garlands], III Scięli dąbek [They cut down the little oak], IV Depce konik [The little horse paws], V Wieczór ciemny się uniża [Dark evening is falling]
- Publisher: PWM Edition.

My Vistula, Grey Vistula / Wisło moja, Wisło szara, Op. 46, folksong for SATB chorus *a cappella* (1981), 4'
- Text: Traditional (Polish)
- Dedication: "Pani Marii Wacholc" [To Mrs. Maria Wacholc]
- Publisher: Boosey & Hawkes for the world.
- Publisher: PWM Edition for Poland.

Lullabies and Dances / Kołysanki i tańce, Op. 47 for violin and piano (1982)
- Dedication: "Mikołajowi w 11. rocznicę urodzin" [to Mikołaj for his 11th Birthday]
- Publisher: Chester Music and PWM Edition for the world.
- World Premiere: 10/3/2003. Bielsko Biała, 8th Polish Composers' Festival, Krzysztof Bąkowski, vn, Anna Górecka, pn

Two Songs of Słowacki / Śpiewy do słów Juliusza Słowackiego, Op. 48 for voice and piano (1983) 19'
- Text: Juliusz Słowacki (Polish)
- Movements: I We łzach, Panie, ręce podnosimy[In Tears, Lord, we raise our hands] II Panie! O którym na niebiosach [Lord, about whom in heavens],
- Dedication: "to Andrzej Bachleda"
- Publisher: Boosey & Hawkes for the world.
- World Premiere: 9/14/1985 in Zakopane, Poland by Andrzej Bachleda (baritone), HM Gorecki (pft)

Three Lullabies / Drei Wiegenlieder / Trzy Kołysanki, Op. 49 for mixed chorus *a cappella* (1984, revised in 1991) 10'
- Text: Traditional (Polish)
- Movements: Uśniże mi, uśnij /Sleep for me, sleep; II Kołysz-że się, kołysz / Rock, baby, rock; II Nie piej kurku, nie piej / Don't crow, rooster, don't crow.
- Publisher: Boosey & Hawkes for the world.
- World Premiere: 8/2/1991 at the Lerchenborg Festival, Denmark by Ars Nova / Bo Holten, cond.

Ah, my Lavender Garland / Ach, mój wianku lewandowy, Op. 50, seven folk songs for mixed chorus *a cappella* (1984)
- Text: Traditional (Polish)
- Movements: I Ach, moj wianku lewandowy / Ah, my Lavender Garland, II Wędrowali trzy panienki /Three girls were wandering; III Taiłam się /I kept my secret, IV Bzi, bzi, bzibziana; V Chcecie wiedzieć/Do you want to know;, VI Pocóżes mię, matuleńku, za mąż wydała /Why have you, mom, married me off; VII Dajże Boże plonowało / Give us, God, a good harvest
- Publisher: PWM Edition.

A Cloud Comes, the Rain Falls / Idzie chmura, pada deszcz, Op. 51, five folk songs for mixed chorus *a cappella* (1984)
- Text : Traditional (Polish)
- Movements: IIdzie chmura, pada deszcz /A Cloud Comes, the Rain Falls; II Gdzie to jedziesz /Where are you going;, III Kiedy będzie słońce i pogoda /When it will be sunny and warm; IV Szła sierotka po wsi [An orphan walked through the village], V Czas nam do domu, dziewczyno /Time to go home, girl.
- Publisher: PWM Edition for the world.

Sundry Pieces / Utwory różne, Op. 52 for piano (1956-61, rev. 1990)
- Movements: I Recitative and Mazurka; II Two pieces, III Three Dodecaphonic Minatures, IV Quasi-Waltz.
- Unpublished

Recitatives and Ariosos 'Lerchenmusik' / Recitativa i ariosa "Lerchenmusik, Op. 53 for clarinet, cello, and piano (1984-85), 40'
- Scoring: clarinet, cello and piano
- Movements: I Lento-Largo. Ben tenuto- Molto piu mosso –Quasi Allegro ma non troppo, II Largo cantabile – dolce, III Andante moderanto man

non troppo-tranquillo- Deciso moto espressivo e ben marcato –Lento assai-tranquillissimo –Piu mosso marcatissimo energico folgorante- Molto tranquillo – Lento cantabile –dolce-tranquillissimo
- Dedicated "Der Lieben Louise Lerche-Lerchenborg gewidmet"
- Publisher: Chester Music and PWM Edition for the world.
- Publisher: Boosey & Hawkes for the world (synchronisation rights only).
- World premiere (incomplete): 7/28/1984 at the Lerchenborg Festival in Denmark by the Danish Trio: Jens Schou, cl/Svend Winslov, vlc/Rosalind Bevan, pft
- World Premiere (complete): 9/25/1985 in Warsaw by
- Jens Schou, cl/Svend Winslov, vlc/ Rosalind Bevan, pft

Five Marian Songs / Zdrowaś bądź, Maryja! Pieśni Maryjne, Op. 54, five songsfor mixed voices (SATB) *a cappella*
- Text: Jan Siedlecki (Polish)
- Movements: Matko niebieskiego Pana / Mother of the heavenly Lord; II Matko Najświętsza! / Most Holy Mother! ; III Zdrowaś bądź Maria! / Hail Mary! ; IV Ach, jak smutne / Oh, how sad; V Ciebie na wieki / You for ever
- Publisher: Boosey & Hawkes for the world.
- World Premiere: 11/13/2005 in Kraków, Poland by the Polish Radio Choir

O Domina Nostra, Meditation on the Black Madonna / O Domina Nostra - Medytacje o Jasnogórskiej Pani Naszej, **Op. 55** for soprano and organ (1982-855, revised 1990), 33'
- Text: Henryk Mikołaj Górecki (Latin)
- Dedication: "These few humble notes I have written to thank for arriving safely – again – ater a dangerous journey. Thanks to Stefania Woytowicz-Rudnicka and her husband Prof. Stanisław Rudnicki – I found my way to Prof Donat Tylman. Then OUR LADY asked OUR LORD, and She was granted her request. It happened in August 1982, composed in October 1982 (the first notes) and in February 1985 - dedicated to Stefania Woytowicz-Rudnicka."
- Scoring: solo soprano and organ
- Publisher: Chester Music and PWM Edition for the world.
- Publisher: Boosey & Hawkes for the world (Synchronisation rights only).
- World Premiere: 3/31/1985 at the 25th Poznan Musical Spring Festival, Stefania Woytowicz soprano, Michał Dąbrowski – organ
- World Premiere, revised version: 7/7/1990, Almeida Festival, London, Patricia Forbes, soprano and Chrisopher Bowers –Broadbent -organ

Pod Twoją Obronę/ Under Thy Protection, Op. 56 for eight-part mixed SATB chorus *a cappella* (1985), 8'
- Text: Traditional Marian prayer (Polish)

- Publisher: Boosey & Hawkes for the world.
- World Premiere: 5/5/2007 at the Bazylika Jasnogórska, Czestochowa, Poland, by the Polish Radio Choir / Chór Polskiego Radia / Włodzimierz Siedlik, cond.

Church Songs / Z pieśni kościelnych for mixed choir *a cappella* (1986), 74'
- Text: Liturgical (Polish)
- Publisher: Boosey & Hawkes for the world.
- Movements: I Zdrowaś bądź Maryja / Hail Mary; II Idźmy, tulmy się / Let's go, hugging III Szczęśliwy kto sobie Patrona/Fortunate is who has a Patron; IV Ludu mój, ludu/ People, my people; V Witaj Pani, Matko Matki / Welcome Lady, Mother of the Mother; VI Zawitaj, Pani świata / Hail Lady of the World; VII; Bądź pozdrowiony/ Praise be to you; VIII, Jezu Chryste, Panie miły / Jesus Christ, good Lord; IX Dobranoc/ Good night; X Matko miłościwa/ O merciful Mother; XI Pozdrawiajmy/ Let us praise; XII Święty, święty,święty /Holy, holy, holy; XIII Tysiąckroć bądź pozdrowiona/ Be praised a thousand times, XIV Krzyknijmy wszyscy/ Let us all shout; XV Witaj jutrzenko/ Hail, Morning Star; XVI Wstał Pan Chrystus/ Lord Jesus has risen; XVII Śliczny Jezu / Beautiful Jesus, XVIII Twoja cześć, chwała / Your glory and praise; XIX Boże Ojcze/ God the father; XX Krzyżu Chrystusa/ Cross of Christ. XXI Ciebie wzywamy/ We call on you
- World Premiere (partial; No. 12 and 18): April 1987, Warsaw Eucharistic Congress, Warsaw Music Academy Choir, Romuald Miazga, cond.
- World Premiere (whole): 6/23/2013 at the St. Francis of Assisi's Church, Kraków, Poland, by the Kraków Singers / Włodzimierz Siedlik, cond.

Na Anioł Pański / The Angelus Bells are Tolling, Op. 57 for mixed chorus *a cappella*(1986), 12'
- Text: Kazimierz Przerwa-Tetmajer (Polish)
- Publisher: Boosey & Hawkes for the world.
- Publisher: PWM Edition for Poland.
- World Premiere: 5/5/2007, at the Bazylika Jasnogórska, in Częstochowa, Poland, by The Polish Radio Chorus, Chór Polskiego Radia / Włodzimierz Siedlik, cond.

For You, Anne-Lill/ Dla Ciebie, Anne-Lill, Op. 58 for flute and piano (1986-90), 12'
- Dedicated "to Anne-Lill Ree"
- Publisher: Boosey & Hawkes for the world.
- Publisher: PWM Edition for Poland.
- World Premiere: 8/4/1990 at the Lerchenborg Festival, Denmark (1pm) by Anne-Lill Ree, flute and Ellen Refstrup, piano

Aria, Op. 59 an opera scene / scena operowa for tuba, piano, tam-tam and bass drum (1987), 15'
- Publisher: Boosey & Hawkes for the world.
- World Premiere: 5/28/1987 Salzburg Festival, Austria; Zdzislaw Piernik tuba, Andor Losonczy piano and Rudolf Schingerlin percussion.

Totus Tuus, Op. 60 for unaccompanied mixed chorus (1987) 11'
- Text: Maria Bogusławska (Latin)
- Dedicated (Polish): "to Holy Father John Paul II for His 3rd Pilgrimage to Mother Country"
- Publisher: Boosey & Hawkes for the world (excluding Poland, Albania, Bulgaria, China, Cuba, North Korea, Vietnam, Romania, Czech Republic, Slovakia, Hungary and the former territories of Yugoslavia and the USSR).
- Publisher: PWM Edition for the rest of the world
- World Premiere: 7/19/1987, at the Victory Square, Warsaw, by the Warsaw Academy of Catholic Theology Choir (for the visit of Pope John Paul II)

Come, Holy Spirit / Przybądź, Duchu Święty, Op. 61 for mixed chorus *a cappella* (1988), 12'
- Music Text: Based on the sequence *Veni Sancte Spiritus* (P)
- Publisher: Boosey & Hawkes for the world.
- World Premiere: 10/11/1993, in Warsaw, Poland by the Catholic Theological Academy Choir, Warsaw / Kazimierz Szymonik, cond.

Already it is Dusk / Już się zmierzcha, Op. 62 for string quartet [String Quartet No. 1] (1988), 16'
- Dedicated "to Kronos Quartet in appreciation"
- Publisher: Boosey & Hawkes for the world (excluding Poland, Albania, Bulgaria, China, Cuba, North Korea, Vietnam, Romania, Czech Republic, Slovakia, Hungary and the former territories of Yugoslavia and the USSR).
- Publisher: PWM Edition for the rest of the world, as listed above.
- World Premiere: 1/21/1989 at the Walker Arts Center, in Minneapolis, Minnesota, by the Kronos Quartet.

Good Night / Dobra Noc, Op. 63 for soprano, alto flute, piano and 3 tam-tams (composed 1988, 1990), 30'
- Text: from Shakespeare's Hamlet (English)
- Dedicated "in memoriam Michael Vyner"
- Movements: I Lento (Adagio) – Tranquillo; II Lento Tranquillissimo; III Lento-Largo, dolcissimo-cantabilissimo

- Publisher: Boosey & Hawkes for the World (excluding Poland, Albania, Bulgaria, China, Cuba, North Korea, Vietnam, Romania, Czech Republic, Slovakia, Hungary and the former territories of Yugoslavia and the USSR).
- Publisher: PWM Edition for the rest of the world.
- World premiere incomplete: 5/6/1990 at the Royal Opera House, London, by Margaret Field, soprano / London Sinfonietta
- World premiere complete: 11/4/1990 at the Queen Elizabeth Hall, London, by Nicole Tibbels, soprano / London Sinfonietta Soloists and Voices

Intermezzo for solo piano(1990) 2'
- Dedicated to "Andenken an Poul Rovsing Olsen"
- Publisher: Boosey & Hawkes for the world.
- World Premiere: 8/3/1990, Lerchenborg Festival, Denmark Rosalind Bevan, piano

Quasi una fantasia, Op. 64 (1990/91) 33' for string quartet [Second String Quartet]
- Movements: I Largo, sostenuto-mesto; II Deciso-energico, Marcatissimo sempre; III Arioso: Adagio cantabile, ma molto expressivo e molto appassionato; IV Allegro, sempre con grande passione e molto marcato
- Dedicated "To Kronos Quartet"
- Publisher: Boosey & Hawkes for the world.
- World Premiere: 10/27/1991 at the Severance Hall, Cleveland, Ohio by the Kronos Quartet
- World Premiere [ballet version]: 11/20/1998, at the Grande Auditorio Gulbenkian, Lisbon, Portugal by Itzik Galili, choreographer / Gulbenkian Ballet

Concerto-Cantata, Op. 65 for flute and orchestra (1992), 22'
- Scoring: 4(II=picc).4.4.4-6.4.3.1-perc:cyms/BD-harp-strings(16-18.14-16.12-14. 10-12.8-10) solo flute also plays alto flute.
- Dedicated "Carol Wincenc dedicato"
- Movements: I Recitative; II Arioso; III Concertino; IV Arioso e Corale
- Publisher: Boosey & Hawkes for the world.
- World Premiere: 11/28/1992 at the Concertgebouw, Amsterdam, by Carol Wincenc, flute / Radio Philharmonic Orchestra / Eri Klas, cond.

Kleines Requiem für eine Polka, Op. 66 / Małe Requiem dla pewnej Polki for piano and 13 instruments (1993), 25'
- Scoring: 1.1.1.1-1.1.1.0-perc:t.bells-pft-strings(1.1.1.1.1).
- Dedicated "Schonberg Ensembel dedicato"

- Movements: I Tranquillo; II Allegro impetuoso-marcatissimo; III Allegro-deciso assai; IV Adagio cantabile
- Publisher: Boosey & Hawkes for the world.
- World Premiere: 6/12/1993 at the Wang Zaal, Beurs van Berlage, in Amsterdam by the Schoenberg Ensemble / Reinbert de Leeuw, cond.

...songs are sung / Pieśni śpiewają, Op. 67 for string quartet [Third String Quartet](1994-2005), 56'
- Title based on a poemby Klebnikov transl. by Bieszczadowski
- Publisher: Boosey & Hawkes for the world.
- World Premiere: 10/15/2005 in the Father Kolbe Catholic Church, Bielsko-Biala, Poland by the Kronos Quartet

...songs are sung, Op. 67 (1995/2005, arr. 2010) 54'
- Scoring: realised for string orchestra by Chris Latham
- Publisher: Boosey & Hawkes for the world.

Lento cantabile for flute, violin and cello (1994), 30"
- Written for Boosey & Hawkes staff

Moment musical for piano (1994)
- Written for the wedding of Ruth Williams and Stephen Gieser

At My Window / U okienka, u mojego, for voice and piano (1995)
Text: Maria Konopnicka (Polish)
World Premiere: 5/28/1995 New York, Andrzej Bachleda, baritone and H.M. Gorecki, piano

Three Songs /Trzy pieśni, Op. 68, for voice and piano (1956/95) 10'
- Publisher: Boosey & Hawkes for the world.

Three Fragments /Trzy fragmenty do słów Stanisława Wyspiańskiego, Op. 69 for voice and piano (1995-96) 10'
- Text: Stanisław Wyspiański (Polish)
- Movements: I Jakże ja się uspokoję / How Can I calm down; II Może z mętów się dobędzie człowieka/ Perhaps from dregs a man will emerge; II Poezjo! Tyś to jest spokojna sjesta / Poetry! You are a calm siesta.
- Publisher: Boosey & Hawkes for the world.
- World Premiere: 2/23/1996 in Zakopane, Poland, by Wanda Warska (voice) Henryk Mikołaj Górecki (piano)

Valentine Piece, Op. 70 for flute solo and little bell (1996) 4'
- Publisher: Boosey & Hawkes for the world.
- World Premiere: 2/14/1996 at the Merkin Concert Hall, New York, New York, by Carol Wincenc, fl

Sanctus Adalbertus, Op. 71, Oratorio for soprano and baritone soloists, chorus and orchestra (1997-98), 55'
- Text: Psalm 115:6 (from the Vulgate, Latin); Henryk Górecki (Latin and Polish)
- Scoring: 4(IV=picc).4.4.4-4.4.4.1-perc(3):2t.bells/tam-t(lg)/BD-3harp-pft.org-strings(min:16.14.12.10.8).
- Publisher: Boosey & Hawkes for the world.
- World Premiere: 11/4/2015, at the ICE Krakow, Krakow, by Wioletta Chodowicz, Artur Rucinski / National Polish Radio Orchestra, Polish Radio Choir, Krakow Philharmonic Choir / Jacek Kasprzyk, cond.

Salve, sidus Polonorum, Op. 72 , Saint Adalbert Cantata / *Kantata o Św. Wojciechu* for large mixed chorus, two pianos, organ, and percussion ensemble (1997-2000), 25'
- Text: Liturgical (Latin), Henryk Mikołaj Górecki (Polish)
- Scoring: large mixed chorus, two pianos, organ, and percussion ensemble 3tam-t/2t.bells/2glsp/BD.
- Movements: I Per Merita Sancti Adalberti /For the Merits of St. Adalbert; II Święty Wojciechu / Saint Wojciech; III Salve Sidus Polonorum / Welcome the Star of Poles.
- Publisher: Boosey & Hawkes for the world.
- World Premiere: 6/21/2000, at the Garden Church, Hannover, Germany, by the chorus and instrumental ensemble from The National Philharmonic, Warsaw / Henryk Wojnarowski, cond.

Little Fantasia / Kleine Phantasie /Mała fantazja, Op. 73 for violin and piano (1997), 13'
- Publisher: Boosey & Hawkes for the world.
- World Premiere: 10/12/1997, Hochschule/Musik&Theater, in Hannover, Germany, by Felicitas Hofmeister, Violin Rohan de Silva, piano

Intermezzo for Wanda and Stefan Wilk for piano (1997), 3'
- Dedicated to "Wanda and Stefan Wilk"
- Composed in Los Angeles on 6 October 1997, unpublished

Five Kurpian Songs / Hej, z góry, z góry! Kóniku bury.Pięć Pieśni Kurpiowskich, Op. 75 for mixed chorus *a cappella* (1999), 24'-25'
- Text: Polish folk songs (Polish)

- Movements: I Hej, z gory / Hey, from the top; II Ciamna nocka/ Dark night/ III Wcoraj, dziwcyno/ Yesterday, girl; IV Z Torunia/ From Toruń; V Wysła burzycka/ The storm came out
- Publisher: Boosey & Hawkes for the world
- Publisher: PWM Edition for Poland.
- World Premiere: 3/30/2003 at the Polish Radio Concert Hall, Warsaw, by the Polish Radio Choir / Włodzimierz Siedlik, cond.

Lobgesang / Hymn of Praise, Op. 76 for SATB chorus *a cappella* and glockenspiel (2000), 9'
- Text: Henryk Mikołaj Górecki, after the Psalms (G)
- Publisher: Boosey & Hawkes for the world.
- World Premiere: 8/13/2000, St Johanneskirche, in Mainz by the Figuralchor Mainz / Stefan Weiler, cond.

Let Them Live and Sing / Niech nam żyją i śpiewają, song for a vocal ensemble (2000), unpublished
- World Premiere: 11/11/2000 Warsaw, Camerata Silesia, Anna Szostak, cond.

Quasi una fantasia, Op. 78, for large string orchestra, based on the second String Quartet (1990/91 arr. 2002) 40'
- Publisher: Boosey & Hawkes for the world.
- World premiere: 10/23/2002 at the Auditorio Nacional, Madrid by the Polish Radio National Symphony Orchestra / Gabriel Chmura, cond.

Dla Jasiunia / For Jasiunio, Op. 79, three little pieces for violin and piano (2003), 4'
- Publisher: Boosey & Hawkes for the world.

Why Have You Come Here, Grey Mist / Po co żeś tu przyszła Siwa Mgło, Op. 80, little pieces for two groups of violins (2003)
- World Premiere: 10/3/2003, Bielsko-Biała, 8th Polish Composers' Festival, Bielska Orkiestra Festiwalowa, Henryk Mikołaj Górecki, cond.

The Song of Katyń Families / Pieśń Rodzin Katyńskich, Op. 81 for SATB chorus *a cappella* (2004), 5'
- Text: Tadeusz Lutoborski (Polish)
- Publisher: Boosey & Hawkes for the world.
- World Premiere: 11/13/2005 in Kraków, Poland, Polish Music Festival, by the Polish Radio Choir, Włodzimierz Siedlik, cond.

Two Tristan Postludes and Chorale (Dwa Postludia Tristanowskie i Chorał) op. 82 for orchestra (2004), 21'
- Orchestrated by Mikolaj Górecki
- Scoring: perc:glsp/t.bells-harp-pft-strings(max:16.14.12.10.8; min:8.6.4.3.2).
- Publisher: Boosey & Hawkes for the world.
- World Premiere: 10/16/2016 at the Lutoslawski Concert Hall, Warsaw, Poland, by Sinfonia Varsovia / Jerzy Maksimiuk, cond.

Kyrie, Op. 83 for SATB chorus, percussion, piano and string orchestra, score and a vocal score (2004-05), 15'
- Text: Liturgical (Latin and Polish)
- Scoring: perc:t.bells/tam-t/BD-pft-strings(16.14.12.10.8).
- Publisher: Boosey & Hawkes for the world.
- World Premiere: 4/21/2014, at the St John the Baptist Cathedral, in Warsaw, Poland by the Polish Radio Choir / Orkiestra Aukso / Marek Mos, cond.

Symphony No. 4, *Tansman Episodes*, Op. 85 for orchestra with obbligato organ and piano (2006), 38'
- Scoring: 4(IV=picc).4.4.4(IV=dbn)-4.4.3.1-timp.perc(3):cyms/glsp/t.bells/BD(sm)/BD(med)/BD/(lg)-org-pft-strings(16.14.12.10.8).
- Publisher: Boosey & Hawkes for the world.
- World Premiere: 4/12/2014 at the Royal Festival Hall, London, London Philharmonic Orchestra / Andrey Boreyko, cond.

B. Film and Theater Music

- **Wieża samotności** [A Tower of Loneliness] (1959), theater music to text by Robert Ardrey (Thunder Rock)

- **Akwarium** [Aquarium] (1959), theater music to text by Andrzej Wydrzyński

- **Papierowa laleczka** [Paper Doll] (1960), song from the play Widok z mostu / A View from the Bridge, by Arthur Miller

- **Jędrek** (1969), music for a short black-and-white film (produkcja Se-ma-for)

C. Górecki's Music Used in Film

Police (1985) feature film directed by Maurice Pialat (from first movement of the Third Symphony).

Fearless (1993) feature film by Peter Weir (from the first movement of the Third Symphony).

Symphony of Sorrowful Songs (1993), experimental documentary by Tony Palmer (with the whole Third Symphony).

Kristin lavransdatter (1995) feature film directed by Liv Ullman, with excerpts from *ODomina Nostra, Beatus Vir*, and second movement from the Second Symphony).

Wit (2001), feature film directed by Mike Nicholls (from the second movement of the Third Symphony).

Basquiat – A Dance with Death / Basquiat – Taniec ze śmiercią (1996) – documentary (with a fragment of the Third Symphony).

Thieves / Ladrones (2007), feature film directed by Jaime Marqués (fragments of the Third Symphony).

The Great Beauty/ La grande bellezza (2013) with fragments of the Third Symphony.

D. Documentary Films about Górecki

Concert /Concerto (1984), documentary film directed by Krzysztof Pulikowski (with Harpsichord Concerto).

Henryk Mikołaj Górecki. Autoportret (1993), documentary film directed by Krzysztof Bukowski.

Master Composers: Henryk Górecki (1996), documentary film. VPRO, The Netherlands.

Henryk Mikołaj Górecki , Please Find (2012), documentary film by Violetta Rotter-Kozera, Silesia Films-Institute Adama Mickiewicza – TVP SA.

◎ BIBLIOGRAPHY ◎

Górecki's Lectures and Writings

Instrumenty perkusyjne, unpublished textbook, handwritten, 1950s. Composer's Archives.

Konwersatorium with H. M. Górecki dedicated to *Beatus vir*, Baranów Sandomierski, September 1979; unpublished material; edited text included in Kinga Kiwała, *Problematyka sacrum w polskiej muzyce współczesnej na podstawie wybranych utworów związanych z osobą Ojca Świętego Jana Pawła II*, M.A. thesis (Kraków: Akademia Muzyczna, 2002).

H. M. Górecki's statement during the General Discussion during the Seminar on *Aktualna sytuacja muzyki religijnej i liturgicznej w Polsce*, in*Muzyka religijna w Polsce. Materiały i studia,*ed. J. Pikulik, vol. X, Warszawa: ATK, 1988.

"Powiem Państwu szczerze..."[I will tell you frankly...] Lecture at the 2nd Musical Meeting in Baranów Sandomierski 1977, reprinted in *Vivo*, 1 (1994): 43-48.

"Już taki jestem zimny drań. Rozmowa z W. Widłakiem," [„I am such a bastard."A conversation with W. Widłak], *Vivo*, 1/11 (1994).

"Moje Podhale, Gawęda przez Marię Baliszewską uwieczniona. Zakopane, listopad 1997."[My Podhale, A Story immortalized by Maria Baliszewska, Zakopane, November 1997]. Interview with Henryk Mikołaj Górecki by Maria Baliszewska, excerpts from the recording of the Polish Radio Tatry, ed. Marcin Trzęsiok. Reprinted in *Scontri* 1 (2013).

"Conversation with USC Music Students,"3 October 1997, translated by Maja Trochimczyk, *Polish Music Journal* vol. 6, no. 2 (2003), http://pmc.usc.edu/PMJ/issue/6.2.03/GoreckiStudents.html

"Remarks on Performing the Third Symphony,"3 October 1997, translated by Maja Trochimczyk, *Polish Music Journal* vol. 6, no. 2 (2003), http://pmc.usc.edu/PMJ/issue/6.2.03/GoreckiThird.html

"Promoting Polish Music" (Speech to the Friends of Polish Music, 4 October 1997), *Polish Music Journal* vol. 6, no. 2 (2003), translated by Maja Trochimczyk http://pmc.usc.edu/PMJ/issue/6.2.03/GoreckiAMP.html

Interviews with Górecki

De Oca Ramon, Montes. "Górecki en capilla: Entrevista" [Górecki on pins and needles: An interviews. *Pauta. Cuadernos de teoria y critica musical* 13 no. 52 (October December 1994): 18-27.

Gmys, Małgorzata and Marcin. "El mundo non consiste únicamente en componer sonidos [Świat niekończy się na układaniu dźwięków], Spanish translation by Abel A. Murcia Rosiano, in *Henryk Mikołaj Górecki Concert Program* to initiate the Polish Year in Spain, Madrid, 23 October 2002, 34-45.

Gmys, Małgorzata and Marcin. "'There's More to Life than the Arranging of Sounds' – Henryk Mikołaj Górecki in Conversation with Małgorzata and Marcin Gmys," English translation of an interview published in Spanish, in Barbara Zwolska-Stęszewska, ed. *Henryk Mikołaj Górecki*. Warsaw: Instytut Adama Mickiewicza, 2008, 33-44.

Gmys, Małgorzata and Marcin."'Music? A Visitor from Another World,' (15 October 2008), Henryk Mikołaj Górecki in Conversation with Małgorzata and Marcin Gmys," in Barbara Zwolska-Stęszewska, ed. *Henryk Mikołaj Górecki*. Warsaw: Instytut Adama Mickiewicza, 2008, 47-53.

Harley, Maria Anna [Maja Trochimczyk]. "On Life and Music: A Semi-Serious Conversation." *Musical Quarterly* 82, no. 1 (Summer 1998). Chapter 3 in this volume.

Howard, Luke. "An Interview with Henryk Mikołaj Górecki." *Paris New Music Review* 2, no. 3 (Summer 1995): 4-7.

Janicka-Słysz, Małgorzata. "'Music is a Conversation.' Henryk Mikołaj Górecki Talks to Anna Wieczorek and Krzysztof Cyran (29 April 2008)," translated by Maja Trochimczyk. Chapter 7 in this volume.

Kominek, Mieczysław. "'I am always myself,' Henryk Mikołaj Górecki in conversation with Mieczysław Kominek,"*Studio* 8 (1993). Translated by Maja Trochimczyk as Chapter 2 in this volume.

Marek, Tadeusz. "Composer's Workshop: Henryk Mikołaj Górecki." *Polish Music* 3, no. 2 (1968): 25-28. Reprinted, with corrections, in Marek & Drew, 1989.

Marek, Tadeusz and David Drew. "Górecki in Interview (1968) -- and 20 Years After." *Tempo*, no. 168 (March 1989): 25-29.

Markiewicz, Leon. "Rozmowa z Henrykiem Góreckim." *Ruch Muzyczny* 6, no. 17 (1962): 6-8.

Markiewicz, Leon. "Conversation with Henryk Górecki,"*Context* 14 (Summer 1997-1998), 35-41. English translation of the 1962 interview by Anya Maslowiec.

Markiewicz, Leon. "Conversation with Henryk Górecki: Leon Markiewicz, July 1962," translated by Anna Maslowiec, *Polish Music Journal* vol. 6, no. 2 (2003), http://pmc.usc.edu/PMJ/issue/6.2.03/Gorecki1962.html. Chapter 1 in this volume.

"Muzyka w muzyce: Diskusja po referatach T. Maleckiej, L. Polonego, H. Lorkowskiej." In *Spotkania muzyczne w Baranowie II: Muzyka w muzyce [1977]*, eds. Teresa Malecka & Leszek Polony, 145-149. Kraków: PWM, 1980.

Payton, Melissa. "Górecki Visit to USC Ends on a High Note." *University of Southern California Chronicle* (20 October 1997): 12.Payton, Melissa. Reprinted in *Polish Music Journal* 6, no. 2 (2003), http://pmc.usc.edu/PMJ/issue/6.2.03/PaytonChroniclereview.html

Trochimczyk, Maja. "'Composing is a Terribly Personal Matter': Henryk Mikołaj Górecki in Conversation with Maja Trochimczyk (Katowice, April 1998)" expanded version of the 1998 interview, translated by Maja Trochimczyk, *Polish Music Journal* vol. 6, no. 2 (2003), http://pmc.usc.edu/PMJ/issue/6.2.03/GoreckiKatowice.html. Chapter 4 in this volume.

Monographs and Dissertations

Bolesławska-Lewandowska, Beata.*Górecki: Portret w Pamięci [Gorecki : A Portrait in Memory]*. Kraków: PWM, 2013.

Bylander, Cynthia E. *The Warsaw Autumn International Festival of Contemporary Music, 1956-1961: Its goals, structures, programs, and people.* Doctoral Dissertation. Columbus: Ohio State University, 1990.

Cary,Christopher W. *Darkness And Light : Henryk Górecki's Spiritual Awakening And Its Socio-Political Context.* M.M. Thesis. Gainesville, Fla.: University of Florida, 2005.

Cizmic, Maria. *Performing pain : music and trauma in 1970s and 80s Eastern Europe.* Ph. D. Dissertation, University of California, Los Angeles, 2004.

Droba, Krzysztof. *Henryka Mikołaja Góreckiego technika komponowania na wielkie zespoły instrumentalne na przykładzie 'Refrenu' i 'Canticum graduum'.* Master's Thesis. Kraków, 1971.

Galeski-Wild, Christiane. *Henryk M. Górecki et ses oeuvres symphoniques.* Master's Thesis. Strasbourg: University of Strasbourg, 1986.

Howard, Luke, B. *"A Reluctant Requiem:" The history and reception of Henryk M. Górecki's Symphony no. 3 in Britain and the United States.* Doctoral Dissertation. Ann Arbor: University of Michigan, 1997.

Henryk Mikołaj Górecki Doktor Honoris Causa Akademii Muzycznej w Krakowie.Kraków: Akademia Muzyczna, 2008.

Jakelski, Lisa Marie. *The Changing Seasons Of The Warsaw Autumn : Contemporary Music In Poland, 1960-1990.* Ph. D. Dissertation, University of California, Berkeley, Fall 2009.

Jakelski, Lisa. *Making New Music in Cold War Poland: The Warsaw Autumn Festival, 1956-1968.* University of California Press, 2016.

Jaraczewska-Mockallo, Krystyna, ed. *Henryk Mikołaj Górecki w piśmiennictwie polskim i obcym: Bibliografia.* Prace Biblioteki Głównej, no. 13. Warsaw: Akademia Muzyczna im. Fryderyka Chopina, 1994.

Jimenez, Ivan, *Textural Depth, Structural Depth, Expressive Depth: Ladders From Line To Sonority In Arvo Pärt And Henryk Mikołaj Górecki,* Ph.D. Dissertation (University of Pittsburgh, 2007).

Jurski, Marek. *Technika dźwiękowa w wybranych utworach symfonicznych Henryka Mikołaja Góreckiego.* Master's Thesis. Gdańsk: Państwowa Wyższa Szkoła Muzyczna, 1975.

Kiwała, Kinga. *Problematyka sacrum w polskiej muzyce współczesnej na podstawie wybranych utworów związanych z osobą Ojca Świętego Jana Pawła II,* M.A. Thesis. Kraków: Akademia Muzyczna, 2002.

Kopacz, Anna. *Symfonie Henryka Mikołaja Góreckiego.* Master's Thesis. Kraków: Państwowa Wyższa Szkoła Muzyczna, 1981.

Kopplin, David, F.*Aspects Of Time In The Music Of Henryk Górecki : The Sacred And The Profane.* Ph.D. Dissertation: University of California, Los Angeles—Music, 1999.

Maciejewski, Bogusław. *H. M. Górecki: His Music and Our Times.* London: Allegro Press, 1994.

Masłowiec, Anna (Anya). *Sonorism and the Polish Avant-Garde 1958-1966.* Ph.D. Dissertation,University of Sydney, 2008.

Masłowiec, Anna (Anya). *The Utmost Economy Of Musical Material : Structural Elements In The Works Of H.M. Gorecki From Refrain To Ad Matrem.* B. Mus.(Hons.) Thesis. Sydney Conservatorium of Music, 1996.

McVey, Roger Dale. *The Solo Piano works of Henryk Mikołaj Górecki.* D.M.A. Dissertation, University of Kansas, Music and Dance, 2004.

Nagórska, Aleksandra. *Trzy Symfonie Henryka Mikołaja Góreckiego.* Master's Thesis. Katowice: Państwowa Wyższa Szkoła Muzyczna, 1981.

Pociej, Bohdan. *Bycie w muzyce. Próba opisania twórczości Henryka Mikołaja Góreckiego [Being in Muisc: An Attempt at Describing the Oeuvre by Hernyk*

Mikołaj Górecki]. Katowice: Akademia Muzyczna im. Karola Szmanowskiego, 2005.

Schwarz, Victoria Leigh. *Brevity created through phrase manipulation in Henryk Mikołaj G'orecki's Miserere.* M.M. Thesis. Colorado State University, 1998.

Szklarska, Kamilla. *An Overview Of The Life, Work And Influences Of Henryk Mikołaj Górecki, With A Structural And Performance Analysis Of The Lerchenmusic, Op. 53 : A Doctoral Essay.* D.M.A. Dissertation, University of Miami, 1999.

Szymura, Justyna A.*The Marian theme in selected compositions by Henryk Mikolaj Gorecki.* M.A. Thesis. California State University, Los Angeles, 2009.

Thomas, Adrian. *Górecki.* Oxford: Clarendon Press /Oxford University Press, 1997.

Thomas, ,Adrian. *Górecki,* Polish translation by E. Gabryś. Kraków: PWM Edition, 1998.

Trochimczyk, Maja, ed. *Henryk Mikołaj Górecki.* Special Issue of the *Polish Music Journal* vol. 6, no. 2 (2003), http://pmc.usc.edu/PMJ/issue/6.2.03/contents.html

Vest, Lisa Cooper. *The discursive foundations of the Polish musical avant-garde at midcentury : aesthetics of progress, meaning, and national identity.* Ph.D. Dissertation,Bloomington: Indiana University, 2014.

Wendland, Andrzej. *Górecki. IV Symfonia Tansman Epizody: Fenomen ŻywiołTajemnica.* Łódź: Instytut Muzyki Polskiej and Stowarzyszenie Promocji Kultury im. A. Tansmana, 2016.

Wilczyński, Marek. *Percussione batteria w twórczości Henryka Mikołaja Góreckiego.* Master's Thesis. Kraków: Państwowa Wyższa Szkoła Muzyczna, 1974.

Zwolska-Stęszewska, Barbara, ed. *Henryk Mikołaj Górecki.* Warsaw: Instytut Adama Mickiewicza, 2008 (a 75th anniversary album). Includes articles by Anna Iwanicka-Nijakowska, Krzysztof Droba and Jakub Banaś, interviews with Małgorzata and Marcin Gmys, and personal impressions by Adrian Thomas, Eugeniusz Knapik, Louise Lerche-Lerchenborg, Jerzy Maksymiuk, Rafał Augustyn, David Harrington, Wojciech Michniewski, Elżbieta Chojnacka, Antoni Wit, Bohdan Pociej and Grzegorz Michalski.

Entries in Reference Works

Droba, Krzysztof. "Górecki, Henryk Mikołaj" Entry in *Encyklopedia muzyczna PWM* (efg), ed. Elżbieta Dziębowska.Kraków: PWM Edition, 1987.

Dziadek, Magdalena. "Henryk Mikołaj Górecki," entry in *Kompozytorzy Polscy 1918-2000,* vol. 2,*Biogramy,* ed. Marek Podhajski. Gdańsk and Warszawa: Akademia Muzyczna im. Fryderyka Chopina in Warsaw and Akademia Muzyczna im. Stanisława Moniuszki in Gdańsk, 2005, 264-270.

Pociej, Bohdan. "Górecki, Henryk." In *The New Grove Dictionary of Music and Musicians,* vol. 7, ed. Stanley Sadie, London: MacMillan, 1980, 539-540.

Thomas, Adrian. "Henryk Mikołaj Górecki," entry in *Musik in Geschichte und Gegenwart,* (2001).

Thomas, Adrian. "Henryk Mikołaj Górecki, entry in *The New Grove Dictionary of Music and Musicias, Second Edition, vol. 10.* London: Macmillan Publishers Ltd., 2001.

Articles, Chapters, Reviews

50lat Warszawskiej Jesieni [50 Years of the Warsaw Autumn]. Warszawa: Związek Kompozytorów Polskich; Międzynarodowy Festiwal Muzyki Współczesnej "Warszawska Jesień", 2007.

50 Lat Zwiazku Kompozytorów Polskich Warszawa: ZKP, 1995.

Alburger, Mark. "Górecki Autumn at USC." *20th Century Music* (December 1997): 24.

Augustyn, Rafał. "Henryk Mikołaj Górecki jako pedagog." *Zeszyt naukowy: Konferencja naukowa p.t. tradycje śląskiej kultury muzycznej* 5, no. 49. Wrocław: Akademia Muzyczna im. Karola Lipińskiego we Wrocławiu, 1990, 167-172.

Baculewski, Krzysztof. *Polska twórczość kompozytorska 1945-1984.* Kraków: PWM, 1987.

Banaś Jakub. "Henryk Mikołaj Górecki – Unwitting Links with the Art of Film," in Barbara Zwolska-Stęszewska, ed. *Henryk Mikołaj Górecki.* Warsaw: Instytut Adama Mickiewicza, 2008, 55-65.

Bauman-Szulakowska, Jolanta, Magdalena Dziadek & Krystyna Turek, eds. *Utwory i publikacje członków katowickiego oddziału Związek Kompozytorów Polskich.* Katowice: Związek Kompozytorów Polskich, 1994.

Bias, Iwona & Urszula Ptasińska. *Spis kompozycji oraz bibliografia prac naukowych i publicystycznuch pracowników Akademii Muzycznej w*

Katowicach. Zeszyty naukowe: Akademia Muzyczna im. Karola Szymanowskiego w Katowicach, vol. 20. Katowice, 1980.

Bocek, Ewa, Andrzej Kornecki & Krystyna Turek. *Kompozytorzy i muzykolodzy środowiska katowickiego*. Katowice: Katowickie Towarzystwo Społeczno-Kulturalne, 1982.

Budzyńska, M. "Pieśni Śpiewają."*Przewodnik Katolicki* (2007).

Chłopecki, Andrzej. "Górecki," entry in *Polska muzyka współczesna*, 2001.

Chłopecki, Andrzej. "Górecki – kompozytor kultowy,"*Polish Culture* 1 (1998).

Chłopecki, Andrzej. "Twardy Ślązak. O znaczeniu muzyki Henryka Mikołaja Góreckiego,"*Gazeta Wyborcza*, 19 September 2003.

Chomiński, Józef M. *Muzyka Polski Ludowej*. Warsaw, 1968. Chapter 7 reprinted in English as "The contribution of Polish composers to the shaping of a modern language of music," in *Polish Musicological Studies*, no. 1 (1977): 167-215.

Chomiński, Józef M . "Muzyka polska po 1956 roku." In *Polska współczesna kultura muzyna 1944-64*, ed. Elżbieta Dziębowska, 61-119. Kraków, 1968.

Chomiński, Józef M -. "Przemiany techniki kompozytorskiej w trzydziestoleciu PRL." *Muzyka* 20, no. 3 (1975): 16-27.

Timothy J. Cooley, *Making Music in the Polish Tatras: Tourists, Ethnographers, and Mountain Musicians*. Bloomington: Indiana University Press, 2005.

Derlińska-Pawlak, Danuta. "Jesień Góreckiego w Los Angeles." *Przegląd Polski* (30 October 1997): 6, 15.

Drew, David. "Górecki's Millions." *London Review of Books* 16, no. 19 (6 October 1994): 9-10.

Drew, David. CD liner notes for *Kleines Requiem fur eine Polka,* Nonesuch CD with *Kleines Requiem für eine Polka*, Op. 66; Concerto for Harpsichord & String Orchestra, Op. 40; and *Good Night*, Op. 63. Nonesuch 9 79362-2, 1996.

Droba, Krzysztof. "Dwie pieśni sakralne." In *Zeszyty naukowe zespołu analizy i interpretacji muzyki* 2. Kraków: Państwowa Wyższa Szkoła Muzyczna, 1977, 185-197.

Droba, Krzysztof. "Jeszcze o III symfonii Henryka Mikołaja Góreckiego." In *Z problemów muzyki współczesnej: Zeszyty naukowe zespołu analizy i interpretacji muzyki*. Kraków: Państwowa Wyższa Szkoła Muzyczna, 1978, 55-65.

Droba, Krzysztof. "Droga do sensu tragicznego: Jeszcze o III Symfonii Henryka M. Góreckiego." *Ruch Muzyczny* 22, no. 15 (1978): 3-4.

Droba, Krzysztof. "Wielkość-Dziwność: O III Symfonii i Koncercie klawesynowym Henryka Mikołaja Góreckiego." *Ruch Muzyczny* 24, no. 10 (1980): 7-8.

Droba, Krzysztof. "Słowo w muzyce Góreckiego." *Ruch Muzyczny* 25, no. 22 (1981): 3-4.

Droba, Krzysztof. "The Music of Henryk Mikołaj Górecki." *Music in Poland* 1, no. 39 (1984): 27-36.

Droba, Krzysztof. "Od Refrenu do Beatus Vir czyli o redukcjonizmie muzyki Henryka Mikołaja Góreckiego." In *Przemiany techniki dźwiękowej, stylu i estetyki w polskiej muzyce lat 70*, ed. Leszek Polony Kraków: PWM, 1986, , 85-97.

Droba, Krzysztof. "Jeszcze o III Symfonii Henryka Mikołaja Góreckiego."*Zeszyt Naukowy* no. 68 ed. E. Sąsiadek. Wrocław: Akademia Muzyczna we Wrocławiu, 1996.

Droba, Krzysztof. "Między wzniosłością a cierpienem, o muzyce Henryka Mikołaja Góreckiego."*Ruch Muzyczny* 25 (2008).

Droba, Krzysztof. "On the Music of Henryk Mikołaj Górecki," in Barbara Zwolska-Stęszewska, ed. *Henryk Mikołaj Górecki*. Warsaw: Instytut Adama Mickiewicza, 2008, 19-30.

Dutka, Elaine. "How USC Nabbed the Great Górecki." *Los Angeles Times* (21 September 1997): Calendar 52, 55.

Dziadek, Magdalena. "Henryk Mikołaj Górecki – źródła i spełnienia,"*Śląsk* 11 (2003).

Dywańska, Dorota. "I wszystko jest zawsze teraz: Archetyp - symbol - sacrum w 'Beatus vir' Henryk Mikołaj Górecki." In *Inspiracje w muzyce XX wieku: Filozoficzno-literackie, religijne, folklorem. Materiały Ogólnopolskiej Konferencji Muzykologicznej, Podkowa Lesna, 1993*. Warsaw: Zwiazek Kompozytorow Polskich, 1993, 177-183.

Erhard, Ludwik. *Contemporary Music in Poland*. Warsaw: Polonia, 1966.

Fisk, Josiah. "The New Simplicity: The Music of Górecki, Tavener, and Pärt." *Hudson Review* 47 (Autumn 1994): 394-412.

Fulkerson, James. "Górecki's Third Symphony is a Transcendent Experience." In *Companion to Contemporary Musical Thought*, vol. 2, eds. John Paynter, Tim Howell, Peter Seymour, and Richard Orton. London: Routledge, 1992, 752-755.

Gąsiorowska, Małgorzata. "Symfonia pieśni żałosnych." *Ruch Muzyczny* 22, no. 3 (1978): 3-5.

Gąsiorowska, Małgorzata. Liner notes for Henryk Mikołaj Górecki, Schwann LP, VMS 1615 (1983).

Gąsiorowska, Małgorzata. "Czas zatrzymany Henryka Góreckiego" [Stopped time of Henryk Gorecki] *Ruch Muzyczny* 27, no. 25 (1983): 3-4.

Ginell, Richard, S. "Los Angeles: USC Symphony: Górecki Symphony No. 3" (reprinted from the *American Record Guide*), *Polish Music Journal* 6, no. 2 (2003), http://pmc.usc.edu/PMJ/issue/6.2.03/GinellAmerRecGuide.html

Gmys, Marcin. "Czarne kwiaty. Henryk Mikołaj Górecki (1933-2010)."*De Musica* 4 (2011).

Maciej Gołąb, *Musical Modernism in the Twentieth Century*, translated by Wojciech Bońkowski. Franfurt am Mein: Peter Lang, 2015.

Górczycka, Monika. "Diagramy H. Góreckiego." *Ruch Muzyczny* 5, no. 21 (1961): 8.

"Górecki, Henryk." *Current Biography Yearbook* 55 (May 1994): 21-25.

Hall, Alan. "Schnittke and Górecki." *Musical Times* 130 (June 1989): 360-361.

Harley, James. "Recent Górecki discs." *Tempo* no. 187 (December 1993): 48-50.

Harley, James. "Recent Górecki." *Tempo* no. 194 (October 1995): 50-52.

Harley, James. "The Górecki Phenomenon: Beyond the Marketing to the Music." *Sonances* (November 1996).

Harley, James. "Górecki Autumn at USC." *MusicWorks* no. 70 (Winter 1998): 49-50.

Harley, James. "Chartin the extremes: Performance Issues in the Music of Henryk Górecki, "*Tempo*no. 211 (January 2000): 2-7.

Harley, Maria Anna [Maja Trochimczyk]. "To Be with God: Catholic Composers and the Mystical Experience." *Contemporary Music Review* 12, no. 2 (1995): 125-145.

Harley, Maria Anna [Maja Trochimczyk]. *Space and Spatialization in Contemporary Music: History and Analysis, Ideas and Implementations*. Ph. D. Dissertation, McGill University School of Music, Montreal, Canada, 1994). Los Angeles: Moonrise Press, 2011.

Harley, Maria Anna [Maja Trochimczyk]. "The Polish School of Sonorism and its European Context," in *Crosscurrents and Counterpoints: Offerings in Honor of Bengt Hambraeus at 70*, ed. Per Broman, Nora A. Engebretsen, and Bo Alphonce. Gothenburg: University of Gothenburg, Sweden, 1998: 62-77.

Harley, Maria Anna [Maja Trochimczyk]. "Górecki and the Paradigm of the Maternal." *Musical Quarterly* 82, no. 1 (Summer 1998).

Harley, Maria Anna [Maja Trochimczyk]. "Spatiality of Sound and Stream Segregation in Twentieth-Century Instrumental Music," *Organized Sound* 3, no. 2 (1998): 147-166. (Includes *Genesis* and Second Symphony).

Hewitt, Ivan. "Singing a New Song." *Classic CD*, no. 34 (March 1993): 36-38.

Hillert, Richard. "The liturgical choral music of Henryk Górecki and Arvo Pärt." *Cross Accent: Journal of the Association of Lutheran Church Music*, no. 7 (January 1996): 16-25.

Homma, Martina. "Das Minimale und das Absolute: Die Musik Henryk Mikołaj Góreckis von der Mitte der sechziger Jahre bis 1985." *Musiktexte* 44 (1992): 40-59.

Homma, Martina. "Reichlich Theorie und Wissenschaft: Polnische Musik und Musiktheorie." In *Deutsch-polnische Ansichten zur Literatur und Kultur 1991*, 280-287. Darmstadt: Deutsches Polen-Institut, 1989.

Howard, Luke B. "Motherhood, Billboard, and the Holocaust: Perceptions and Receptions of Górecki's Symphony No. 3,"*The Musical Quarterly* 82, no. 1 (spring 1998): 131-159.

Howard, Luke B. "'Laying the Foundation:' The Reception of Górecki's Third Symphony, 1977-1992"*Polish Music Journal*, vol. 6 no. 2 (2003). http://www.usc.edu/dept/polish_music/PMJ/issue/6.2.03/Howard.html

Howard Luke B. "Henryk M. Górecki's Symphony No. 3 (1976) as a Symbol of Polish Political History."*The Polish Review* 52, no. 2 (2007): 215-222.

Iwanicka-Nijakowska, Anna. "A Biographical Note," in Barbara Zwolska-Stęszewska, ed. *Henryk Mikołaj Górecki*. Warsaw: Instytut Adama Mickiewicza, 2008, 3-13.

Jacobson, Bernard. *A Polish Renaissance*. London: Phaidon Press, 1996.

Jakelski, Lisa. "Górecki's Scontri and Avant-Garde Music in Cold War Poland," *The Journal of Musicology* 26, no. 2 (Spring 2009): 205-239.

Jaraczewska-Mockałło, Krystyna, ed. *Henryk Mikołaj Górecki w piśmiennictwie polskim i obcym: Bibliografia* [Henryk Mikołaj Górecki in Polish and Foreign Literature: A Bibliography]. Warsaw: F. Chopin Academy of Music, 1994.

Jarociński, Stefan. "Polish Music after World War II." *Musical Quarterly* 51, no. 1 (1965): 244-258.

Jarociński, Stefan ed. *Polish Music*. Warsaw: Państwowe Wydawnictwo Naukowe, 1965.

Jurski, Marek. "Kantata op. 26 Henryka Mikołaja Góreckiego na organy — technika dźwiękowa i ekspresja." In *Organy i muzyka organowa*, ed. Paweł Podejko, 227-238. Gdańsk, 1975.

Kaczyński, Tadeusz and Bohdan Pociej. "Dwugłos o Refrenie." *Ruch Muzyczny* 10, no. 23 (1966): 6-7.

Kiwała, Kinga. "Wokół muzyki chóralnej *a capella* Henryka Mikołaja Góreckiego, *Przybądź Duchu Święty* op. 61,"*Pro Musica Sacra* 12 (2014).

Kopplin, David. "The Concept of Time in the Music of Henryk Górecki,"*Polish Music Journal* vol. 6, no. 2 (2003), http://pmc.usc.edu/PMJ/issue/6.2.03/Kopplin.html

Kostka,Violetta. "Elementy narodowe w muzyce Henryka Mikolaja Góreckiego," In: *Wspólczesna muzyka estońska w kontekście muzyki europejskiej*, ed. by Monika Bakowska-Lajming. Gdańsk, 2002.

Kozinn, Allan. "Górecki: Symphony No. 3." *Opus* 3, no. 1 (December 1986): 34.

Lebrecht, Norman. "Publishers Feud over Popular Pole." *Classical Music Magazine* 16, no. 2 (27 March 1993): 5.

Lee, Jan Patrick. *Musical Life and Sociopolitical Change in Warsaw, Poland: 1944-1960*. Doctoral Dissertation. Chapel Hill: University of North Carolina, 1979.

Lindstedt, Iwona. *Dodekafonia i serialism w twórczości kompozytorów polskich XX wieku* [Dodecaphony and Serialism in the Oeuvre of Polish Composers of the 20th Century]. Lublin: Polihymnia, 2001.

Lindsteadt, Iwona. Sonorystyka w *w twórczości kompozytorów polskich XX wieku* [Sonorism in the Oeuvre of Polish Composers of the 20th Century]. Warsaw: Wydawnictwa Uniwersytetu Warszawskiego, 2010.

Lissa, Zofia. *Music in People's Poland: Sketchesand Monographs*. Warsaw: Polish Interpress Agency, 1973.

MacDonald, Ian. "Górecki." *Classic CD*, no. 27 (August 1992): 51.

MacDonald, Ross. "Górecki: Symphony No. 3." *Classical Music Magazine* 16, no. 1 (February 1993): 38.

Maciejewicz, Dorota. "Między jednością a różnorodnością: Analizując 'Muzyczkę II' Henryka Mikołaja Góreckiego." *Muzyka* 39, no. 3 (1994): 89-104.

Malecka, Teresa. "O koncercie klawesynowym Góreckiego." In *Mieczysławowi Tomaszewskiemu w 60-lecie urodzin*, ed. T. Malecka. Kraków, 1984, 108-113.

Malecka, Teresa. „Między symfonią a pieśnią. Próba analizy integralnej *Symfonii pieśni żałosnych* H. M. Góreckiego," in:*Muzyka w kontekście kultury*, ed. M. Janicka – Słysz, T. Malecka, K. Szwajgier (Kraków: Akademia Muzyczna, 2001), 798.

Malecka, Teresa. „III Symfonia i Beatus vir – faza szczytowa w drodze twórczej Góreckiego,"in*Dzieło muzyczne i jego rezonans,* ed. Anna Nowak (Bydgoszcz: Akademia Muzyczna, 2008).

Malecka, Teresa. "O rezonowaniu historii w życiu i twórczości Henryka Mikołaja Góreckiego in *Dzieło muzyczne i jego rezonans,* ed. Anna Nowak (Bydgoszcz: Akademia Muzyczna, 2008).

Malecka, Teresa. "Henryk Mikołaj Górecki. Styl późny," *Res Facta Nova,* 2010, 11 (20), 135-150.

Malecka, Teresa. "Henryk Mikołaj Górecki wobec myśli Jana Pawła II,"*Ruch Muzyczny* 9 (2011).

March, Ivan, Edward Greenfield & Robert Layton. "Górecki, Henryk." In *The Penguin Guide to Compact Disks and Cassettes,* new ed. London: Penguin Books, 1994.

Marek, Tadeusz. "The Copernican Year in Polish Music." *Polish Music* 8, no. 1 (1973): 3-9.

Markiewicz, Leon. "O Zderzeniach, radości i . . . katastrofiźmie." *Ruch Muzyczny* 4, no. 21 (1960): 10-11.

Markiewicz, Leon"*Choros I* Henryka Góreckiego." *Ruch Muzyczny* 8, no. 21 (1964): 8-9.

Markiewicz, Leon. "*Elementy* H. Góreckiego." *Ruch Muzyczny* 9/17 (1965): 9.

Markiewicz, Leon. "Bolesław Szabelski on his 70th Birthday." *Polish Music* 2, no. 1 (1967): 10-14.

Markiewicz, Leon. "Główne tendencje twórcze w katowickim środowisku kompozytorskim." *Muzyka* 19, no. 2 (1974): 22-30.

Maslowiec, Anna (Anya). "'The Utmost Economy of Musical Material:' Structural Elements in the Works of Górecki from *Refrain* (1965) to *Ad matrem* (1971),"*Contact*14 (1999). Rreprinted in *Polish Music Journal* vol. 6, no. 2 (2003),http://pmc.usc.edu/PMJ/issue/6.2.03/Maslowiec.html

McLellan, Joseph. "Górecki's Symphonies and Sympathies." *Washington Post* (5 March 1995).

Mellers, Wilfrid. "Round and About Górecki's Symphony No. 3." *Tempo,* no. 168 (March 1989): 22-24.

Michalski, Grzegorz, Ewa Obniska, Henryk Swolkień & Jerzy Waldorff. *Dzieje muzyki polskiej.* Warsaw: Interpress Publishers, 1977

Miller, Thomas A. "Reviews: Górecki." *Absolute Sound* 18 (Winter 1993): 181.

Mirka, Danuta."Góreckiego Musica Geometrica,"*Dysonanse* 1 (1998), reprinted in English translation as"Górecki's Musica Geometrica,"*The Musical Quarterly* 87, no. 2 (summer 2004): 305-332.

Moody, Ivan. "Górecki: The Path to the Miserere." *Musical Times*, 133 (1992): 283-284.

Moody, Ivan. "Górecki, Pärt, Tavener." *Gramophone* 72 (December 1994): 137.

Moor, Paul. "Górecki: Already It Is Dusk." *Musical America* 111, no. 6 (November-December 1991): 46-47.

Morrison, Dave. "Henryk Górecki: Miserere." *WIRE Magazine* (January 1995): 56-57.

Morton, Brian. "Symphony No. 3." In *The Blackwell Guide to Recorded Contemporary Music*. Oxford: Blackwell, 1996, 238-244.

Ochlewski, Tadeusz, ed. *An Outline History of Polish Music*. Warsaw, 1979.

Palmer, Tony. "The Unknown Hero who Outsells Madonna." *YOU Magazine* (4 April 1993): 14-21.

Patkowski, Józef and Anna Skrzyńska, eds., *Horyzonty Muzyki*, Biblioteka Res Facta, vol. 1. Kraków, PWM, 1970.

Perlez, Jane. "Henryk Górecki." *New York Times Magazine* (27 February 1994): 32-35.

Pisarenko, Ogierd. "Ta sławna płyta." *Ruch Muzyczny* 37, no. 9 (1993): 7.
Pociej, Bohdan. "Epitafium Henryka Góreckiego." *Ruch Muzyczny* 3, no. 6 (1959): 10-13.

Pociej, Bohdan. "Zderzenia Henryka Góreckiego." *Ruch Muzyczny* 4, no. 18 (1960): 7.
Pociej, Bohdan. "Ad matrem Henryka Mikołaja Góreckiego." *Ruch Muzyczny* 17, no. 3 (1973): 3-5.

Pociej, Bohdan. „Kosmos, tradycja, brzmienie" [Cosmos, Tradition and Sonority] *Ruch Muzyczny* 15 (1973): 3-5.

Pociej, Bohdan. "Recitatywy i ariosa Henryka Mikołaja." *Ruch Muzyczny* 30, no. 3 (1986): 6-7.

Potter, Keith. "Górecki: Symphony No. 3." *BBC Music Magazine* 3, no. 3 (November 1994): 74.

Pysh, Gregory M. "The Choral Music of Henryk Górecki." *Choral Journal* (December 1997): 33-38.

Rapoport, Paul. "Górecki: Symphony No. 3." *Fanfare* 7, no. 1 (September-October 1983): 188-189.

Rappoport-Gelfand, Lidia. "Sonorism: problems of style and form in modern Polish Music." tr. Jennifer M. Goheen, *Journal of Musicological Research* 4, nos. 3/4 (1983): 399-415.

Rappoport-Gelfand, Lidia -. *Musical Life in Poland: The Postwar Years 1945-1977.* tr. Irina Lasoff. New York: Gordon and Breach, 1991.

Rhein, John von. "Chicago Choruses: Górecki Miserere." *American Record Guide* 57, no. 4 (July-August 1994): 41.

Ross, Alex. "Górecki." *Fanfare* 17, no. 2 (November-December 1993): 245-247.

Sandow, Greg. "Celebrating the Surprises That Are Górecki's Gift." *Los Angeles Times* (1 October 1997): F3 , *Polish Music Journal* vol. 6, no. 2 (2003), http://pmc.usc.edu/PMJ/issue/6.2.03/SandowLATimes.html

Scott, Patrick.*Songs of Stones.*Program notes for all-Górecki concert, "Songs of Stones" by Jacaranda: Music on the Edge, Santa Monica, November 19-20, 2011.

Schwarz, K. Robert. "Symphony No. 3." *Rolling Stone* (29 April 1993): 65.

Siedlik, Włodzimierz, "Henryk Mikołaj Górecki i jego muzyka,"*Pro Musica Sacra* 10 (2012).

Silverton, Mike. "Górecki: Already It Is Dusk." *Fanfare* 15, no. 3 (January-February 1992): 222-223.

Silverton, Mike.. "Góecki [sic]: Symphony No. 3." *Fanfare* 16, no. 1 (September-October 1992): 247.

Silverton, Mike."Górecki, Bryars, Satie, Milhaud." *Fanfare* 17, no. 6 (July-August 1994): 290-291.

Šišková, Hana. "When music meets nation: Henryk Mikołaj Górecki's music as an example," *Musicologica,* online journal, 2015. http://www.musicologica.cz/studie-brezen-2012/when-music-meets-nation-henryk-mikolaj-gorecki-s-music-as-an-example.

Stearns, David Patrick. "Górecki: Symphony No. 3." *Stereo Review* 57 (September 1992): 93, 96.

Stegemann, Michael. CD Liner note to Henryk Mikołaj Górecki, Koch-Schwann CD, 3-1041-2 (1993).

Stewart, Michael. "Górecki." *Gramophone* 70 (April 1993): 44, 47.

Strickland, Edward. "Górecki, Symphony No. 3." *Fanfare* 11, no. 1 (September-October 1987): 205-206.

Swed, Mark. "The Three Holy Minimalists." *Los Angeles Times* (8 January 1995): Calendar.

Swed, Mark. "Górecki Festival Begins With Searing Early, Late Works." *Los Angeles Times* (2 October 1997).

Swed, Mark. "Górecki's Third Is All His Own: Music Review" *Los Angeles Times*, 6 October 1997), reprinted in *Polish Music Journal* vol. 6, no. 2 (2003), http://pmc.usc.edu/PMJ/issue/6.2.03/SwedLATimes.html

Swed, Mark. "So Ver Still but Moving: Music Review" (Third String Quartet). *Los Angeles Times* (20 February 2007), Calendar section.

Swed, Mark. "Henryk Górecki's Quirky, Final Major Musical Statement,*"Los Angeles Times*, 18 January 2015, http://www.latimes.com/entertainment/la-et-cm-la-phil-review-20150119-column.html.

Sykes, Debra. "Henryk Mikołaj Górecki." *Musicworks* no. 62 (1995): 52-53.

Sykes, Debra. "From Monks to Modernity: Spiritual seekers canonize a Polish avant-gardist." *The Georgia Straight* (Vancouver paper, March 3-10, 1995).

Szczurko Elżbieta. "Aspekty transcendencji w tworczości Henryka Mikołaja Góreckiego I Krzysztofa Pendereckiego,"*Studia Bydgoskie* 3 (2003).

Taylor, Tim. "Górecki." *American Record Guide* 54, no. 6 (November-December 1991): 68.

Taylor, Tim."Górecki." *American Record Guide* 56, no. 6 (November-December 1993): 111.

Thomas, Adrian. "The Music of Henryk Mikołaj Górecki: The First Decade." *Contact* 27 (Autumn 1983): 10-20.

Thomas, Adrian. "A Pole Apart: The Music of Górecki Since 1965." *Contact* 28 (Autumn 1984): 20-31.

Thomas, Adrian. "Henryk Mikołaj Górecki." Liner notes to H. Górecki, Olympia CD, OCD 313 (1988).

Thomas, Adrian. *Henryk Mikołaj Górecki*. Promotional brochure. London: Boosey & Hawkes, 1988.

Thomas, Adrian. "Górecki: A Place at the Top." *Classic CD*, 32 (1992): 20-22.

Thomas, Adrian. "Granieten monumentaliteit en heldere lucht." In *Holland Festival Almanak*, 52-58. Amsterdam, 1993.

Thomas, Adrian. "Górecki: Symphony No. 3." Liner notes for Henryk Górecki: Symphony No. 3, EMI CD 5 55368 2 (1995).

Thomas, Adrian. "'Intense Joy and Profound Rhythm:' An Introduction to the Music of Henryk Mikołaj Górecki"*Polish Music Journal* vol. 6, no. 2 (2003),http://pmc.usc.edu/PMJ/issue/6.2.03/ThomasIntro.html

Thomas, Adrian. "Henryk Górecki: Polish Pioneer," introductory essay and program notes in the *Total Immersion: Henryk Górecki* Program Book for BBC Symphony Orchestra Festival, 2015.

Thomas, Adrian. "On Reflection" Introduction to a 7-CD set *Henryk Górecki – A Nonesuch Retrospective* (January, 2016).

Thomas, Adrian. "On Polish Music..." blog with many entries about current events, festivals, concerts, and recordings of Górecki. https://onpolishmusic.com

Thomas, Adrian. *Polish Music since Szymanowski* (Cambridge and New York: Cambridge University Press, 2005).

Thomas, Adrian. "Boundaries and Definitions: The Compositional Realities of Polish Sonorism," *Muzyka* 53, no. 1 (2008): 7-15.

Tompkins, David G. *Composing the Party Line: Music and Politics in Early Cold War Poland and East Germany* (Purdue University Press, 2013).

Trochimczyk, Maja "Bogurodzica Reborn: A Medieval Anthem in Contemporary Polish Music," in *Mittelalter-Sehnsucht?*, ed. Dorothea Redepenning and Annette Kreutziger-Herr. Kiel, Germany: Wissenschafts-verlag Vauk Kiel KG, 2000, 131-152.

Trochimczyk, Maja, ed. "Reviews of the Górecki Autumn Festival,"*Polish Music Journal* 6, no. 2 (2003),http://pmc.usc.edu/PMJ/issue/6.2.03/GoreckiReviews.html

Trochimczyk, Maja, ed. *Program of "Górecki Autumn" Festiva.l Polish Music Journal* 6, no. 2 (2003)http://pmc.usc.edu/PMJ/issue/6.2.03/Goreckiprogram.html

Trochimczyk, Maja. "Henryk Mikołaj Górecki at 70,"*Polish Music Journal* vol. 6, no. 2 (2003),http://pmc.usc.edu/PMJ/issue/6.2.03/trochimczyk6_2.html

Trochimczyk, Maja. "Witold Lutosławski and *musique concrète:* The Technique of Sound Planes and its Sources," in *Lutosławski: Music and Legacy*, Edited by Stanisław Latek and Maja Trochimczyk. (Montreal: Polish Institute of Arts and Sciences in Canada; Cracow: Polish Academy of Arts and Sciences, 2014).

Tyrała, Robert. "Kulturowy i religijny kontekst twórczości kompozytroskiejHenryka Mikołaja Góreckiego (zm. 2010). Niebiańskie polany jako przesłanie jego kompozytorskiej twórczości." *Pro Musica Sacra* 9 (2011).

Vroon, Donald. "Górecki: Symphony of Plaintive Songs (No. 3)." *American Record Guide* 51, no. 3 (May-June 1988): 32-33.

Vroon, Donald. "Górecki: Symphony of Sorrowful Songs." *American Record Guide* 52, no. 4 (July-August 1989): 46.

Vroon, Donald. "Górecki: Symphony of Sorrowful Songs." *American Record Guide* 55, no. 4 (July-August 1992): 136-137.

Walsh, Michael. "Top of the Pops: A Symphony?" *Time*, U.S. Edition (8 March 1993): 64.

Walsh, Michael. "Not Just a One-Tune Man." *Time*, U.S. Edition (20 September 1993): 84.

Warnaby, John. "Henryk Mikołaj Górecki." *Musical Opinion* 116 (4/1993):138.

Warnaby, John. "The Essential Górecki." *Tempo* no. 185 (June 1993): 49-50.

Waskowska, Teresa. "Sukcesy muzyki polskiej w Danii." *Ruch Muzyczny* 28, no. 22 (October 1984): 23-24.

Whealton, Stephen Allen. "Górecki: Symphony No. 3." *American Record Guide* 46, no. 6 (September 1983): 23.

Wierzbicki, James . "Henryk Górecki," *St. Louis Post-Dispatch*, July 7, 1991.

Wilk Wanda. "Behind the Scenes" (reprinted from News of Polonia, 22 October 1997) *Polish Music Journal* vol. 6, no. 2 (2003), http://pmc.usc.edu/PMJ/issue/6.2.03/WilkPolonia.html

Witherden, Barry. "Górecki." *Classic CD* no. 65 (September 1995): 78.

Wright, David. "Henryk Mikołaj Górecki." *Musical Times* 134 (2/1993): 82.

Zagorski, William. "Górecki." *Fanfare* 14, no. 5 (May-June 1991): 116.

Zuziak Władysław. "Związki twórczości HenrykaMikołaja Góreckiegozmyśląjana Pawła II." *Pro Musica Sacra* 9 (2011).

◎ NOTES ABOUT CONTRIBUTORS ◎

Krzysztof Cyran, born 1973, in Kraków, Poland, graduated with honors from the Academy of Music in Kraków in Theory of Music and Classical Guitar. He went on to complete his Ph.D. there in Theory of Music – his doctoral dissertation was entitled „Canon and Postmodernism in Polish Religious Music at the Turn of the 20th to the 21th Century." The subject was Polish contemporary religious music around year 2000, with the examples chosen from oeuvre by K.Penderecki, H.M. Górecki, W. Kilar, P. Szymański, P. Łukaszewski, P. Mykietyn and others. He currently works as an assistant lecturer at the Faculty of Musical Composition, Interpretation and Education at the Academy of Music in Kraków. He specializes in contemporary Polish music as well as Polish folk music – both traditional and new. He has also been interested in the history of Western church music. Dr. Cyran has published scholarly research in Polish and English, and he regularly attends international and interdisciplinary conferences (Great Britain, Lithuania, Poland). Other activities include concert presentations for children, in cooperation with the Kraków Philharmonic. Occasionally, he also performs classical repertoire as a guitarist. In 2016 he was awarded the Medal of Merit for Polish Culture.

Małgorzata Gmys completed cultural studies in 1989-92 in Wrocław, and in 1997 received her M.A. in musicology from the Adam Mickiewicz University in Poznań. She worked for the Henryk Wieniawski Music Society in Poznań, organizing many concerts and competitions. In 1998-2001, she also helped organize four theatre festivals entitled "Malta." Since January 2001, she has worked at the Polish Radio 2 classical music station, organizing annual music festivals and coordinating the work of the radio ensembles. Since 2001 to 2010, she also served as an assistant to Henryk Mikołaj Górecki and accompanied him on several travels. In 2008-2013, upon the invitation of Mariusz Treliński, she was the representative of the artistic director of the Grand Theater- National Opera. Since 2014, she has worked in the Office of Culture and National Heritage for the President of the Republic of Poland.

Dr hab. Marcin Gmys (b. 1970) is a Polish musicologist, music critic, professor and Vice Director of the Institute of Musicology at the Adam Mickiewicz University in Poznań. He finished his PhD dissertation in 2001 and serves as editor-in-chief of the journal *Res Facta Nova: Texts about Contemporary Music*; he is also the president of Association De Musica, Vice President of the Program Council for Music at the Institute of Music and Dance in Warsaw, and the president of the editorial committee of the

Complete Works of Feliks Nowowiejski, initiated in 2016 in Kraków by PWM. His main specialty is the history of music from the 19th to the 21st centuries and he is also interested in the borderlands of music and other arts. He regularly writes for the Grand Theater-National Opera, National Fyderyk Chopin Institute, as well as for the literary journal *Zeszyty Literackie*. He also occasionally collaborates with the Second Program of the Polish Radio as a co-author of music broadcasts, for instance the cycles of *Romanticism Known and Unknown; Mieczysław Karłowicz – Singer of Modernist Melancholy,* and *Gustav Mahler. My Times will Come.* Dr. Gmys is the author of over 200 publications, both scholary and popular, and of a series of books: *Poetyka teatru operowego Ferruccia Busoniego* [Poetics of Ferruccio Busoni's operatic theatre] (2005); *Mieczysław Karłowicz: An Eulogist of Modernist Melancholy* (2007); *Technika teatru w teatrze i jej operowe konkretyzacje* [The Technique of Theater in Theater and its Operatic Embodiments] (1999); *The Music of Liszt and Mahler: Interpretation, Context, Reinterpretation* (2013); and *Karol Kurpiński i Romantyczna Europa* (Warsaw, 2015). His "habilitationschrift" book *Harmonie i dysonanse: Muzyka Młodej Polski wobec innych sztuk* [Harmonies and dissonances: Young Poland music and other arts] (2012) received the Chalice Award from the President of the Adam Mickiewicz University in Poznań as the best scholarly work of 2013; two years later this book received the main prize in the competition of the National Center of Culture as the best scholarly book about Polish music.

Dr. Luke B. Howard, a native of Australia, holds M.A. in musicology from Brigham Young University (1994) and Ph.D. in musicology from the University of Michigan (1997) with a dissertation on the history and reception of Henryk M. Górecki's Third Symphony. Dr. Howard has served on the faculties of the Department of Music at Minnesota State University Moorhead and the Conservatory of Music at the University of Missouri Kansas City. He joined the faculty of Brigham Young University in 2002 as an Associate Professor in the School of Music. Dr. Howard's research focuses on appropriations of classical music in popular culture, and he has published his work in major journals including the *Musical Quarterly, Paris New MusicReview, Periphery,* and *Context.* He contributed an essay to the groundbreaking volume *Postmodern Music: Postmodern Thought,* and has presented his research at national and international conferences in England, Finland, Trinidad, Australia, and throughout the United States. He is a recording reviewer with *American Music* and has written book reviews for *Polish Music Journal* and *Musicology Australia.* He is also an active program annotator and pre-concert presenter.

Dr. Kinga Kiwała is a music theorist, M.A. in Philosophy, assistant professor in the Department of Musical Work Theory and Interpretation at the Academy of Music in Kraków. Her research interests focus on contemporary Polish music, issues of the 'sacred' in music, as well as philosophy and aesthetics of music (especially phenomenology). Her studies are of an interdisciplinary nature – in these research projects, she focuses on presenting relations between music and word, music and philosophy, aesthetics, music and other arts. In 2013, she published a monograph, *A Symphonic Work in the Perspective of Polish Phenomenological Concepts. Lutosławski. Górecki*. Her output also includes several dozen research articles. She participated in conferences and symposiums in Poland and abroad. Dr. Kiwała is a scholarship holder from the Minister of Science and Higher Education (Scholarship for Outstanding Young Scientists), and she received several awards for her scholarly activities. She has also served as a member of concert program committees and juries.

Mieczysław Kominek serves as the Director of the Polish Music Information Centre at the Polish Composers' Union in Warsaw, Poland, and oversees the Union's library, including many manuscripts and documents of contemporary Polish composers. He published many articles and several books on the history of recording industry in Poland, as well as numerous reviews and program notes for contemporary music concerts.

Prof. dr hab. Teresa Malecka is the head of the Documentation Center of Kraków Composers' Output at the Academy of Music in Kraków and editor-in-chief of a scientific journal *Theory of Music. Studies, Interpretations, Documentations* edited by the Academy of Music in Kraków. Research areas: Russian music (Rimski-Korsakov, Mussorgski); contemporary Polish music (Penderecki, Górecki, Bujarski); theory of music: word–sound relationships and relationships between the arts seen from a semiotic perspective. Prof. Malecka is the author of books: *Słowo, obraz i dźwięk w twórczości Modesta Musorgskiego* [Word, Image and Sound in Musorgsky's output] (1996), *Zbigniew Bujarski. Twórczość i osobowość*, [Zbigniew Bujarski. Output and Personality] (2006), as well as a number of articles in Polish and European publications. She is also the organizer and the participant of international congresses in Poland and abroad. Member of the Polish Composer's Union: Societe Internationale d'Histoire Comparee du Theatre, de l'Opera et du Ballet; the Artistic Board of Beethoven Festivals; the Board of the European Centre of Krzysztof Penderecki's Music. Since 2010 she has also served as a member of the Council of National Centre of Science; since 2014 - of the the Scientific Board of National Museum in Kraków and in 2014 – 2017 - of the jury of Hieronim Feicht Competition for the best musicological dissertation.

Leon Markiewicz is a Polish musicologist, researcher and college professor. In 1979-1981 he served as the president of the Karol Szymanowski Academy of Music in Katowice, where he started his music studies in 1949-1955. He received his Ph.D. in 1970 from the Institute of Musicology at the

University of Warsaw, and his "habilitation" degree in 1997 from the Institute of Arts of the Polish Academy of Sciences in Warsaw – based on a book about Bolesław Szabelski. Markiewicz published any books and articles extensively about Polish composers (Szabelski, Grzegorz Fitelblerg, Michał Spisak, and Karol Szymanowski) as well as music education issues, and the history of the Silesian music culture.

Anna (Anya) Maslowiec completed her Honours Degree in Musicology in 1995 at the Conservatorium of Music in Sydney, and her postgraduate work in 2009, under the supervision of Professor Peter McCallum, with a project on contemporary Polish music. Her research area is the sonoristic movement in Polish music after 1945. Her work appeared in *Contact* and *Polish Music Journal*, as well as *Ruch Muzyczny*.

Maja Trochimczyk, Ph.D., is a music historian, poet, photographer, and non-profit director born in Poland and living in California (www.trochimczyk.net). She published six books on music: *After Chopin: Essays in Polish Music, The Music of Louis Andriessen, Polish Dance in Southern California, A Romantic Century in Polish Music, Lutoslawski: Music and Legacy, and* most recently *Frédéric Chopin: A Research and Information Guide* (rev. ed., 2015). She also published 27 peer-reviewed articles in such journals as *Musical Quarterly, Computer Music Journal, Leonardo, American Music,* the *Polish Review, Polish American Studies,* and *Muzyka,* as well as 18 book chapters in edited volumes on Chopin, Lutoslawski, women composers, Polish music after 1945, and ecomusicology. Hundreds of her articles and poems appeared in English, Polish, as well as in German, French, Chinese, Spanish and Serbian translations. She also published six books of poetry. Dr. Trochimczyk taught history at McGill University and the University of Southern California, and read papers at over 80 national and international conferences (in Poland, France, Germany, Hungary, U.K., Canada, and the U.S.) She received awards and fellowships from the American Council of Learned Societies, Social Sciences and Humanities Research Council of Canada, USC, McGill University, MPE Fraternity, Polish American Historical Association (Swastek Award, Creative Arts Prize, and Distinguished Service Prize), City and County of Los Angeles, and Poland's Ministry of Culture (medal for the promotion of Polish culture abroad). The founder of Moonrise Press, Trochimczyk also serves as Secretary and Communications Director for the Polish American Historical Association.

Andrzej Wendland is a musician, musicologist, editor and publicist. A graduate of the Instrumental Departmetn of the Academy of Music in Łodz, he also studied music theory and composition. He won many prizes at international competitions as a performer and composer in Poland, Italy and

Greece. In 1980-1986, Wendland served as a lecturer of the Academy of Music in Bydgoszcz. He collaborated with the Polskie Wydawnictwo Muzyczne PWM as the author of the series „El Maestro" He also collaborated with the Professional Music Press and published articles in many music magazines in Poland, Germany, France, Italy, Great Britain and Japan. He is the author of books: *Gitara w twórczości Aleksandra Tansmana*[Guitar in the Oeuvre of Aleksander Tansman] (Łódź, 1996) and*Górecki. IV Symfonia Tansman Epizody. Fenomen, Żywioł, Tajemnica [Gorecki. Symphony No. 4 Tansman Episodes, Phenomenon, Elements, Mystery]* (Łódź 2016). He is the founder and artistic director of the Tansman Festival –International Festival and Competition of Musical Individualities. Mr. Wendland is the recipient of many honors and prizes, including the medal „Zasłużony Kulturze Gloria Artis" from the Polish government, 2015.

Anna Wieczorek is a music theorist, Ph.D. student at the Academy of Music in Kraków (Poland). The area of her scientific interest is contemporary Polish music based on religious background. Her master thesis concerned Henryk Mikołaj Górecki's output with a focus on the concept of motherhood in his work. Currently, she is focused on her dissertation about the genre of 'Te Deum' in Polish music in the 20th and 21st centuries by composers such as Penderecki, Palester, Schaeffer, Kurylewicz and Kilar. She is supervised by professor Teresa Malecka. Ms. Wieczorek is an author of scholarly articles and an participant in Polish and international (Kowno) conferences and symposiums.

◎ INDEX ◎

12-tone system/technique – 65, 101, 104, 107, 114, 120, 344.

Africa – 40.

Alberti bass – 13.

Already It Is Dusk – 116-7, 131-2, 191, 234-5, 237, 238, 240, 244, 318.

Anna (Anne, Saint) – 258, 260.

Argentina/Argentinian – 40, 219-20.

Augustyn, Rafał – 134, 329.

Austria/Austrian – 29-30, 101, 130, 184.

Avant-garde – 14, 77, 104-5, 107, 111-13, 116, 119, 253, 263, 281, 321, 323, 325, 345.

Bach, Johann Sebastian – 14-5, 24, 30, 48, 49, 63, 67, 72, 82, 102, 130, 156, 316, 328, 332.

Bachleda, Andrzej – 22, 25, 132, 268, 278-282.

Bacewicz, Grażyna – 136, 227.

Baird, Tadeusz – 112, 116.

Baroque – 72, 265, 319.

Bartók, Béla – 63, 72, 101, 103-4, 126, 130, 134, 301, 328.

Beethoven, Ludwig van – 15, 30, 49, 65, 67-9, 70-1, 83, 85, 88-90, 102, 129, 130-4, 156, 171, 234, 244-5, 262, 267, 270, 273, 275, 301, 304, 319, 348.

- Fidelio – 49, 88

- Piano Sonatas – 67-9. 85,

- Piano Concerto No. 4 – 131-2, 244, 270.

- String Quartets – 67-9.

- Third Symphony, Eroica – 71. 245, 267.

- Seventh Symphony – 83.

- Ninth Symphony – 88, 102, 262.

Bellini, Vincenzo – 48, 49.

Belorus/Belorussian – 188.

Benedicamus Domine (chorale) – 116, 235-8, 241-2.

Berg, Alban – 103.

Berlin –115.

Biegon, Bernard – 90.

Bielsko-Biała – 79, 80, 136-7, 277, 289, 305, 307.

Bieszczadowski, Mikołaj – 75-6.

Błażusiak, Helena Wanda – 74-5, 127, 215-7, 219, 231, 308.

Bogurodzica – 50-6, 59, 129, 130, 176-7, 318, 341.

Bogusławska, Maria – 194, 195.

Bohemian – 53.

Bolivia/Bolivian – 40.

Boosey & Hawkes – 81, 76, 109, 197-8, 209, 328.

Boulez, Pierre – 7, 14, 320.

Brahms, Johannes – 4, 30, 130, 300, 308, 332.

Bruckner, Anton – 300.

Buddhism – 185, 193,

Bydgoszcz – 59, 95, 124, 189.

Cage, John – 7, 115.

Cantabile – 231, 232, 247, 285, 287, 333, 340, 341.

Carlyle, Thomas – 336, 337.

Carpenter –24, 73.

Catholic – 114, 130, 133, 135, 137, 184-5, 188-9, 190, 206-7, 214, 219, 253, 259, 307, 316.

Chłopecki, Andrzej – 20, 310, 351, 352.

Chicago – 35.

Chochołów – 16, 17, 74, 270, 297, 314.

Chomiński, Józef – 85, 106.

Chopin, Fryderyk – 4, 14, 15, 30, 31, 46-9, 54, 65, 70, 84-5, 88, 91-2, 103, 129, 130-2, 136, 160, 221, 223, 234-7, 244-7, 253, 263, 266-7, 275, 299, 300, 314, 318-9, 348.

- Impromptus – 262.

-Mazurka Op. 17, No. 3 – 221, 235, 246-7, 266, 318.

- Nocturnes – 50.

- Sonata in B-flat Minor, Op. 35 – 245.

Chorale – 49050, 94, 129, 131, 149, 160-3, 164-5, 234, 241, 321, 333.

Christmas – 44, 69, Carols – 46, 69.

Constructivism – 104, 119, 120, 237, 263, 344, 345.

Copernicus, Nicolas / Kopernik, Mikołaj – 121-3, 144-174, 323, 327.

Credo – 96.

Czech – 29-30, 38, 52, 101, 272.

Czernica – 29, 101

Częstochowa – 49, 50, 55, 59, 129, 196, 189, 190, 192.

Debussy, Claude – 9, 71.

Dejmek, Kazimierz – 84.

Dębski, Krzesimir – 136.

Droba, Krzysztof – 101, 119, 121-2, 145-6, 151-6, 166, 172, 237, 241, 349.

Dvorak, Antonin – 130.

Easter – 190, 258, 333.

Electronic music – 8, 105.

Elsner, Józef – 85.

Elzenberg, Henryk – 317, 322-5, 346.

Erhardt, Ludwik – 3, 4, 21.

Evangelisti, Franco – 10.

Feicht, Hieronim – 50-1, 85, 177.

Folklore – 18, 29, 38, 39, 50, 56, 101-4, 159, 166, 225-6, 249, 255, 268, 276-7, 326, 338, 350.

France/French – 11, 38, 118, 221.

Franciscan – 14, 16, 50, 273.

Galica, Wincenty – 74.

Garner, Art – 90.

Gąsienica, Tadeusz – 93.

Gdańsk – 59.

Genes – 30, 101, 132.

Gestapo – 73, 125, 127, 216.

Germany/German – 38, 40, 53, 91, 101, 115, 127, 188, 219, 221, 276, 282, 297, 298, 307.

Gołachowski, Stanisław – 31.

Golden Section – 63, 65, 149, 160.

Gorzkie Żale – 95, 258.

Górale/Góral – 16-7, 37, 47, 132-3, 247, 277, 290, 297.

Górecka, Anna (daughter) – 102, 115, 281.

Górecka, Jadwiga (wife, nee Rurańska) – 102, 104, 115, 178.

Górecka, Otylia (mother) – 102, 199, 200. See also *Ad Matrem*

Górecki Henryk Mikołaj – Works

- *Ah, My Lavender Garland*, Op. 50 – 226, 236.

- *Ad Matrem*, Op. 29 – 62-3, 104, 118-9, 120-1, 136, 143, 145, 166, 176, 193-5, 197, 199, 204-10, 211, 217,-8, 222, 228, 231, 261, 263,-4, 303, 324, 340.

- *Amen*, Op. 35 – 121, 145.

- *At My Window* (song) – 33, 317.

- *Beatus Vir*, Op. 38 –59-60, 90, 124, 129-30, 135, 145, 141, 154, 189, 218, 248, 252,

256, 261, 263,-4, 267, 307, 310, 313, 317, 328, 345.

- *Blessed Raspberry Songs,* Op. 43 – 33, 317.

- *Broad Waters,* Op. 39 – 235, 254.

Cantata, Op. 26 – 118.

- *Canticum Graduum,* Op. 27 – 117, 318, 322.

- *Chorale in the form of a Canon* – 234, 321.

- *Choros I,* Op. 20 –117-8, 120.

- *Concerto-Cantata,* Op. 65 –328, 342, 345.

- Concerto for 5 Instruments, Op. 11 – 106.

- Concerto for Harpsichord and String Orchestra, Op. 40 –17, 177, 260, 263, 270, 328, 335, 339.

- *Church Songs* – 46-9, 50, 54, 56, 131, 176, 190-1, 204, 236, 237, 253, 236-9, 260-1, 313, 318, 345.

- *Diagram IV,* Op. 18 – 5-6, 8.

- *Epitafium,* Op. 12 – 9, 106-11, 120, 339.

- *Euntes Ibant and Flebant,* Op. 32 – 118, 121, 145, 317.

- *Five Pieces,* Op. 13 – 263.

- *For You, Ann-Lill,* Op. 58 – 282.

- *Genesis,* Op. 19 – 5, 8, 107-111, 120, 300, 308, 320, 345.

- *Good Night,* Op. 63 – 271, 282.

- *Intermezzo,* 282, 304.

- *Kleines Requiem für eine Polka,* Op. 66 – 121, 131,-4, 212, 269, 270-3, 282, 328, 333, 335, 339, 342, 345.

- *Kyrie,* Op. 83 – 96, 205, 313, 343, 345.

- *Little Fantasia /Kleine Fantasie,* Op. 73 – 131, 282.

- *Lobgesang,* Op. 76 – 308.

- *Lullabies and Dances,* Op. 47 – 178.

- *Lullaby,* Op. 9 – 104, 178.

- *Marian Songs,* Op. 54 – 176, 190-1, 204, 236, 257, 308, 313, 317-8.

- *Miserere,* Op. 44 – 124, 145, 177, 189 308, 313, 317.

- *Monologhi,* Op. 16 – 5, 64, 107, 113, 120.

- *Muzyczka III /Musiquette III,* Op. 25 – 117.

- *Muzyczka IV / Musiquette IV,* Op. 28 – 117, 177, 345.

- *My Vistula, Grey Vistula,* Op. 46 – 235, 255.

- *O Domina Nostra,* Op. 55 – 60, 119, 124, 176, 192-4, 198-9, 217-8, 228, 313.

- *Old Polish Music,* Op. 24 –115-6, 118, 130, 191, 235, 237, 239, 240, 242, 244, 321, 324.

- *Four Preludes,* Op. 1 – 104, 245, 263, 308.

- *Recitatives and Ariosos, Lerchenmusik,* Op. 53 – 67, 131, 244, 270, 304, 332, 342.

- *Refrain,* Op. 21 – 16, 18, 117-8, 120, 136, 149, 151, 259, 324, 344.

- Piano Sonata No. 1, Op. 6 – 104, 282.

- *Salve Sidus Polonorum,* Op. 72 – 52, 124, 307, 313.

- *Sanctus Adalbertus,* Op. 71 – 52, 59, 60, 124, 307, 313, 345.

- *Scontri,* Op. 17 – 4-8, 9, 14, 16, 18, 93, 104, 107-8, 113-4, 120, 142, 323, 326, 344.

- Sonata for Two Violins, Op. 10 – 18, 106.

- Sonatina in One Movement, Op. 8 – 104.

- 3 Songs, Op. 3 – 33, 104, 176, 199-204, 228, 230, 218, 261.

- *Song of Katyń Families,* Op. 81 – 256.

- *Songs of Joy and Rhythm,* Op. 7 – 6, 9, 318.

- String Quartet No. 1, *Already it is Dusk,* Op. 62 – 131, 235, 244.

- String Quartet No. 2 *Quasi Una Fantasia,* Op. 64 – 66, 131, 245, 348.

- String Quartet No. 3 *...songs are sung* – 80, 88, 131, 135-7, 268, 345.

- Symphony No. 1 *1959* –9, 107-8, 111, 113, 177, 326.

- Symphony No. 2, *Copernican* – 59, 121, 123, 132, 144-174, 235, 263, 313, 326-7.

- Symphony No. 3, *The Symphony of Sorrowful Songs* – 13-22, 56, 60-1, 73-6, 91-

3, 121, 126, 129, 131-6, 143, 175-233, 237, 245, 247, 267, 275-309, 318, 325, 327.

- *Symphony No. 4, Tansman Episodes* – 135, 142, 177, 308, 310-351.

- *Three Fragments*, Op. 69 – 136.

- *Three Lullabies*, Op. 49 – 6, 178, 225.

- *Three Pieces in the Old Style* – 14, 115, 321.

- *Toccata*, Op. 2 for piano – 104, 263.

- *Totus Tuus*, Op. 60 – 124, 145, 176, 293-6, 198, 199, 217, 218, 228, 257, 261.

- *Two Little Songs*, Op. 33 – 177.

- *Two Songs of Lorca*, Op. 42 – 33, 75-6.

- *Two Songs of Słowacki*, Op. 48 – 33.

- *Two Sacred Songs*, Op. 30 – 104, 121.

- *Two Tristan Postludes and a Chorale*, Op. 82 – 320, 342, 345, 348.

- *Under Your Protection*, Op. 56 – 176.

- *Valentine Piece*, Op. 70 – 4, 282.

- *Variations*, Op. 4 – 4, 282.

- *Wratislaviae Gloria* – 160.

Górecki Mikołaj (son) – 102, 115, 328, 329.

Górecki, Roman (father) – 102.

Gromada, Thaddeus –36-7, 132, 276-9, 280.

Grunwald – 53, 54.

Haydn, Joseph – 57, 130, 301.

Heller, Michał, Father – 87, 88, 92.

Herbert, Zbigniew – 68, 317, 322, 329, 336, 338, 340.

Herling-Grudziński, Gustaw – 317, 322.

Hitler, Adolf – 4.

Holoubek, Gustaw – 84, 89.

Holocaust – 95, 129, 212, 285.

Holy Cross Lament – 125-6.

Hummel, Johann Nepomuk – 48, 49.

Immaculate Conception –188, 190-1.

Italy/Italian – 95, 221, 307.

Ives, Charles – 130, 134.

Iwaszkiewicz, Jarosław – 95.

Jadwiga (Saint) –59, 60.

Japan/Japanese – 40, 94.

Jew/Jewish – 38, 142, 188.

John Paul II, Pope – 96, 124, 135, 155, 188, 195, 256, 257, 259, 308, 343.

Kaczyński, Tadeusz – 20.

Kalamarz, Wojciech, Father – 257.

Kant, Immanuel – 158, 166-8, 173-4.

Kantor, Tadeusz – 4.

Kapela /folk ensemble – 131, 277-8, 314, 341.

Karłowicz, Mieczysław – 75, 136.

Katowice – 25, 29, 35, 45, 54-7, 58, 60m 64, 87, 89, 101-2, 104, 112, 115, 134-5, 137, 139, 143, 154, 189, 200, 236, 295, 297, 299, 307, 311, 320, 344, 346

Kazimierz Dolny – 35

Kątski, Apolinary – 84.

Kedroń, Jane (Janina) – 32, 36, 42, 132, 277-81.

Kenya – 28.

Kilar, Wojciech – 17, 37, 53-4, 133, 136.

Khlebnikov, Vladimir – 81.

Kilanowicz, Zofia – 290, 295-7, 307.

Knapik, Eugeniusz – 119, 134, 135.

Kolbe, Maksymilian – 59.

Kolberg, Oskar –61, 130, 225-6, 236, 318.

Kołakowski, Leszek – 85, 89.

Konieczny, Zygmunt – 136.

Konopnicka, Maria – 33, 190, 304, 317.

Kraków (Cracow) –35, 48, 59, 81, 87, 95, 137, 254, 257, 296, 297

Krenz, Jan – 67, 136.

Kresy/Borderlands – 30.

Kronos Quartet – 66, 69, 80, 136, 137, 349.

Krzanowski, Andrzej – 134, 135.

Krzesany – 17. 37. 133.

Kujawiak – 46.

Kujawy – 53.

Kurpie – 16, 46, 129, 130, 215, 226, 235, 254, 314, 318.

Lament – 125-6 (Holy Cross), 127, 208, 212, 219, 227, 231, 247, 258.

Laude digna prole (chorale) –149, 160, 235.

Ligeti, György – 134, 323.

Litanies – 147, 185, 193, 198, 217.

London – 18, 76, 1289, 136, 142, 275, 289, 295, 301, 309

London Sinfonietta – 76, 128, 275, 295.

Loreto Litany – 185, 193, 198

Los Angeles – 22, 43, 138, 142, 222, 275-309

Lullaby – 46, 61-2, 104, 178, 199, 223-228.

Lwów/Lviv – 74.

Mahler, Gustav – 134, 300.

Majakovsky, Vladimir – 14, 28.

Malecka, Teresa – 87, 88, 145, 154, 155, 157, 159, 165, 234-274.

Markiewicz, Leon – 3-11, 101, 104, 113, 135, 320.

Mars – 41-2, 287, 305.

Mazovia/Mazowsze – 31, 54, 225, 226, 304.

Mazurka – Folk 46, 255; Szymanowski – 95, 262; Chopin – 46, 50, 85, 91-2, 225, 235-7, 245-7, 262, 266, 318.

Medieval – 124, 129, 130, 163, 204-5, 235, 237.

Meditation – 60, 146, 148, 155, 164, 172, 192, 228, 261, 272.

Menuhin, Yehudi – 28.

Messiaen, Oliver – 10, 25, 71-2, 96, 104, 114-15, 118, 130, 134, 328, 332.

Michalska, Ewa – 35, 136.

Michalski, Grzegorz – 45, 323.

Mickiewicz, Adam – 32, 50, 66, 91, 103.

Miłosz, Czesław – 89, 91.

Modal/Modality – 129, 145, 165, 241, 244, 245, 249, 255, 257, 260, 267.

Moniuszko, Stanisław – 136.

Monteverdi, Claudio – 319, 324.

Mozart, Wolfgang Amadeus – 13-5, 30, 50, 72, 89, 90, 96, 130, 156, 182, 275, 299, 300, 301, 319

Mrowiec, Karol, Father – 170.

Mycielski, Zygmunt – 21, 112.

New Jersey – 132, 277-8, 286.

New York – 33-4, 136, 144, 276, 278.

Nikodemowicz, Andrej – 20.

Nocturne – 50, 75, 91.

Nono, Luigi –10, 104, 112.

NOSPR – National Symphony Orchestra of the Polish Radio – 297, 320.

Norwid, Cyprian Kamil – 32, 33, 50, 73, 91, 190.

Oberek/Obertas – 46, 255.

Obrochta, Bartuś (Bartłomiej) – 37, 38, 133.

Obrochta, Władek (Władysław) – 93.

Ottoman Empire – 53.

Paderewski, Ignacy Jan – 136, 138.

Panufnik, Andrzej – 53, 54, 116.

Paris (Paryż) – 10, 11, 111, 114, 115, 136.

Paganini, Nicolo – 93.

Palester, Roman – 115.

Palestrina – 15, 95.

Pascal, Blaise – 173, 351.

Patkowski, Józef – 3, 105.

Penderecki, Krzysztof – 69, 136, 164.

Pentatonic chord/scale – 123-4, 149, 152, 158, 164, 265.

Peterson, Oscar – 90.

Picasso, Pablo – 4.

Pisarenko, Olgierd – 20.

Pociej, Bohdan – 35, 143, 146, 154-5, 158, 163, 172, 236, 253, 346-8, 350-1.

Podhale – 4, 11, 16-7, 37, 47, 57, 58, 73, 74, 80, 82, 83, 95, 101, 133, 137, 235, 247-8, 253, 266, 277, 281, 297, 305, 314, 315,

Polish Radio – 105, 295, 297, 312, 315.

Polish language – 94, 182, 184, 318.

Postmodern – 168-9, 270, 338.

Prayer – 25, 97, 114-5, 124, 146-7, 173, 176, 185, 190-2, 198-9, 205, 216-18, 223, 227, 230, 259-60, 264, 266, 313, 333.

Protestant – 49, 185.

Psalms – 121, 124, 130, 146-7, 156, 171, 199, 256, 317.

Puccini, Giacomo – 130.

Raciborz – 29, 101.

Recording – 18, 40-1, 76, 80-1, 106, 111, 119, 128, 136, 275, 285, 289, 294-7, 301, 303.

Renaissance – 129, 133, 319.

Romanticism/Romantic – 32, 33, 68, 71-2, 75, 103, 202, 265, 286, 317, 319, 334.

Rosary – 147, 185, 198,

Ruch Muzyczny – 3,4, 20, 21, 63 and notes 128, 146, 161, 320, 347.

Romanian – 38.

Russia/Russian – 25, 30, 38, 82, 95, 118, 184, 188,

Rybnik – 29, 101, 102, 137.

Rydułtowy – 102,

Sandomierz – 34, 35.

Schoenberg, Arnold – 6, 270, 302.

Schubert, Franz – 15, 30, 65, 83, 92, 96, 130, 223, 213, 275, 300-1,

  - *Winterreise* – 83

  - *Wiegendlied* – 213

Schumann, Robert – 30, 130, 170, 332.

Scriabin, Alexandre – 70.

Siedlecki, Jan, Father – 258.

Sienkiewicz, Henryk – 53-4, 91.

Sikorski, Kazimierz – 85.

Silent Night – 69.

Silesia – 29-31, 38, 54, 101, 127, 130-1, 133, 135-6, 219, 314.

Silesian Philharmonic – 295, 297, 311.

Skierkowski, Władysław – 46, 56, 235, 248-9.

Slavic – 40, 184, 254.

Słowacki, Juliusz – 32-3, 91, 104, 163, 190, 201-2, 230, 317.

Sonorism/Sonoristic – 117, 120, 260, 320, 345.

Spain/Spanish – 38, 75.

Spisak, Michał – 115.

Spisz – 74.

Spohr, Louis – 48.

Stabat Mater –54, 62, 63, 94, 95, 126, 204-5, 208, 213, 228, 229, 248.

Stokowski, Leopold – 67.

Strauss, Richard – 71.

Stravinsky, Igor – 9, 14, 95, 15, 118, 171, 300, 301, 324.

Sweden – 18, 107.

Szabelski, Bolesław – 54, 89, 102, 104.

Szymanowski, Karol – 4, 15, 30-2, 46-7, 47-50, 56, 70,72, 75, 83, 91, 93,-5, 102, 104, 130, 132, 135-7, 204, 213,234-250, 262, 273, 296, 304, 314, 318, 319, 341, 346.

- Stabat Mater – 54, 62, 63, 94, 95,248.

- Mazurkas – 262.

- Third Piano Sonata – 72.

Tansman, Aleksander – 137, 142, 177, 308, 310-351.

Tarkovsky, Andrei – 25.

Tatar – 38.

Tatry (Tatra Mountains) – 4, 16, 17, 33, 37-8, 47, 72, 75, 8,0, 82, 93, 101-2, 130, 132-3, 253m 276-8, 280, 315-16.

Tchaikovsky, Piotr – 95, 275.

Television – 28, 42, 312.

Teutonic Knights – 53, 91.

Thomas, Adrian – 56, 68, 113, 135, 137, 143, 144, 148, 157, 176, 199, 244-9, 266-7, 270, 282, 299, 303, 321.

Tischner, Józef, Father – 87, 316.

Tomaszewski, Mieczysław – 154, 155, 163, 164, 170, 236, 241, 244, 253, 268, 273, 334, 345, 350.

Tonal/Tonality – 92, 124, 128-9, 145, 165, 245, 255, 260, 263, 266, 268--9, 273, 323, 333, 344.

Toruń – 59.

Tradition – 13, 21, 29, 32-3, 37, 93, 114-7, 126, 129, 131, 133, 146-7, 156-7, 159-166, 170, 180-2, 184, 193-5, 202, 213, 226, 229, 234-261, 265-6, 268, 313-5, 317-9, 341-4, 348.

Transcription – 66.

Translation – 75-6, 81, 94-5.

Trochimczyk, Maja – 12, 22-44, 45-65, 101-143, 175-233, 275-309, 344.

Tuwim, Julian – 104, 107, 201-3, 231, 311, 317, 338, 340.

Tymoszowka – 30, 95.

Ukraine/Ukrainian – 38, 74, 95, 188.

Upshaw, Dawn – 76, 128, 129, 275, 295, 297, 301.

Urbanowicz, Andrzej – 4.

Van Gogh, Vincent – 4.

Vedova, Emilio – 4.

Vespers – 59.

Vienna – 130.

Wacław of Szamotuły – 116, 133, 191, 234-7, 240.

Wadowice – 74, 219.

Wagner, Richard – 71, 130, 300, 319, 329, 34203, 348.

Parsifal – 71, 130.

Ring des Nibelungen – 320, 342.

Warsaw (Warszawa) – 9, 13, 35, 56, 50, 54, 66, 95, 103, 105-7, 112-13, 128, 136, 137, 138, 256.

Warska, Wanda – 34-5, 136, 277.

Washington, D.C. – 35, 137.

Webern, Anton – 10, 14, 55, 103-4, 113.

Weir, Peter – 75.

Wendland, Andrzej – 142, 213, 304, 310-352.

Whole-tone Chord/Cluster – 123, 149.

Wiedza Powszechna – 31.

Wieniawski, Henryk – 136, 290.

Wincenc, Carol – 304, 332.

Witkiewicz, Stanisław, "Witkacy" – 4.

Wnuk-Nazarowa, Joanna – 320.

Woytowicz, Stefania – 89, 129, 294, 295.

Wujek, Jakub, Father – 159.

Wyspiański, Stanisław – 33-5, 136, 317.

Xenakis, Iannis – 104, 115, 118, 134, 324.

Zakopane – 17, 22, 26, 31, 32, 35-6, 66, 73-4, 78, 80, 95, 115, 127, 135, 137-9, 216, 231, 279, 280-1, 297, 314, 340.

Ząb – 66, 80, 131, 276, 297, 331, 340.

Zieliński, Tadeusz – 21, 63, 248.

Zinman, David – 76, 128-9, 275, 285, 294-5, 297.

ZKP (Związek Kompozytorów Polskich/Polish Composers Union) – 105-7, 111, 112, 128, 138.

www.ingramcontent.com/pod-product-compliance
Lightning Source LLC
Chambersburg PA
CBHW021814300426
44114CB00009BA/175